THE POLICE AND POLITICAL
DEVELOPMENT IN INDIA

The Police and
Political Development in
 INDIA

DAVID H. BAYLEY

PRINCETON UNIVERSITY PRESS
PRINCETON, NEW JERSEY
1969

This book has been composed in Linotype Caledonia

Printed in the United States of America by
Princeton University Press

To Chris, Jenny, and Tracy

Preface

This book is intended primarily for two audiences: people interested in comparative politics and people interested in Indian studies. The book attempts to ask questions about the nature of political development that would profit by genuine comparative treatment. Indeed, it is only by asking questions about the police and political development in other cultural or national contexts that meaningful theories may be worked out. It is hoped this book contributes to the comparative enterprise by posing important questions and assaying initial answers on the basis of Indian experience. At the same time, the book attempts to provide a thorough, general treatment of police for the person interested in India as such. The last major work on the Indian police was J. C. Curry's excellent book written in 1932. Students of Indian affairs know very little about the police. They are aware of their existence, to be sure, and sometimes deal with them. The police loom for scholars, students, and the Indian public as a whole as a rather forbidding specter in the background of daily life. They know almost nothing about their history, organization, or procedures. The present work attempts to fill this gap, to bring the story told almost exclusively by former British officials up-to-date, and to examine the conformity between contemporary police activities and the requirements of the post-independence democratic order.

This project grew out of a general intellectual preoccupation with the manner in which India has coped with establishing a balance between political freedom and the maintenance of stable order. Field research began in 1963 when I was appointed a Senior Research Fellow of the American Institute of Indian Studies. Their generous grant allowed me to spend the year 1963-1964 in India. The work of that year had two aspects. First, I undertook a pilot survey of public reactions to the police. Second, I began extensive interviews with officials about police problems. In this way I hoped to put two sides of a story together—to find out how the police were perceived by the public, and what kinds of contacts were established, and how police problems were perceived by professionals charged with responsibility for law enforcement. My interviews in several parts of India were with I.P.S. and I.A.S. officers, as well as members of the judiciary. Although I spoke with I.P.S.–I.A.S. officers at many stages of career advancement, from senior secretaries to probationers, I made a particular point of interviewing officers who were holding or had recently held operational charge in a district.

The year in India convinced me of the possibility of doing a large survey of public opinion and the police. In 1965 I was given a grant to put my plan into effect. The survey was organized in the early autumn of 1965 and was conducted, as had been the pilot survey, by the Indian Institute of Public Opinion, New Delhi. I spent the autumn of that year in India working with the staff of the I.I.P.O. preparing samples and questionnaires.

The Indian Institute of Public Opinion undertook a very demanding and sensitive task with open-mindedness, imagination, and energy. Although the results of the survey itself must serve as the best evidence of the quality of their work, I should like to say that I found it of a high order. Moreover, their consideration and hospitality were overwhelming. To Eric da Costa, director, Joginder Singh Yogie, and the entire staff, my very deep thanks.

I also used the autumn months of 1965 to complete the course of personal interviewing with officials that I had begun the previous year. I talked with officers from every state and of every rank level from inspector-general to assistant superintendent of police. I have not been able to interview men of non-I.P.S. rank, due largely to lack of time as well as language competence. This failure represents a major gap in my knowledge of the Indian police. Indeed, as I shall point out later, information about subordinate ranks is generally lacking among official sources and deserves systematic study.

Many people doubted that a foreign scholar would be well accepted in India if he attempted to study the police. For understandable reasons, the police of any country are cautious about publicity. I have often wondered how an Indian political scientist would be received in the United States if he announced he wanted to study the police and political development. This book is implicitly a tribute to the reality of an open society in India. The project was invariably received with consideration and accepted on its imputed merits. I must admit that at best I had expected only grudging cooperation. To my surprise and delight, I found officials eager to discuss the problems of law enforcement and not only to share their own experiences and insights but to suggest ways in which the research might be utilized to help them. In sum, officials were anxious to help me learn about their problems and as a result to help them learn in turn how more effectively to accomplish what they were charged with doing. I cannot possibly thank adequately the scores of officials who gave unstintingly of their time, energy, and hospitality. I am profoundly in their debt. It is my earnest hope that in writing this book I repay their trust in some measure by contributing to the development of the Indian police and to the larger responsibility of administering justice under law, tasks to which these men are singularly dedicated.

During the course of any extended research project many people contribute to its development and eventual completion. Often they do so in ways that they might not even recognize as being helpful. Support comes in so many forms that one can never acknowledge all of it or give credit where it is due. I am grateful to the Graduate School of International Studies, University of Denver, for providing me with financial support and secretarial assistance. Graduate research assistants Tilden LeMelle, David Chamberlin, and Bill Bramble helped to put masses of statistical data in usable form, as well as assisting in preparing the punch-card decks for initial analysis. Mr. V. P. Singh translated a host of Vidhan Sabha debates and prepared a valuable analysis of them. Professor John Horn displayed endless patience in steering me through the intricacies of factor analysis and prevented despair when programs failed to run as expected. The staff of the computer center worked efficiently and with kindness to assure that man and machine could cooperate productively, a point that was not always certain. Mrs. Jerri Arendt and Mrs. Lorraine Tappan put my drafts, with their innumerable tables, into presentable order. To all these people, I am most grateful.

My thanks to my wife and daughters can never be adequately expressed. They offset the loneliness of scholarly enterprise, the moments of doubt and frustration, and shared with me the fascinating, arresting, delightful, saddening, and sometimes shattering experiences of life in India.

DAVID H. BAYLEY
Denver, Colorado
April, 1969

Contents

Preface　vii

Introduction　3

ONE
THE POLICE AND POLITICAL DEVELOPMENT

1. *Role of the Police in Political Development*　11

TWO
THE INDIAN POLICE—CHARACTER AND SETTING

2. *Structure and Development*　35
3. *The Indian Police Today*　58
4. *The Criminal Setting*　97

THREE
CRIMINAL INVESTIGATION

5. *The Record*　123
6. *The Process*　149

FOUR
THE POLICE AND THE PUBLIC

7. *Public Contact with the Police*　183
8. *Public Perspectives on the Police*　199
9. *Determinants of Public Perspectives*　220
10. *The Maintenance of Public Order*　248
11. *Corruption and the Police*　283
12. *University Students and the Police*　307

FIVE
ADMINISTRATORS, POLITICIANS, AND PANCHAYATI RAJ

13. *The Police and Civilian Administration*　349

14. *Police and the Politicians*   364
15. *Police and Village Government*   385

SIX

CONCLUSION
16. *The Police and the Political System:
An Assessment*   409

Appendices
Appendix A. SURVEY METHODOLOGY AND ANALYSIS   427
Appendix B. QUESTIONNAIRE ADMINISTERED
TO THE PUBLIC   435
Appendix C. QUESTIONNAIRE ADMINISTERED TO
UNIVERSITY STUDENTS   450

Selected Bibliography   465

Index   479

List of Tables

1. Sanctioned Strength of Police, 31 December, 1960   61
2. Growth of Police, Selected States, 1950-1960   64
3. Comparative Ratios of Police to Population and Area in India, United States, and Great Britain   65
4. Police Strength by States   66
5. Expenditure on Police Force by States   68
6. Comparative Police Strength in Major Cities   70
7. Criminal Statistics for States and Centrally Administered Territories   104
8. Clearance and Conviction Rates of Crime—1963   126
9. Persons Guilty as Percentage of Arrests   127
10. Clearance and Conviction Rates in India—1963   128
11. Percentage of Population Seeking Police Assistance   129
12. Public Views of Police Misbehavior   142
13. Contact with Police Analyzed by Education and Income   192
14. Attitudes of Others Toward the Police   204
15. Clustering of Negative Evaluations of the Police   207
16. Unpleasant Contact with the Police   210
17. Negative Personal Experience with the Police   211
18. No Contact and No Recognition Factors   217
19. Bangalore: Sample Composition   221
20. Tumkur: Sample Composition   222
21. Kanpur Residents: Sample Composition   223
22. Kanpur Rural Migrants: Sample Composition   224
23. Contact Questions Analyzed by Background   234-235
24. Contact Questions Analyzed by Caste   236
25. Personal Experience with Crowd-Control   273
26. Public Views of Corruption in the Police   285

27.   *Data on Universities Sampled*   309
28.   *Background Data on Students*   311
29.   *Distribution of Students by Curricula*   313-316
30.   *Student Attitudes Toward Demonstrations*   332
31.   *Student Experience with Crowd-Control*   334

THE POLICE AND POLITICAL
DEVELOPMENT IN INDIA

Introduction

THE purpose of this book is to examine the role and function of the police in contemporary India. This purpose is informed by a particular concern, namely, the formative role that police play in the maintenance and development of a political system. The point of the book is not to determine how effectively police control criminal activity or preserve law and order. That is the perspective a criminologist employs. Nor is the point to determine how the police are organized to carry out their tasks or to assess how performance might be improved. That is the perspective an expert in public administration employs. My concern is with the impingement of police activities upon the working of a political system, which means those processes by which Indian society regulates itself. My perspective is that of the political scientist, and in particular of the student of political development. The basic question becomes, then, how do police activities affect the nature of social, and predominantly formal, self-regulation? And, in the Indian case, does what the police do reinforce or subvert the establishment of stable democratic processes?

The perspective employed in this book is unfamiliar. Neither scholars nor public officials are accustomed to asking if what the police are called upon to do and the manner they choose to do it affects the nature of political processes. The police have been thought of customarily as a passive instrument in the hands of government. The practice has been to examine how well they worked or the manner of their working, but always within the framework of their formal purpose—the preserving of acceptable conditions of social order. Other groups in society—such as the military, civil service, students, or interest groups—have been studied with a view to assessing their role in political life. The police, despite their ubiquity and identification with government, have curiously been neglected. Because the perspective of this study is novel, the first task must be to determine how the police might play a formative role in political life. Only by perceiving clearly the range of opportunities for influence can one begin to study successfully actual effects. Part I will explore this topic.

The importance of studying the impact of the police upon the community, as well as police problems generally, has begun to be understood in several countries. Years of neglect seem to be giving way to informed inquiry, although the trend though encouraging is not yet massive. In Great Britain and the United States, the Royal Commission on the Police in 1962 was the first official body to undertake a careful appraisal. It saw the need not only to examine traditional problems of administrative structure, recruitment, accountability, and conditions of service but the need to examine public perceptions of police activity and the policeman's perceptions of himself and his relations with the community. In America President Johnson, activated by growing concern about crime and civil disorder, in 1965 appointed a presidential commission to conduct a comprehensive study of America's law-enforcement machinery and the problems it faced. The urgency of the commission's work had been underscored by serious and unheralded riots in major cities, by restiveness among the nation's youth, and by public confrontations between reformers and police. Through anxiety and now through study people are becoming sensitized to the critical role police play in a community. What has been the fitful concern of isolated scholars and officials has become a preoccupation of the public and their spokesmen. Whether concern will produce substantial programs for improvement or even comprehensive study is problematic. Nonetheless, the logjam of ignorance shows some sign of breaking up.

There are many kinds of police in the world, and many different kinds of functionaries who perform policing roles. By "police" I shall be referring to employees of the community, for the most part uniformed, whose special purpose is to ensure that the community's laws are observed and who do so by initiating the process through which sanctions are applied. The police may be distinguished from other agents of the community who enforce law, employ force, or wear uniforms by (a) having an exclusively domestic mandate and (b) being the initial point of contact between citizen and enforcement machinery. British and American policemen are prototypes of this model. So too are Indian policemen.

Standard studies of the police, concentrating upon what police do, their rules, organization, internal management, pay, and perquisites, are based upon data obtained from official documents, interviews with policemen, and first-hand observation.

The discussion of Part II of this study, where history, organization, and criminal problems of the police are discussed, is based largely on information of this kind. However, in order to measure police impact, one must go further. It is necessary to examine how police activities touch other people, groups, and structures. This requires finding vantage points outside the police organization from which to observe its operations. There are many of these, as we shall see in Part I. Certainly the most important of these vantage points is with the public. What relations have they with the police? When do they appeal to the police for help? What kinds of demands do they make of the police? What kinds of judgments about police behavior does the public make? When do citizens complain and to whom? Do they feel an obligation to lend assistance to the police? Are their attitudes toward the police based on personal experience with the police or inherited tradition? Do they know much about the police and are they on terms of personal familiarity with any of them? Do they think the police do an effective job? In short, if one wants to know how police relate to a community's members, one must go to the public and find out. There are two ways of doing this. One may live in a community and observe, or one may employ survey techniques and ask individuals to talk about their own experiences. Unless a community is small or a great number of observers are used, observation suffers from being episodic and limited in coverage. With survey techniques a larger population is covered with built-in provisions for representativeness. Survey operations are the technique I have adopted for gaining access to public responses.

Three thousand six hundred interviews were allocated for the survey. Two thousand four hundred of them were devoted to the general public, twelve hundred to university students. Four samples of the general public were selected: (a) rural people, (b) urban people, (c) second-generation urban residents, and (d) migrants to urban areas. The choice of samples was dictated by several hypotheses which the survey was designed to explore. These will be discussed in Chapters 7 and 8. University students were organized into four samples, each one coincidental with a single university in a different part of the country. The data from all eight samples could be compared with one another in various combinations.

The general public samples were drawn from Bangalore city in Mysore state; rural Tumkur district in Mysore state; and Kanpur city in Uttar Pradesh state. In 1960, at the last decennial census, Bangalore was India's sixth largest city with a population of about 1,200,000. Kanpur was the eighth largest city with a population of close to one million. Tumkur district is located about sixty miles northwest of Bangalore. It is predominantly rural. The four student samples were drawn from Delhi University, Allahabad University, Osmania University, and Bangalore University. General public samples were drawn from lists of eligible voters—the electoral rolls. University samples were chosen from lists of matriculated students furnished by the universities.

Survey methodology has its own peculiar shortcomings. Let us examine five points at which it may be challenged. First, since it is impossible in most cases to interview every member of a population one is interested in, one must select a subpopulation —a sample—that is representative of the whole. Drawing a sample must be done very carefully. If it is not representative, data obtained from the survey cannot be interpreted as applying to the whole. Any conclusions drawn are limited by the biases of the sample. A check on the representativeness of the Indian samples has been made using census data in the case of the general public and official data on higher education in the case of university students. An estimation of the representativeness of the samples will be found in Chapters 7 and 12 for general public and students, respectively. Second, there is always a great temptation to extend survey conclusions based on one sampled area to others of a superficially similar kind. For example, in the present instance no attempt was made to construct a representative all-India sample. The question naturally arises whether data from Bangalore or Kanpur would be similar to data obtained in Bombay or Calcutta. This may in fact be the case. That survey areas may be representative of larger population or similar areas elsewhere may be strongly felt, but unless it can be proven, the applicability of survey generalizations to other areas should not be asserted dogmatically. Third, what guarantee is there that people respond honestly to the questions they are asked? There is none at all. People may glibly dissemble their true experiences or feelings or they may simply refrain from giving any answer whatsoever even though they hold strong views. An interviewer is a stranger, and may be perceived as an interloper, nuisance, or threat. Whenever responses are inhibited or distorted, surveys do not obtain reliable information about what people think, know, or experience. Fourth, even if people respond forthrightly and honestly, survey questions may be ambiguous, and this fact may go unperceived by the researcher and his interviewers. If respondents and researcher diverge in their interpretations of the meaning of an item, the researcher quite literally doesn't know what the respondent is talking about. His conclusions are bound to be mistaken. Fifth, surveys record verbal responses. They do not record physical behavior. What a person says he is or does may be quite different from what he is or does in fact. Strictly speaking, surveys can show only what people say in an interview situation. The coincidence between verbal and physical behavior may be questioned.

These are the logical limitations of the use of survey data. The extent to which they apply in the present instance must be determined by the reader for himself. The soundness of the methodology itself, the care and foresight with which the survey has been conducted, can be judged from Appendix A. Reliability may also be judged by comparing data from the survey with data from other surveys or from other information-gathering techniques. Since this is the first survey in India to focus exclusively on the subject of the police, comparable survey data simply do not exist. A few previous surveys had one or two items that provide comparisons, but they are exceptions. Information from other kinds of observers is fragmentary and focuses more on police actions than public responses. Readers will inevitably—sometimes despite their best intentions—fall back on what they expect the situation to be. When they do this, they may be well informed or very poorly informed. In principle validation of this kind is neither inappropriate nor unfair. Empirical facts from whatever sources should be set side by side and examined. I should like, however, to caution the reader about elevating any methodology, especially implicit ones, above another. This is particularly true in the present case, when information of any kind is so sadly lacking. All methodological techniques have limitations. The reader should be cautioned against overlooking the mote in his own eye in looking for the beam in mine.

I said earlier that the prime concern of this project was to determine whether and to what extent police activities impinged on the operation of the Indian political system. In fact this purpose cannot be carried out entirely with the information at hand.

In order to do so it would be necessary to obtain data about the police and the political system over a period of time. Only in this way could one determine whether changes in one were associated with changes in the other. There is an alternative procedure, at least in principle. One could compare the Indian situation with those in other countries. This is impossible to do, not only because international data are almost entirely lacking but because intercultural differences are so great as to cast serious doubt on the meaningfulness of comparisons. Processes of interaction between police and politics may be qualitatively different between cultures and nations. Most of the data obtained in the present study presents a snapshot of the contemporary situation. It is limited to a single point in time. The survey data, for example, reveal what people did and thought in 1965-1966. This information cannot help us to understand what happened between the police and public in 1947 or 1900. Most of the primary source data utilized, whether official or private, tends to concentrate on what the police have done; it gives only occasional insights into how the public, or any other component actor of the political system, was responding. This study, therefore, cannot demonstrate conclusively the influences police exerted on the system. It can only present presumptive evidence, patterns of association at one moment in time, from which tentative hypotheses of mutual effect may be worked out.

Part I, as I have explained, explores in an a priori fashion how any police force might affect the encapsulating political system. Part II describes the development of the Indian police system, its contemporary organization, and the salient criminal problems with which it must deal. Part III examines procedures and problems of criminal investigation. Part IV explores police operations as they affect the Indian populace and presents survey data to determine the responses of the public to the police. Part V examines the interaction of police and specific agencies or actors important in contemporary political life, such as the bureaucracy, politicians, rural police, and panchayat institutions. Part VI is devoted to conclusions.

ONE

THE POLICE AND POLITICAL
DEVELOPMENT

1 · *Role of the Police in Political Development*

It is generally accepted that the nature of police activities provides an important clue to the character of a political regime. A government's evaluation of itself as democratic would hardly be allowed to go unchallenged if the police severely restricted public meetings and political demonstrations or resorted readily to physical force and intimidation in order to prevent crime. A "jack-booted tread" and imperious knocking at the door late at night have become symbols of political repression. Similarly, a police force that conducts its operations openly and with little violence and that members of the public do not hesitate to approach in time of personal need is considered supporting evidence that political life is free and unconstrained. There is a common expectation, then, that the nature of police activities and the nature of government are coincidental. For many people this expectation is founded upon their understanding of the concepts of police and government. Their expectation of coincidence is supported by a tautology. Police are the leading edge of government regulation; what they do is part and parcel of government's activity; police and government could no more be separated than knife and knife-edge. While this is not an improper way of defending the expectation of coincidence, it is a restrictive one, for it asserts a relation only between concepts and not between empirical events. If an empirical relation is being asserted, then one must realize that it is logically possible that the character of police and government may diverge. Police are only one among many agencies of government. A government could be capricious and arbitrary while the police conscientiously acted within the provisions of codified law. Or a government might be dedicated to the voluntary ordering of political opinion and support, shrinking from any hint of coercion, while the police callously overrode individual rights in conducting a battle against crime and did not hesitate to use force and violence against suspects. Granting that there is more to the relation between the character of government and police than logical entailment, one must then ask how likely it is that police and government may develop independently of the other with respect to the character of their operations.

Casting through the histories of nation-states, does one find that political despotism is always reflected in the behavior of the police? On the other hand, does the glow of freedom in a democratic state burnish the image and activities of the police? Russia, with an unrelieved history of political repression under Czars and commissars, has been noted for its cruel police methods. In Great Britain, by contrast, representative democracy has been associated for almost 150 years with an evenhanded police force self-consciously eschewing the use of force against public and criminal alike. But what of France and the United States? *"Les flics"* have a reputation for arbitrariness seemingly independent of the character of the regime in power. In America lawlessness and violence are a fabled part of the past, and as a result police go fully armed. Yet the United States also boasts a commitment to democratic institutions second to none and has an impressive record of achievement to give substance to the claim. If one could construct an index of the character of political life and an index of the character of police operations, would one find that there was a close correlation between the two?

"People get the government they deserve." By extension, people must get the police they deserve. According to the theory implicit in this popular formulation, government reflects the character of its society. There is no point in wringing one's hands if government is repressive, inefficient, or corrupt. It could not be otherwise since people generally are not sufficiently disturbed to protest and reform. The police can only be what the public will allow. Government passively reflects society; the police, as an agency of government, are the creatures of both.

There are three relevant terms in this analysis: society, government, and police. Using more fashionable terminology, the variables may be described as environment, system, and agency within the system. The passive theory of political development maintains that environment determines the nature of the system and of the agency within the system. It is most unlikely, therefore, according to this formulation, that police would develop independently of the system.

As a theory of social process the foregoing formulation is clearly false. Government may indeed operate differently from what the public expects, requires, or wants. Government may be the instrument of an elite which imposes its will on a majority by the use of force. Force substitutes for consent, and the leeway obtained by force allows government to depart substantially from what the mass of the people are capable of on their own. "People get the government they deserve" is a bit of folklore that could only seem plausible in a nonauthoritarian society. Today the world is being treated to the spectacle of radical social changes being undertaken by elite governments. They are shaping the social supports that are necessary to the more assured continuation of their own identity. It is like Archimedes' principle for moving the world. The government, in many new states, is a lever resting on a fulcrum composed of a very small segment of society. This small segment is trying to get purchase through government on the rest of society so as to provide a more sure footing for that very government. This is not to argue that government has an unlimited capacity for remaking its encapsulating society. It certainly has not. But it is to assert that a government is not a passive creation of society.

Can as much be said for the police? How likely is it that the police may maintain a character in some respects divergent from government and from the social environment too? Moreover, is it possible for the police to play a formative role in shaping their own environment—which in this case would be both the political system and the social environment? The possibility has not received the attention it deserves. The military and the civilian bureaucracy have been examined for the formative role they can play. The police have not been. Yet there is no reason in logic to believe that their role may be less eventful in affecting the course of political development. The unwillingness to entertain this possibility may be explained by the tendency to associate police and government more intimately together than other agencies. Surely, though, if bureaucracy and government are not identical, police and government are not either. Sir Charles Reith, prominent historian of Anglo-Saxon police development, has long maintained that the establishment of Peel's police in England in 1829 brought about a fundamental reshaping of English society. If the British people are law-abiding today, he has said, it is due in overwhelming measure to the effect the "new police" had on attitudes toward law, crime, and the responsibilities of the citizenship. The model behavior of British police, a byword around the world, is not a reflection of a deep-rooted, primordial love of order among the British people. In fact, before 1829 such qualities were distinctive by their absence. The British love of order and respect for law is the result of model behavior on the part of the British police in spite of appalling conditions of crime, vice, public insecurity, and individual apathy, hostility, and indifference to law enforcement.[1] Reith disagrees strongly with American historians who blame the record of lawlessness, brutality, and corruption in the United States on defects of American character, and who then argue that one should not expect different behavior from the police. A prime cause of lawlessness, brutality, and corruption in the United States, in Reith's view, is the law-enforcement machinery itself. Were the police efficient, incorruptible, and law-abiding, American society would enjoy a new birth of order and domestic tranquillity. Indeed, if exemplary behavior were maintained by the police over a period of time these so-called traits of American character would vanish. Reith is more extreme than anyone in the extent to which he believes police may play a formative role in society. But it would be unwise to neglect the possibility that they may have some innovative function to perform. So far, at least in scholarly writings on political development, this possibility has been neglected.

There are several presumptive reasons for thinking police can exert a formative influence in political life, at least in comparison to the contributions of other agencies. First, they are thoroughly and widely visible. Since they are uniformed, their activities are difficult to disguise; since their responsibilities permeate all corners of social activity, they are brought into contact with everyone. Other government servants touch only very specialized parts of human life and when they do so they attract little public attention. Second, police possess a near-monopoly on the instruments of force. They are society's regulators, imbued with power denied to everyone else. This creates around them an aura of apprehension, of anxiety, of fear. They are imbued with an emotional significance that does not attach to other agents of government. Third, they have responsibility for safeguarding the most basic elements of human life. Theirs is the power to protect or not to protect, to save or not to save. Moreover, they intrude into individual lives at moments of stress and tribulation. Policemen are identified with the

[1] Charles Reith, *A Short History of the British Police* (London: Oxford University Press, 1948); and *The Blind Eye of History: A Study of the Origins of the Present Police Era* (London: Faber and Faber, 1952).

greatest of life's crises. Fourth, police are immediately identified with law. In many respects they are more important than
law, for they implement its strictures and decide when it is to
be applied. Whether government is by men or by law depends
to a marked extent on the nature of the police.

Perhaps these reasons explain why police and government cannot be considered separately by many people. If government is
regulation, then police personify government. But, then, if government can affect its own environment, the police can do so too,
simply because the police are the most ubiquitous, visible, and
important of governmental agencies for the average citizen.

For the student of police and political development there are
two questions, not just one, that must be answered: (1) how
does the social and political environment affect the police, and
(2) how do the police affect the social and political environment? The possibility of reciprocal interaction between the police, on the one hand, and political system and social environment, on the other, must be entertained. In practice the interaction means that police may engage in behavior reinforcing
or subverting the established political system. One must not,
however, get caught in a chicken-and-egg paradox. The proposition of interaction does not assert that change can be initiated
by an agency in society without some supporting requisites
in that society. Nor does it assert that police can initiate and
long sustain behavior radically divergent from society generally.
The point of the analysis is not to seek a *primum mobile*. All
that is necessary to the argument is to recognize that social
change may be brought about by government instrumentalities, among them the police, just as these instrumentalities are in turn influenced in their activity by the surrounding
environment.

Of the two questions, the second—how do police affect the
social and political environment—is the more difficult to answer.
This is in part because the focus of impact—society or government—is more diffuse than when asking how society affects the
police. For example, how does one assess the influence of policemen upon all persons they contact? The police, by contrast,
are relatively more homogeneous, certainly less extensive, and
so the job of studying them for effects generated by environment
is easier. Moreover, the question of how the police affect the
social and political environment is difficult to answer because
people are unaccustomed to considering it. Acceptance of the

possibility that police may exert a formative influence on political development is an essential first step to discovering whether they do so in fact. Then it becomes possible to specify the means by which the police affect political life and the social environment. In the next section some of the more important formative links between the police and political development will be explored.

How the Police Affect Political Development

Police can play a formative role in political development by virtue of what they do, how they do it, what they are, and what they do to each other. I shall consider each of these in turn.

In the analysis that follows no claim is made that police always exert the effects imputed, nor that the modalities discussed are the only ways in which they may exercise an effect. The analysis is neither exhaustive nor empirical; it is suggestive and a priori. It is intended to stretch the mind to the possibilities of interaction. A point of influence is considered to exist if (a) choice is possible with respect to the nature of the police activity in question, and (b) one can produce a plausible hypothesis linking police activity and wider effect. The possibility of doing differently on the part of the police and the possibility of influence are both essential to the analysis.

A. What Police Do

Police affect political development through the things they do, the nature of the actions they perform. These actions, which are not all of a kind, impinge upon society at different points. Both the nature of the activity and its point of contact with the political system affect its influence on political development.

1. The police bear primary responsibility for maintaining stable conditions of social life. Whether they do so or not determines to a large extent the fortunes of any development effort. This is particularly obvious for economic development. Insofar as the form and pace of economic development condition political enterprise, the police, by maintaining conditions compatible with economic development of whatever character, affect the form of political interaction in the future. Order and security are essential conditions of economic growth. Property must be protected; contracts upheld; peculation curtailed; the opportunity to work safeguarded; and the fruits of one's labor

secured for enjoyment. The balance between order and violence, lawlessness and order, security and insecurity, is held by the police; they critically determine whether development will prosper.

2. Police may play a role directly in the political life of a nation. They do so in many ways. Most obviously, they may choose to participate directly in top-level policymaking. They normally possess a preponderance of force in domestic society, and they may use it, or the threat of it, to influence the character and composition of government. Police have often lent support, if only through inaction, to the forceful overthrow of governments; the reward for services has been membership in the resulting junta. Even where government is not in part their creature, police may generate a political role for themselves by the shrewd use of latent power. The police become one of several important constituent groups supporting government and they develop leaders expected to move in high councils of state so that policy reflects a police point of view. Even without participating directly in policymaking, police can significantly shape government activity. They do this by affecting the composition of national leadership. Police have been known to use their powers to harass and frustrate politicians unfavorable to them. Permission to hold public rallies, parades, or to use loudspeakers on public streets may be denied these leaders. Rallies may be dispersed at the first hint of enthusiasm as a menace to public order. Or leaflets and pamphlets may be confiscated as subversive. Candidates favorable to the police, on the other hand, may be given every consideration and may even be lent conveyances the better to visit electors. Perhaps most subtle of all, police possess an almost unlimited ability to intervene in politics and policy implementation by standing aside. For example, protection of a politician too independent of police wishes may be tardy in coming; his rallies may be broken up by hooligans before the police arrive; his family, friends, and supporters may be victims of attack, pranks, or criminal acts always while the police are occupied elsewhere. If popular elections are part of politics, then with police connivance the dead may vote and the living vote more than once.

The police can also influence politics by failing to support the implementation of policy decisions already made. Suppose, for example, that government decrees land is to be distributed to peasants. Police may allow landowners to intimidate peasants having the temerity to apply for new holdings. Or if a stricter tax law is inaugurated, police may allow its provisions to be flagrantly disregarded; tax collectors may be subjected to brutal physical attacks or summons to tax delinquents may never be served.

Police may also affect political development by the patterns of political competition they allow to grow. By what they do or do not do they help to establish norms for the conduct of remonstrance. The quantity of violence, for example, in politics is in part their responsibility. They regulate the vociferousness of demonstrations and the disruptiveness of agitation. The police determine, at least initially, whether a stump politician is exercising his right of free speech or is a public nuisance or a threat to public order. A society subject to periodic outbursts of violence, to ambuscades and arson in the pursuit of political ends, to civil disobedience and sabotage will surely develop in quite a different way from a society in which violence is rare and relations among individuals proceed on the basis of stable expectations about the means of contention.

At the other end of the scale, police influence in politics may be carefully regulated by law and custom. In Anglo-Saxon countries police have become uniformed technicians in enforcing law. They are subordinate to civilian officials who bear the prime responsibility for determining law-and-order policy. Even their role as an interest group may be cautiously circumscribed. They may not be allowed to form voluntary associations. They may be denied a collective voice in establishing wages and conditions of service. In particular, the right to strike may be denied them. Some countries have even gone so far as to exclude them from the full privileges of citizenship by disqualifying them from voting. Their political role, even as individuals, is reduced below that of other citizens.

3. Police influence political life through administration. They may be entrusted with administrative tasks far beyond the normal concept of police duties. They may license shops, inspect buildings, supervise fire services, issue permits, run laboratories, check immigration, issue passports, register births and deaths, run industrial plants (especially those producing equipment used by police), collect taxes, solicit for public undertakings, manage hospitals and schools, direct construction of roads, and supervise public health programs. Even without participating

themselves in general government administration they may influence it through acts within their own domain. They may bring pressure to bear upon civil servants to perform as police wish or they may allow others to bring improper pressure to bear without raising a hand in protection. They hold an even tighter rein over administrators when they are granted authority to investigate administrative actions or administrative personnel. Criminal acts by civil servants outside their work are generally subject to police investigation; should this also be the case with criminal acts while in the performance of duty? Who, for example, should investigate charges of bureaucratic corruption—the police or a civilian agency? More seriously, police may be given authority to examine charges of malfeasance and inefficiency. Their access to administration becomes then almost limitless and they may be tempted to impose their own standards of procedural as well as substantive propriety.

4. The police influence political life by what they do generally in society and the relations they establish with the public. Even assuming that the task of police is considered minimally as maintaining law and order and limiting criminal activity, it is a mistake to conceive of police duties as being all of one kind. Several important determinations affect their substantive actions, and some of these determinations are made by the police themselves. The decisions that are made involve (a) the emphasis that is to be given to different aspects of the prevention-containment task; (b) the laws that are to be given priority in enforcement; (c) the rules that must be established to guide police in applying laws to specific persons and situations; and (d) the number of enforcing functions that are given the police to perform. Let us look at each of these.

The first question that arises is how should time be divided between providing protection and inflicting punishment. Efficiently tracking down and arresting criminals is like locking the barn door after the horse has escaped, except insofar as speedy punishment serves as a deterrent to future crimes. If police address themselves to the preventive task, however, they quickly become involved in a range of activities calling for quite different skills than are required for criminal investigation. They must begin to publish brochures and deliver lectures on household security; they must visit schools to conduct traffic safety clinics; they must sponsor courses in personal safety for working girls and taxi drivers. Given limitations in resources, which task should come first—prevention or punishment? The image of police held by the public may be profoundly affected by the answer to this question.

The police frequently perform duties that are not strictly a part of maintaining law and order and limiting criminal activity. Through these non-criminal contacts the police influence attitudes. Police very often serve as a ready source of information about all kinds of things—from bus schedules to rules for pets—and they are called upon to handle many personal emergencies—such as finding lost children, rescuing cats from trees, removing dead animals from the street, providing medical attention, and seeking help for the destitute or abandoned. They also undertake welfare services. They supervise athletic programs, youth clubs, hobby societies; they run summer camps, police bands, and outings to historical monuments. In underdeveloped countries they are exhorted to contribute labor to village development projects, to assist in dispensing medical information, and to aid in relocating the dispossessed.

Police themselves are divided about the effects of undertaking tasks not strictly related to law enforcement. Most policemen would probably echo the sentiment of the Maharashtra Police Commission in 1964:

"The first and foremost duty of the police in a democratic welfare state is the maintenance of law and order. All other roles are subsidiary. It is not desirable to fritter away the energies of the police force, already overworked, by asking them to shoulder responsibilities which do not fall within the above category."[2] But the police need the cooperation and goodwill of the public in order to accomplish the basic task of maintaining law and order. How can they most successfully gain this essential regard? If they confine themselves to criminal investigation they deal largely with criminals. They run the risk of becoming punitive functionaries whom the public meets only as a last resort in situations of great stress. Would a surer way to develop sympathy with the lot of a policeman and a greater awareness of a citizen's own responsibilities for law and order be to "fritter" time away in non-criminal contacts? Whatever the answer to this question, the fact is that the image of the police will be af-

[2] Government of Maharashtra, *Summary of Recommendations of the Maharashtra State Police Commission*, 1964 (Bombay: Government Central Press, 1964), p. 32.

fected as a result and with it the image of the rest of government as well.[3]

Another critical variable in what police do is how they define the scope of the police function. Should they handle all restraining and punitive chores of government? Are they to be responsible for inspecting motor vehicles, unsafe premises, liquor establishments, and the condition of firearms? Should they direct traffic and issue parking tickets? There are consequences here for the structure of administration, especially for the degree of centralization, as we noted before, but also for the regard members of the public have for the police. In situations of danger individuals are often grateful for police intervention; this opinion might change to anger and resentment if they always encounter police wherever government moves to regulate their activity. This in turn might influence whether the mass of the people identify with the police against wrongdoers or with lawbreakers against the police.

The police also possess an enormous amount of discretion in the laws they choose to enforce. Laws are usually so numerous that police cannot hope to enforce all of them equally. They must make judgments about which are most important. Are all infractions of motor vehicle laws equally serious? Should as much attention be given to public nuisances and noise abatement as to protection of property and the maintenance of order at public events? In most countries if vice laws were studiously enforced the police would have very little time left over for investigating more serious criminal activity. But if all laws cannot be enforced all the time, then how are the police to be guided in what they choose to do? Should they take their cues from society or should they follow the dictates of their own conscience? The police exercise discretion too in the choice of when and against whom laws are to be applied. When is the juvenile to be arrested and when simply cautioned? In the United States gambling in a country club by the elite of

[3] Dr. A. L. Goodhart in a note of dissent to the Royal Commission on the Police supported the view that the surest way of obtaining public cooperation is to demonstrate efficiency in criminal investigation and crime prevention. If the people have faith that the police will be able to accomplish these essential tasks, they will be more willing to offer assistance even to the point of enduring infringements of their liberty. Great Britain, *Royal Commission on the Police, 1962: Final Report*, Cmnd. 1728, pp. 157-181. Professor Michael Banton discusses this view in *The Policeman in the Community* (New York: Basic Books, Inc., 1964), p. 160, and argues that in the United States at least the effects are as Dr. Goodhart predicted.

a community is often overlooked, while gambling by the Negro waiters of the same club for much lower stakes in a minority neighborhood attracts the attention of the vice squad. The seriousness of an offense, and consequently the response of the police, varies with the people involved. Pilfering by a starving child in a crowded market may be winked at; shoplifting by a woman with a record of convictions for petty criminal acts produces immediate action. A fist-fight among business executives in a well-to-do nightclub may earn a charge of assault, while a free-swinging brawl by sailors in a waterfront bar earns a night in jail for drunkenness. Even assaults with a deadly weapon may be shrugged off by the police if the perpetrators are lower-class people, while they would occasion arrest and a sensational trial if those involved were wealthy or prominent.

Laws are not self-starting—delicate acts of judgment are required and these choices are made by policemen on the spot. Whose code of conduct are they to enforce? In underdeveloped countries the contest may be between modernizers and traditionalists. When land is distributed from large landholders to landless peasants, the success of the venture may depend upon whether the police put the full weight of enforcement muscle behind the reforms or whether they allow covert noncompliance. Similarly, when squatters in new industrial towns erect dwellings on unused land, the police must decide whether to turn a blind eye or protect the property rights of absentee landlords. Police usually deny that they have discretion; but in the minds of the public, whatever the police may say, the police are considered friendly or hostile agents depending on whose side they seem to be supporting. Respect for law is rarely prized in the abstract; it is good and bad laws which attract support or condemnation, and this depends upon point of view and personal interest. Police are an instrument for achieving conformity between human behavior and human prescriptions. Even by doing nothing at all the police cannot avoid choosing sides and appearing to adopt one or another philosophy of life.

Enforcement of law involves detection, investigation, judgment, and punishment. The number of these functions police handle themselves has important effects for the appearance of justice in any country. In the United States and Great Britain executive agents of law are carefully separated from judicial ones. One agency provides the facts; another evaluates them.

The administration of punishment, too, is separated from police work and entrusted to another establishment. Attitudes toward law may change significantly depending upon whether the police are investigators, judges, juries, jailors, or hangmen.

In summary, considering the task of the police simply as law enforcement, the police may exercise discretion with potential political significance with respect to the emphasis given to prevention as opposed to punishment; the kinds of laws enforced; the occasions on which any law is enforced; and the number of law-enforcing functions combined in the hands of the police.

B. How Police Do It

Police influence by their manner as much as by what they do. Several qualitative elements in contact between police and public are particularly important.

1. Where is the locus of initiative between police and public? Police may seem a passive instrument that the citizen must activate in order to secure needed assistance. Sometimes the activation process requires considerable effort. Police create the impression that they come if they must, not because they want to. On the other hand, police may create an image of being actively sympathetic. They respond before being required. In many countries the impact of a police force grasping at opportunities to display initiative would be difficult to exaggerate; it would be startling certainly, shocking perhaps, and might possibly lead to a whole new conception of the possibilities for government in human affairs.

2. Are the police secretive or open? Secretiveness breeds suspicion and fear; people fill in what they don't know with what they imagine or the worst of what they are told. In attitudes as with currency, there seems to be a tendency for the bad to drive out the good. Moreover, commendable traits in the police may be obscured by secretiveness. What good is efficiency if the aggrieved party is not aware that he is being taken care of efficiently. Police forces must not only be good; they must be seen as being good.

3. How are members of the public treated by the police in individual contacts? Are the police formal or informal, familiar or stiff, rude or polite, responsive or uninterested, well-spoken or coarse, abusive or considerate, restrained or overbearing, intimidating or solicitous, brutal or peaceful, and so forth?

That the police do treat people differently in different circumstances is attested by many observers of police behavior. For their own self-protection policemen feel justified in varying their approach. Since a single miscalculation can result in injury and death to the policeman, it has always seemed presumptuous for outsiders to attempt to set down rigid rules of procedure for policemen to abide by. Furthermore, there has been very little serious study of public responses to different approaches by the police. Neither policemen nor observers are confident that they can predict the effects that a particular demeanor may have on individuals contacted. Take the single cases of the use of force by policemen. Does the readiness of police to use force call forth hostility and violence in the general public, and particularly among suspects, or is readiness to use force essential to prevent a greater amount of violence from the public and suspects? It is illuminating to note that police authorities in the United States and Great Britain proceed on the basis of diametrically opposed theories in this matter, for the British policeman does not carry a firearm, the American policeman always does. Police authorities in Britain believe that to go armed, to prepare visibly for war, would trigger a greater amount of violence in those they contact; American police, on the other hand, believe that their sidearm is an essential deterrent, and that without it they would be helpless in enforcing the law. But even American policemen are not consistent in their theories about the proper use of force; they admit tacitly that readiness to appeal to physical violence on their part must be carefully meshed with circumstances. They say that the kid-gloves approach diminishes respect for law enforcement; that if criminals, or would-be criminals, no longer respected—or feared —the police they would be more likely to engage in violent criminal acts. At the same time, policemen are aware that against crowds force must be applied in gradual increments—too much too soon can precipitate a riot. Policemen tell, too, of the need to keep talking and avoid physical violence when facing a hostile crowd with a prisoner. If the crowd is not to be pushed into violent action against the policemen, the policeman must preserve an appearance of being a human being, not a machine of force. His humanity—like a slender thread of sympathy between aggressor and victim—is his only shield.[4] So it is one thing to know

[4] William A. Westley, "The Escalation of Violence Through Legitimation," *The Annals*, March, 1966, p. 123.

what one approves of himself in the way of police demeanor; it is quite another to stipulate with confidence what any particular manner will achieve in terms of public response. The need for research is critical. Perhaps even more critical is a greater willingness to admit honestly that one does not know how the public—a varied creature—will always respond to police contacts. On the part of both police and their critics there is a great deal of dogmatic assertion, which in turn prevents the cooperative study that alone can resolve questions of police behavior and public response.

4. Do the police act impartially? Does the lower class person get the same kind of attention as the college president? Are the police as keen to stop lawbreakers in minority neighborhoods as they are in higher class suburbs? Minority leaders in the United States continually criticize the double standard employed by police. The police are portrayed as being agents of the power structure, not as servants of all the people. Tough but seemingly arbitrary police actions may encourage lawlessness far more than a more gentle but strictly impartial policy.[5]

C. What the Police Are

Police affect society through the individual contacts they have with fellow citizens; they also affect society as a corporate entity, by virtue of what they are and what they require of society. Three modes of influence are involved: demonstration effect, creation of external economies, and generation of demand.

By exhibiting certain characteristics the police develop an image; they stand for something; and if what they stand for is insecurely rooted in society, or is totally new, the police may confirm its establishment by the example they set. For instance, police may serve as living proof of the possibility of creating a truly national instrument of government; they may be one of the few agencies acting in the name of the nation even though composed of individuals from many subnational groupings. The police serve a symbolic role, representing a nation yet to be, developing national heroes, and giving a sense of pride in country by means of parades, reviews, and athletic competitions.[6]

[5] Yale Kamisar, "On the Tactics of Police-Prosecution Oriented Critics of the Courts," *Cornell Law Quarterly*, XLIX, 1964, pp. 456-457.

[6] Morris Janowitz, *The Military in the Political Development of New Nations* (Chicago: University of Chicago Press, 1964), pp. 80-83, notes this

The police may exert a profound influence simply because of the relations they publicly establish with other elements of government. Do they show themselves willing to work with a new national leadership? Do they work in harness with civilian bureaucracy? Police may also set an example by means of the techniques they employ to accomplish their objectives. In an underdeveloped country police are sometimes an island of modernity, eager to use the latest technical devices, organized on the basis of merit rather than status, and experimenting with functionally specific role-playing. A local example of the utilization of these techniques may embolden others to innovate too. People in any country, whatever its stage of development, look over their shoulders for new ideas to use in solving their own problems, for the courage to do what they think is required, or simply for an example that will allow them to convince others of the sensibleness of their own plan. An underdeveloped country has fewer centers of innovation than a Western country and consequently the police may be a more persuasive example.

Because of what they are, the police may create for themselves, or urge society to create, what they require in order to function properly. In the one case they create external economics; in the other they generate demand. Police forces sponsor development of chemical and seriological laboratories; they urge universities to establish criminology curricula or courses on public administration and police management; they support the development of communication networks; they establish educational qualifications for recruitment, thus creating a market that educational institutions must take into consideration in training young men and women; they institute their own schools and training establishments; they urge the manufacture of protective devices against criminal activity, as well as the paraphernalia needed for efficient detective work; and they may vigorously support the establishment of many kinds of welfare facilities, such as canteens, public housing, hospitals, and maternity services.

D. What Police Do to Each Other

Police affect political development by what they do to each other in becoming and remaining policemen. The police force

---

symbolic role in the case of the military. He believes it contributes to building national self-esteem.

in some countries has been an important avenue of upward social mobility; it has allowed men to escape from depressed conditions of minority status. The police have served as a melting pot, by developing a sense of national identity overcoming particularistic loyalties to subnational groups. In order to be a policeman the recruit may have to learn a specialized skill, such as radio maintenance, accounting, photography, office management, typing, and so forth. The sense of one's position in society and one's relation to political agencies can certainly be affected by police membership. It has long been recognized that occupational membership influences views about society. Face-to-face interaction conditions general attitudes more thoroughly than any other means. Policemen may become more aware of the possibilities for action through government, the opportunities— perhaps even the necessity—for creative political action. They may be led to see government as acting in behalf of many people or only in the interests of a few. They may be imbued with the notion that government employment is an opportunity for service to the nation or is a chance to feather one's own nest. Membership in the police may affect their view about whether people should be told or asked to do something in the interests of the nation. The police may generate the outlook that they are guardians of a uniquely correct blueprint for national development and that civilians are too blind, stupid, or self-centered to perceive what is required for national greatness. Finally, older policemen may convince recruits that social conditions are not impermeable, that change is possible, that life contains dynamic potentialities.

It is entirely possible of course that the organization will play no formative role in molding individual predispositions. The human clay brought to it, rather than being reshaped, contaminates the organization, making it incapable of doing differently from what society endorses. The capacity to acculturate depends largely on isolation from the surrounding community. The military possess this ability to a higher degree than the police. The police, due to the nature of their work, must mingle with the public. Also, they are not as a rule separated from their families. Nonetheless, like any occupational group they may develop a distinctive subculture. Because the police so often come to feel like a group apart, the opportunities for acculturation to a divergent pattern are probably greater than for most other occupational groups in the society.

In all these ways, the police may become a nexus of influence upon the nature of political life in any country. They may not always do so, and the influence they exert may often be quite marginal. But the possibility for influence exists, and should not be disregarded.

PROBLEMS OF ANALYSIS

After having established the modalities through which the police may affect the political system, the job for the analyst of political development is to establish prescriptions for the kind of behavior by the police that will most efficiently serve whatever goals of political development he wants achieved. The problem is, however, that there are enormous intellectual difficulties to be surmounted before precise specifications can be made. Some of these difficulties can be illustrated by giving an example. Let us assume that a police policy is to be established that should contribute to the development of a democratic political regime. What would appear to be the reasonable rules that should regulate the way police act in political life, in administration, toward the public, upon one another, and as a group setting an example, in order to achieve a democratic polity? One might argue a priori as follows.

First, the police should be studiously nonviolent; they should go to great lengths to avoid the use of force. Force produces bitterness and hostility on the part of the public. The use of force by the police forfeits public cooperation, which is essential to a law-abiding society and alienates people from government generally. Second, a police force cannot operate across the grain of what people want them to enforce. Respect for law is an essential ingredient of democracy; for the police to try to operate autonomously, without consideration for the desires of the people, would cheapen law and encourage the public to make common cause with lawbreakers against the law. The police must choose to enforce substantially what the public will permit and support. Third, police must close the gap that may grow in any society between those who enforce the law and those against whom it is enforced. Especially where an impersonal rule of law is something new, it is essential that the police demonstrate their common humanity with the citizenry at large. Law must be seen as a creative, public-serving engine, not only as a restricting one. One way of achieving this is for police to join with the public in accomplishing non-enforcement goals. They may cooperate in community work projects, set up youth clubs, promote programs of village health and hygiene, and assist in distributing food to undernourished children. Fourth, the police must recruit from every geographical region of the country and from every social stratum or group. The police can help to create that modicum of national unity which undergirds any democratic regime. If police become identified with any particular group they will lose the support of the rest of the people, perhaps lending force to the ever-present whisper that government is by "them" and not "us." Fifth, a national democratic government seems to require a growing, modern economy. A high-performance economy in turn demands skills— the level of skill development that underlies increasing specialization of function. Then, too, democracy itself may require an educated population capable of participating intellectually in complex and abstract national issues. The police, therefore, should recruit and train men who will be able to fit comfortably into a technological society and who will be several cuts above the general population in educational attainments.

Eventually a set of principles could be constructed that would specify the nature of police activity at every point at which police affect political development, so as to confirm that development in the direction of freedom-conserving institutions. Even a brief inspection of the five principles previously suggested quickly indicates how slender a reed is logic separated from fact. Any notion that there is a single "democratic police policy" must be examined with great caution. The first difficulty is that we do not yet know how to choose among contributions of different kinds that the police might make to political development, each of which calls for different, sometimes incompatible, policies. For example, it seemed reasonable to argue that police should use physical force with great restraint and prudence; that the use of force aggravates the cleavage between ruler and ruled. However, law and order, peace and security, are themselves requisites for a stable political life. It may be necessary to choose between allowing stultifying acts of civil disobedience by significant segments of society or a firm, tough-minded police policy that does not allow laws to be trampled contemptuously underfoot. How does one balance these desiderata? Similarly with the argument that police cannot operate across the grain of what the public will accept in law enforcement. Surely any modernizing elite will enact laws designed to lead people into new forms of interaction. Resistance will be encountered, but progress in the long run can only be achieved through overcoming inevitable reluctance to accept new ways. It is necessary to balance enforced conformity against destructive hostility generated in the process of separating people from the past. Which consideration has higher priority?

The second major difficulty in constructing a democracy-reinforcing police policy involves the ambiguity of results that may flow from any specific policy prescription. It was argued that one way of closing the gap between police and public is to have the police engage with the public in the performance of common tasks. Civilians might be brought into police work, as auxiliaries or volunteer workers, and the police might serve in civilian, especially welfare, lines of endeavor. But does the public gain a higher respect for the police and for the process of law enforcement by participating in such activities with the police? Even if police can spare the time without jeopardizing the efficiency with which they defend life and property, do people come to respect law-enforcement functions by working with policemen in building a school? In another case, many people argue that the police should be strictly impartial in the implementation of laws—law should be impersonal. But perhaps law needs to be individualized to be respected? The policeman should treat the first offender more leniently than the habitual offender. The juvenile whose home life is excellent, whose parents will readily assume responsibility for him, should receive different treatment from the juvenile whose mother is a drunkard and whose father is in jail. Is respect for law, and for the police, more successfully built through police who act like automata, never allowing explanations from individuals to have an effect, or through police who may modify their behavior, especially in the case of arrests, because of the particular circumstances of the case or of the individual?

Both because our knowledge of priorities in accomplishing political development of a specified character is quite limited and because many policies may have contrary effects, all the a priori prescriptions earlier suggested may be challenged as being subverting of democratic evolution in some countries. Our knowledge of the requirements of democracy and of the nature of the effects of police activities must be improved considerably before we may be confident about what police should do in order to help secure the blessing of liberty to a developing nation.

Research, therefore, must proceed in two directions: (a) that of general political development and (b) that of the impact of police on political structures and public behavior. The latter task is perhaps the simpler, although the methodological problems involved will not be overcome easily. In order to make recommendations about police policy, we must know what type of police behavior produces what kind of effects. This kind of information can only be obtained by studying police activity in its relations with politically relevant groups over a period of time. If we can do that, for police in different cultures, we are halfway to the goal of linking police and political development. With this information, there is point in asking if police in a particular country are contributing to or detracting from the growth of a regime of a given character.

TWO

THE INDIAN POLICE—CHARACTER AND SETTING

2 • *Structure and Development*

THE Indian police system compared to systems in other countries has three distinguishing features.

First: the police are organized, maintained, and directed by the several states of the Indian union. There are today sixteen state police forces in India. Although the central government has some police agencies under its authority, such as the Central Bureau of Investigation (C.B.I.) and the police forces of centrally administered territories, these forces are in the nature of residuary police forces. They are not expected to bear the primary burden of police work in the country; they complement state agencies as well as providing enforcement muscle in the implementation of exclusively central government tasks. At the same time, the authorizing legislation for the state-based police forces is very similar from state to state. The result is that there is diversity in operational control combined with remarkable organizational similarity. India has managed to avoid both the fragmentation of police under a system of local control, such as in the United States with its forty thousand separate forces, and the rigidity of a national police force directed by a central government.

Second: the Indian police system is horizontally stratified. Like military forces, the police are organized into cadres depending upon rank—commissioned officers, noncommissioned officers, and men, although these are not the precise terms used in India. Appointment to N.C.O. rank is partly by promotion from below and partly by lateral entry through direct recruitment. Promotion from N.C.O. rank to officer status is not impossible but it is rare. The principle of horizontal stratification affects more than the organization of ranks. It accounts also for the relations between the central and state governments with respect to police administration and for the distribution of police powers among ranks. The officer cadre, known as the Indian Police Service (I.P.S.), is recruited, organized, trained, and disciplined according to national legislation. The officers belong to one of the two all-India services and for the purpose of internal organization, as opposed to operational control when on duty, are subject to central government authority. Moreover, police power and authority, that is, what a policeman is allowed to do in the line of duty, differs with rank. Different police powers are assigned by law to be carried out by different ranks of policemen. This practice is in marked contrast to that of Great Britain where the constable, the lowest ranking policeman, possesses all the authority any policeman can have. Horizontal stratification, then, is reflected in rank structure, relations between levels of government with respect to police personnel, and the distribution of legal authority among policemen.

Third: the police in each state are divided vertically into an armed and an unarmed branch. This is a functional division. The unarmed police staff the police stations, go on patrol duties, and prevent and investigate crime. The armed police are employed for those duties which require the presence of constituted physical force, such as guard duties at banks and the quelling of civil disturbances. The armed police are housed in barracks, trained in weapons handling and drill, and live a quasi-military life. But they are part of each state's police force and are officered by men of the I.P.S. Great Britain and the United States have solved the problem of police and armament in two different ways; India has found yet a third mode. In the United States all policemen are armed as a matter of course; in Great Britain none is. The Indian arrangement recognizes the value of having policemen uncontaminated by arms but also recognizes that it is necessary to have ready at hand a well-trained body of police capable of responding with overwhelming force.

These are the three primary structural characteristics of the Indian police. They distinguish the Indian system from other systems in the world. How has the system developed to its present form? Since India has had a prolonged colonial experience, which structural forms are indigenous and which are imported? Finally, how are these principles worked out in terms of organization and legislation? These questions will be answered in the following sections.

POLICE DEVELOPMENT PRIOR TO 1947

Throughout all of Indian history, even into the present time, one can discern two distinct police systems, a rural village-based system and a system emanating from the dominant locus of imperial power at the moment. In fact Indian police history can be written largely in terms of attempts to create an imperial system linking the indigenous fragmented system to the imperium and making it both efficient and responsive to orders from the imperial capital. Since India is and has always been a country of villages, it is not surprising that the basic unit of the traditional police system is the village. Responsibility for policing rested with the headman who was usually assisted by a watchman and sometimes by a special police helper (e.g., the *patel* of western India). Village security and prevention and detection of crime were in the hands of the headman. He was also responsible for the detection and capture of local villagers who committed crimes in other areas. Many accounts of this system[1] mention that the headman was required to make up out of his own pocket the value of property stolen and not returned. External security for the village was often obtained by negotiating to pay "protection money" to a threatening band or to a criminal tribe if one was resident in the area.[2] Whether the headman was autonomous or was responsible to higher local authority depended upon the structure of landholding. If there was a dominant landowner, as was often the case, responsibility for policing rested with the landowner and the headman acted as his agent, both for police and for revenue purposes. But where landholding was more evenly distributed or where a dominant landowner was indolent or remote, the headman represented the pinnacle of the only police authority most Indians knew.

The rural police system is as old as recorded Indian history and has continued unchanged by the tides of conquest, consolidation, and anarchy that have swept over India in the past millennia.[3] As we shall see, the village headman or local landowner might be contacted by the subordinate officials of the imperium but his relations to his fellow villagers and his duties within the village were not touched. Rather he was simply held

[1] West Bengal, Home (Police) Department, *Report of the Police Commission, West Bengal, 1960-1961* (Alipore: Superintendent Government Printing, 1964), p. 4; and J. C. Curry, *The Indian Police* (London: Faber and Faber, 1932), pp. 19-23.

[2] John Matthai, *Village Government in British India* (London: T. Fisher Unwin, Ltd., 1915), Chapter 4, notes an instance of villagers revolting against the price of protection charged by local criminal tribes. This was near Madura in what is now Madras states in 1896-1897. Considerable agitation resulted and some serious rioting.

[3] See, for example, A. L. Basham, *The Wonder That Was India* (London: Sidgwick and Jackson, Ltd., 1954), Chapter 4.

accountable for what he had been doing all along. Only once, and that comparatively recently, have relations within the village been affected by an imperial power. This departure was made by the British and began in the early nineteenth century. Whether the authority of the traditional system has been wholly undermined and lost is a question that will be taken up later. The other great empires—Maurya, Gupta, and Moghul —were content to establish contact with the autonomous villages but not to reorder policing within them. The details of structure as well as the names of agents within the imperial organization changed from empire to empire, but the traditional police system persisted mutely.[4] The empires were administered autocratically through a system of agents extending from capital to province, from province to subdivision, and from subdivision to landowner and/or headman. Officials at any level combined in their own persons all the functions necessary to the empire. They were military commanders for internal security, revenue collectors, judges, magistrates, and chiefs of police.[5] This tradition of functional concentration was carried on by the British in the position of district collector and has only recently been challenged.[6]

The cities and towns had a more elaborate police system, and because they were centers of trade and communication were always tied more closely to the imperial administrative structure. The head of town police administration was the *kotwal*, a word which comes down to us in the name given in many Indian towns today for the central police station, the *kotwali*. Although the post may go back to Mauryian times, the clearest description of its activities comes from Moghul sources, especially the *Ain-i-Akbari* or diary of Akbar (1556-1605). The kotwal was to raise and maintain a police force, to regulate night patrolling, to maintain surveillance over visitors, spies, and migrants, to arrest criminals, to keep the prison, and to eliminate prostitution and consumption of alcoholic beverages.[7] It is

---

[4] "In the rural areas no new arrangements appear to have been introduced by the Moghuls: they remained, as from time immemorial, under the headman of the villages and their subordinate watchmen." West Bengal Police Commission, p. 5.

[5] Curry, p. 22.

[6] The separation of executive and judicial functions was made official policy in the late 1950's and was completed in most districts within the next five years.

[7] Jadunath Sarkar, *Mughal Administration* (Calcutta: M. C. Sarkar and Sons, Private Ltd., 1963), pp. 57-60; and Sir Edmund C. Cox, *Police and*

clear from commentaries that the kotwal was the unacclaimed ruler of many towns. The position was coveted by many, particularly for the opportunities it provided for extortion and receiving of bribes. The kotwal is usually pictured as being ruthless, cruel, arbitrary, and effective when it was in his interest to be.[8]

Indian police history can be seen then as the expansion and contraction of an imperial power always set upon an impermeable stratum of village institutions. Structures came and went, but there was no qualitative evolution from one imperial high-point to another. In terms of ensuring the security of life and property, the imperial agents of law and order played the more important role. Village policing was essentially a self-regulatory mechanism tied closely to the internal power structure of village society. Its external defense capabilities were extremely limited, being composed of village defense parties if the men would dare, or of the passive ability to bribe a threatening band into passing on. When an imperial power was in decline, life became hazardous in the extreme. The effects of imperial disintegration may be seen in this picture of life around Delhi at the beginning of the nineteenth century:

"Now at Delhi, now at Meerut or Agra or elsewhere a strong ruler would enforce order, and establish security for miles around. But everywhere he went he would see men armed, with shield and sword, with musket or with a stout wooden *lathi* or stave. In those days only the strong man armed could guard his goods, and then only until a stronger than he should come."[9]

It was a time when armed bands of freebooters roamed the countryside—Pindaris, Marathas, Afghans, and bandits and adventurers of all kinds—and villages settled disputes over stolen property and cattle by means of surprise raids on one another at night.

Only an efficient and well-organized imperial power could free the countryside from such anarchy. Yet even when this was achieved the peasant was hardly free from oppression and in-

---

Crime in India (London: Stanley Paul and Co., n.d.), Chapters 3 and 4.

[8] The position of *kotwal*, and particularly his arbitary power, in towns in central India during the early nineteenth century is described in fictional form in Meadows Taylor, *Confessions of a Thug* (London: Oxford University Press, 1916). The novel was first published in 1839.

[9] Percival Spear, *Twilight of the Mughals* (Cambridge: At the University Press, 1951), p. 6.

security. The difference between a period of imperial regnum and interregnum was the difference between a single familiar exploiter and a multitude of itinerant unfamiliar exploiters. The exactions of subordinate officials were hardly likely to seem much less capricious to a peasant than the appearance of a gang of robbers. Whether the severity of the demands in each was much different would be very important but very difficult to determine. Police in all periods of Indian history have been represented as oppressive and unfair, like this comment on the policeman of the late eighteenth century: "Extortion and oppression flourished unchecked through all gradations of officials responsible for the maintenance of law and order."[10]

The British first came to India in 1609 when Captain Hawkins, trader for the East India Company, landed at Surat. More than a century and a half passed before the Company began to play a role in the processes of government. It was content to compete for trading concessions, to set up its warehouses and commercial colonies, and to vie for favors at the courts of the Moghuls and lesser rulers of the interior. The Battle of Plassey in Bengal in 1757 marked the beginning of a new phase in Company activity. It proved that the interloping British possessed sufficient force of arms to defeat local rulers. The British required stability, and if it was not provided they were fully competent to provide it for themselves. So the British began to move into the void created by the gradual dissolution of the Moghul empire.[11] The subsequent history of administrative development under the British can be broken neatly into two periods of approximately equal length: 1757 to 1858, Battle of Plassey to Government of India Act, and 1858 to 1947, Government of India Act to independence.

The first hundred-year period was a time of groping for the most efficient solutions to the institutional problems of ruling an expanding colonial empire. As far as police were concerned, it was a time of experimentation in which the British sought the solutions to two problems. First, the perennial question faced by any imperial authority in India, what use should the rul-

[10] Government of India, *Report of the Indian Police Commission, 1902-1903,* p. 5.

[11] The British undoubtedly hastened the collapse of the Moghul empire. They certainly undermined any chance of its reinvigoration. For a discussion of the British impact on Moghul institutions, see Percival Spear, *Twilight of the Mughals* (Cambridge: At the University Press, 1951) and *The Nabobs* (paperback edition, London: Oxford University Press, 1963).

ing power make of the traditional rural police? Second, how should the imperial administration be organized with respect to its different and most important functional responsibilities, namely law and order and revenue collection? Neither of these problems was clearly perceived nor consistently articulated at the time, but gradually, by a process of trial and error, solutions to both were found.

By 1792 the Company felt they could no longer overlook the incidence of crime, brigandage, and unrest in its three "presidency" provinces, Bengal, Bombay, and Madras. It became apparent that the village system was inadequate by itself and that an imperial power had to assume some role in maintaining law and order. Accordingly, in 1792 Lord Cornwallis, governor-general of India, took police administration out of the hands of the large landowners (the *zamindars*) and established in their place a police force responsible to agents of the Company. Districts were divided into parts and over each a police official, known as a *darogha*, was placed. The darogha was to raise and direct a force of men known as *barkandazes*, literally "lightning throwers" because they were armed. The darogha was accountable to the district judge and was in turn responsible for supervising the village headmen. The kotwal remained in charge of police administration in the towns.

The darogha system did not measure up to expectations. Crime continued to mount and social conditions became even more unsettled. The darogha was unable to exercise control over village police. The darogha and his men were a force apart, the creation of alien authority; they could not command the assistance of local castes and traditional leaders as a hereditary landowner could. Moreover, the darogha system was undermanned. Even if the integrity of the traditional system had not been destroyed, the new arrangement was stretched much too thin. But it should be understood also that the reforms in police administration were only one aspect of more fundamental changes in the whole process of criminal justice management. A new system of courts was established in which the standard of proof was much higher than that demanded by village *panchayats* or Moghul courts. Convictions became increasingly difficult to get. Punishments were rendered less cruel and were no longer administered summarily. Indefinite jail sentences were abolished and prisoners suddenly found themselves comparatively well treated.[12] Perhaps because the darogha's arrogance and tyranny were so clearly to be seen by any district officer, he was saddled with the entire blame for the deteriorating conditions in the countryside. There was a spate of special commissions, minutes, and weighty reports, all of them castigating the darogha arrangement. In 1814 the Company formally ordered the system abolished and a return made to the traditional method of village policing.[13]

The decision amounted to renouncing the Company's attempt to police through a force of its own and to go back to a system already found wanting. Perhaps the evils of the present seemed more serious than those of the past. If the darogha was the culprit, then nothing would do except to eliminate him. Ironically, however, the British soon discovered that they could not even abandon completely the new but discredited darogha system. The Company's order was that the darogha and his force were to be disbanded; that supervisory power over village police was to be exercised by the collector, the chief executive officer in each district.[14] The collector,[15] as the name indicates, was an officer of the revenue service. Without daroghas he could remain in touch with law-and-order conditions only through the subordinate officers of his own department. This was in fact what was done in Madras and Bombay.[16] In Bengal, however, the collector was in a peculiar predicament. As a result of Lord Cornwallis' "Permanent Settlement" in 1789, there was no subordinate revenue establishment, or not much of one. In order for the collector to supervise village police he had no recourse but to work through the darogha. So in Bengal the

[12] *Indian Police Commission, 1902-1903*, pp. 3-14.

[13] Curry, pp. 23-24.

[14] Orders to this effect were promulgated in Madras in 1816 and in Bombay in 1828. *Ibid.*

[15] The title for this post varies from place to place. Today he is collector in Andhra Pradesh, Bihar, Gujarat, Kerala, Madhya Pradesh, Madras, Maharashtra, Orissa, and Rajasthan; deputy commissioner in Assam, Jammu-Kashmir, Mysore, Punjab, and Uttar Pradesh; and district magistrate in West Bengal. David C. Potter, *Government in Rural India* (London: G. Bell and Sons, Ltd., 1964), p. 6.

[16] Sir Thomas Munro described the system in Madras in these words: "We have not in most places reverted to the old police of the country, executed by village watchmen, mostly hereditary, under the direction of the heads of the villages, *tehsildars* [minor revenue officials] of districts and the collector and magistrate of the province. The establishments of the *tehsildars* are employed without distinction either in police or revenue duties as the occasion requires." Quoted in Curry, p. 28.

darogha was, as a matter of necessity, retained and somewhat reformed.

The darogha system had not been without its supporters. Perhaps one of the most engaging was John Beames who gave a colorful description of the darogha of Bengal in his book *Memoirs of a Bengal Civilian*.[17] They ruled their territories, said Beames, like little kings. Their misdeeds were legion and always went unpunished, for who would have the temerity to report him to the collector. The darogha's powers of harassment were enormous; he could have a person indicted for harboring a bad character or failing to assist an officer in arresting a criminal. Obtaining witnesses presented no problem to the darogha. Beames also credited the daroghas with being splendid detectives. They were close to the people and were themselves wily and unscrupulous enough to meet the criminal on his own ground. The "new police," by contrast, after 1861, were quite inferior in detective ability. They were "overdrilled" and "overregulated." Their failure in criminal investigation, thought Beames, was inevitable:

"And fail we did, ignominiously for some years, until the new police learnt to use the 'extra-legal' methods of the old police without being found out. Even after they had got into the way of their work this new police was not after all very much better than the old, in spite of the flourish of trumpets with which it was introduced."[18]

The uneven abolition and reform of the darogha worked no miracles. Crime, especially dacoity, civil unrest, and insecurity, continued unabated. Officers of the Company seemed powerless to meet the challenge, as if held in thraldom by a choice between an inefficient darogha system which had been rejected and a village police system which was grossly ineffective. It is perhaps not an accident, therefore, that the impetus for a solution came from outside the established provinces and from a man who was not a conditioned Company servant. In 1843 the territory of Sind, now in West Pakistan, was conquered for the Company by Sir Charles Napier. As far as police were concerned Sind was tabula rasa. It had neither a village police system nor the remnants of a centralized revenue administration. Sir Charles, who had come to India in 1841, used as the model

[17] John Beames, *Memoirs of a Bengal Civilian* (London: Chatto and Windus, 1961), pp. 140-141.
[18] *Ibid.*, pp. 144-145.

for policing in Sind the Royal Irish Constabulary. He was undoubtedly familiar with Peel's Metropolitan Police Force but the Royal Irish Constabulary fitted more exactly the requirements of the situation he faced. Napier created a separate police organization directed by its own officers. Direction throughout the territory was in the hands of an inspector-general of police; in each district with the superintendent. The superintendent was accountable to both inspector-general and collector, for the collector remained the ranking Company officer in each district. Thus responsibility for law and order was assumed by government through the collector, but the mechanics of police administration was entrusted to a new, functionally specific department.[19]

Bits and pieces of the Sind experiment were adopted during the next few years in other parts of India. In Punjab, after its annexation in 1849, the Company set up a police establishment separate from the village system. It was divided into two branches, a military police and a civil detective force. Bombay and Madras moved more slowly to establish a Company-maintained police but they did adopt the principle that police and revenue administration should be separated, with the senior district police officer serving as lieutenant for security affairs to the collector.[20]

The Mutiny broke out in 1857, shocking the British into full realization of the responsibilities of imperial domination in so vast a territory. It ushered in a period of agonizing reassessment, the results of which set the seal on administrative development for a hundred years. Reforms that had been maturing for many years with pragmatic, bureaucratic thoroughness were suddenly enshrined in law. The Government of India Act, passed in 1858, abolished the proud Company and transferred governance of India to the Queen in Parliament. The great Indian legal codes were enacted: the Code of Civil Procedure in 1859, the Indian Penal Code in 1860, and the Code of Crim-

---

[19] There was another precedent for a force of this kind, although it was little noted at the time of its development. In 1818 Captain Outram, later Sir James, conquered Kandesh in the northern Deccan. The area was inhabited by a tribe of wild and primitive hill people known as Bhils. In 1827 Outram organized them into a force of some six hundred strong to guard government installations, escort treasure and prisoners, guard jails, and perform general police work. They were armed and given uniforms similar to the Company's sepoys. The system seems to have worked well, but it was not copied in the rest of India. Cox, pp. 65-66.

[20] This step was taken in Bombay in 1853 and Madras in 1859.

inal Procedure in 1861. Finally, a police commission was appointed in 1860 to study exhaustively the police needs of country and government. The result of the commission's deliberations was the Police Act of 1861.[21]

The police commission of 1860 established the following principles of police organization: (1) military police were to be eliminated and policing was to be entrusted to a civil constabulary; (2) civil police were to have their own separate administrative establishment headed by an inspector-general in every province;[22] (3) the inspector-general was responsible to the provincial government as the superintendent was to the civilian collector; and (4) the superintendent was to supervise village police. The principles of the Police Act were neither revolutionary nor particularly novel. They were an extension to all of British India of arrangements already found useful in several areas. The darogha, for example, did not disappear; he became the sub-inspector of police.[23] The significance of the act lay in the fact that it provided authoritative answers to the two questions implicit in British experimentation during the previous hundred years, namely, what should be the relations between imperial and rural police and how should imperial police administration be coordinated with other functions of imperial authority.

As if this colossal outpouring of energy and legislation had exhausted the spirit of innovation, the British during the second hundred years of rule made no structural reforms in police administration. It was a time of consolidation, of trying to work more successfully the machine already developed. There was organizational motion but this was a matter of tidying up, tinkering with, and elaborating upon existing arrangements. Imperial police relations with the rural police and with other agencies of imperial government remained fixed in the mold of 1861. It should be noted that the new structure applied only to British India, which in extent covered about two-fifths of the land mass of the subcontinent. The rest of the area, the India of the princely states, got on very much as it had for ages.

[21] The act applied to all British India except Bombay and Madras. These two provinces already had police acts almost identical to the central act. *Indian Police Commission, 1902-1903*, p. 115.

[22] The post of I.G.P. was not established in Bombay presidency until 1885. Cox, p. 71.

[23] Philip Woodruff, *The Men Who Ruled India*, Vol. II: *The Guardians* (paperback edn., 1963; London: Jonathan Cape, 1954), p. 52.

Occasionally the British were asked to help in refashioning a police force or indeed in cutting one out of whole cloth. And of course there was some demonstration effect from British India. Nonetheless, progress was slow or nonexistent and assimilation of these areas into an all-India police system along the lines of the Police Act of 1861 would become an awkward problem for the new Indian government after independence.

Although the police commission in 1860 had been opposed to military police their need was almost universally recognized —indeed most district officers considered them indispensable— and they were gradually accommodated within the system. In fact it would be more accurate to say that military police never really went out of existence. A clear separation was made between military forces utilized for police duties and an armed reserve of the police force. The former was eliminated; the latter was kept. Considering that one of the "substantial and senior tasks of government"[24] was the preservation of law and order and that communal disturbances, village faction fights, and depredations of sizable robber bands were common occurrences, the continued development of armed police is hardly to be wondered at. Other specialized forces grew as well, such as the railway police, river police, and the frontier police.

Affected by the example of the London Metropolitan Police, the three presidency towns of Madras, Bombay, and Calcutta developed a police organization centering around a police commissioner. These great port-cities had unique problems, problems quite unlike those of the rural regions surrounding them. Consequently it seemed sensible to treat them as separate units. The presidency police were forces unto themselves; the commissioner reported directly to the provincial government and not through the inspector-general of police. Furthermore, the commissioner combined for law and order purposes the powers of the district magistrate and superintendent of police. The presidency cities were treated as urban districts, but with the commissioner of police acting as his own district magistrate.[25]

Several attempts were made to regularize recruitment, pay-

---

[24] W. H. Morris-Jones, *The Government and Politics of India* (London: Hutchinson University Library, 1964), p. 21.

[25] Police arrangements for Bombay, Calcutta, and Madras were first ordered by Act XIII of 1865, amended by Act XLVIII of 1860. Later special police acts were passed for each city: Calcutta Police Act, 1866, Madras City Police Act, 1888, and Bombay Police Act, 1902. *Indian Police Commission, 1902-1903*, p. 65.

ment, and duties of the village police, beginning with the Village Chowkidari Act of 1870. A particularly nagging problem was the question of the kind and amount of authority over village police to be exercised respectively by provincial government and village panchayat. By stages the power of panchayats, that is, the villages themselves, was gradually eroded and supervisory powers passed to the superintendent and the district magistrate. Today there are indications that this trend may be reversed. I shall examine the status of village police in greater detail later, including the question of whether they are an effective police agency.[26]

In 1902 Lord Curzon, Viceroy of India, set up a new police commission to make a searching inquiry into the functioning of the police. The commission found a great deal to criticize. The criticism, though, was directed at failure to achieve high levels of performance and not at the system itself. The new commission strongly endorsed the organizational principles established in 1861. Consequently one finds no recommendations for substantial organizational changes in the report of 1902. Something of the candor of the commission's report may be seen in this observation, which has become a benchmark for evaluation of the police and has been repeated endlessly in literature on the Indian police:

"The police is far from efficient; it is defective in training and organization; it is inadequately supervised; it is generally regarded as corrupt and oppressive; and it has utterly failed to secure the confidence and cordial cooperation of the people."[27]

The stinging judgments of the police commission of 1902 actually hide several quite remarkable accomplishments. The

[26] See Chapter 15.

[27] *Ibid.*, p. 150. In fairness to the police at the turn of the century one must mention that there were opposing, or at least less harsh, opinions. One experienced British officer has said: "As a body, the police come in for abuse and wholesale suspicion altogether in excess of their demerits. Nevertheless, in spite of all defects, the fact remains: life and property are more secure than they were under any previous regime; serious crime is committed with far less impunity than it ever was a quarter of a century ago; there is less crime; and protection of life and property is as complete as in England." Major-General Fendall Currie, *Below the Surface* (London: Archibald Constable and Co., 1900), pp. 221-222. The views of the commission and of Currie are not exactly in opposition, because each has assumed a different standard for comparison. Currie notes the very substantial progress made over previous regimes; the commission, by the nature of its charge, is compelled to measure the police by what should have been achieved.

"Chemical Examiners' Department" of the Punjab, and later of other provinces, was the precursor of modern forensic science laboratories.[28] India is one of the first nations to provide systematic training of a high quality for officers and aspirants to high rank. France alone preceded India in establishing such a scheme, and its program was not as extensive.[29] Finally, the fingerprint system used round the world today was developed in India by an inspector-general of police in Bengal, Sir Edward Henry.[30]

The development of formal criminal investigation departments lagged somewhat behind progress in Great Britain. A C.I.D. organization was established in Great Britain in 1878. Although some of the larger Indian cities had small detective departments at that time, criminal investigation organizations at provincial level were not established until after the report of the police commission in 1902.[31] About the same time one of the most romantic investigating agencies in Indian history was disbanded. This was the famous "Thuggee and Dacoity Department."[32] A dacoit was, and is, a rural bandit operating in a band of five or more; a "thug" was a ritual strangler who preyed on travelers, dedicated his booty and murders to the goddess Kali, and whose distinguishing tools were a silk scarf and pickaxe.[33] The "Thuggee and Dacoity Department" was founded in 1830. It was directed from 1835 to 1839 by Colonel William Henry Sleeman, later known as "Thuggee Sleeman" the man who eliminated the "thug" menace from India. The department had

[28] John Coatman, *Police* (London: Oxford University Press, 1959), p. 228.
[29] *Ibid.*
[30] Sir Edward Henry was a civilian administrator by training, an officer of the I.C.S. It was common during this period for top officers of the police to be appointed from outside the police establishment. After serving as inspector-general, Sir Edward was brought to London in 1903 where he was appointed commissioner of police, a post he held until 1919.
[31] Curry, pp. 151 ff.
[32] The spellings for the title of this department vary. The Indian Police Commission, 1902-1903, referred to it as the "Thagi and Dakaiti Department."
[33] The story of the discovery of this vicious form of crime and of its suppression is a fascinating one. It is briefly recounted in Curry, *The Indian Police*, pp. 151 ff. For a more lively and thorough treatment, see Meadows Taylor, *Confessions of a Thug*, a fictionalized diary of a thug based on the author's own experience; John Masters, *The Deceivers* (Penguin Books, 1955), for a first-rate novel; and the memoirs of the man responsible for the suppression of "thuggee," Sir William Henry Sleeman, *Rambles and Recollections of an Indian Official* (London: J. Hatchard and Son, 1844), which is also out in other editions.

outlived its usefulness by 1860, as the police commission of the time recognized, but whether for reasons of inertia or nostalgia, it was kept until 1904.[34]

In the twentieth century the struggle for independence soon began to catalyze all development, administrative or political. For the police it brought their most agonizing time of trial. The independence struggle pitted police against national movement, Indian policeman against Indian freedom-fighter. Because the police bore the brunt of repressive activities, memories were planted in the minds of people that even today fundamentally affect relations between the two. Apart from emotions and attitudes, the major effect the nationalist struggle had upon the police was to compel greater speed in taking Indians into the officer cadre. The police commission of 1902 had recommended that educated Indians be admitted to the police at officer level. Hitherto Indians could rise only to the rank of inspector of police, the senior N.C.O. position. A new rank was now created especially for Indian officers—deputy superintendent of police, immediately below the rank of superintendent. But the deputy superintendent was not a part of the Indian (Imperial) Police; he was at the top of the provincial, or subordinate, service. The educated Indian stopped in rank where the European officer began. The tide of indianization could not long be resisted, however, certainly not by such transparent devices. In 1920 the Indian (Imperial) Police was thrown open to Indians and the following year entrance examinations for the service were given in India as well as England.[35] Indianization was by no means rapid even so, and in the police it was even slower than in other imperial services. For example, by 1931, half the district magistrates in the country were Indian, only one out of five superintendents of police were.[36]

The police legacy left by the British to independent India had several elements. First, they bequeathed the structure of the police system. The system today has been handed down virtually intact from the reforms of 1861. Second, they bequeathed perceptions, attitudes, and predispositions toward the police on the part of both public and policymakers which re-

[34] C. W. Steward, "Editor's Introduction" to Taylor, *Confessions of a Thug*, p. xi.
[35] Government of Bihar, *Report of the Police Commission* (Patna: Secretariat Press, 1961), p. 9.
[26] Curry, p. 88.

main vital today. Thirdly, they bequeathed a concept of the role police should play in Indian society. That is, "proper" police duties today are very much what were considered "proper" police duties under the British. Moreover the two great questions of British police experimentation—relations of government police with village constabulary and relations among agencies, one of them police, within government—continue to dominate debate about contemporary police organization. The continued importance of these questions, of course, is not due to the perspicacity of the British but to the persistence of social needs and administrative structures.

DEVELOPMENT AFTER 1947

In 1947 the police in West Bengal abolished the 'lal pugree,' or red turban, symbol of British rule.[37] India was free.

Colonial domination was replaced by a representative democracy with parliamentary and federal features. National elections now determine the members of parliament and of the state legislatures, the only lawmaking bodies in the country. The dominant party or coalition of parties selects from its ranks in parliament and legislatures the prime minister and state chief ministers, the chief executive officers of the union and states, respectively.[38] These officers, with the advice of their legislative supporters, choose the candidates to be appointed to direct the major agencies and departments of government. Police affairs are handled for the central government by the Ministry of Home Affairs, for the state governments by the Home Departments. Immediately below the ministerial level come the ranks of permanent government employees or civil servants. The senior civil service posts go to members of the I.A.S. (Indian Administrative Service); the pinnacle of achievement in each ministry or department being the post of secretary. Therefore, the ranking civil servant in police affairs is the secretary of the Ministry of Home Affairs, or the secretary of the Home Department. It is

[37] West Bengal Police Commission, p. 234.

[38] This is not technically true. The president of India and the governor of each state are the chief executive officers in law, but they have little real power. They personify the country or the state, as the case may be, and actions are taken in their name. But, with only minor exceptions, they are bound to accept the advice of the elected officials. For a full discussion of the nature and functioning of Indian government, see Morris-Jones, *The Government and Politics of India.*

to the Home Department in each state that the inspector-general of police is responsible.

Independence brought revolutionary changes in the political structure of government, it brought none of any consequence to the structure of police administration. The three structural characteristics distinguishing the contemporary police system—control by state governments, horizontal stratification, functional specialization between armed and unarmed police—had been developed before independence. Independence required of the police only that they accommodate themselves to a new political context; it affected the manner in which they were held accountable and not the way they were organized to accomplish police purposes.

According to the constitution, police are state subjects. States have exclusive power over their control and regulation.[39] The central government may enter the police field only in connection with establishing and maintaining a "Central Bureau of Intelligence and Investigation."[40] As with the British, there is no national police force; police are directed by governmental units limited in their territorial jurisdiction. Several small territories in India are centrally administered—such as Tripura, Manipur, and the Andaman and Nicobar Islands—and for them the central government maintains a police force. These forces may be used only within those areas.

The division of power between central and state governments is not immutable. It can be modified.[41] However, in law, and so far in practice, the states have retained control over raising, maintaining, and directing the preponderance of police forces in India. The central government does, however, exert a special form of direction over one part of these forces. The Indian Police Service, or superior officer cadre, is one of the two all-India

[39] Government of India, *Constitution*, Seventh Schedule, list II, item 2.
[40] *Ibid.*, list I, item 8.
[41] There are three ways of affecting the division of power. First, the government of India may declare a state of emergency, subject to ratification by parliament, in which case it may enact legislation with respect to any item on the list reserved for the states. *Ibid.*, articles 352-360. Such a proclamation was issued in October, 1962, when the Chinese invaded northern India. Second, any combination of states may allow parliament by vote of their legislature to intervene in matters on the state list. Third, the Council of States or upper house of parliament may empower, by a two-thirds vote, the central government to co-opt items on the state list. It is possible, therefore, that if a government at the center had the votes in either the upper or lower house, it could nullify the division of power set forth in the constitution.

services. The other is the Indian Administrative Service (I.A.S.). They are successor services to the Indian police and the Indian civil service of British days. Their regulation is a central subject.[42] The central government determines the selection and conditions of service of all I.P.S. officers. The states determine the selection and conditions of service for all lower ranks. Because conditions of service are set by the central government, officers, although they act under the immediate direction of state authorities, are immune from threats directed against the terms of their livelihood.

The union government possesses two police forces of its own. The first is the Central Reserve Police. This is an armed reserve used mostly for guarding frontiers and for assisting states in times of emergency, such as during widespread public disorder or against large dacoit bands. The Central Reserve Police had been created under legislation passed in 1949,[43] thus just escaping the limiting stipulations of the new constitution with respect to union government and police.[44] By 1964 there were fourteen battalions in the force.[45] The Central Reserve Police is directed by an inspector-general in the Home Ministry, New Delhi. Acting within the only area of police activity allowed it by the constitution the union government has set up its second police force, namely, the Central Bureau of Investigation and several forensic institutions. The Central Bureau of Investigation (C.B.I.) was formally established in April, 1963. It subsumed the older Delhi Special Police Establishment which became the Investigation and Anticorruption Division of C.B.I. The government also maintains a central fingerprint bureau, a central detective training school, and a central forensic science laboratory, all of them located in Calcutta.

The union government, through the Ministry of Home Affairs, has played an informal role in police affairs which is of some im-

---

[42] *Ibid.*, list I, item 70.

[43] Central Reserve Police Force Act, 1949.

[44] It was laid down in Sagar Mal *v.* The State, 1951 All. 816, by the Allahabad high court that distribution of legislative powers under article 246 of the constitution does not affect laws which were in existence and in force prior to the promulgation of the constitution. The central government could not raise a Central Reserve Force today. In the same way such legislation as the Police Act of 1861 remains in effect even though the states can pass supplementary legislation if they wish. R. B. Sethi, *The Police Acts* (2nd ed.; Allahabad: Law Book Company, 1959), p. 11.

[45] A. R. Nizamuddin, "Unarmed Police for India" (Mt. Abu: Central Police Training College, 1962).

portance. The Home Ministry annually convenes a conference of state inspector-generals of police. The group has no formal authority but serves as a forum for the discussion of mutual problems and setting forth of policy directives for the guidance of state governments and police forces around the country. The Home Ministry has from time to time provided special assistance, in the form of money or experienced personnel, to states with special security problems. In 1955-1956, for example, it provided for the deputation of officers experienced in dacoity work to a large anti-dacoity operation in the area where Uttar Pradesh, Madhya Pradesh, and Rajasthan come together.[46] The Home Ministry supervised the creation of zonal police reserves, pools of armed police to be used in times of emergency by the contiguous states forming each of India's four zonal councils.[47] Zonal police reserves and contingents of state police too may be deputed, with state consent, to service with the central government. The southern zonal reserve was sent north during the brief war with Pakistan in 1965. A battalion of Mysore special reserve police went to Nagaland in 1964.[48] And any tourist in Kashmir can observe the words "Punjab Police" stenciled on vehicles and equipment of khaki-clad armed policemen. Finally, states perform some police tasks which are properly the responsibility of the union government. States with international borders must maintain frontier surveillance. This can become an appreciable burden; Rajasthan, for example, has one thousand miles of border with Pakistan. Then, certain pieces of union legislation, such as the Arms Act and the Foreigners Act, can only be effectively implemented by a pervasive police agency, meaning in practice the state police forces. The union government has begun to recognize that it is unfair to demand of states that they support these activities themselves, and it has begun to share costs through a system of monetary grants. The amount of money given by the union government to the states is not, however, a matter of public record.

Legal underpinning for state police forces is provided by both central and state enactments. In West Bengal, by way of illustration, there are four laws dealing explicitly with the police,

[46] S. R. Nigam, *Scotland Yard and the Indian Police* (Allahabad: Kitab Mahal, Private Ltd., 1963), p. 116.

[47] Government of India, Ministry of Home Affairs, *Report*, 1963-1964, p. 13, refers to them as "Common Police Reserves."

[48] Government of Mysore, *Annual Administration Report of the Department of Police*, 1964, p. 65.

one central and three state: Police Act, 1861, West Bengal Police Act, 1952, Calcutta Police Act, 1866, and Calcutta Suburban Police Act, 1866. Most of the states have some police legislation of their own, usually a state police act. The relevant central acts were of course passed before passage of the new constitution.[49] Immediately after independence India was faced with the task of extending the provincial systems to the newly assimilated princely states. Some of these states, such a Hyderabad, Baroda, and Gwalior, had relatively effective, well-organized forces.[50] The majority, however, were below performance-levels in the provinces. An already difficult situation was complicated quickly by the campaign for States' Reorganization, begun in 1952, which pressed for a redrawing of internal political boundaries. The campaign was successful, and in 1956 fifteen states were created where formerly there had been twenty-six. Rational planning in the police was vexed, then, not only with assimilation of princely states but uncertainty stemming from confusion over what the boundaries of each state would be. "Wait and see" became the creed of the period. In Mysore state, to take an extreme case, five different police acts were in operation in different parts of the state after States' Reorganization.[51] A uniform police act for Mysore was not passed until 1964.

As far as city police administration is concerned the commissioner system has been expanded from the former presidency towns to Hyderabad, Ahmedabad, and Bangalore. The Maharashtra Police Commission recently recommended that Nagpur and Poona should employ the system too.[52] With the growth of urban areas, police administrators will increasingly want to separate, insofar as possible, urban policing from rural policing. One may expect the next few years to bring several more additions to the group of cities with commissioners. As in British days, the commissioner of police is in effect the inspector-gen-

[49] See footnote 44.

[50] Curry, pp. 50-52; and S. T. Hollins, *No Ten Commandments: Life in the Indian Police* (London: Hutchinson, 1954), Chapter 29, especially pp. 301-302.

[51] H. Veerabhadriah, "An Insight into Police Administration," *Studies in State Administration*, ed. G. S. Halappa (Dharwar, Mysore: Karnatak University, 1963), p. 319.

[52] Government of Maharashtra, *Summary of Recommendations of the Maharashtra State Police Commission, 1964* (Bombay: Government Central Press, 1964), p. 1. The Uttar Pradesh Police Commission considered adopting the commissioner system in Kanpur and Lucknow, but decided against it.

eral of police for a city. He reports directly to the state government. Furthermore, he is not responsible to a district magistrate but combines the police powers of superintendent and D.M. The commissioner system is based upon the recognition that urban police problems should be treated separately from rural ones. At the same time, it is essential that there be close cooperation between the urban and rural forces. In the past, especially under the British, the two sets of forces tended to be aloof from one another. They recruited separately, had different pay scales, different uniforms, and became preoccupied with different forms of crimes, certainly different technical problems in coping with crime. This situation has been considerably alleviated since independence. Conditions of service have been made more uniform between them, there is now a greater exchange of personnel, and cooperation in handling state police problems is much closer.[53]

So far, we have examined how the police are organized and who directs them. Equally important is how they can be directed in the line of duty and who determines that. The primary set of empowering laws are the all-India legal codes—the Indian Penal Code and the Code of Criminal Procedure. Criminal law and criminal procedure are matters of concurrent jurisdiction between the center and the states.[54] Amendments to the codes must be enacted by the union parliament; supplementary criminal legislation may be enacted by state legislatures. The federal division of powers affects certain categories of criminal liability. For example, the states exclusively legislate with respect to the production and sale of intoxicating liquor.[55] Prohibition offenses, therefore, are crimes by virtue of state determination. Regulation of "arms, firearms, ammunition, and explosives" is a union concern.[56] The Arms Act of 1959 is a central act applied throughout India. The states are exclusively responsible for public order.[57] This is a vast responsibility and accounts for many of the regulatory provisions found in state police acts. Preventive detention is partly reserved to the central government and partly shared with the states, depending upon the interests in defense of which it is employed.[58] As a result the states are

[53] See West Bengal Police Commission, Chapter 5.
[54] *Constitution*, list III, items 1 and 2.
[55] *Ibid.*, list II, item 8.
[56] *Ibid.*, list I, item 5.
[57] *Ibid.*, list II, item 1.
[58] *Ibid.*, list I, item 9, and list III, item 3.

prohibited from enacting preventive detention legislation in order to safeguard, *inter alia*, the security of India, but they may do so in order to maintain public order. As it happens, the center has enacted a Preventive Detention Act conferring powers on state officials. The states thus possess executive powers under a central act which they could not have given to themselves through their own state legislatures. The situation may seem complicated, as it is apt to be in any federal arrangement, but it is far less complicated than it would be without the all-India codes. But for these, criminal law would be as much of a thicket as it is in the United States. Even so, in a state like West Bengal there are eighty-two acts in addition to the codes which confer power on the police.[59]

The principle of supervision of police by civilian administrative authority has been preserved, except of course in the cities which have commissioners of police. The Police Act of 1861 stated that administration of police was to be vested in the I.G.P. at provincial level and superintendents at district level. The superintendent was to hold his charge "under the general control and direction" of the district magistrate.[60] The phrase "under the direction and control" has been subjected to searching examination and interpretation time and time again. It is now commonly assumed to mean that the superintendent is independent with respect to internal management of the force. The D.M.[61] is responsible for the correct use of that force in coping with security problems of a district. This is not to say that the D.M. will actually initiate directives for its use. The precise manner in which the D.M. exercises "general direction and control" has caused and continues to cause discomfort on the part of the police. As the question is often put, is the superintendent to be a colleague of the D.M. or a subordinate? Whatever the descriptive rhetoric, it is quite clear that ultimate responsibility belongs today to the D.M.[62] From the point of view of a subordinate police officer, there are two hierarchies with supervisory authority over police activities—a police hierarchy culminating in the I.G.P. and a civilian hierarchy running from D.M. to the secretary of the Home Department.

[59] See comment of the West Bengal Police Commission, p. 37, and the list in Appendix VIII, *Police Regulations, Bengal* (Vol. I).

[60] The Police Act, 1961, section 4.

[61] District Magistrate (D.M.) is here used synonymously with Collector.

[62] See Chapter 13 for a discussion of the relations between the I.P.S. and I.A.S., superintendent and collector.

What is particularly striking about contemporary police structure is its permanence. Its fundamental principles of organization have remained fixed for over a century. This suggests two questions: is the system still capable of coping effectively with the basic tasks of police responsibility, and is the system as compatible with a democratic political state as it was with a colonial one? These two questions provide the themes for much of the following discussion.

3 • *The Indian Police Today*

IN THE previous chapter we noted three distinguishing features of police in India and saw how the police system fitted within the constitutional and legal framework of modern India. Now we shall examine the nature of that police force in detail. How is the force organized to carry out the tasks entrusted to it? What is its command structure? What is the nature of the linkage between an individual police station in some remote rural area and the inspector-general in the state capital? What kinds of specialized police are there? How are both men and officers recruited to the police service? How are they trained and under what conditions do they serve? How many police are there, and how are they distributed with respect to functional as well as geographical divisions?

The bulk of the Indian police, those that bear primary responsibility for the prevention and investigation of crime and for the preservation of public order, are organized on the basis of subnational territorial units—that is, states. The central government, as we have seen, has only residuary police forces. These are the Central Bureau of Investigation and the Central Reserve Police. A description of the police of India properly focuses, therefore, on state police organizations.

QUANTITY AND DISTRIBUTION OF POLICE

Within state police forces a firm division exists between armed and unarmed police.[1] Unfortunately, in statistical tables or commentaries this distinction is not always made. Since they per-

---

[1] A firm distinction exists in terms of function but this is not always reflected in official statistics. Sometimes other criteria are employed in distinguishing armed from unarmed police. Although the unarmed police do not carry firearms, a weapon is sanctioned against the post in most states. The weapon will be kept at the police station, at district headquarters, or in the state armory. In Punjab, for example, classification as armed police is done on the basis of posts against which a weapon is issued. As a result, figures for police strength in Punjab show more than 90 percent are armed police. Their figures are, therefore, very misleading. Punjab represents the most serious departure from general practice. Comparisons between strength of armed and unarmed police may be made between most other states without serious distortions occurring.

form very different duties, failure to distinguish between them when commenting on the size of the police force, particularly if an argument is to be made about the adequacy of their numbers, leads to very misleading conclusions. The unarmed police, or civil constabulary, staff the police stations and the departments of criminal investigation. They are uniformed but unarmed, although they may carry a short baton or sometimes a bamboo staff called a *lathi*. They are the police with which the public has contact in the normal course of affairs. They hunt for lost children, investigate crimes, patrol streets, regulate traffic, interpose in village quarrels, and generally respond to the articulated needs of the mass of the people for police assistance. They are to be found distributed across the face of India, in metropolis, city, town, and remote village. The armed police, on the other hand, live in cantonments concentrated at a few points throughout each state. They do not have daily contact with the public. They do not respond to calls of assistance from individuals but to orders from superior officers based upon perceptions of need. They usually act as a group and exercise hardly any individual discretion. The armed police provide officials with a reserve striking force to be used when the unarmed constabulary loses control of a situation or finds itself overwhelmed. They embody a clearly defined threat of physical force. They allow for an escalation of force without recourse to armed units outside the police organization. It is very much as if a contingent of the national guard in the United States were permanently assigned to the police of each state. Armed police are not exclusively engaged in quelling public disturbances. They serve as guards for specie shipments, jails, escort of prisoners, and government buildings and installations. They are often employed on what is referred to as general *"bandobust." Bandobust* means arrangements and is most commonly used in referring to police preparations for public affairs drawing large crowds, such as festivals or athletic events. The armed police undoubtedly spend more time performing such mechanical duties than in the more dramatic activity of restoring public order. In most states the armed police are recruited and trained separately from the unarmed police. There may be some transferring back and forth but it is comparatively rare.[2]

[2] Bihar differs from most states in requiring that constables serve at least five years in the district armed police before being posted to a police station as an unarmed policeman. Bihar Police Commission, 1961, p. 34.

Armed police are not all of a kind. In most states a distinction is made between district armed police and special armed police reserves. The district armed police (D.A.P. in many states) is a force of armed policemen quartered in each district usually at district headquarters, under the control of the district superintendent. The specialized forces are under the immediate command of the inspector-general through a deputy inspector-general, and are concentrated at one or two points in the state. They may have heavier armament than the D.A.P. and they are often utilized for special sorts of enforcement actions. The Bihar military police, for example, is equipped with rifles with one-mile range, while the D.A.P. has muskets with a range of about one hundred yards. There is also a Bihar mounted military police, with headquarters at Arrah.[3] West Bengal has two armed police groups in addition to the D.A.P.: the state armed police reserve, which has within it an industrial area reserve force, and the Eastern Frontier Rifles, stationed at Salua in Midnapore district. Madras has its Malabar special police and Mysore the Mysore special reserve police force.

It should be understood that when I refer to armed police I am including special armed police units as well as district armed police. This usage conforms to practice in official reports.

In 1960 the strength of the police in India was just over half a million men.[4] Approximately two-fifths of them were armed police, three-fifths unarmed.[5] See Table 1.

[3] Bihar Police Commission, p. 34.

[4] The use of Indian statistics on the size and growth of police forces presents several difficulties. The basic documents for information about the police, or crime for that matter, are the annual *Police Administration Reports*. Unhappily there is often a delay of several years before they are issued. Moreover, in some states since the declaration of emergency in 1962, the amount of information they contain has been reduced. Even more distressing for the scholar, there seems to be no single library in India maintaining an up-to-date collection of state police administration reports. This statement applies even to central depository libraries such as the library of the Ministry of Home Affairs, the Central Secretariat Library, Parliament Library, and the library of the Central Police Training College. Summary statistics for all of India are collected by the Ministry of Home Affairs, New Delhi, and are published in their annual reports. Again perhaps as a result of the emergency, the last figures published for the entire country were for 1960, appearing in the Home Ministry's 1961-1962 report. Finally, with disturbing frequency one finds discrepancies in reported totals given in different documentary sources. For example, the Home Ministry reported the total sanctioned strength of police in Madras, December 31, 1960, as 33,428. The police administration report for Madras reported total sanctioned strength as 29,148. Even within reports there may be discrepancies. Wherever possible I have tried to use figures from the most basic source.

[5] Ministry of Home Affairs, *Report*, 1961-1962, p. 23. These figures are

TABLE 1

SANCTIONED STRENGTH OF POLICE, 31 DECEMBER 1960

Name of State	Armed	Unarmed	Total
Andhra Pradesh	13,964	27,667	41,631
Assam	9,823	6,937	16,769†[sic]
Bihar	14,468	18,098	32,566
Gujarat	13,957	17,358	31,315
Jammu-Kashmir	1,156	5,115	6,231 [sic]
Kerala	5,746	7,531	13,277
Madhya Pradesh	8,986	31,621	40,607
Madras	9,629	23,799	33,428
Maharashtra	24,295	37,908	62,203
Mysore	6,528	17,949	24,478
Orissa	4,725	9,828	14,553
Punjab	33,175*	1,079	34,254
Rajasthan	12,275	20,628	32,885 [sic]
Uttar Pradesh	25,050	39,824	64,874
West Bengal	17,288	31,746	49,034
Andaman and Nicobar Islands	256	559	815
Delhi	8,975	2,677	11,652
Himachal Pradesh	2,504	38	2,542
Manipur	964	933	1,897
Pondicherry	283	342	625
Tripura	1,017	903	1,920
	215,057	302,540	517,597

* Punjab has used a different classificational scheme for distinguishing armed from unarmed police. See footnote 1, page 58.

† The addition is wrong, as it is for Jammu-Kashmir and Rajasthan.

SOURCE: Ministry of Home Affairs, *Report*, 1961-1962, p. 23.

The total expenditure on police was just over 850 million rupees (approximately $113 million).[6] By budget year 1963-1964 police expenditure had gone up 32 percent.[7] Outlays on police made up 7.86 percent of all state government budgets in 1960; by 1964 the proportion was 7.28 percent. During the Third Five-Year Plan, 1961-1966, India was to spend just over

for "sanctioned strength" of the forces as opposed to "actual strength." Examination of state police reports shows that sanctioned and actual strength are only slightly different. And, curiously, the figures for actual strength, especially for the ranks above head constable, are very often larger than the figure for sanctioned strength.

[6] India, Ministry of Information and Broadcasting, *India: A Reference Annual, 1961* (New Delhi: Ministry of Information and Broadcasting, 1961), pp. 391-498. The figure was Rs. 855,385,000. For the conversion to dollars I have used the official exchange rate of 7.50 rupees to the dollar.

[7] *Ibid.*, 1964, pp. 353-400. In 1964 the expenditure was Rs. 1,131,265,000.

ten thousand crores of rupees in development investment.[8] India then would have spent about twenty billion rupees per year on development investment compared to about one billion on police, or about one-twentieth as much as on economic development.

It is very difficult to determine accurately the growth of police forces in India except for a few very recent years. The British controlled only part of the subcontinent so their figures do not nearly represent an all-India total. Independence was bought at the cost of a loss of territory to Pakistan; assimilation of princely states added area; and very soon thereafter States' Reorganization redrew internal governmental boundaries. The Home Ministry did not issue a meaningful all-India figure on police until 1956. In 1956, there were 431,362 policemen in India. By 1960 the police forces had grown by about 20 percent or at the rate of 5 percent per year. During this period the unarmed police grew more rapidly than the armed police— for the armed police a total growth of 13.5 percent or 3.5 percent per year, for the unarmed police 23.9 percent or 6 percent per year. There are indications that the relative rates of increase of armed and unarmed police may have changed significantly since 1962, the year of the emergency. One knowledgeable Home Ministry official told me in 1965 that the size of the armed police reserve had in fact doubled since 1962. While this amount of growth seems extreme, a change in this direction is plausible considering the external and domestic circumstances which had to be faced.

Some states have experienced very little change in the extent of their territory in the last fifty years and for them it is possible to trace police growth over longer periods. In Uttar Pradesh, for instance, the sanctioned strength of the police in 1930 was 33,615.[9] In 1960 it was 64,874, or almost double the former figure. Population in the same period grew by 48.1 percent.[10] In 1930 Bihar and Orissa taken together had a force of

[8] India, Planning Commission, *Third Five-Year Plan* (n.p., n.d.), p. 59. A crore is ten million; a lakh is one hundred thousand. In most places I have converted the Indian designations to their Anglo-Saxon equivalents. This has not been done if the more familiar term in a specific context, even among Westerners, is the Indian one. This is the case in discussing outlays under the Plans.

[9] J. C. Curry, *The Indian Police* (London: Faber and Faber, 1932), p. 347.

[10] From 49 million to 73 million. India, *Census of India: Final Population Totals, 1961* (Delhi: Manager of Publications, 1962), pp. 6, 8-9. The

14,365;[11] in 1960 the combined strength was 47,119, a growth in thirty years of 328 percent. Population grew by 46 percent.[12] Other assessments of growth rates may be made for unchanged states since independence. Uttar Pradesh and West Bengal between 1950 and 1960 experienced an overall growth in police of 10 percent, 1 percent per year. Orissa had a slightly higher yearly growth rate, 1.9 percent. Bihar and Assam expanded their forces quite dramatically during this period; Bihar by 80 percent and Assam by 87 percent. (See Table 2.) It is noteworthy that in the three states which experienced modest growth the unarmed police grew more rapidly than the armed. But in the two states that had unusual rates of growth— Bihar and Assam—the armed police grew more quickly than the unarmed.

Thus, from 1950-1960, for those parts of India with stable boundaries, police growth has been at least 1 percent a year; much higher rates of growth are attributable to very rapid expansion of the armed police; and in only one of these areas— Assam—did armed police bulk larger than the unarmed by the end of the period. While one cannot claim that these areas are representative of state development in the decade of the 1950's, they do account for 42.1 percent of India's total population and 27.3 percent of the land area.[13]

In 1960 there was one policeman for every 848 persons and one policeman for every 2.27 square miles of territory. By way of comparison, in Great Britain in 1961 there was one policeman for every 565 persons and for every 0.883 square mile.[14] In the United States in 1960 there was one policeman for every 526

---

annual police administration report, Uttar Pradesh, 1940, gives the total strength at 33,131, indicating that little increase took place between 1930 and 1940. The annual report, 1959, gives total strength (actual) at 52,584. Yet a year later the Home Ministry cites Uttar Pradesh police strength at 64,874. Can the police force have grown by twelve thousand men in one year? This is another example of the difficulties encountered in using existing statistical documents. To make the puzzle even more aggravating, the Uttar Pradesh Police Commission, 1960-1961, agrees with the total given by the Home Ministry for 1960. So it would appear that the force did grow by twelve thousand men, or 23 percent in one year.

[11] Curry, p. 347.

[12] *Census of India: Final Population Totals, 1961*, pp. 8-9.

[13] Based on *Census of India*, 1961, pp. 5-6.

[14] Computed from figures given in Great Britain, *Royal Commission on the Police, 1962, Final Report*, Cmnd. 1728 (London: Her Majesty's Stationery Office, 1962), pp. 187-191.

TABLE 2

GROWTH OF POLICE, SELECTED STATES, 1950-1960[*]

	Uttar Pradesh	Bihar	West Bengal	Orissa	Assam
Total in 1950	58,591	17,763	44,412	12,226	8,923
Armed	23,457	1,443	16,263	4,611	3,821
Unarmed	35,434	16,293	28,149	7,615	5,117
Total in 1960	64,874	32,566	49,034	14,553	16,769
Armed	25,050	14,468	17,288	4,725	9,832
Unarmed	39,824	18,098	31,746	9,828	6,937
Total percentage increase	10.2	80.3	10.4	19.0	87.8
Armed	10.9	910.0	6.32	2.48	150.7
Unarmed	12.4	11.2	9.22	29.0	35.4

[*] Informants tell me that growth patterns have been different in southern states. They have been more willing to expand the unarmed police and have been reluctant to expand the armed police. This point must be considered unestablished, however, until hard data are made available.

SOURCES: Home Ministry, Report, 1961-1962, p. 23. Home Ministry, Report, 1951-1952.

people and every 15.22 square miles.[15] (See Table 3.) India, then, has half again as many people per policeman as the United States or Great Britain. There is one very important qualification that needs to be made. In the ratio just cited armed and unarmed police have been combined. If one is interested in civil constabulary, that is, the kind of police that make individual contact with the public, then the Indian ratio must be adjusted. In 1960 the ratio of unarmed police to population was one to 1,450; the ratio of unarmed police to areas was one to every 3.89 square miles. There are, then, three times as many people per civil constable as in the United States or Great Britain.[16]

In 1960, the state of Uttar Pradesh had the largest police force, Jammu-Kashmir had the smallest. Armed and unarmed

[15] The police population ratio was given in United States Justice Department, Federal Bureau of Investigation, Uniform Crime Reports, 1960 (Washington: U.S. Government Printing Office, 1961), p. 105. The figures used in the report are not complete for all the United States; they cover 40 percent of the rural area and 73 percent of urban areas. Ninety-six percent of the population is covered. See page 26.

[16] An Indian police officer gives as the same ratio for Japan, one for every 600 persons; for France, one per 562; and for Germany, one per 448. K. G. Ramanna, "Police Forces of India and Their Cost—A Preliminary Study," Transactions, October, 1962, p. 3.

TABLE 3

COMPARATIVE RATIOS OF POLICE TO POPULATION AND AREA IN
INDIA, UNITED STATES, AND GREAT BRITAIN

	India	United States	Great Britain
Police	517,597	195,109	90,874*
Population	439,235,000	179,323,175†	51,439,900‡
Area (in square miles)	1,178,000	2,977,128§	88,142
Ratio of policemen to population	(a) Total police: 1 per 848 persons (b) Unarmed police: 1 per 1,450 persons	1 per 526 persons‖	1 per 565 persons
Ratio of policemen to area	(a) Total police: 1 per 2.27 (b) Unarmed police: 1 per 3.89	1 per 15.22	1 per 0.883

* As of December 31, 1961.
† As of April, 1960.
‡ As of June 30, 1961.
§ Minus Hawaii and Alaska.
‖ U.S. police figures are for 40 percent of rural area and 73 percent of urban communities, covering 96 percent of the population. See *Uniform Crime Reports*, p. 26.

SOURCES: *Census of India*, 1961, Final Population Totals; *Home Ministry Report*, 1961-1962; *Uniform Crime Reports*, 1960; *Royal Commission on Police*, 1962, pp. 87-91; *Columbia Lippincott Gazetteer of the World* (New York: Columbia University Press, 1952); *World Almanac* (New York: Newspaper Enterprise Association, Inc., 1967).

police have been considered together. The most populated state did, then, have the most police. But the correlation immediately breaks down. Bihar was second in population but eighth in numbers of police. The more significant comparison is of numbers of people per policeman. Bihar in fact had the least favorable ratio in all India—1,425 persons for each policeman. (See Table 4.) Bihar, Orissa, Kerala, Uttar Pradesh, and Madras all had more than one thousand people for each policeman. The most satisfactory situations were in Jammu-Kashmir, Punjab, Rajasthan, Maharashtra, and Gujarat (from 568 to 660 persons per policeman). When the situations were compared more meaningfully with respect to *unarmed* police only, the five states with the least favorable ratios remain the same. The five

TABLE 4

POLICE STRENGTH BY STATES*

State	Ratio: armed police per unit unarmed	Rank by ratio of armed per unarmed (highest to lowest)	Police per unit population	Rank by ratio: police per unit population (highest to lowest)	Area per policeman (in square miles)	Area per unarmed policeman (in square miles)	Ratio: population per unarmed police	Rank by population per unarmed police (highest to lowest)
Andhra Pradesh	0.54	9	864	7	2.55	3.83	1,300	8
Assam	1.42	1	709	10	2.8	6.80	1,701	4
Bihar	0.80	3	1,425	1	2.06	3.71	2,565	1
Jammu-Kashmir	0.26	14	568	15	N.A.‡	N.A.‡	696	14
Kerala	0.76	4	1,263	3	1.13	1.99	2,245	2
Madhya Pradesh	0.28	13	795	8	4.21	5.40	1,020	12
Madras	0.40	11	1,010	5	1.50	2.11	1,420	6
Maharashtra	0.64	5	635	12	1.91	3.22	1,040	11
Mysore	0.36	12	961	6	3.01	4.13	1,310	7
Orissa	0.48	10	1,205	2	4.13	6.12	1,785	5
Punjab	3.03†		593	14	1.38	43.8	18,820	
Rajasthan	0.59	7	613	13	4.02	6.40	975	13
Uttar Pradesh	0.63	6	1,137	4	1.75	2.85	1,850	3
West Bengal	0.54	8	711	9	0.69	1.06	1,100	10
Gujarat	0.80	2	660	11	2.31	4.16	1,190	9

* Calculations based upon data for 1960.

† Punjab has used a different classificational scheme for distinguishing armed from unarmed police. See footnote 1, page 58.

‡ Not Available.

states with the most favorable police to population ratio change somewhat. They are now Jammu-Kashmir, Rajasthan, Madhya Pradesh, Maharashtra, West Bengal, and Gujarat. Omitting Punjab, the states with the highest ratios of armed to unarmed police were, in descending order, Assam, Gujarat, Bihar, Kerala, and Maharashtra. Again excepting Punjab, only Assam had more armed than unarmed police. The states with the least armed police per unarmed were Jammu-Kashmir, Madhya Pradesh, Mysore, Madras, and Orissa.

In the foregoing comparisons the state of Jammu-Kashmir stands out like a sore thumb. It has the smallest force and the smallest proportion of armed to unarmed police. Yet it is well known that substantial out-of-state police elements have been in the area for some time. What is more, the central government maintains an armed militia in Kashmir numbering in excess of ten thousand men. The totals for effective police in Jammu-Kashmir should certainly be larger than shown in official figures. Correspondingly, the armed police totals for some other states should be reduced to allow for units on deputation to Jammu-Kashmir.

In 1964 Maharashtra and Uttar Pradesh spent more money on police than any other states. They both spent about 140 million rupees (almost $19 million).[17] The smallest outlay for police was in Kerala, just under 30 million rupees (about $4 million). (See Table 5.) Police expenditures made up the largest portion of a state's budget in Assam, 14.5 percent, followed by West Bengal (8.60 percent) and Maharashtra (8.54 percent). Uttar Pradesh ranked ninth among the states in proportion of outlay on police to total budget. Mysore, Kerala, and Orissa had the smallest proportionate outlays. More revealing are figures which show the relation between expenditure on police and number of people in a state. Per capita expenditure on police was highest in Jammu-Kashmir (Rs. 3.96), Assam (Rs. 3.43), Punjab (Rs. 2.50) and Maharashtra (Rs. 2.50). For India altogether, the per capita expenditure was Rs. 1.94. The lowest per capita expenditure was in Orissa (Rs. 1.18), Bihar (Rs. 1.22), Uttar Pradesh (Rs. 1.43), Mysore (Rs. 1.58), and Kerala (Rs. 1.37). There are indications that during the period since independence expenditure on the police as a proportion of

[17] *India: A Reference Annual*, 1964, pp. 352-400. The smallest outlay was in fact in Jammu-Kashmir, but for reasons given above, Jammu-Kashmir should be considered a special case.

TABLE 5

EXPENDITURE ON POLICE FORCE BY STATES

State	1960 Police budget (LAKHS)	1960 Percent of total budget	1964 Police budget (LAKHS)	1964 Percent of total budget	1960 Rank by percentage of budget assigned police, 1964	1960 Cost per police-man Rs.	1960 Rank by expenditure per police-man (highest to lowest)	1960 Cost per citizen Rs.	1960 Rank by expenditure per citizen on police
Andhra Pradesh	640.55	7.43	625.58	4.96	12	1,583	9	1.78	9
Assam	408.15	9.96	804.64	14.5	1	2,433	1	3.43	2
Bihar	567.66	7.47	650.75	7.38	7	1,743	5	1.22	14
Gujarat	398.81	7.73	608.29	7.25	8	1,273	15	1.98	8
Jammu-Kashmir	141.23	10.66	135.20	5.58	11	2,266	2	3.96	1
Kerala	231.68	4.87	299.61	4.27	14	1,744	4	1.37	11
Madhya Pradesh	633.43	9.41	754.11	7.78	6	1,559	10	1.95	7
Madras	589.63	6.79	748.62	5.58	10	1,763	3	1.75	10
Maharashtra	992.21	9.06	1440.45	8.54	3	1,595	8	2.50	4
Mysore	372.45	4.46	450.30	4.43	13	1,521	11	1.579	12
Orissa	208.47	4.89	300.79	4.22	15	1,432	13	1.18	15
Punjab	508.28	8.12	847.49	7.90	5	1,483	12	2.50	3
Rajasthan	468.04	10.08	559.78	8.0	4	1,423	14	2.32	6
Uttar Pradesh	1055.58	7.63	1339.85	6.49	9	1,627	7	1.43	13
West Bengal	841.24	8.62	1039.14	8.60	2	1,715	6	2.40	5
Territories	496.44	—	440.52	—	—	—	—	—	—
Total (All-India)	8553.85	7.86	11,312.65	7.28		1,652		1.94	

SOURCES: India, *A Reference Annual*, 1961, pp. 391-498.   India, *A Reference Annual*, 1964, pp. 352-400.
For Police size, see Table 1. Census Totals, 1960, p. 5.

total state budget has declined, although the total amount spent on police in every state has risen.[18] This is certainly true for the period between 1960 and 1964. This is another way of saying that while state expenditures generally have risen, and have risen under every head, non-police expenditures have grown more rapidly. The most rapid increases almost certainly are to be found in education, welfare, and development.

India's major cities have more policemen per unit of population than is the case for the country as a whole. The first three cities in population—Bombay, Calcutta, and Delhi—have ratios more favorable than either London or New York. Size of police establishment is not correlative with amount of population. Delhi, third in size, has proportionately the largest police force. Calcutta is second in both. Bombay, first in overall size, is third in police establishment. Madras seems to have done least well by its population. Although it is fourth in total size, it ranks below Kanpur, eighth in population, in ratio of police to population. (See Table 6.)

Judged by proportionate size of police force India has done as well as the West, if not somewhat better, in her major cities but has done much less well than the West overall. In India there has been relative neglect of the non-urban community. To put it another way, there is much greater disparity over the country as a whole with respect to the number of police per unit of population than is the case in the United States or Great Britain.

OTHER POLICE FORCES

The bulk of police duties are handled by the state police, armed and unarmed branches. In addition to these there are auxiliary police units that assist the regular police in particular circumstances. There are three categories of these: (a) railway police, (b) rural police, and (c) volunteer police. These will be discussed in turn.[19]

---

[18] See the comment of the Bihar Police Commission, 1960-1961, p. 236.

[19] It might be worthwhile in passing to note the strength of the central government's police forces, namely the Central Bureau of Investigation and the Central Reserve Police. At the end of 1963 the C.B.I. had 1,039 policemen; it also had 1,505 other staff engaged in clerical, technical, or prosecution work. India, Ministry of Home Affairs, Special Police Establishment (Investigation and Anti-Corruption Division), Central Bureau of Investigation, *Annual Report*, 1963, Appendix IV, p. 34. In 1964 the Central Reserve Police was reported to have fourteen battalions. An Indian battalion numbers on the average about one thousand men. Therefore the Central Reserve

TABLE 6

COMPARATIVE POLICE STRENGTH IN MAJOR CITIES

City rank size	Cities	Police size* (sanctioned)	Population	Proportion of people to one policeman	Rank by portion: people to police
1	Greater Bombay	14,813	4,152,056	280.5	3
2	Calcutta	14,031	2,927,289	208.3	2
3	Delhi state†	11,652	2,359,408	202.1	1
4	Madras city	4,019	1,729,141	431.0	5
8	Kanpur district	2,678 (in 1959)	971,062 (Town group) 976,291 (District)	363.0	4
6‡	Bangalore	2,003	1,206,961	603.0	6
	London	20,683 (Dec. 31, 1961)	8,147,150	393.0	
	New York	24,626 (Dec. 31, 1960)§	7,781,984 (For 1960)§	315.5	

* Figures are for 1960 unless otherwise specified.
† Population for Delhi: Town group and Delhi state are given as same in basic figures.
‡ This list omits Hyderabad which is India's fifth largest city.
§ *World Almanac*, 1966, p. 351.
SOURCES:
  Calcutta, West Bengal Police Commission, Appendix XI, p. 75 (1961).
  Madras, Annual Police Administration Report, 1960, Statement E.
  Uttar Pradesh Annual Report, Statement E.
  Bangalore, Mysore Police Administration Report, Statement E.
  Bombay, Annual Bombay Report, 1960, Statement E.
  London, Final Report, Royal Commission, p. 190.
  New York, Uniform Crime Reports, 1960, p. 112.

The railway police are composed of two forces which are easy to confuse. They are the Railway Police and the Railway Protection Force. The Railway Police is a special branch of the state police. Control of it is exercised through one or more deputy inspectors-general of police. The purpose of the force is to prevent and investigate crime committed on the railways or within railway property. The Railway Protection Force is a sep-

---

Police would have had about 14,000 men in 1964. Together, C.B.I. and Central Reserve Police made up approximately 3 percent of the total police strength in the country.

The central government has other specialized forces which I have chosen to overlook since they do not perform normal police functions. They are the Indo-Tibetan Border Force, the Border Security Force, and the India Reserve Battalions. The Railway Protection Force will be discussed later.

arate police agency directed and financed by the railway administration itself. Its duties are wholly to guard and protect railway property as well as property entrusted to the railways. It has replaced the railway watch-and-ward staff of bygone days.[20]

How should a country organize its police forces so as to be most effective in preventing crime on its railroads? There are several possibilities. The entire system, or elements within it, may be given its own police staff with exclusive jurisdiction over crime on the railroads. There would then be two police forces in the country, one for railroads, another for everything else. Alternatively, a country may give its primary police force jurisdiction over railways. Why, it might be asked, should railways be singled out for special treatment? The answer is that a nation's police force is usually organized in terms of certain, often small, territorial areas. Railroads, however, cover vast distances, crisscrossing many police jurisdictions. Unless there is a national police force, the fight against railway crime may not be effectively coordinated. Since Indian police are operationally organized on the basis of districts, it was obvious that criminal problems of the railways could not be coped with successfully by district police. At the same time, to give the railways their own police would create, it was felt, unmanageable problems of coordination and control. So a special branch of the state police was created to deal with crime on the railways within each state. The United States faces a similar problem in controlling highway safety. Plainly this responsibility cannot be left entirely to each city, town, or even county police force. The areas are simply too small. In most states in India the railway police organization is subdivided into sections or railway "districts." In Bihar, for example, there are two railway districts with headquarters at Muzaffarpur and Patna.[21] In Uttar Pradesh there are five, with headquarters at Agra, Lucknow, Gorakhpur, Moradabad, and Allahabad.[22] At the same time, the essential but

[20] The contemporary force is authorized under an act of parliament, the Railway Protection Force Act of 1947.

[21] Bihar Police Commission, Chapter 7.

[22] Uttar Pradesh Police Commission, Chapter 8. Since railway police are part of the state police force they are not usually distinguished in statistical tables. Thus, some proportion of every state's force should be understood to be permanently on railway duty, just as some proportion of them are in armed police. Officers and men transfer between the railway police and district police. In Bihar, for instance, out of 32,566 police in 1960, 1,228 were with the railway police. Bihar Police Commission, p. 270. Actually,

mechanical duty of guarding railway property has been entrusted to the railways themselves, for which purpose they have created their own security force. The Railway Protection Force is comparable to security forces maintained in the United States by institutions or businesses.

There are several difficulties with existing arrangements. Cooperation between the railway police and the district police is uncertain and haphazard. Each force puts its own problems first and is not enthusiastic about helping the other. There are often peculiar jurisdictional problems that hamper effort. The railway police do not have the power of search in the districts outside the railway rights-of-way or railway property.[23] Their investigators are dependent upon the district police for this activity. In Maharashtra the jurisdiction of the railway police runs only between the right-of-way limits and the two outer traffic signals of each station. In some states an offense taking place on a running passenger train falls to the investigating unit of the railway police, while an offense on a running goods train is a matter for the district C.I.D.[24] Similarly, some states have established a prosecuting staff solely for railway affairs, others require the railway police to rely upon the district prosecuting staff.[25] There will never be an entirely neat and simple solution to this puzzle. Functional specialization and geographical specialization are bound to conflict at some points.[26] The payment of the railway police has become an item of contention too. At present the state governments pay for the "crime" part of railway police duties, the railway administra-

---

171 of these were in the "leave and training reserve" of the railway police.

[23] The Police Commission, 1902-1903, recommended that they be given this power but it has never been implemented.

[24] For two discussions of problems of railway police and district police, see Syndicate of I.P.S. Officers, "An Appropriate Police System for India," *Transactions*, April, 1964, pp. 1-89, and Syndicate of I.P.S. Officers, "Railway Crime," *Transactions*, April, 1965, pp. 159-199.

[25] Uttar Pradesh, Rajasthan, Andhra Pradesh, and Madhya Pradesh have a separate railway prosecuting staff. "Railway Crime," p. 198.

[26] A study group of I.P.S. officers at the Central Police Training College has made what seems a sensible suggestion, at least as an experiment. They suggest that district police be given concurrent jurisdiction and responsibility over railway matters. The railway police would have their own specialty, but they would be considered as a wing of the district police for use in coping with railway crimes. Thus, the superintendent would be clearly responsible for participating in solving railway crimes, especially within his district. He would not be able to ignore the responsibility as is now often the case. In this way greater cooperation between the two forces would be achieved. "Railway Crime," p. 195.

tion pays for the "order" part. It is quite obvious, of course, that police cannot be divided permanently according to whether they perform "crime" or "order" duties. When the question of increasing staff comes up, the states contend the need is due to increased "order" duties, the railway administration counters that it is due to augmented "crime" needs. The result is that new staff is not sanctioned.[27] Finally, there are indications that railway police personnel are not up to the standard in the districts. It has even been suggested that railway police are the "dumping ground" for unwanted and inferior personnel of the district police.[28]

The second auxiliary group is the rural, or village, police. Village police are essentially watchmen, responsible for patrolling the community at night and for notifying nearby police authority of criminal acts, suspicious activity, or public unrest. They may also be employed in performing simple, routine administrative tasks, such as keeping a register of births and deaths or in helping to collect land revenue.[29] Village police are known by several names, *chowkidar* and *patel* being the most common. By and large the rural police are subjected to a system of dual control: accountability to the collector and pay in the hands of a local government body. They are appointed, disciplined, and, if necessary, dismissed by the collector. They are paid partially by the state and partially by the local community, usually through a panchayat. Immediate supervision of their activities falls to the district police.[30] They are poorly and irregularly paid and must eke out a living through some supplementary occupation. In Uttar Pradesh they are paid Rs. 5 a month;[31] in Bihar, 1958, a chowkidar got Rs. 15 a month and a dafadar Rs. 17.[32]

Every police commission since 1860 has criticized them

[27] The study group to which I referred in the previous footnote has suggested that costs be divided half and half between railway administration and state government.

[28] *Ibid.*, p. 194.

[29] The Bihar Police Commission, 1961, pp. 204-205, has recommended that they not be so employed in the future.

[30] Bihar Police Commission, 1961, pp. 202-205; West Bengal Police Commission, 1960-1961, pp. 55-57; Uttar Pradesh Police Commission, 1960-1961, Chapter 7.

[31] Uttar Pradesh Police Commission, Chapter 7.

[32] Bihar annual police administration report, 1958. A dafadar is for all intents and purposes a chowkidar, although he has a bit more "rank," as well as some modest supervisory powers over other chowkidars.

strongly. For example, the recent West Bengal Police Commission said:

"Chaukidars and dafadars are generally recruited from the lower stratum of society and many of them are illiterates and aged persons who are generally cultivators living within their beats."[33] The annual police administration report of Bihar in 1959 observed that ". . . the chaukidars continued to provide an extremely weak foundation to the police system in the rural areas." They are also the butt of a good deal of wry humor, indeed they are almost a stock figure of fun in India:

". . . pasi by caste, thief by birth, hence selected to catch thieves and protect the villagers' property. His badge of office, a brass-bound *lathi*, or club, a leather belt, and a chronic irritation of the larynx from sundown to sunrise. His leisure moments, when not perambulating the village making horrible noises, are occupied in assisting neighboring chowkydars to carry out previously planned burglaries."[34] For the moment it is not necessary to enter into a discussion of the strengths and weaknesses of the rural police; it is enough to identify the force and distinguish it from other police units. But it should be borne in mind that their future is uncertain. India is confronted once again with one of the great thematic questions of its police history: how should policing of rural areas be handled, and especially, what should be the relation between a locally-directed village police force and an imperial force representing state or central government authority?[35]

The third auxiliary group is composed of the various volunteer police organizations. The most important of these are the Home Guards and the Village Volunteer Forces, also known as Village Defense Parties and Village Resistance Groups.[36] Home Guards are members of the public holding permanent employment outside the police establishment who are subject to mobilization by the state government in time of local emergency, such as during a serious riot, flood, or unusual festival. They are trained to do auxiliary police work and to become the nucleus of emergency aid units. Home Guards receive training initially upon recruitment and are given periodic refresher courses there-

[33] Page 56.

[34] Fendall Currie, *Below the Surface* (London: Archibald Constable and Co., 1900), p. 32.

[35] This question is taken up again in Chapter 15 when I discuss the police and Panchayati Raj.

[36] In Uttar Pradesh the analogous force is called the Prantiya Rakshak Dal.

after. They are paid for their time while training and on duty. In Bihar, for instance, a Home Guard in training receives a daily allowance of one rupee a day plus a ration allowance of forty rupees a month. When called up for duty, he gets the same ration allowance and a duty allowance of one rupee and a half a day. He will also be given a journey allowance and free uniform.[37] Nine states had Home Guard units in 1960, in total just under a million men.[38] As a consequence of the emergency in 1962, all states and territories now have Home Guard units. The central government makes some contribution to the states for their support.

Village Volunteer Forces, Village Defense Parties, or Village Resistance Groups are small bodies of men, locally recruited, who are instructed in the elements of village defense, permitted to wear distinctive badges or armbands, trained in drill, and encouraged to take upon themselves some responsibility for the security of the immediate area in which they reside. These groups have done particularly useful work in areas of heavy dacoit activity. In Bengal, which had forty thousand groups in 1960 comprising over a million men, the police credited the Village Resistance Groups with the steady decline in the incidence of dacoity. Financial assistance by state governments is slight; sometimes they contribute crude weapons, such as spears or staves, or they may contribute generally to defray the expenses of a group.

Metropolitan areas may have their own volunteer organizations. Calcutta has its Special Constabulary composed of civilians who are called upon to assist the police from time to time. They may help to keep order at a sporting event or a major festival. Calcutta also has Vigilance Parties which are the urban equivalent of Village Resistance Groups.

COMMAND ORGANIZATION (*see diagram on page 76*)

The Indian Police Service and the state police services overlap at the rank of assistant superintendent of police and deputy superintendent of police, respectively. An assistant superintendent and a deputy superintendent perform the same duties but they are the bottom and top of their respective services. A

[37] Bihar Police Commission, p. 133.
[38] Ministry of Home Affairs, *Report*, 1961-1962, p. 24, gives the figure as 998,348. However, 913,425 of these came from only one state—Uttar Pradesh.

certain proportion of I.P.S. vacancies are held open to appointment by promotion from the state services.

Inspectors, sub-inspectors, and assistant sub-inspectors are known as non-gazetted officers; they are the N.C.O.'s of the Indian police. There is some ambiguity in the use of the word "officer": it may refer to gazetted ranks only or it may refer to all persons in supervisory capacities, from inspector-general through sub-inspector.

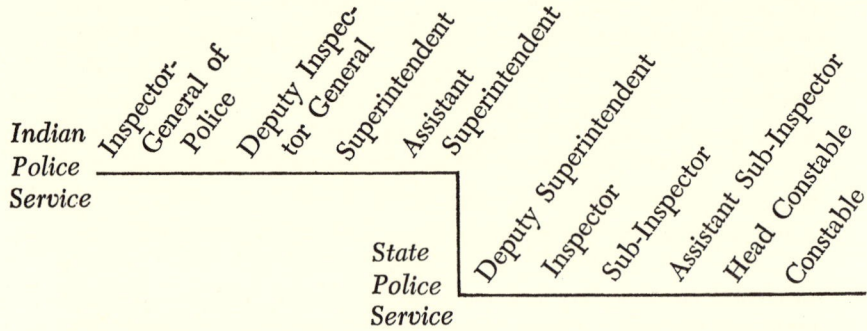

At the end of December, 1963, the I.P.S. had an authorized strength of 1,258 and an actual strength of 1,078.[39] Approximately two-tenths of 1 percent of the total Indian police force was made up of I.P.S. officers, making one I.P.S. officer for approximately 480 non-gazetted officers and men.[40] Generally, between 6 and 7 percent of the force are composed of officers of all kinds; 93 to 94 percent of all policemen in India are, therefore, constables or head constables. Thus, in 1960, there would have been about 33,600 officers of all kinds, a thousand of which would have been I.P.S., and about 483,000 constables and head constables.

At the top of the police pyramid are the state inspectors-general of police. These posts must be filled by I.P.S. officers.[41]

[39] Ministry of Home Affairs, *Report*, 1963-1964, p. 1.

[40] Some state figures are available. In Madras in 1960, out of a force of 28,933, 1,793 were officers, about 50 of them I.P.S. Thus, 6.2 percent of the force were officers of all kinds; 0.175 percent of the force was I.P.S. In Mysore in 1964, 6.25 percent were officers, 0.24 percent were I.P.S.; Madhya Pradesh in 1960, 7.08 percent officers, 0.27 percent I.P.S.; Bihar in 1960, 6.63 percent officers, 0.218 percent I.P.S. Computed from Ministry of Home Affairs, *Report*, various years, and several annual police administration reports from different states.

[41] The British, however, even into the present century, often appointed non-uniformed civil servants to the post. The West Bengal Police Commission, 1960-1961, indeed saw considerable virtue in introducing a civilian

An inspector-general will be assisted by deputy inspectors-general and assistant inspectors-general. The latter is not a rank but a position. In some states there are also "additional inspectors-general," but this is rare. The work of the police organization under the I.G.P. is organized according to geographical and functional criteria. States are first divided into territorial ranges. In Uttar Pradesh there are seven with from six to nine districts in each.[42] Bihar has four ranges with about four districts in each. Each range is headed by a deputy inspector-general. Deputy inspectors-general also direct the statewide functional offices of the police, such as armed police, C.I.D., or railway police. The range deputy inspector-general serves primarily in a supervisory capacity, providing a link in the chain of command, but especially of coordination and information-gathering between the district superintendent and the I.G.P.

Apart from the individual police stations themselves, perhaps the most important unit in police organization is the district headquarters, directed by a superintendent of police. The district headquarters is the hub of Indian police organization: this is the level at which command discretion has been vested so as to mediate between general directive and specific circumstance. Indian districts are like American counties with respect to their position in the governmental hierarchy, although they tend to be much larger in extent. On the average, an Indian district contains about 3,600 square miles and a population of over a million and a quarter people. This is a considerable trust for any superintendent, and most of them achieve this position in their early or middle thirties. In addition to providing administrative services, the district headquarters has a large jail and storehouses for clothing, equipment, arms, and ammunition. Constabulary are recruited and partly trained there. Armed police, and sometimes mounted police, will have their "lines" or barracks nearby. Each headquarters will have a permanent C.I.D. staff who will work throughout the district as needed.

Districts are organized into subdivisions, then into police circles, and finally into police stations. A subdivision is super-

---

from time to time, more or less as a leaven in the otherwise flat cake of a career police force.

[42] The ranges are Varanasi, Gorakhpur, Lucknow, Kanpur, Bareilly, Meerut, and Agra. Uttar Pradesh Police Commission, Chapter 4.

vised by an assistant superintendent of police or a deputy superintendent. Below the subdivision is the police circle composed
of groups of contiguous police stations. In Bengal, for example,
in the early 1960's, there were seventeen districts, forty-seven
subdivisions, one hundred and twenty-six circles, and three hundred and one police stations.[43] The police circle is usually directed by an inspector. Stations, or *thanas* as they are known, are
under the supervision of a sub-inspector. Larger towns and
cities will be divided into divisions and then into police stations. Police stations in towns are frequently under the direction of an inspector rather than a sub-inspector.

In addition to police stations most states have what are
known as outposts. They are of two kinds, "registering" and
"watch-and-ward" outposts. The latter is far more common.
Both are normally under the supervision of an assistant sub-
inspector. Watch-and-ward outposts serve a "scarecrow" function
and may handle the investigation of less serious offenses.
They are found in areas where a police presence is advisable
but which do not warrant a full-fledged station. They are often
found in border areas. Registering outposts have jurisdiction in
all offenses, although they are directed to notify the nearest police station as soon as possible.

The average jurisdiction of a police station is about two hundred square miles, covering one hundred villages, and with a
population of approximately 75,000 persons.[44] There is, of
course, considerable variation in different parts of the country.
Jurisdictions tend to be larger in the north, smaller in the south.
In West Bengal, with a high density of population,[45] there are
106,000 people per police station and each station is responsible
for 122.4 square miles of territory on the average.[46] In Calcutta the territory for each station is much smaller but the number of persons is about the same, 104,000 per station.[47] In
Rajasthan, with a low density of population[48] there are 4,210 peo-

---

[43] West Bengal Police Commission, p. 27.

[44] I am indebted for these figures to A. R. Nizamuddin, "Unarmed Police
in India" (Mt. Abu: Central Police Training College, 1962), p. 12. Statistics on the number of police stations all over India can be built up from
state data. Nizamuddin must have been using a figure of 5,890 or there-
abouts for the number of police stations in India.

[45] 1,032 per square mile.

[46] West Bengal Police Commission, Appendix VII, p. 58.

[47] *Ibid.*, Appendix XI, p. 75.

[48] 153 per square mile.

ple per station,[49] and one station for each 271 square miles of area. Normally, throughout India, a station is staffed by one sub-inspector, one head constable, and seven constables.[50] Along with the district headquarters the station is probably the most important level of police administration. The station-house officer (S.H.O.) has a substantial charge; he *is* police administration for areas amounting almost to small kingdoms. He is responsible for the protection of property, surveillance of bad characters, preservation of law and order, execution of writs, patrolling of roads, arrangement of fairs and bazaars, supervision of rural police, drilling of subordinates, maintenance of records, and the investigation of crime.

India is a country of great distances and poor communication. This means that police affairs are difficult to supervise adequately and that personnel of stations, especially in rural areas, exercise an enormous amount of discretion. It also means that police are one of the most pervasive governmental agencies in the country. One authority has noted that in the mid-1950's police stations were third only to primary schools and post offices in their proximity to all villages. Police stations were on the average about eight miles from any village. Hospitals were the same; telegraph offices were almost twelve miles away and railway stations were twenty miles away.[51] These statistics give added meaning to a question raised earlier, what kind of socializing effect might the police have in a comparatively isolated milieu such as this? Certainly the number of contacts most rural people have with government is still comparatively slight, although there is no question that they have increased enormously since the beginning of the Five-Year Plans. Still, the police are there all the time; development experts and advisors come

[49] Using the figure of 489 police stations, Rajasthan, Police Department, *The Police Centenary*, 1961 (souvenir booklet), p. 31. There are also 795 outposts.

[50] Nizamuddin, *op.cit.*, p. 12. These figures for station-house strength may be too low. Other police officers say that the normal strength is not less than one sub-inspector, two head constables, and twelve constables. Once again, there are no authoritative figures available based upon actual studies of practices in several states.

[51] Reinhard Bendix, *Nation-Building and Citizenship* (New York: John Wiley and Sons, 1964), p. 258. Based on Cabinet Secretariat, National Sample Survey, No. 45, *Report on Indian Villages* (Tenth to Twelfth Round, December, 1955-August, 1957), 1961, p. 9.

and go, their presence is occasional and unpredictable. The police are there, for and as the government, day in and day out. Is it reasonable to expect that Indian police play a larger role in affecting attitudes toward government precisely because the number of offsetting or complementary experiences with government are comparatively few? One would certainly be unjustified in discounting the possibility that police, by virtue of their ubiquity and the relative lack of other sorts of official contacts, may be playing a much more important socializing role in political development in India than would be the case in more developed countries.

Many, perhaps most, police stations do not have telephone communication with district headquarters. Radio grids are expanding but they are even less well developed at the present time than telephone communication. The difficulties of road travel are obvious when one notes that in 1961 India possessed a total of 440,626 miles of surfaced and unsurfaced roads. Unsurfaced roads were 67.7 percent of the total.[52] Unsurfaced roads are rarely all-weather roads and are subject to deep pitting and scarring. The government estimated that in 1964 there were thirty-six miles of road for every one hundred square miles of area.[53] The government has projected a twenty-year road development scheme designed to raise this figure to fifty-two miles per one hundred square miles of area. *If this goal is achieved,* villages in "developed and agricultural" areas would be four miles from surfaced roads and 1.5 miles from any road; villages in "semideveloped" regions would be eight miles from surfaced roads and three miles from any road; and in "underdeveloped and uncultivated" areas villages would be twelve miles from surfaced roads and five miles from any road. This is the goal to be achieved in twenty years; the situation currently is about half as good. Can one doubt that adequate supervision of policemen in rural areas may be a sometime thing or at most accomplished with considerable difficulty? Or can one doubt that while policemen are handicapped in fulfilling their responsibilities to the citizens of their bailiwicks, they are caught with them in a situation of relative isolation which can enhance the sense of authority and power of the one over the other?

[52] *India: A Reference Annual*, 1964, p. 314.
[53] *Ibid.*, p. 317.

The Indian Police Service

Unlike the police system in Great Britain and in most of the United States, the Indian police are divided into stratified layers containing different ranks to which admission is gained primarily by direct recruitment. With minor variations among states and with some provision for promotion from one level to another, one may be recruited as a constable, attaining maximally the rank of head constable; one may be recruited as a sub-inspector, or assistant sub-inspector, attaining the rank of inspector; one may be recruited as a deputy superintendent of police, where he will likely stay; or one may be recruited to the Indian Police Service at the rank of assistant superintendent of police, attaining maximally the rank of inspector-general. The senior supervising ranks are composed then of I.P.S. officers and deputy superintendents of police. Deputy superintendents are recruited by the public service commissions of their respective states; I.P.S. officers are members of one of the two all-India services and are recruited nationally by the Union Public Service Commission. Each year about one-fourth of the vacancies in the I.P.S. are held open to entry from the state services by promotion from the rank of deputy superintendent.

Because direct recruitment is possible at a senior supervisory level, the educational attainments of Indian police officers are higher than that found in the United States or Great Britain. As we shall see, all I.P.S. officers must have university degrees. Very few recruits to police in Great Britain or the United States do. The British Royal Commission on the Police, 1962, noted that there was *no* recent instance of a university graduate entering the police service.[54] "While the service attracts a substantial number of grammar school boys, most of them belong to the lower half of those who leave the grammar school at the age of sixteen."[55]

The strength of the I.P.S. was fixed in 1960 at 1,258; that of the I.A.S. at 2,278. In 1963 there were 1,078 I.P.S. and 1,928 I.A.S. officers. Who are these men who direct the fortunes of the In-

[54] *Final Report*, p. 93.

[55] *Ibid.* The Royal Commission defended the system of promotion from the force, but was concerned about the lack of higher educational training of recruits and recommended higher pay for recruits and, especially, that less time be spent as a constable by men of greater abilities and qualifications. *Ibid.*, pp. 93-95.

dian police? What qualifications must they have? How are they trained? And what kind of careers do they undertake?

In the past several years between 50 and 70 new officers have been recruited to the I.P.S. every year.[56] In order to qualify for entrance into the I.P.S. the candidate[57] must be between twenty and twenty-four years old; he must be a citizen of India; he must be a graduate of an approved university; and he must be in good physical health with no apparent mental or physical defects.[58] It is not enough that the candidate have simply graduated from a university, he must have a degree in arts, science (but not a science degree in technology or chemical engineering), commerce, agriculture, or in civil, mechanical, or electrical engineering.[59]

The heart of the recruitment process is the written and oral examination. All candidates for the I.P.S. and the I.A.S.[60] must be examined in three compulsory subjects: the ability to write an essay in English, general comprehension of English, and general knowledge. I.P.S. candidates must write two optional papers, selecting from a list of twenty-two. These subjects cover the major areas of liberal arts training, including Sanskrit and foreign languages. Candidates for the I.A.S. and the Indian Foreign Service must write three optional papers from the same list, plus two additional papers from another list for which the standard of passage is higher than that required for the optional papers. Thus, the I.A.S. and Foreign Service candidates are examined in a total of three more subjects, two of them at higher standard than is required for an I.P.S. entrant. Candidates who pass the written examination sit for a personality test. This is an oral interview designed to ascertain how the candidate

[56] Ministry of Home Affairs, *Report*, for several years. I.A.S. recruitment has run between 85 and 100 each year.

[57] There is no formal prohibition against women applying for the I.P.S. The word "candidate" rather than "man" is used in describing necessary qualifications. None have been appointed so far, and it would be most unlikely that they would be. There are several women in the I.A.S.

[58] India, Union Public Service Commission, *Notice*, 1965, pp. 6-7. The age requirements are relaxed for certain categories of persons, such as scheduled castes and tribes, expatriates from Ceylon, refugees from Pakistan, and so forth. Every year five or six members of scheduled castes and tribes join the I.P.S.

[59] Certain LL.B. and B.L. degree-holders are admissible too.

[60] Actually candidates for all-India services, the Indian Foreign Service, and Class I services of the central government take these tests. I have focused on the requirements for the I.P.S. and, by way of comparison, on the I.A.S.

conducts himself in a situation of personal interaction. It is not an oral examination. In 1963, which is not unrepresentative, 7,113 persons applied for the examinations for I.P.S., I.A.S., and Class I central services. Of these, 4,282 appeared for the written examination, of whom 852 were declared eligible for the personality test. Of these, 417 were finally recommended for appointment.[61]

There seems to be little question that appointment as an I.A.S. officer is more prestigious than appointment to the I.P.S. Although there are no statistics on this, many observers believe that the majority of I.P.S. officers took I.P.S. appointment when they failed to achieve I.A.S. eligibility. That is, they sat for five optional papers rather than two. If a person does sit simultaneously for I.A.S.-I.P.S., he must specify in advance which of the two optional papers are to apply to I.P.S. admission; he is not allowed to take five papers and then select the highest two to apply to I.P.S. candidacy. Even allowing for the greater attractiveness of an I.A.S. career, competition for I.P.S. appointment is very keen indeed. In 1963 the selection rate for I.A.S., I.P.S., and Class I posts taken together was one out of every seventeen candidates.[62] The I.A.S. may enjoy an edge in attractiveness but the floor of selection for all-India services is sufficiently high that the I.P.S. does truly qualify as an elite service.

At the same time it would be important to know something about the attractiveness of a career in all-India service in comparison to careers outside government. Does the government get the pick of the crop or do many, perhaps the best, young men and women go into business and professions? All evidence indicates that government does draw from the most able and best qualified. Government employment, especially in an all-India service, enjoys enormous prestige. As a government study group said in 1959: "There is the honour and prestige—somewhat attenuated in recent years but still considerable; and there are opportunities for full and continuous use of talent, and for the exercise of influence in the shaping of public policies and programs."[63]

[61] India, Union Public Service Commission, *Fourteenth Report* (for the period April 1, 1963, to March 31, 1964), pp. 5 and 35.

[62] *Ibid.*, p. 35.

[63] India, Ministry of Finance, *Commission of Enquiry on Emoluments and Conditions of Service of Central Government Employees, 1957-1959 Report*, p. 85. This commission is referred to generally as the "Central Pay Commission." It will be so referred to in the rest of this book.

Margaret Cormack found in her survey of university students that the most highly esteemed career was in the all-India services.[64] Business has not yet achieved a high status reputation, and indeed is regarded by many persons with considerable suspicion. Careers in business and professions certainly appear more risky to young men and women; the securer path is to be found in government service. In fact, considering the bleak prospects of employment for most college graduates, a career in government is regarded by many graduates as the be-all and end-all of occupational attainment. The Central Pay Commission, soon after its appointment in 1957, became concerned with whether the quality of entrants into all-India and Class I central services was slipping. The Home Ministry undertook several studies to find out. The studies showed that from 1947 to 1957 there had not been a decline in the standard of achievement on written examinations of the top 350 candidates each year. Moreover, from 1950 to 1957, for every vacancy in an all-India or Class I service there were three candidates applying with first-class degrees, and that one out of every four persons with a first-class degree appeared for the competitive examinations for government service.[65] There is no reason to believe that this situation has materially changed since that time.[66]

The judgments that have been made about the quality of recruits to the I.P.S., and I.A.S. are relative to India. One should really like to know how good an Indian university degree is. This question becomes particularly arresting when one considers the many assessments of deterioration in the performance of In-

[64] Margaret L. Cormack, *She Who Rides a Peacock* (New York: Praeger, 1961), pp. 133 ff. Curiously, however, she found that while "Indian administration and government services" ranked highest among occupations preferred, "police officer, district superintendent of police" ranked fifteenth, after such occupations as engineer, lecturer, professor, lawyer, important political leader, and social worker. It is not at all clear from her data whether the I.P.S. does enjoy the prestige of the I.A.S. When student respondents thought of "Indian administration and government services" did they include the I.P.S. or not? And can one accept at face value putting district superintendent of police below social worker, political leader, and teacher? If one can, then being a police officer, even though it is a post in an all-India service, carried a much different prestige value than its sister service.

[65] Central Pay Commission, pp. 85-86.

[66] On the basis of their Delhi state survey Professor Eldersveld *et al.* found the prestige of government employment among the public "tremendously high." People would rather work for government, provided of course that rates of pay were similar. *The Citizen and the Administrator in a Developing Democracy* (Glenview, Illinois: Scott, Foresman and Company, 1967), pp. 28–29.

dian educational institutions. Perhaps most recruits do have a first-class degree but are these as indicative of real achievement as was the case before independence or as is the case at a university in Great Britain or the United States? How much does an Indian degree weigh against a school-leaving certificate in Great Britain or a high school diploma in the United States? I cannot pretend to answer this question. I may say, as a partial answer, that I.P.S. officers in personal conversation display a breadth of interest and knowledge, as well as analytic skill, that has continually impressed me. To talk to an I.P.S. officer is, in the vast majority of cases, to talk to an educated man. Although the opinion is exceedingly impressionistic, I do not believe an American high school graduate or even many college graduates would show up as well.

Why do people join the Indian Police Service? What are its particular benefits? What is the nature of the career one may expect?[67] Base pay for a junior officer in the I.P.S. begins at Rs. 400 per month (about $53). By and large, junior officers are those occupying positions below the superintendent of police. A higher scale is provided for officers from superintendent and up. This scale begins at Rs. 740 per month. By yearly increments of first sixty and then fifty rupees per month an officer may achieve, after twenty-five years service, a salary of Rs. 1,300 per month ($173). I.A.S. officers begin at the same base pay but then advance by slightly larger jumps until at the end of the service they may be earning Rs. 1,800 a month ($240). Many posts, S.P. level and above, are subject to special rates of pay. A commissioner of police in Bombay and Calcutta starts at Rs. 1,800 and may earn as much as Rs. 2,000 per month. I.P.S. officers may be awarded dearness allowance (D.A.) in addition to their base pay. Dearness allowance is a monthly increment awarded to government employees automatically in proportion to their salary and the cost of living as compared with a base year. A high-salaried employee will draw proportionately less D.A. than a lower salaried employee. I.P.S. officers may be given

[67] Conditions of service are governed by the All-Indian Services Act, 1951. The government is empowered under the act to make rules and regulations concerning recruitment and conditions of service as circumstances require. All rules must be laid before parliament, which may, in turn, modify them as it sees fit. For a complete compendium of rules and regulations for the all-India services, see India, Ministry of Home Affairs, *Hand Book of Rules and Regulations for the All-India Services* (3rd ed., corrected to September 1, 1962).

housing if it is available, for which they pay a nominal rent. Unfortunately, housing is not nearly plentiful enough, especially in larger cities, and officers frequently are forced to find housing for themselves. For this housing they will likely pay a good deal more than the 10 percent of their salary which is considered a fair expenditure.[68] Most district superintendents, inspectors-general, and commissioners of police will be provided with a house —most of them built before 1947—but members of their staffs will be lucky indeed if accommodation is made available. I.P.S. officers and their families are entitled to free medical care at government hospitals. Officers are also given various special allowances, for uniforms, travel, special duty, and so forth.

An I.P.S. officer, after completing his training, will normally be posted to a district as an assistant superintendent of police in charge of a subdivision. He will hope to be appointed district S.P. in six to ten years. He will not remain a subdivisional officer during all the intervening time, but will be posted to district headquarters or perhaps to central police offices at the state capital. After attaining the rank and post of superintendent he may serve on deputation to the central government, perhaps with the C.B.I. or at a forensic institution. His ambition will be to serve as deputy inspector-general attached to the state inspector-general's office. The pinnacle of his career would be to become state I.G.P. During the 1960's promotion possibilities at the upper levels have become limited. This is because of the emergency recruitment to the I.P.S. which took place in the late 1940's as a result of the loss at independence of British and Muslim officers. There is now a glut of officers all the same age and rank lodged at about the ranks of deputy inspector-general and senior superintendent. This situation will be eased in another ten years. I.P.S. officers must retire at age fifty-eight and may retire after thirty years of service. Retired officers are paid in proportion to years of service and amount of pay at time of retirement. In no case will they earn a pension amounting to even one-half their pay at final posting. Families of officers who have died may receive a pension not to exceed Rs. 150 per month for a period not to exceed ten years.[69]

[68] The Central Pay Commission reported that in 1957 only 24.4 percent of Class I and Class II central government employees were provided housing. Comparable figures for a later date, or by services, are not available.
[69] I have been told that this was recently liberalized so that widows of officers could get a pension for life. I have not yet seen formal notification.

Upon appointment to the Indian Police Service a probationer is sent to the National Academy of Administration, Mussoorie, for a five-month "foundational course" given to all candidates appointed to all-India or Class I central services. The training received there is designed to orient the recruit to problems of general administration, Indian history, law, and philosophy of development. It is also hoped that some esprit de corps, as well as camaraderie, will be instilled among the members of the senior services. Interservice rivalry has been an irritant in the past and it still mars administrative relations from time to time.[70] The recruit then goes to the Central Police Training College, Mt. Abu, in Rajasthan, where he undergoes intensive training in police matters.[71] The regimen is stiff, involving instruction in technical police subjects, such as criminal procedure and methods of investigation, language, and martial skills and athletics. The course lasts one year, culminating in a tour of police installations and facilities throughout India and a demanding final examination.[72] Probationers must also demonstrate competence in written and spoken Hindi. I.P.S. officers are recruited nationally and are then assigned to state cadres, to which they will be attached— except when on deputation—for the remainder of their careers. Current practice is to assign half of the probationers to states other than those in which they grew up. This practice is designed to break down provincial barriers and to create a genuinely all-India outlook. After passing their final examination probationers report to their state police forces. There they are familiarized with the peculiarities of each state organization, are assigned briefly to each phase of police work—from beat patrol to motor transport maintenance—and are instructed in the language of their new state, if they are not already familiar with it. The burden of language training upon the new recruit may be very great; a police officer must after all be able to speak

[70] See Chapter 13 for a discussion of I.P.S.-I.A.S. relations.

[71] Plans call for the college to be moved to Hyderabad in the near future.

[72] The final examination is divided into two parts: (a) law and police work, and (b) drill, sports, and practical subjects. The former is made up of Indian criminal law; Constitution of India; police procedure and administration; crime and criminals; investigation; medical jurisprudence; plan drawing and map reading; and observation including portraits. The latter comprises physical training; infantry drill; weapon training and musketry, including rifle and revolver; lathi, sword, and tear smoke drill; equitation; stable management; motor transport, and wireless training. India, Ministry of Home Affairs, Notification: *The Indian Police Service (Probationers' Final Examination) Regulations,* 1965.

colloquially with persons of his adopted state. One can imagine the effort that might be required for a Punjabi, raised on Hindi, to learn Tamil or Malayalam in a year. Probationary status lasts for two years, after which the recruit is confirmed as an I.P.S. officer or terminated.

Non-I.P.S. Officers and Men

The state police services are composed of ranks from constable to deputy superintendent. The points of lateral entry are at the levels of constable, sub-inspector (or assistant sub-inspector where this rank exists), and deputy superintendent. In most cases, some proportion of vacancies at these levels is held open to appointment by promotion. Constables are recruited by the district S.P.; sub-inspectors usually by a special police committee in which the S.P. plays a large part; and deputy superintendents by the state public service commission. Non-gazetted officers serve interchangeably in armed and unarmed police. The amount of movement between armed and unarmed police for constables varies from state to state. In West Bengal and Madhya Pradesh they are recruited to each wing separately; in Bihar they serve first in the armed police and later in the unarmed; and in Orissa, as well as several other states, there is no hard-and-fast division and a man may move from one to the other if he obtains permission.

Sub-inspectors (or assistant sub-inspectors) must have passed at least the matriculates examination and in many states must have a university degree.[73] The comparable level in the United States is sergeant, and certainly very few American sergeants possess a B.A. degree. The minimum qualifications for constable vary so much that generalization is quite difficult.[74] Constables are generally recruited between the ages of eighteen and twenty-five; minimum physical standards are prescribed, usually specified in terms of height and chest measurement; and they must be of good families. Literacy is now insisted on as a prerequisite for recruitment.[75] Standards for this may not be very

[73] A degree is required in West Bengal and Mysore; one year of university work as a qualification has been recommended by the Bihar Police Commission, pp. 160-161.

[74] Syndicate of I.P.S. Officers, "Training of Constables in Modern Set-Up," *Transactions*, April, 1965, p. 41.

[75] "An Appropriate Police System for India," pp. 32-34, and West Bengal Police Commission, p. 132.

high. The West Bengal Police Commission said that the "present practice is to demand a modicum of literacy in a vernacular language."[76] Some states insist on formal education even as high as eighth-class standards.[77] Mysore, for example, requires education to the sixth form or five years from school-leaving.[78] All the police commissions that have reported have expressed concern about the level of education in the constabulary. It is apparent from them that most constables are only just literate —some indeed may still have difficulty in writing much more than their names.[79] The police commissions of West Bengal, Bihar, Maharashtra, and Uttar Pradesh recommend formal education at least through primary school and hopefully through junior high school.[80] For constables in the armed police most commissions consider the ability to read and write sufficient.[81] As in the case of superior officers, exceptions are made for members of scheduled castes and tribes.

While I.P.S. officers are better educated than their counterparts in the United States or Great Britain, constables are very much below the standard for constables or patrolmen in the West. This is another illustration of an often-made generaliza-

[76] Page 109.

[77] *Ibid.* Indian "standards" correspond to American "grades." There are usually four years of primary school, three years of middle school, and four years of high school. Indian students enter universities then after eleven years of primary and secondary schooling, not twelve years as in the United States.

[78] Police officers in Mysore told me that in practice this means they are barely literate.

[79] Although the standard of education in the constabulary seems minimal today, police officers unanimously attest that educational quality has risen appreciably in the past ten years or so. This is an indication of the standards that prevailed under the British. One might note that in some British provinces—Bihar, for instance—a distinction was made between "writing constables" and all others. One authority states that of officers and men together in 1907, only 54.1 percent could read and write. Sir Edmund C. Cox, *Police and Crime in India* (London: Stanley Paul and Co., n.d.), p. 215, In the late 1900's very few could read and write. S. M. Edwardes, *The Bombay City Police* (London: Humphrey Milford-Oxford University Press, 1923, p. 60), notes that in 1885 in a force of 1,521 in Bombay city only 110 officers and 297 men could read and write. And Curry, *Indian Police*, p. 68 ff., says that in 1930 most constables were still totally illiterate.

[80] Uttar Pradesh, p. 92; Maharashtra, recommendations, p. 5; Bihar, p. 160; West Bengal, p. 132.

[81] Mysore in 1963 actually reduced the standard demanded for recruitment of constables to the armed police. It had been education to the eighth standard and it was reduced to fourth standard. The reduction was due to difficulties experienced in obtaining enough recruits with the higher qualifications.

tion about Indian society: that along any continuum—wealth, taxation, levels of education—extremes are apt to be much farther apart than in a developed nation.

Competition for recruitment to ranks of sub-inspector and constable is keen. Police officers rarely complain of lack of applicants. But they do complain about the quality of the lot that does apply. Choices have to be made among young men the vast majority of whom only just meet minimum standards. Police officers tend to believe that a job with the police is a last resort for most recruits. Certainly the higher the educational level of an individual the less likely he is to choose it. Officers believe that they get a large proportion of "rejects," men who have tried and failed in other occupations.[82] In Mysore, for the rank of sub-inspector in 1962-1964 at least four times the number of men applied as were needed for the vacancies advertised.[83] Recruitment of constables is made by the district superintendent. There are two procedures: enlistment days may be advertised and the nearby government employment exchange may be notified to send around qualified young men. Selection is apt to be rough and ready—a tape measure for height and chest expansion, cursory physical examination by a civil surgeon, attestation of literacy or education, and some indication of earnestness and integrity usually by means of a written "chit" from a village headman or influential neighbor or a verbal recommendation from another policeman. The quality of any batch of recruits depends upon the needs of the moment and alternative opportunities for work. Thus if jobs are plentiful and economic conditions good or the force is understaffed, standards of recruitment will suffer.

Who are the men of the constabulary? Where do they come from? What castes predominate? What families repeatedly send their young men to the police? It is a distressing fact that hardly anything is known about these matters. Perhaps the greatest gap in knowledge about the Indian police is at just this point. Although many people have impressions—such as that 50 percent

[82] "The Training of Constables," p. 39. This group of I.P.S. officers suggested that recruitment be made from young men, as close to eighteen years old as possible, so that they might be molded to an appreciation of police early in life. In this way the police would not have to depend on the older "rejects."

[83] Statement provided by the Office of the Inspector-General. In 1962 there were 50 vacancies, 251 applicants; 1963, 80 vacancies, 317 applicants; 1964, 60 vacancies, 248 applicants.

of Calcutta policemen are from Uttar Pradesh and Bihar or that most constables come from agricultural classes[84]—there is an appalling lack of hard data. What is needed is a thorough search of personnel records of the constabulary and the subordinate officer corps in order to determine precisely who the men of the Indian police are. Personnel records will only take one part of the way; it would be necessary as well to examine a random sample through survey techniques. Only in this way, for example, could information about caste be uncovered. Since independence there has been, according to police officers, a broadening of the base of recruitment. Today one finds more castes, especially depressed ones, represented in the force. But how many of which kinds? One doesn't know. There is a maddening reluctance to discuss caste in India, particularly by government servants in relation to the performance of governmental agencies. I.P.S. officers generally say that they have found no correlation between the community of a policeman and ability to perform police duties well.[85] Nor do they find it necessary, except in a few peculiar circumstances, to assign men to duties taking community—in the sense both of caste and religion—into account. It may be, of course, that I.P.S. officers are reluctant to admit to findings on their part which smack of bias against one group or another. Officers deny ever considering caste in the appointment of constables, a job which they have to do themselves individually. They would certainly not want to ask a candidate his caste outright; that might be resented very deeply and could lead to great embarrassment for the officer. Caste affiliation is officially noted only in the case of members of scheduled castes and tribes who thereby are allowed to claim certain exemptions and favors in recruitment. It is hard to believe that community is either not known or not considered to some degree. Officers have the names of the candidates —an indication of caste in many areas—and they usually have some information about the man himself from a relative or friend. Rarely do applicants for jobs in India come unsupported; they are usually backed by somebody already in the estab-

[84] Syndicate of I.P.S. Officers, "Welfare in Police," *Transactions*, November, 1965, p. 7.

[85] Occasionally respect for the old "martial" castes will show through: that the Marathas are tougher, Rajputs and Jats do better in the armed police, hillmen in Assam are particularly good in the armed police. But these views are exceptional by their presence. Generally no hint of unequal evaluation is evidenced.

lishment. That caste is a force of consequence in India today, few people would deny. It strains credulity, therefore, that a responsible officer would not pay some attention to the caste of the candidate if only out of consideration for the morale of the force. If caste is as pervasive in its influence as is generally accepted, can a police force operate effectively if it does not reflect the caste composition of the area in which it must act or is utterly heterogeneous in caste makeup?

The total emoluments of a constable each month vary from about sixty rupees to just over one hundred.[86] The computation of returns to a constable is complicated by the fact that base pay is only a part of total income. West Bengal provides a representative example. Base pay for a starting constable is forty-five rupees a month, with increments of one rupee for each year of service for the first fifteen years, then one-half rupee increments each year for the final ten years of service. Thus he begins at forty-five rupees and ends at sixty.[87] But he also gets a dearness allowance of thirty rupees per month which, with other emoluments to which he may be entitled, gives him about seventy-five rupees per month, even for a beginning constable. Kerala and Punjab also begin with a base pay of forty-five rupees per month. Other states, such as Madras, Mysore, and Bihar, have raised or are soon going to raise the starting pay to sixty-five rupees a month while recomputing the rate for special allowances.[88] The number of special allowances is quite bewildering: dearness allowance, dearness pay, special allowances for housing, uniforms, clothing for people in C.I.D., horse allowance in hill areas, food allowance during travel with police parties, special pay for instructors, for hazardous duty, and so forth. Police in India do not get additional pay, however, for extra duty. Policemen are often called upon to do longer stints in a day, but they are not given any consideration for it.[89] Sub-inspectors begin with a base pay which is two to three times that of a constable. For instance, in Rajasthan a constable begins at thirty rupees a month, plus a dearness allowance of twenty rupees and dearness pay of ten, while the sub-inspector begins at one hundred rupees a month plus a dearness allowance

[86] M. M. Singh, "Minimum Wage for a Policeman," *Transactions*, October, 1962, p. 12.

[87] West Bengal Police Commission, p. 134.

[88] See Bihar Police Commission, p. 167, and West Bengal Police Commission, p. 134.

[89] "Welfare in Police," p. 5.

of twenty-five rupees and dearness pay of fifteen.[90] The annual income, with allowance, of a constable comes to just below one thousand rupees a year (about $133). A sub-inspector's pay is about three thousand rupees a year ($400). It is interesting to note that the Central Pay Commission, Government of India, recommended in 1959 that the lowest pay acceptable for a government servant, taking into consideration all grades from secretary to peon, was seventy rupees a month with ten rupees extra for dearness allowance.[91] Constables, then, begin with pay just below the minimum acceptable for the lowest central government employee.

A constable's salary of one thousand rupees per year, which is a slight overestimation, is about 70 percent of the average salary of factory labor.[92] Indian per capita income in 1963-1964 was Rs. 370.7. Assuming that a constable supports a family of five —which was the average household size in 1960—per capita income in his family would be only Rs. 200.[93] According to official figures, rural households expended Rs. 247 per person in 1960 and urban households Rs. 334.6.[94] Since the size of rural and urban households was respectively 5.2 and 4.8 persons, total average household expenditure would be Rs. 1,275 in rural areas and Rs. 1,600 in cities. A constable could not support an urban or a rural family at the national level of average household expenditure. Among working class families, a family income of Rs. 60-90 a month places that family in the lowest 20 percent in Bombay and in the second lowest quartile in Delhi, Madras, and Calcutta.[95] Even by Indian standards, police constables are miserably paid.[96]

[90] *The Police Centenary*, p. 41.

[91] Central Pay Commission, p. 206.

[92] *Times of India, Directory and Yearbook, 1964-1965* (Bombay: *Times of India*), p. 332.

[93] Government of India, *India, A Reference Annual, 1965* (Delhi: Ministry of Information and Broadcasting, 1966), p. 160, reporting figures from the Fifteenth Round of the National Sample Survey.

[94] *Ibid.*

[95] *Ibid.*, p. 161.

[96] In Great Britain and the United States, too, income of the lowest ranking policemen tends to be below the national average for wage earners. The Royal Commission on the Police reported that the maximum pay of a police constable in 1960 was about 5 percent below average industrial earnings (Interim Report, p. 56). Average household income in 1964 was twenty-four pounds per month (*U.N. Yearbook of Labour Statistics, 1966*, p. 675). A British policeman could earn about half as much. Income per household in the United States, 1960-1961, was $6,719 a year. Median annual salary for a patrolman in large cities in 1967 was about $5,300 (President's Com-

Among the many welfare schemes for policemen perhaps the most important are housing and medical treatment. Housing, especially in larger towns and cities, uses up an exorbitant amount of a constable's salary. Accordingly state governments, with central government help, have undertaken substantial housing construction schemes.[97] Despite all the effort, in not one state do even 50 percent of constables live in rent-free housing. Some southern states—Mysore, for example—are approaching 50 percent; the situation is better generally in the south than in the north.[98] Most constables are provided a house allowance, usually quite inadequate, in lieu of government housing.[99] Policemen and their families are generally supposed to get free medical treatment; policemen usually get some attention, their families rarely do. Again, the efforts to remedy the lack of hospitals and dispensaries have been noteworthy; the need is so great, however, that even more heroic efforts will be required to redeem the promise of the regulations. In some places special medical facilities for policemen and their families have been constructed. In others, wards in civil hospitals have been reserved for their use.

Policemen must retire at the age of fifty-five, except in Uttar Pradesh where it is fifty-eight. Sometimes an earlier retirement age is specified for persons in armed branches of the police due to the greater physical exertion involved in that kind of work.[100] Pension schemes are meager, being paid only to persons who receive a disabling wound in action beyond normal call

---

mission on Law Enforcement, *Challenge of Crime in a Free Society*, p. x). Besides satisfying elementary conditions for sustaining life, the critical question about pay scales is whether, given employment supply and demand, existing wage rates in any society attract men of sufficient caliber and character to perform the tasks required of them. This is an immensely complicated question.

[97] During the budget year 1963-1964 the central government advanced loans to states for police housing to a total of Rs. 26,400,000. Since the inception of the grant scheme, early 1960's, a total of almost 210 million rupees had been given the states by 1964. That is about 28 million dollars. Ministry of Home Affairs, *Report*, 1963-1964, p. 16.

[98] "Welfare in Police," p. 9.

[99] For example, in Mysore constables receive a housing allowance per month of Rs. 5.50 in cities and towns with a population over 200,000 inhabitants, and in other parts of the state they receive Rs. 4. Sub-inspectors receive respectively Rs. 12 and Rs. 8 per month. Figures provided me by the Office of the Inspector-General, Mysore, 1965.

[100] Men of the Bihar military mounted police retire normally at age forty-five; in the D.A.P. at fifty. They may apply for a five-year extension. Bihar Police Commission, pp. 174-175.

of duty or to families of men who died prematurely from performing especially hazardous work. Routine illness, or even wounds and retirement after a lifetime of service are not regularly recompensed.

Constables receive training in police work extending over a period of six to nine months. Some states have special training centers for constables—Uttar Pradesh, for example, has thirteen —but in many of them the bulk of the training is imparted at district headquarters under the general supervision of the superintendent. Sub-inspectors are usually trained at a subordinate officers' training school—in Bihar at Hazaribagh, in Uttar Pradesh at Moradabad, in Maharashtra at Nasik. There is considerable room for improvement in the standard of instruction. Most states are almost completely without training manuals and pamphlets. So far there are no uniform training syllabi for all India, the result being that there is tremendous variation in the content of training from state to state and even within states.[101] Little attention is given to formal training after a man has begun his career as a policeman. If a state does provide for refresher courses, they are commonly made available only once in a man's career and involve a course not exceeding one month in duration, usually provided at district or circle police headquarters.[102]

Upon appointment as constable a man is generally posted within his home district but never, or very rarely, to his home police circle or station. Sub-inspectors must be posted outside their home districts. The chances of promotion within the subordinate police are quite small. In Madras, for example, chances of promotion from constable are only one in twenty in the unarmed police and one in fourteen in the armed police.[103] In Bihar the vast majority of constables retire at the rank they began, only 12 percent of them achieving promotion to head constable.[104] Eldersveld, *et al.*, found in Delhi state that 60 percent of police constables had held their present position for longer than ten years with no advancement.[105] In Bihar, 18 percent of sub-inspectors will be promoted, the average pe-

[101] The Intelligence Bureau, C.B.I., has prepared a draft syllabus for constable training which, it is hoped, will become a model for the states. For a description of a syllabus for training constable recruits see West Bengal Police Commission, Appendix XXVII, pp. 120-121.

[102] "Training of Constables in Modern Set-Up," pp. 56-57.

[103] *Ibid.*, p. 57, citing reply of the Government of Madras to their query.

[104] Bihar Police Commission, p. 187.

[105] *The Citizen and the Administrator in a Developing Democracy*, p. 72.

riod of waiting being thirteen to fifteen years.[106] In West Bengal 6 percent of constables will be promoted, 15 percent of head constables, and 12 percent of sub-inspectors.[107] Promotion possibilities are correlative with status in rank, I.P.S. men enjoying the greatest opportunities for advancement, constables the least.

All in all, the subordinate ranks—accounting for 94 percent of all police in India—are only slightly educated, bare literacy being the norm; are paid as poorly as the lowest central government employee; will normally not serve more than twenty miles from home; will remain at the very rank to which they were recruited; will be helped minimally, if at all, in the event of untimely illness, hurt, or death; and will retire on a minuscule pension, again, if it is paid at all. It will be necessary to examine what the effects of these prospects are upon the ability of the Indian police to perform the tasks allotted to them and required of them in the contemporary world.

[106] *Bihar Police Commission*, p. 187.

[107] Promotion prospects are no better in Great Britain. One authority notes that 80 percent of British police are constables and only 12 percent are sergeants. Only 8 percent of those recruited as constables can expect to be promoted to sergeant. Ben Whitaker, *The Police* (Harmondsworth: Penguin Books, Ltd., 1964), p. 103.

4 • *The Criminal Setting*

THE primary purpose of a police force is to ensure the continued existence of those elements of personal life and of social process that society considers valuable. A police force may of course do many other things, from rendering aid in times of natural calamity to sponsoring boys' clubs, but its essential function is protective. Crime is the name by which threatening activities emanating from persons within society are known. Crime is socially defined; its content shifts among societies and within a single society over time. Moreover, crime has an indefinite number of gradations, from quite trivial departures from established norms to very serious breaches profoundly and emotionally shocking to members of that society. A police force is organized in terms of a criminal context. The criminal is the focus of a policeman's attention. It is important, therefore, in studying the police of India that one understands both the magnitude of criminal activity and its nature.

THE INCIDENCE OF CRIME

How much of what kinds of crime is there in India? How is crime distributed with respect to time and to physical and human geography? What comparisons can be made concerning the incidence of crime between India and other countries? In order to answer these questions it is necessary to examine statistics about crime. In India, and indeed in most countries, this immediately leads to difficulties. There are two sorts of problems in using Indian criminal statistics. First, there are technical problems involving the collection, transmission, computation, and presentation of data. Here one is concerned with proper handling of whatever data are collected. Second, there are problems involving the adequacy of any data collected by police reporting agencies.

Statistics on Indian crime originate in police stations, they are collected into district reports at the office of the superintendent. From the mosaic of district reports a state report is compiled and made available to the public as part of the annual police administration reports. These reports contain detailed tables of all offenses under the Indian Penal Code as well as special and local laws; the body of the report discusses these findings, noting trends in the incidence or nature of crime. A summary for all India is published each year by the Ministry of Home Affairs under the title *Crime in India*.[1] Unhappily both public sources—state reports and *Crime in India*—are flawed. The center's published figures sometimes do not agree with those of the state it refers to; state reports will cite the incidence of crime differently in different sections of the report; and when a state report recapitulates a feature of the criminal situation from another year it may disagree with figures cited in that previous year.

In order to guard against basing conclusions on statistics that have been faultily reported or presented, I have sought to obtain the most basic published sources. This means, whenever possible, the state annual police administration reports. And within them I have used figures contained in their summary tables (presented as appendices) and not figures reported either in graphs or in the body of the text. Since I have not been able to obtain or see copies of these reports from all states, I am forced to rely on *Crime in India* for all-India figures. I do so with considerable reservation.[2]

Even when all technical problems of collection and presentation are solved, important questions concerning the adequacy of crime statistics remain. Whatever the country the basic problem is that crime is not self-authenticating. It must be found out, and that requires human agency. Either the police must discover it or the public must report it.[3] What the police discover—meaning report as a crime—is affected greatly by police procedures and public concern. It may also be affected by referral practices, circumstances, social class, time, and place.[4] If

---

[1] The first number was issued for 1953.

[2] I know of no library in either the United States or India which has a complete collection of state police administration reports.

[3] Marvin E. Wolfgang, *Crime and Race* (New York: Institute of Human Relations Press, American Jewish Committee, 1964), pp. 22-24, cites several studies from the United States showing "that offenses committed by normally law-abiding citizens are far in excess of the number known to the police or committed by persons actually taken into custody." Nor are their offenses trivial; they involve serious felonies. One study showed that two-thirds of the men and three out of ten women polled were guilty of having committed one or more of fourteen felonies.

[4] *Ibid.*, p. 24.

reporting is made easier or a larger force is deployed, crime rates may rise. Similarly, if the public becomes concerned about some particular form of crime, police may begin to arrest offenders rather than just warning them. Figures on prostitution, homosexuality, and gambling are notoriously unstable this way. Even in Great Britain, which has a good reputation for competence in obtaining statistics, one noted criminologist and former police officer has said:

"But among those who have actually watched the machinery for compilation at what might be called the feeding end, it must be difficult to keep a straight face when the figures come out every year."[5]

Police officers often have a vested interest in minimizing the amount of crime that occurs within the area of their responsibility. A low crime rate reflects well upon an officer; a high crime rate may be used as evidence that he is not efficient.

"Unfortunately over the past decade the tendency has grown to judge the work of districts and police stations purely by the figures of crime and not by the inherent quality of the work of superintendents of police and station-house officers in the field of detection and prevention. Naturally officers of all ranks wish to have good remarks about their work because their future career and promotion depend upon such remarks. The temptation therefore of keeping the crime figures low is very great and hardly an S.P. carries on a crusade to detect unregistered cases and getting [sic] them registered."[6]

So officers encourage or condone the practice of minimizing offenses—a felony becomes a misdemeanor, a murder an unnatural death, a riot an affray, and major robbery a petty theft. The results of minimization and non-registering of cases were shown graphically in the state of Uttar Pradesh. Many observers, as well as the Uttar Pradesh Police Commission, have noted the anomaly of gradually decreasing amounts of crime during the decade of the fifties when the population was increasing.[7] In 1961 the state undertook a stern campaign to ensure com-

---

[5] Quoted in John Barron Mays, *Crime and the Social Structure* (London: Faber and Faber, 1963), p. 24.

[6] Statements of B. N. Mullick, former director of the Intelligence Bureau, Ministry of Home Affairs, quoted in Abraham Varghese, "Practice and Precepts in Police Work," *Transactions*, November, 1964, p. 65.

[7] See Government of Uttar Pradesh, *Report of the Uttar Pradesh Police Commission*, 1960-1961 (Allahabad: Superintendent Printing and Stationery, 1962), pp. 6-7.

plete recording of all crimes coming to the attention of the police. The effect was startling. Total reported crime between 1960 and 1961 went up by over 50 percent.[8] Comparing the first quarter of 1961 with the first quarter of 1960 the Police Commission noted an increase in dacoities of 78 percent, robberies 98 percent, riots 73 percent and murders 23 percent.[9]

But the problem goes beyond policemen themselves. Unless a police force is ubiquitous, crime can only be recognized if it is reported by the citizen, whether as victim or witness. There are many reasons why people may be reluctant to do so. The offense may be too trivial; the distance to a police station may be too great; the expectation of productive outcome too meager, as in the case of cycle thefts; reporting may expose the individual to harassment from the criminal or his friends; the individual, family, or group may not welcome the intrusion of outsiders and prefer to handle the matter themselves; the offense may be embarrassing to the victim, as is the case in sex offenses; and, finally, there may be neither victim nor witness who feels that a wrong has been committed, as in narcotics cases, prostitution, gambling, and some kinds of sex deviation. It is probably true that the more serious the offense the less likely it is that it will not be reported. Many police officers use this thought as a poultice to their consciences. But as the figures from Uttar Pradesh have shown, too many serious crimes seem to be going unrecorded to justify complacency. Two American anthropologists residing in a village of western Uttar Pradesh, not far from Delhi, tell of the unreported murder of an illegitimate baby by the father of the wronged girl. They conclude that "murder of such children is evidently accepted as a necessary step for the preservation of family honor."[10] Few observers, Indian or American, have failed to comment on the reluctance of villagers to break ranks in the face of outside intervention and also of the ability of powerful village leaders to arrange matters to suit their convenience. Many villagers are in the habit of taking disputes, even when criminal offenses are involved, to the village panchayat, or council. They not only do not think to take them to the police, they would rather not do so, preferring to

[8] The figures were 64,131 in 1960 and 100,798 in 1961.

[9] Uttar Pradesh Police Commission, pp. 6-7.

[10] Leigh Minturn and John T. Hitchcock, "The Rajputs of Khalapur, India," ed. Beatrice B. Whiting, *Six Cultures—Studies in Child Rearing* (New York: John Wiley and Sons, 1963), pp. 303-304.

trust to the decisions of respected and familiar leaders. While it would be unwise to overstate the point, there is little doubt that a great deal remains hidden from the prying eyes of the police.[11] Two items in the public opinion survey provide clues to the amount of unreported crime in India. Respondents who had been victims of crimes were asked whether they had reported the matter to the police. Ten percent or less of respondents in each sample had been the victim of a crime. Of these, most said they had reported to the police. However, not less than 25 percent of them had failed to make a report. Among Kanpur rural immigrants, almost as many had reported as had not. Respondents were also asked whether they knew of instances when crimes had been committed but the people involved had not reported the matter to the police. About one in ten of all respondents knew of such an instance. Urban people were more aware of this, rural migrants next, and rural residents least of all. Generalizations from these figures are very risky. One would have to assume that the areas surveyed are representative of all India and that respondents knew about real crimes, not fancied crimes. Still, the absolute numbers involved in unreported crimes would seem to be considerable.

The incidence of serious crime against persons and property reported to the police in 1948 was approximately 179.4 per 100,000 people.[12] In 1963 it was 143.6 per 100,000.[13] In abso-

[11] In the United States the President's Commission on Law Enforcement and the Administration of Justice reported in 1967 that the incidence of crime was appreciably above that shown in official figures. It based its findings on a public survey of 10,000 respondents. See *The Challenge of Crime in a Free Society* (Washington: U.S. Government Printing Office, 1967), pp. 20-22.

[12] This figure requires an explanation:

1. The crime figure used is for total cognizable crime under Classes I-V of the I.P.C. A distinction is made in India between cognizable and noncognizable crime. Cognizable crime is more serious than noncognizable. A police officer has a duty to prevent cognizable offenses and may arrest an offender or potential offender without a warrant. For noncognizable offenses an arrest warrant is required, as it were after a court has taken "cognizance" of it. These terms make the same kind of distinction that felony-misdemeanor do in the United States. Cognizable offenses, then, are serious offenses.

However, not all cognizable offenses are delineated by Classes I-V of the I.P.C. It is fair to say that the offenses listed in Classes I-V of the I.P.C. account for the most common offenses against persons and property; they are the kind of offenses that would be listed in a model criminal code anywhere in the Western world. Class I comprises offenses against "The State, Public Tranquillity, Safety and Justice"; Class II, "Serious Offenses against Persons"; Class III, "Serious Offenses against Persons and Property, or

lute terms crime hit a high in 1949, with 640,000 reported cases. Crime declined steadily through 1955, when it began a gradual ascent. The 1949 high was not surpassed until 1962. *In 1963, the last year under review, there were only four thousand more cases of reported cognizable crime under the I.P.C. than in 1949, although the population had grown by over 25 percent, or about 107 million persons.* The pattern of crime development in India is certainly surprising. Rising crime rates are the rule among nations of the world and an almost static incidence of crime measured in absolute terms is unheard of. From Bihar

---

against Property only"; Class IV, "Minor Offenses against the Person"; and Class V, "Minor Offenses against Property." Offenses under other laws may also be cognizable. For example, offenses under prohibition acts, the Drug Act, Arms Act, Suppression of Immoral Traffic in Women and Children Act, and so forth.

Thus, by using the figure for cognizable offense under Classes I-V, I have understated the total amount of crime in India, but I have accounted for all serious crime that would normally be recognized against persons and property in a Western country.

2. However, I have used the figure for cognizable crime *reported* to the police. Reported cases are to be contrasted with true cases: a reported case is an unverified report of a crime, a true case is a reported case which has been investigated by the police so as to determine whether the report is correct. Figures for true cases give a more accurate picture of actual crime. I have used figures for reported crime because it tends to be the more common statistic in Indian documents. But it should be understood that using figures for reported cases does overstate the amount of crime. By and large, verified cases run about 10 percent less than reported ones. This is a gross approximation; I have seen true cases as much as 18 percent less than reported and as low as 5 percent less. It would be useful to study the relation between true and reported cases, but the exercise is not worth doing until the quality of statistics has been approved.

All in all, I have erred on the side of overstating serious crime against persons and property. This is significant since, even so, the incidence of serious crime in India is dramatically lower than in the United States or Great Britain.

3. For population in 1948 the figure of 351,518,622 was used. This figure was computed by taking the 1950 census figure and subtracting from it three years' worth of population increase based on the yearly average increase during the 1940's. See Government of India, *Census of India: Final Population Totals* (New Delhi: Manager of Publications, 1962), p. 9.

4. The source for reported cognizable crime is *Crime in India*, 1953, p. 1. *Crime in India* has never given a complete explanation of the figures it represents. It refers to its all-India figure as being for "total cognizable crime." But it clearly is not this. Bombay city, for example, has a total cognizable crime figure alone which is almost this every year. The figure that is in fact being used, though this is never mentioned, is for cognizable crime under Class I-V of the I.P.C.

[13] Based on adjusted population for 1963, which I compute to be 458,-095,082, using the yearly increase of the 1950's.

comes an indication that the situation is even more startling. The Bihar Police Commission noted that in 1912 the police registered 53,324 cognizable cases. In 1960, although the population had almost doubled, the police registered 63,122 cases. Some Indians, especially politicians, have taken considerable pride in the unique pattern of criminal development—it only shows once again the more pacific nature of the Indian people as well as their essential regard for law, life, and property. Others are less charitable, seriously questioning the accuracy of official statistics. Is India sui generis with respect to crime or are the figures suspect? The question cannot be answered authoritatively yet. It is easy to criticize existing statistics, but is it fair to assimilate India to a wider world pattern—a pattern most clearly documented in the Western world—and to ignore the possibility of critical uniqueness?

Looking at 1963 in detail there were 658,800 cases of serious crime reported under Classes I-V of the Indian Penal Code. Just over 530,000 of them proved to be true. Over 700,000 persons were taken into custody, or about 157 for each 100,000 persons. (See Table 7.) The Indian crime rate for serious "true" crimes against persons and property would be 115.6 per 100,000 in 1963.[14] In England and Wales in 1963, for every 100,000 people there were 2,382.7 indictable offenses known to the police.[15] The Federal Bureau of Investigation in the United States gives the crime rate in 1964, based on seven categories of crime[16] as 1,361.2 per 100,000 people.[17] In 1963 the rate was 1,226.2. The American and English indices were computed on the basis of much fewer crimes than was the Indian, and still the Indian rate

[14] The point should be underscored that these figures represent crime under Classes I-V of the Indian Penal Code. There are many more crimes each year, indeed many more cognizable crimes. Total cognizable crime is easily ten times as much. This may be demonstrated by examining state records, which carefully separate cognizable offenses according to classes of the I.P.C. and special and local laws. If total cognizable crimes were used to compute the rate, it would be easily 1,200 per 100,000 of population. Nonetheless, the smaller figure, based on Classes I-V of the I.P.C., does represent the most common and most serious offenses against persons and property. They certainly include all the offenses that the F.B.I. uses to compute the crime rate for the United States.

[15] Great Britain, Home Office, *Criminal Statistics: England and Wales*, 1963, Cmnd. 2525, p. 16.

[16] Murder and non-negligent manslaughter, forcible rape, robbery, aggravated assault, burglary, larcency over $50, and auto theft.

[17] U.S. Department of Justice, Federal Bureau of Investigation, *Uniform Crime Reports for the United States*, 1964 (Washington: U.S. Government Printing Office, 1965), p. 3.

TABLE 7

CRIMINAL STATISTICS FOR STATES AND CENTRALLY ADMINISTERED TERRITORIES

States	Cases reported during the year	Total true cases	Cases convicted	Volume of crime	Rank in criminal rate (highest to lowest)	Persons arrested	Persons con- victed
Andhra Pradesh	34,460	27,243	16,434	95.8	13	39,445	21,156
Assam	19,268	16,589	3,613	162.28	5	32,960	5,600
Bihar	63,785	51,326	6,276	137.30	8	73,475	14,527
Gujarat	32,526	29,192	6,597	157.63	6	42,290	10,884
Jammu-Kashmir	3,822	2,627	418	107.0	12	5,842	747
Kerala	16,105	12,979	4,649	95.27	14	20,421	5,607
Madhya Pradesh	79,547	72,293	21,308	245.6	1	70,313	31,601
Madras	56,477	46,880	27,629	167.7	4	52,259	30,342
Maharashtra	49,493	44,932	13,328	139.8	7	54,446	20,775
Mysore	25,824	22,203	8,395	109.49	11	37,322	11,900
Nagaland	283	213	84	73.9		220	107
Orissa	23,723	19,574	5,493	135.1	9	24,477	9,600
Punjab	18,452	15,219	5,355	90.8	15	23,798	8,988
Rajasthan	27,040	19,081	4,986	134.1	10	34,411	9,029
Uttar Pradesh	132,220	101,300	19,598	179.29	2	114,187	42,400
West Bengal	55,055	48,679	7,314	172.1	3	82,825	11,846
Andaman and Nicobar Islands	211	201	68	332.0		147	83
Delhi	14,373	13,692	2,465	540.6		7,977	3,131
Himachal Pradesh	1,442	1,076	399	106.72		1,881	583
Laccadive, Minicoy and Amindivi Islands	2	2	2	8.3		—	—
Manipur	1,702	1,225	97	218.19		1,169	168
Tripuria	2,990	2,728	313	261.82		3,529	515
Total	658,800	549,254	154,821	134.8		723,394	239,589

SOURCE: *Crime in India*, 1963, pp. 32-39.

is lower. It is clear, *accepting each country's official figures*, that the incidence of serious crime in India is very much lower than in the United States or Great Britain. Indeed, serious crime is more than ten times more numerous per unit of population in these Western countries than in India.

Referring to 1963, among cognizable offenses the most common form of crime was theft (33.2 percent of all cognizable crime).[18] The next most prevalent was housebreaking (20.8 percent), followed by rioting (4.27 percent), cattle theft (3.57 percent), criminal breach of trust (2.8 percent), murder (1.63 percent), cheating (1.34 percent), robbery (1.16 percent), kidnapping and abduction (1.05 percent), and dacoity (0.75 percent).[19] To Western eyes the unusual items are rioting and cattle theft. The prominence of the former suggests that armed police may not be out of place in contemporary India and the latter that crime in India may come in an unusually wide assortment.

Punjab has the lowest crime rate in India, 90.80 per 100,000; Madhya Pradesh has the highest, 245.6.[20] The Madhya Pradesh rate is unusual enough to warrant study by experts: it is well above the Indian average, has been so for over a decade, and is more than sixty-five points above the next highest state, Uttar Pradesh. The explanation does not seem to be a greater concentration of policemen, because it ranks eighth in India in this respect. With respect to the distribution of various forms of crime in 1963, Madhya Pradesh, Gujarat, and Assam had a much higher proportion of murders than other states.[21] Uttar Pradesh was close behind. The highest incidence of dacoity was in Madhya Pradesh, followed by Uttar Pradesh, West Bengal, Assam, and Bihar. The southern states—Madras, Mysore, Kerala, and Andhra Pradesh—had very little at all. Nor did Punjab, Rajasthan, Maharashtra, or Orissa. Dacoity is plainly concentrated in the north-central and northeast parts of India.[22] Assam had the highest incidence of rioting in 1963, just shading West Bengal. Bihar, Jammu-Kashmir, and Uttar Pradesh were next in order.[23] Robbery was more prevalent in Rajasthan, West Bengal, and Gujarat.[24] Finally, cattle theft—which may seem nostalgic

---

[18] Theft is the taking of movable property without the owner's consent. *Indian Penal Code*, section 378.

[19] *Crime in India*, 1963, pp. 4-5. [20] *Ibid.*, pp. 32-39.
[21] *Ibid.*, pp. 40-41. [22] *Ibid.*, pp. 56-57.
[23] *Ibid.*, pp. 96-97. [24] *Ibid.*, pp. 64-65.

to Westerners but is deadly serious in India—was proportionately greater in Madhya Pradesh, Uttar Pradesh, and Rajasthan (about twice the national average). In fact, so high were the proportions in these three states that all other states fall below the national average.[25]

Conforming to the worldwide pattern, crime rates are higher in urban areas. Calcutta has a crime rate more than four times that of the country as a whole. In order of decreasing crime rates, the rank in 1963 among the eight most populated cities was Calcutta, Kanpur, Delhi, Bombay, Madras, Ahmedabad, Bangalore, and Hyderabad. The range is from 700 to 193 per 100,000. Accepting crime figures from India and the United States and Great Britain at face value, crime rates even in India's largest cities are only one-third the national rates in the United States, England, and Wales.

THE INDIAN CRIMINAL SCENE

Crime in India is bewildering in its variety; the police must cope with a range of crime as diverse as any in the world. While people are vicious to one another in India in much the same ways that they are in the West, what distinguishes the Indian scene is the enormous variety of circumstances within which crime becomes manifest. It is the richness of social and geographical conditions that gives to Indian crime its incredible and fascinating heterogeneity. Only in a country which, as someone has remarked, is advancing in uneven stages from the first to the twentieth centuries could one have cattle thievery and insurance frauds, dacoity and stock swindles, murder for witchcraft and vehicular homicide.

Murder in India is generally committed among persons acquainted with one another.[26] Its causes are intimate in the sense of having to do with the nature of everyday relations among people living closely together. An Indian saying has summed up the causes of murder as "Zan, Zar, and Zamin"—lust, loot, and land. But this explanation is not complete. One must add motives having to do with considerations of propriety, right-behavior, and pride. In an impersonal society, buffets to a person's

---

[25] *Ibid.*, pp. 80-81.
[26] For a discussion of evidence supporting this point, see Edwin D. Driver, "Interaction and Criminal Homicide in India," *Social Forces*, December, 1961, pp. 153-158.

pride are borne by the individual alone; in a village community they are a matter of common knowledge, seemingly cherished by the entire community and touching one's family and close friends. They threaten the entire ground of social being. Only factors of this kind can explain the openness, the viciousness, and the conspiratorial group-participation characteristic of so many Indian murders.[27] Police authorities commonly list the motives of murder as land disputes, love intrigues, domestic quarrels, jealousy and revenge, and considerations of gain. In some states witchcraft figures prominently as a cause of murder.[28] Belief in witchcraft is still prevalent among the tribal communities, and it leads to murder when someone fears he has been selected as a target for witchcraft. Such people kill, they fully believe, in self-defense.[29]

Because of the wild and remote conditions of so much of India murders may go undetected or be marked down as "unnatural deaths." Proper postmortems may be delayed for days, if performed at all, obliterating clues as to the true cause of death. Every year many people die of snakebite, savaging by wild animals, drowning, and falls from heights. Among other forms of life-taking, suicide seems to be growing, especially among the relatively well-to-do of the urban centers. Infanticide is not un-

[27] Here is an example which is not atypical. In a village near Sringeri police station, Mysore state, 1958, eight men entered the house of a neighbor and chopped to death the man of the house, his wife, and their six sleeping children. The murderers were promptly arrested and two immediately confessed. The cause of the crime was jealousy, relative loss of face in the village community, and bitterness stemming from a dispute over land. The murdered man had moved to the community ten years before. He had prospered and soon became influential in village life. His neighbor resented the growing prestige and wealth of the "intruder." Jealousy festered and spread. The fields of the two rivals abutted and finally, inevitably, there was a dispute over the boundary. The new man won the suit and bitterness etched the soul of the loser. Finally he and his friends could stand the situation no longer, and in the night they embarked on their ugly act. For other comments on this theme, see Justice G. D. Khosla, *The Murder of the Mahatma* (London: Chatto and Windus, 1963), p. 9.

[28] Bihar, *Report on the Administration of the Police in the State of Bihar for the Year 1959* (Patna: Secretariat Press, 1960), p. 14, gave a breakdown of the causes of murder as follows: witchcraft, 6.8 percent; land disputes, 11.7 percent; love intrigues and domestic quarrels, 17.3 percent; jealousy and revenue, 7.7 percent; and considerations of gain, 7.1 percent. Attributed to other causes were 43.4 percent.

[29] Crimes with superstition as an underlying cause tend to be concentrated in southern Bihar, Orissa, Madhya Pradesh, and western Maharashtra —the areas of greatest tribal concentration. Syndicate of I.P.S. Officers, "Superstition and Crime" (Mt. Abu: Central Police Training College, 1963), p. 5.

common, most cases involving illegitimate births, although some proportion is made up of unwanted female children. *Satti*— self-immolation by wives on the funeral pyres of their husbands—is now a thing of the past.

In any society there is a large amount of violence to persons not resulting in death. Dacoits in rural India especially embody this threat as do goondas of the urban areas. Goondas are urban "toughs," a floating population of men living on the fringes of the criminal world, willing to undertake a strong-arm task, spoiling for fights, providing very often the "shock troops" for urban riots. They are unscrupulous, vicious men who can be hired to break up union meetings, to intimidate the supporters of a rival political candidate, or to extort money from tradesmen in return for protection. In rural India physical violence most commonly stems from village factions—fights and private quarrels, in addition to dacoities. There are a surprising number of riots—by definition involving five or more people—in rural areas. In 1963, for example, there were over 19,000 true cases, and almost 160,000 people were arrested.[30] This subject will be discussed separately later. Besides beatings, house-burning and crop-burning are used as a means of avenging oneself on a rival. The opportunity to set fires, particularly to thatch roofs, is almost limitless and it takes little ingenuity and no equipment.

In urban areas authorities are becoming increasingly concerned about unmannerly and rude behavior to young women. Young men congregate near girls' schools and colleges or near bus stops and make provocative remarks, stare brazenly, and jostle against the women. In Delhi these men are called "Eve-teasers," in Calcutta "roadside Romeos." Public opinion is mounting against them, for their behavior touches a cord in most adult men who are fathers or brothers in their own right with a strong sense of obligation toward the women in their families. If "Eve-teasing" continues, its perpetrators may one day find themselves given very short shrift by police, courts, and an aroused public.

Crimes against property are widespread but they are usually petty in nature. Very few burglaries, dacoities, or thefts net over a hundred rupees. One interesting change in the pattern of burglary in towns is the growing shift to daytime operations, when tenants of houses can be counted on to be at work. Po-

[30] *Crime in India*, 1963, pp. 36-37.

lice must now provide day as well as night patrols, adding greatly to their burdens. The amount of property stolen each year due to petty thievery and pilfering is enormous but the enormity is a function of the numbers of people involved and not of the scale of each taking. Because the standard of living is so low in India, objects which in the West would attract no attention are a standing temptation. If an object can be moved, it can be stolen, and it can be sold. The railroads are particularly subject to petty thievery. Iron keys, electric light bulbs, fans, hooks, fittings of all kinds, luggage on platforms, and coal piled in yards are all stolen. One estimate of the value of railway fittings stolen in 1960-1961 was just over 2,300,000 rupees (about $303,000).[31] This figure is admitted to be an understatement. Other thieves concentrate on bazaars, where they loiter, filch, and run. Small children are often used for this purpose, bringing stolen items to their parents who wait in nearby streets sometimes with sacks over their shoulders for use in carrying home the loot.[32] The theft of telegraph wire, for the copper in it, is very common in India and indicates once again that the value of an object depends upon the level of well-being in the surrounding society. Special acts of parliament have been passed to cope with this form of crime but it continues to rise sharply.[33] In 1958 there were 4,071 cases; in 1962 6,715.[34] Telegraph lines are easily accessible, the spot for cutting can be chosen for maximum safety to the thief, no special knowledge is required, the stolen goods are easily transported —often after being cut into very short lengths—and quickly disposed of by melting. Setting aside the cost in terms of interrupted communications, the value of copper wire thefts in terms of replacement cost comes to over a million rupees a year (about $133,000).[35]

An immemorial practice still in vogue is the administration of stupefying drugs to persons a criminal intends to rob. Most

[31] Syndicate of I.P.S. Officers, "Railway Crime," *Transactions*, April, 1965, p. 188.

[32] See Shankar Sahai Srivastava, *Juvenile Vagrancy: A Social-Ecological Study of Juvenile Vagrants in the Cities of Kanpur and Lucknow* (New York: Asia Publishing House, 1963), p. 176, for a description of bazaar thievery in Kanpur.

[33] The Telegraph Wires (Unlawful Possession) Act, 1950, and the Telegraph Wires (Unlawful Possession) Amendment, 1962.

[34] Shyam Lal (I.P.S.), "A Study into the Problem of Copper-Wire Thefts in India," *Transactions*, April, 1964, pp. 1-3.

[35] *Ibid.*

states report some cases of this each year. Bihar, for example, reported 72 in 1959.[36]

Conditions in rural India are particularly suitable for crimes against property. Houses are made of mud, through which holes can easily be dug; many dwellings have no doors and hence no locks; electricity is still rare in the countryside—after dark the kerosene lamps with their small orange glow provide the best illumination; people have yet to develop the banking habit, preferring to bury money in the earth or to buy women's gold jewelry; firearms are few and villagers timorous after dark; and the police are far away, pursuit unlikely. The practice of decking children and women in valuable ornaments is perennially responsible for brutal murders and maulings by criminals who lie in wait or entice them to secluded parts. The village does have some deterrent capabilities. Villagers normally will stand together against outsiders—if the outsiders are not too numerous or too well armed; it is impossible for an outsider to come into the village without being noticed; people come and go at all hours in an Indian household and homes are rarely completely unattended; and, finally, Indian villages are inhabited by what seem like hosts of mongrel dogs whose inquisitiveness is only outdone by their ability to howl.

In many parts of India the police must deal with criminal tribes. These groups are not really tribes at all, but are offshoots of lower castes.[37] "Criminal tribe" refers to a group, often itinerant, which has as one of its customary occupations some form of crime, always against property. Partly because the determination of what groups are criminal is a nice matter of judgment, there are no accurate figures on the number of them in India today. Delhiwala Bauriahs, Sansis, Bhatus, Kanjars, Karwal Nats, and Minars are accepted examples of criminal tribes.[38] The Kanjars of southeast Rajasthan, for example, train their children in techniques of housebreaking, resisting police torture, and disguising their activities when stealing produce from fields by im-

[36] Annual Reports, 1959, p. 15. S. M. Edwardes, *Crime in India*, pp. 38-40, notes that poisoning for gain is mentioned in the Laws of Manu. He cites the following figures for cases of use of drugs in 1921 in British India; 91 cases in Uttar Pradesh, 38 in Punjab, and 23 in Madras.

[37] Verrier Elwin, *Maria Murder and Suicide* (2nd ed.; London: Oxford University Press, 1950), p. 3. Note also that Elwin's *A New Deal for Tribal India* (New Delhi: Ministry of Home Affairs, 1963) makes no mention of criminal tribes at all.

[38] See J. C. Curry's remarks in *The Indian Police*, Chapter 10, about criminal tribes in British India.

itating the noises of wild animals. The women are powerful in the tribe and often engage in prostitution. They have developed an argot, as well as signs, which are only intelligible to members of the tribe.[39] The old Criminal Tribes Act required members of these tribes to report to the nearest police station at specified intervals and also to request permission before leaving an area. This act was replaced in 1954 by the Habitual Offenders Act, and many police officers complain of the difficulty in applying it to criminal tribes. Rather than having power automatically with respect to any member of a tribe so designated, police must now wait until a member has been convicted often enough to qualify for the label habitual offender. The good ones, police officers point out, rarely get caught. And before they are they may do considerable damage.

A dacoity is robbery—that is, theft with violence—committed by five or more persons.[40] It is the most publicized form of crime in India today. Movies have been made about it, often romanticizing dacoit leaders in the Robin Hood image; large interstate police campaigns have been mounted to drive them out of infested regions; India's leading saint, Venoba Bhave, made a celebrated tour of a notorious dacoit area, the Chambal Ravines, in northern Madhya Pradesh, in a vain effort to make them give up their evil ways; police careers have been broken and state administrations seriously embarrassed by their depredations; village defense parties have been sponsored and arms licenses liberalized in order to strengthen the helpless village; villagers are terrorized by them; and newspapers delight in reporting their activities. So great is their hold on the public's mind that police officers will congratulate themselves if the number of dacoities decreases whatever happens to other forms of crime. Dacoity is most prevalent in northern Madhya Pradesh, Uttar Pradesh, Bihar, and West Bengal. In 1963 there were 4,759 true cases of dacoity. The number of dacoities decreased in the middle and late 1950's, hitting a low in 1959 and 1960. The number has risen since then but not in proportion

[39] D. P. N. Singh, "Kanjars of Rajasthan," *Central Police Training College Magazine*, November, 1964, pp. 80-89.

[40] *Indian Penal Code*, section 391. The word dacoity conjures up a picture of gangs descending on a house or a village, guns firing and eyes aflame. There is something to this picture but it is overdone. Actually, some dacoities are really only burglaries in which the inmates of the house have been awakened and give resistance, thereby precipitating the violence necessary to the designation dacoity.

to population, so the incidence per capita is still declining. Hardly a day goes by that a dacoit attack is not reported in the press. Sometimes a prominent dacoit leader is killed, more often it is the innocent who lose their lives, sometimes accidentally, sometimes deliberately, and from time to time with great cruelty. Dacoits may single out one house for attack or surround, intimidate, and pillage an entire village. Some dacoit bands are permanent organizations; they exist only to steal. Others are short-term arrangements of convenience made up of men without work, or underworked, who have insufficient resources to support themselves or their families. The number of dacoities rises in times of crop failure and of economic distress; dacoities are also less frequent during the busy seasons of an agricultural year, at planting and harvest.

Reflecting the growing mechanization of life in India, dacoits are beginning to develop in a new direction. There is a rising incidence of robbery of motor vehicles on major arterial roads. Cars and even buses have been held up on the Grand Trunk Road in West Bengal, Bihar, and Uttar Pradesh. Roads must traverse isolated areas; they are narrow and in bad repair, necessitating slow speeds; and they are dark, completely unlighted, and virtually unpatrolled by the police. The chances of success are all with the criminals. Government officials in parts of these states have been known to demand armed police escorts when forced to travel at night.

The opportunities for fraud, cheating, and swindling are as numerous as the activities of human beings. Because the social milieu is so varied in India, so also are the forms of fraud and cheating. Checks are forged or fraudulently cashed, spurious organizations or business enterprises solicit money in exchange for worthless promises or certificates; rail shipments are misappropriated or falsely damaged and insurance collected; university and government examinations are taken by substitute candidates; textbooks are pirated and privately printed for wholesale distribution; and claims are put forward for dead or nonexistent persons. What makes cheating in India so fascinating to the Western observer is the juxtaposition of the most sophisticated frauds, utilizing business mechanisms of the most modern kind, with swindles built upon rank superstition at the very limit of credulity. One story of gullibility will suffice. In the late summer of 1964 a short man clad in a black coat and yellow turban came to the door of a house in Bangalore. With a sincere but agitated manner, he informed the head of the household that an evil spirit was hovering over the house and that if ritual offering were not made soon the daughter of the house would surely die. The family became thoroughly frightened and begged the man to tell them what they could do. The solicitous visitor said he wasn't sure himself but did know of a holy man who might be persuaded to come and help. The stranger undertook to find out, and promised to return in three days. He was as good as his word, for on the evening of the third day he showed up with a venerable holy man in tow. The father was told that "puja" would have to be performed, the ritual offering consisting of various items belonging to the daughter, such as a sari, scarf, ornamented plate, gold necklace, and so forth. The father consented and the family, excepting the father, was ordered to go out into the courtyard. Then the holy man and his accomplice put the various objects into a pot. The father was directed to turn his back while spells were recited and the pot was placed in a hole in the earth floor. The two men finished the "puja" and promised to return the next day to exhume the pot and determine whether the signs were propitious. Needless to say, they did not return and the family became suspicious. Upon digging up the pot they discovered that the gold necklace with pendant, worth fifteen hundred rupees, was missing.[41]

An almost universal form of petty cheating is traveling without tickets on the railroads. In the budget year 1962-1963, for example, over eight million people were detected traveling without tickets, and this was only a small fraction of the number who actually did.[42] Ticket inspectors are forced to travel in teams and are often reinforced by railway police because there have been numerous instances of inspectors being threatened, manhandled, or beaten by whole carloads of irate travelers. No stigma seems to attach to the offense; certain classes of persons, such as beggars, students, frequent travelers, and railway employees, think they may travel free as a matter of right. In part the habit of free rail travel was learned during the independence struggle when people were urged not to pay fares as a protest against the British government. Economic reasons un-

[41] This story was reported to the press by the commissioner of police, Bangalore, at his weekly press conference, September 22, 1965. India has no monopoly on gullibility. Almost any police officer, whatever the country, can recount stories of incredible simple-mindedness.

[42] "Railway Crime," pp. 167-168.

doubtedly play some role, although railway fares are hardly exorbitant. But, most important, traveling without tickets seems to have become a custom, a habit, and as long as the chances of detection are fairly small, there is little incentive to change.

Cattle theft, an antique form of crime in the West, is a matter of deadly seriousness in India. Police learn early that the surest way to arouse hostility in the peasantry is to display a cavalier attitude toward cattle theft. In 1963 there were 21,649 true cases of cattle theft and almost 20,000 people were arrested. In an agrarian society where many people live on the cheerless threshold of starvation, "cattle are all," as one police officer expressed it. Cattle are as important as children, perhaps more so, and grown men, gnarled by toil, will weep bitterly over the loss of their stock. Some cattle thefts become cases of "cattle-napping" when the thief, rather than disposing of the animals himself, lets it be known through an intermediary that they will be returned for a ransom. Because cattle are so highly prized, they become the objects of malicious mischief directed against their owners. Poison is one means often employed.[43]

In most societies certain forms of pleasure are considered either obnoxious in themselves or conducive to harmful results for the individual, those acquainted with him, or society at large. These are labeled vices and the police are called upon to eliminate them or at least to keep them out of sight. Vice in India primarily involves gambling, prostitution, and the consumption of addictive drugs and alcohol. Gambling, by and large, is a private or small-scale affair. Upper class people wager over cards or dice in their homes or clubs. Gambling establishments capable of serving ten or twelve people at the most will be found in many cities; there is no special prestige to be earned in frequenting such places and they draw patrons from the lower middle class and below. There are also "floating" games to be found whenever people may congregate easily, not too publicly, and without suspicion, such as a railway yard, a riverbank, or the corner of a common. Gambling on the cotton market is fairly common and one sometimes hears of gambling on the time of the monsoon. So far, at least, the organization of games of

[43] Madras, 1961, reported 88 cases of cattle poisoning, against 111 the previous year. Madras, *Report on the Administration of the Police of the Madras State*, 1961 (Madras: Controller of Stationery and Printing, 1963), p. 7. In 1959, Bihar reported 353 cases of mischief by killing cattle; it did not specify the means employed. *Report on the Administration of Police*, 1959, p. 16.

chance is a matter of individual initiative and has not been constituted as large business ventures.[44]

Trustworthy information about the extent of prostitution, as with any form of vice, is unobtainable. Its antiquity in India —as in any society—is unquestioned, being mentioned in the Rig Veda and Kautilya's *Arthasastra* among others. Prostitution is more common in urban areas, although promiscuity and the profligacy of widows in rural areas are more than fictional constructions. Certain areas of many towns are noted for being the haunts of prostitutes. Public solicitation, however, is rare and is certainly much less common than in the West. Action against prostitution is authorized under the Suppression of Immoral Traffic (in Women and Girls) Act, 1956. Calcutta police reported 1,451 brothels and disorderly houses officially known to them in 1958.[45] The police in Delhi registered sixty cases against 115 pimps and 143 prostitutes in 1960. They also uncovered fifteen "private brothels" engaged in "clandestine prostitution."[46] Some cities have special squads which investigate prostitution. Officers admit that these squads serve as an independent check on the activities of station-house officers who may otherwise suppress knowledge of it for a price. Concern with prostitution among the police does not seem to be great; they consider it simply one more task to be performed. Many officers do, however, believe that it is growing and will be a larger problem in the future. Authorities are particularly concerned with inhibiting the activities of procurers, that is, the traffic in young women and girls leading to careers in prostitution. Enticing and sometimes kidnapping young girls, even buying unwanted female children, for later sale to houses of ill fame has been known since the British period.[47] *Crime in India* in 1963 noted cryptically that elopement and enticement of young women were being reported as cases of kidnapping and abduction and, most revealingly, that in Madras and Ahmedabad, which had higher rates for these, the increase was not due to

[44] Srivastava, *Juvenile Vagrancy*, pp. 164-171, describes games of chance played by the lower castes and vagrants in Kanpur.

[45] Government of West Bengal, Home (Police) Department, *Annual Report on the Police Administration of the City of Calcutta and its Suburbs, 1958* (Alipore: Superintendent, Government Printing, 1961), p. 33.

[46] Delhi, *Annual Administration Report*, 1961-1962 (Delhi: Director, Public Relations, Delhi Administration, 1962), p. 6.

[47] See Edwardes, *The Bombay City Police*, pp. 162-165, and Currie, *Below the Surface*, Chapter 13.

gang activity. The implication was plain that gang activity is not unexpected. Girls who are homeless, destitute, and without family are the favorite mark of the procurer. The protection of these vulnerable young women is one purpose of the 1956 act. It provides for the establishment of "protective homes" to which girls and prostitutes may be sent by a magistrate for such period as he may determine. In these homes rehabilitation may be attempted or those who have not yet succumbed to prostitution may be trained in a skill that can provide for their minimum needs.

The addictive drugs most in use are opium and hemp derivatives, such as charas, ganja, and bhang.[48] Opium is smoked or eaten; charas is smoked; ganja and bhang are usually drunk, although bhang is occasionally smoked. Drug consumption seems to be mostly by members of the poor and laboring classes, though this finding is inevitably impressionistic and may simply indicate a greater official concern with its incidence among those classes. There are very few cases each year of prosecution in connection with handling or use of drugs. Madras city, for example, had only sixteen cases concerning drugs in 1961, against almost 26,000 connected with alcohol. Bombay city in 1960 registered twenty-nine cases under the Drugs Act, fifty persons arrested, compared with over 96,000 under prohibition laws.[49]

Far and away the largest vice problem is the consumption of alcoholic beverages. Six states have a statewide prohibition policy—Bihar, Gujarat, Kerala, Madras, Maharashtra, and Uttar Pradesh; one state has none—West Bengal; and the remainder have prohibition in some sections but not in others.[50] Not only is the prohibition net tattered in places but where it does exist it is applied with varying degrees of rigor. Prohibition imposes an enormous burden on the police who are called upon to shut off the supply of illicitly distilled liquor, to prevent its shipment, and to discover its sale and consumption. The following examples indicate the magnitude of the task. Of all cognizable

[48] India, Planning Commission, *Report of the Prohibition Enquiry Committee, 1954-1955* (New Delhi: Manager of Publications, 1955), pp. 18-22.

[49] Maharashtra, Home Department, *Annual Administration Report of Greater Bombay Police, 1960* (Bombay: Director, Government Printing and Stationery, 1963), pp. 35 and 43.

[50] India, Ministry of Information and Broadcasting, *India: A Reference Annual, 1964* (New Delhi: Ministry of Information and Broadcasting, 1964), pp. 104-108.

offenses reported to the police in Mysore in 1958, 29 percent involved prohibition.[51] In 1960 almost one-fifth of all cognizable offenses registered in Bombay were for infractions of prohibition laws.[52] Moreover, police officers believe, whatever their views about the rightness of prohibition, that it is one of the most important occasions for corruption within the police.

Organized crime does not seem to have come to India, not even in connection with vice rackets. Crime is largely an individual or local group undertaking; each operation is limited in scale and is not manipulated by organizations with authority over a large area. However, the day of local control may be drawing to a close. Many police officers are quietly alert to a development they consider logical and inevitable.

Juvenile delinquency has been given little attention until quite recently.[53] Nor has much care been given to investigating the size of the problem. Between 1958 and 1959, while total cognizable crime declined, national figures for juvenile delinquency increased by 61 percent.[54] It is clear that figures were reflecting increased official attention and not a profound deterioration in youthful morality. Few cities and only one state, even today, have specialized police agencies to deal with juveniles.[55] The agencies are understaffed, rarely having more than ten full-time officers employed.[56] The volume of work these few agencies handle is very small relative to the need. Bombay's juvenile police detachment handled 608 cases in 1962.[57] In all of India in 1963, 16,432 cases of cognizable crime were officially credited to juveniles.[58] In other words, of all cognizable crime 2.5 percent was committed by persons under twenty-one. By comparison, in England and Wales in 1963, 23.7 percent of per-

[51] Mysore, Home Department, *Annual Administration Report of the Department of Police of the Mysore State, 1958* (n.p., 1961), p. 27. Total cognizable crime was 250,241; of these, 23,418 were offenses under Classes I-V of the I.P.C. There were 72,804 prohibition offenses.

[52] 491,967 cognizable offenses were recorded against 96,803 prohibition offenses. See pp. 43 and 89 of the 1960 Annual Report on Police Administration.

[53] Juvenile delinquency is officially defined as crime committed by persons under twenty-one years old.

[54] *Crime in India*, 1958, 1959.

[55] The single state is Bihar.

[56] R. Deb (I.P.S.), *Role of the Police in Combating Juvenile Delinquency in India* (Mt. Abu: Central Police Training College, 1964), pp. 22-29.

[57] *Ibid.* He further reports that the juvenile units in Ranchi and Patna handled forty cases between August, 1961, and September, 1962.

[58] *Crime in India*, 1963, p. 28.

sons found guilty of offenses were under twenty-one.[59] In the United States in 1964, 20.5 percent of all persons arrested were under eighteen years of age.[60] The magnitude of the juvenile problem is still unappreciated in India and is not revealed in official figures, although steps are being taken to remedy the situation. It may be, as some spokesmen for India have claimed, that crime in India is less of a problem than in more developed nations and that, by the same token, participation in it by youths may be dissimilar also. However, until statistical reporting becomes more accurate this proposition will have to be taken on faith. Moreover, the first step in moving to test it will be to develop a greater concern and a greater willingness to look the situation squarely in the face.

PUBLIC PERCEPTIONS OF INSECURITY

The survey of public opinion and experience, conducted in Bangalore city, Tumkur district (Mysore state), and Kanpur in Uttar Pradesh, shows that about one out of ten adult males has been the victim of a crime. The incidence was one in ten in Kanpur and Bangalore, but only one in one hundred in Tumkur and five in one hundred among rural migrants to Kanpur. City dwellers experience crime more often, which accords with the official statistics on the incidence of crime. About the same proportion of people know someone personally who has been the victim of a crime. Most of the crimes experienced are minor, thefts being the most common. The rest are a sprinkling of domestic and neighborhood disputes, pickpocketing, and harassment or physical abuse from hooligans. Rural respondents in Tumkur were asked whether their village had ever been troubled by dacoits. Only 11.2 percent of respondents said that their villages had. One would expect the figure to be higher in the north, but no evidence is available because a northern rural sample was not included.

Five items in the survey were designed to demonstrate the sense of security among the Indian public. Respondents were asked (a) whether the area was safe to live in; (b) whether it was safe to keep valuables, such as money and jewelry, in the

[59] Computed from figures given in *Criminal Statistics: England and Wales*, 1963, p. ix.

[60] Computed from figures given in *Uniform Crime Reports for the United States, 1964*, p. 108.

house; (c) whether it was safe to travel within the village or neighborhood; (d) whether it was safe to travel outside the village or neighborhood; and (e) whether the individual thought it would be a good idea to own a firearm. Factor analysis shows that the first three of these items are closely associated together. The factor loadings were 0.60 or above. In every sample, one factor is defined primarily in terms of these items. In other words, an individual's sense of security generally, his sense of the protection afforded by his home, and his sense of safety in moving about the immediate vicinity are consistently associated, and seem to define a dimension of security-insecurity. Only in the case of Kanpur residents was the desire to own a firearm part of this dimension. For Kanpur rural migrants the items were combined by pairs in two factors, with desire for a firearm associated with insecurity in traveling about the immediate vicinity at night.

The effect of the personal experience (or near-personal experience) of being the victim of a crime on the individual's assessment of the security of the area does not appear to be great. While there is always some association, it is generally slight, about 0.20, except in the case of Kanpur rural migrants. In the latter instance there were heavy loadings on the security factor. Among Kanpur rural migrants, anxiety about security is associated very heavily with having a friend who was a victim of a crime. Generally most of the people who are fearful about their security have not been the victim of a crime nor do they know anyone personally who has been.

Nine out of ten people in all of the samples show no anxiety about their security generally. About 20 percent of people doubt the safety of their homes as far as keeping valuables is concerned. Not more than 21 percent of any sample expressed fear about moving around their immediate residential area, whether in villages or cities. A larger percentage, however, have doubts about safety away from their immediate environment. This conforms to expectations, since unfamiliar areas are likely to appear less secure to the traveler. City dwellers— Kanpur and Bangalore—were expressly asked whether they were concerned about the women in their families moving around on the streets without an escort. Over a third of all respondents—all of whom were males—did say they were concerned. Thus, while men are not terribly anxious for themselves, they are anxious on behalf of the women in their families.

The survey included a question about the perceived need to own a firearm, and this item was used as a possible measure of insecurity. It was not associated with the other security items; it did not help to define the security-insecurity factors. One interesting sidelight, however, is the clear indication of a very substantial latent demand for the possession of firearms. Not more than 5 percent of any sample admitted owning a firearm. Many more may have had them, but if they had failed to register them they may have been unwilling to admit possession. Nonetheless, while a very small proportion admitted owning firearms, close to a half of all respondents said they thought it would be a good idea to have one for protection. Rather surprisingly, the need seems to be felt more keenly in the urban areas than in the rural ones. Exactly half of all Bangalore respondents wanted a firearm; among Kanpur residents the proportion was only fractionally less. In Tumkur, on the other hand, 35 percent indicated a desire to have a weapon, while among Kanpur rural migrants 41 percent agreed. A rising standard of living coupled with more liberal licensing regulations could bring about an enormous increase in the ownership of firearms.

Because comparative data about perceptions of security are so sorely lacking, it is difficult to put the Indian findings into perspective. Operating wholly impressionistically, it does not seem that Indians are especially fearful in their surroundings. Few of them are very much concerned on this score. Few of them have been the victims of a crime, and those who have have not experienced very serious crimes. There is, however, considerable concern about the safety of women in public streets. This is a hidden issue, the effects of which might suddenly be felt as in anomic outrage against the abuse of women or in support for punitive legislation in defense of women in public places.

THREE

CRIMINAL INVESTIGATION

5 • *The Record*

THE core of police activity is the investigation of crime. Measures designed to prevent crime, no matter how stringent, will sometimes fail and then the police will be judged by their ability to detect the culprit and bring him speedily to book. But the police cannot be successful in criminal investigation through their own unaided efforts. Crimes are rarely committed in the presence of police officers; police are dependent on members of the public for information about the occurrence of crime and the circumstances involved. Furthermore, the relations between investigator and member of the public are apt to be strained and difficult however charitable the attitudes are on both sides. Police must intrude into the innermost interstices of private lives. They come and stand within homes, in kitchens, in vegetable gardens, in courtyards; they stand between brothers, fathers and sons, mothers and sons, between friends, among colleagues. The police intrude for a purpose sanctioned by society; and though their behavior is regulated by law, they bring to bear an impersonal, alien mandate which may be at odds with the intensely personal situation revealed by the crime. Whether the police succeed in their task and whether society, not as an abstraction but in its component human parts, continues to support police objectives depend in large measure on the quality of relationship established between investigator and contacted individual.

The following two chapters will discuss the record and the process of criminal investigation in India. The first chapter will describe police organization for investigation and evaluate the quality of investigations generally. The second chapter will describe the manner of police investigation and prosecution. It will focus especially upon the nature of police contacts with the public. It will describe the reaction of the public to this contact and will evaluate the results of interaction from the point of view both of investigation efficiency and of fostering respect for the processes of law.

THE RECORD OF INVESTIGATION

In judging the effectiveness of investigative efforts, most authorities rely on a comparison between the number of offenses known to the police and the number of these offenses for which someone was arrested. Another measure is the number of offenses known to the police that result in conviction. For evaluation of police efficiency the number "cleared by arrest" is deemed preferable because arrest is exclusively a police matter. Whether a person arrested is actually convicted depends upon activity within courts and outside the responsibility of the police. It is apparent, however, that "cleared by arrest" indicates only that the police have decided that a case has been terminated by the arrest of someone, not necessarily that the guilty individual has in fact been captured or has been punished for his action.

It is important, too, not to confuse efficiency and desirability of police conduct. A police force may capture many criminals, but if it does so by brutal methods, invading privacy, and trampling individuals' rights in the dirt, efficiency may be bought at too great a cost. A high rate of convictions or of arrests in relation to crimes committed may not be a good thing. By judging officers solely on the basis of unfeeling ratios undesirable police behavior may be encouraged. Police are to serve the ends of justice; the acquittal of an innocent accused should be as important as the conviction of the guilty. The statistical record of any police force must always be illuminated by an evaluation of the methods employed.[1]

For India as a whole the results of investigation appear to have remained constant from the early 1950's to the present day. The number of cases in which conviction was achieved to number of true cases investigated[2] has varied within a range of 26 to 31 percent.[3] In 1963, for example,[4] 28.23 percent of all true

---

[1] Comment on the tyranny of statistics is commonplace in literature on the police, whether in India or elsewhere. The harmful effects of relying too much upon them in evaluating the work of policemen is generally recognized, but the temptation to do so seems to be overwhelming. For comment on misuse of statistical criteria at various points in Indian police history see Fendall Currie, *Below the Surface*, pp. 207-208; the Indian Police Commission, 1902-1903, Chapter X; and Maharashtra Police Commission, Recommendations, 1964, p. 22.

[2] Cognizable crime.

[3] *Crime in India.*

[4] The last year for which data had been published by the time of writing.

cases investigated ended in convictions. A figure comparable to "cleared by arrest" was not produced in all-India official reports until 1959. *Crime in India* reported that charge sheets were laid in 52.5 percent of all true cases in 1959; and in 50.6 percent in 1958.[5] This means that in just over half of all crimes known to the police persons were arrested and charged with the offense.[6] The "cleared by arrest" figure has remained within a percentage point or two above fifty since that time. The Indian record is significantly better than that of Great Britain or the United States. England and Wales in 1963 had a clearance rate of 43.1 percent for all indictable offenses.[7] In the United States, the clearance rate for serious crime was 26.5 percent.[8] And while the Indian clearance rate appears to have remained steady during the late fifties and early sixties, the rates in the United States, England, and Wales have declined steadily.[9]

As in the West, the Indian clearance rate is highest for serious offenses against the person—murder, assault, and rape—and lowest for crimes against property. In 1963, the clearance rate for murder in India was 66.5 percent; in the United States, 91 percent; and in England and Wales, 92.2 percent.[10] In 1963 the clearance rate for robbery was 49.4 percent in India; 39 percent in the United States; 43 percent in England and Wales.[11] In India in 1963 the clearance rate for kidnapping and abduction cases was 65.9 percent; for ordinary theft, 42.5 percent; for housebreaking, 28 percent.[12] (See Table 8.)

High clearance rates may hide shoddy detective work. While it is unfair to hold the police completely responsible for whether a suspect is convicted or not, nonetheless the police do pro-

[5] Page 12.

[6] Indian statistics distinguish between cases reported to the police and true cases. Sources in Great Britain and the United States do not make this distinction, but simply talk about offenses known to the police. I shall assume that a case known to the police in Great Britain or the United States is a verified report, thus a "true case" in Indian terminology.

[7] *Criminal Statistics England and Wales, 1963*, p. viii.

[8] *Uniform Crime Reports*, 1964, p. 20. The rate in 1964 was 24.5 percent.

[9] For example, in 1938 the clearance rate in England and Wales was 50.1 percent; in 1957, 47.2 percent; in 1958, 45.6 percent; in 1959, 44.7 percent; in 1960, 44.4 percent; in 1961, 44.7 percent; and in 1963, 43.9 percent. Ben Whitaker, *The Police* (Harmondsworth, England: Penguin Books, Ltd., 1964), p. 39.

[10] *Uniform Crime Reports*, 1963, p. 21; *Criminal Statistics England and Wales, 1963*, computed from information found on p. 20; *Crime in India*, 1963, computed from information found on pp. 40-41.

[11] *Ibid.*

[12] Computed from *Crime in India*, 1963.

TABLE 8

CLEARANCE AND CONVICTION RATES OF CRIME—1963

Crime	Clearance rate	Conviction rate to known offenses
Murder	66.5	40.55
Kidnapping and abduction	65.9	24.85
Dacoity	55.1	24.85
Robbery	49.4	21.12
Housebreaking	28.0	18.56
Cattle theft	51.1	29.62
Ordinary theft	42.5	27.11
Riot	82.2	25.6
Cheating	66.5	32.91

SOURCE: Computed from figures given in *Crime in India*, 1963.

vide the prosecution with both suspect and evidence. It may happen that the police close a case prematurely. That is, they arrest someone on reasonable suspicion who in fact later turns out either to be innocent or impossible to convict on the flimsy evidence available. In making comparisons among nations, it is important therefore to determine whether the courts back up the clearance rates produced by the police. In the present instance we have found that clearance rates in India are higher than in the United States or England or Wales. One would have to discount this finding considerably if it were discovered that Indian courts failed to convict a much larger proportion of people arrested than was the case in Western countries. This does not happen to be true. In the United States in 1963, 29.3 percent of persons arrested for serious offenses were found guilty of serious crimes.[13] In India, 33.2 percent of the number of persons arrested were convicted. With one exception among five kinds of serious crime in each country, the Indian ratio of per-

[13] *Uniform Crime Reports*, 1963, p. 97. Actually this figure was computed for a sample of the nation. The clearance rate for the country as a whole was 26.5 percent, for the sample 24.1 percent. For the present purpose, however—demonstrating the significance of clearance rates in judging police efficiency—the figures provided by the sample will do. Note that I have not said that 29.3 percent of persons arrested for serious crimes *in any year* were found guilty. In both India and United States, totals are given each year for numbers of persons arrested, charged, tried, and convicted. But there may be considerable time between arrest and trial. People arrested one year may not be tried until the next. However, if rates are stable over several years, one can treat the ratio computed for convicted/arrested in any given year as being for the same people.

sons found guilty to persons arrested is higher than the American ratio. (See Table 9.) Thus, insofar as clearance rates indicate police efficiency and on the basis of official statistics, the Indian police are more efficient than the American in criminal investigation.

TABLE 9

PERSONS GUILTY AS PERCENTAGE OF ARRESTS

	United States*		India
Overall	29.3		33.2
Murder	33.6		35.3
Robbery	32.4		26.3
Breaking and Entering	25.8	Housebreaking	56.2
Larceny	34.6		46.5

* Based on 1,679 cities, population estimated 52,329,000. Total clearance rate 24.1, or 2.4 percent below national average.

SOURCE: *Crime in India*, 1963, *Uniform Crime Reports, 1963.* Computations made by the author.

Among the states of India there has been a remarkable variation in clearance and conviction rates. (See Table 10.) The range of clearance rates is from 85.5 percent (Kerala) to 34.02 percent (Bihar). Conviction rates range from 60.3 percent (Andhra Pradesh) to 12.23 percent (Bihar).

With an all-India clearance rate of slightly more than 50 percent and a conviction rate between 25 and 30 percent, it is disturbingly apparent that crime does indeed pay in India, as it does in most countries of the world.

Has police efficiency changed significantly since independence? The information available is sketchy and no firm conclusions can be drawn. In Uttar Pradesh during the later 1930's the percentage of convictions to investigations was about 20 percent.[14] In 1963 there were 19.34 percent convictions for every true case. No change, then, whatsoever. In Madras there seems to have been an improvement. In 1941, the conviction rate for cognizable crime was 46.1 percent;[15] in 1950 it was 40.6 percent,[16] and in 1963 the rate was 58.9 percent.[17] In Calcutta between 1945 and 1958 there was a minor improvement, from an 18.27 percent

[14] *Annual Police Administration Report,* 1940, pp. 12-14.
[15] *Report on the Administration of Police of the Madras State, 1950,* a graph.
[16] *Ibid.,* computed from Statement AA, Part I.
[17] *Crime in India,* 1963.

TABLE 10

CLEARANCE AND CONVICTION RATES IN INDIA—1963
TOTAL COGNIZABLE CRIME

States	True cases	Cases in which charge sheet was laid	Clearance rate* (percent)	Cases convicted	Conviction rate per true case investigated* (percent)
Andhra Pradesh	27,234	22,183	82.0	16,434	60.4
Assam	16,589	9,105	54.9	3,613	21.8
Bihar	51,326	17,458	34.0	6,276	12.2
Gujarat	29,192	19,318	66.2	6,597	22.6
Jammu-Kashmir	2,627	1,763	67.1	418	15.9
Kerala	12,979	11,091	85.5	4,649	35.8
Madhya Pradesh	72,293	36,057	50.0	21,308	29.4
Madras	46,880	38,139	79.3	27,629	59.0
Maharashtra	44,932	25,494	56.8	13,328	29.3
Mysore	22,203	16,472	74.1	8,395	37.8
Nagaland	213	117	55.0	84	39.4
Orissa	19,574	10,951	56.0	5,493	28.0
Punjab	15,219	9,612	63.1	5,355	35.2
Rajasthan	19,081	11,084	58.1	4,986	26.1
Uttar Pradesh	101,300	35,747	35.0	19,598	19.3
West Bengal	48,679	17,450	35.8	6,827	14.0
Total	530,321	282,041	53.2	150,990	28.4

* Computations made by the author.
SOURCE: *Crime in India*, 1963, pp. 32-33.

conviction rate to 22 percent.[18] In West Bengal, however, there has been a very noticeable decline since 1938 in the number of convictions. In 1938 convictions were secured in 83.76 percent of cases; in 1960 convictions were obtained in only 49.7 percent.[19] Whether the decline indicates a deterioration in police ability or higher standards of probity applied by judges is not apparent.

As a result of police activity, slightly more than one million people are sent to prison in India each year. Approximately half of these are persons convicted of crimes and the other half are persons detained in police "lockups" or awaiting trial.[20]

[18] *Annual Report on the Police Administration of the Town of Calcutta and its Suburbs, 1945 and 1958,* computed from Statement AA, Part I.

[19] *West Bengal Police Commission,* p. 18.

[20] Government of India, Home Ministry, Central Bureau of Correction Services, *Social Defence,* Vol. IV, no. 1, January, 1964, pp. 33-34. In 1960 the total number of persons admitted to jail in the year was 1,149,000. This figure excludes Jammu-Kashmir. The total in 1959 was 1,134,000.

According to the Home Ministry[21] there were 344 convicts and undertrials admitted for each 100,000 of the population in 1960. For most of the persons sentenced (84.3 percent), the length of stay was less than six months. Those sentenced for more than six months but less than two years comprised 11.2 percent. Only 3.5 percent were to serve more than two years; and only 0.8 percent were given life sentences.[22] Death sentences are awarded to about 200 persons a year.[23] Death sentences are carried out by hanging.

THE INITIATION OF AN INVESTIGATION

According to the survey findings, about 90 percent of the population have never been victims of a crime. Theft is the form of crime most commonly experienced. A residual group (1 or 2 percent) have experienced violence upon their persons.

Over India as a whole, about 10 percent of the people have gone to the police for help. (See Table 11.) In all but a few of these cases the people went to the police in connection with a criminal situation—they had been victims of a crime, they were

TABLE 11

PERCENTAGE OF POPULATION SEEKING POLICE ASSISTANCE*

City	Segment of Population	
Mysore	Rural	Urban
Yes	5.3	16.7
No	94.2	83.2
Kanpur city	Residents	Rural Migrants
Yes	24.2	12.1
No	75.8	87.9

* Survey question: Have you ever gone to the police for help?

[21] *Ibid.*, p. 37.
[22] *Ibid.*, p. 39.
[23] There were 210 in 1960. *Ibid.*, p. 56. The annual reports of the Ministry of Home Affairs give figures on the number of petitions of mercy received from persons under sentence of death, and these figures substantiate the conclusion that about 200 persons each year suffer sentence of death. In 1960, 67 persons were hanged in Uttar Pradesh, 45 in Punjab, 32 in Madras, 26 in Andhra Pradesh, 14 in Kerala, 9 in Maharashtra, 7 in Madhya Pradesh, 4 in Mysore, 3 in Gujarat, and 3 in Delhi. None were executed in Bihar, Orissa, or West Bengal.

reporting a crime in the neighborhood, or they perceived a threatening situation, as when people were being harassed by hooligans or a violent dispute was likely to break out between landlord and tenant. Urban people have gone to the police more frequently than rural people. In other words, about 10 percent of the Indian population have gone to the police at some time or another on their own initiative and with the expectation of a police response that was important to them personally.

The survey sought to provide a measure for the amount of unreported crime in India. Respondents were asked if they knew of instances when crimes had been committed but people did not report them to the police because they were afraid of getting involved. On the average between 10 and 15 percent of the sample did know of such instances. This does not of course mean that crimes were not in fact reported or that crimes had even occurred; this question simply measures whether Indians know of people who did not report what they thought was a crime. In most cases what were not reported were thefts and the activities of hooligan elements, such as street fighting and the threatening or beating of people by gangs.

When a crime occurs in India, how is police intercession initiated? The average police station is responsible for two hundred square miles of territory. Since the telephone grid over India is incomplete, in the vast majority of instances the police find out that a crime has occurred when someone comes to the station house. Sometimes a police officer may be in the vicinity, but more commonly it will be necessary for someone to travel several miles—even as many as twenty or twenty-five—in order to get police help. He will travel by all means of conveyances, relying heavily on bullock cart, horse, bicycle, or foot over dirt roads in bad repair and subject to every whim of the weather. Policemen themselves are seldom provided with any better transportation, and, except in cities, will have to join their informant in walking or riding a bicycle to the scene of the crime. Throughout most of India the time between the commission of a crime and the arrival of the police is measured in hours and not in minutes. Delay in police arrival is one of the reasons why it is so difficult to keep the scenes of crime undisturbed. Curious neighbors and friends simply cannot be kept away for any length of time; and if someone known to the neighborhood has been killed, people will want to make proper disposition of the body. Nor are police themselves in instantaneous touch with one another. Many police stations are still without telephone connections to either circle or district headquarters. Radio facilities are spreading but there are still districts without them, to say nothing of individual police stations. Communication with the police, and among police, is largely a matter of piecing together an assortment of surface modes of communication.

The situation in cities and towns is much better, if only because distances are so much shorter. Most major cities have now established central telephone switchboards, control rooms, and radio networks. They often have several mobile radio patrols as well. Even so, it is probably fair to say that most crimes come to the attention of the police through face-to-face contact across the desk of the officer on duty.[24]

When a report of a crime comes into a police station, the station-house officer decides whether it requires investigation. If the offense is noncognizable the police cannot investigate without an order from a magistrate. If the case is cognizable—that is, serious—the police may investigate at their own discretion. However, investigation is not mandatory.[25] The station-house officer may have reason to believe that the possibility of harm is remote or that the amount of harm threatened is slight;[26] he may conclude that the complaint is spurious or that a trivial occurrence has been exaggerated in order to get police intervention in a private quarrel.[27] Police cannot be held accountable in law for refusing investigation. Officers must record in writing their failure to investigate a complaint of what seems to be a cognizable offense. This ensures that willful disregard of duty or obvious favoritism can be checked by senior police officers, but it does not eliminate the rancor generated in a complainant who finds the police unwilling to leave the station house and venture into the heat and dust for a reason the complainant considers important enough to have brought him to the station.

[24] Delhi, with a population close to three million, has three positions on its central switchboard to handle all incoming calls. It also has nine radio-equipped police vans. William H. Parker, Chief of Police, Los Angeles, *Report to the Ministry of Home Affairs of the Government of India Through the United States A.I.D. Mission to India,* 1965, p. 5.

[25] See section 156, Code of Criminal Procedure.

[26] Section 95, Indian Penal Code.

[27] The Uttar Pradesh Police Commission believes that station-house officers have too much discretion in deciding when to make an investigation; they recommended that a study be undertaken to make police response more automatic. See page 69.

The decision to investigate is made most often by a sub-inspector, since in most rural police stations—which means most stations in India—the station-house officer is of this rank. In serious offenses he will make the investigation himself; in other cases he will deputize a subordinate. Each state makes its own rules as to the ranks that can investigate a complaint and conduct an investigation. Usually no one below the rank of sub-inspector can do so. There is considerable evidence, however, that head constables and even constables often make investigations.[28] Charges against suspects can only be laid by someone of the rank of sub-inspector (or assistant sub-inspector) and above; a head constable may do so only if the station-house officer is away and then only in minor offenses. Constables accompany investigating officers, and do the donkey work of running errands, but they should not make investigations on their own hook.

The organization of the police for criminal investigation work depends on the nature of the police administrative unit. At district, circle, and station-house levels there is no separation between investigating and enforcing staff. Local police officers must be jacks-of-all-trades: one moment they may be supervising traffic or breaking up a fight, at the next they are collecting evidence at the scene of a murder. Detective work is simply one duty among many. Specialized detective staffs exist only in the offices of state inspectors-general and commissioners of police in major cities. These are designated Criminal Investigation Departments (C.I.D.). The C.I.D. is organized into two branches, the Crime Branch and the Special Branch. The C.I.D. Crime Branch usually performs three functions: (a) assisting in the investigation of particularly important crimes anywhere in the state or city; (b) investigating crimes that cover a wide area, such as dacoities, smuggling, counterfeiting, and copper-wire thefts; and (c) gathering and studying information about the nature, incidence, and trend of crime. Detective staff from the C.I.D. may intervene where they wish, although as a rule they are asked for by a superintendent when he finds he needs special talent

[28] See Bihar Police Commission, pp. 103ff., and Government of India, Law Commission of India, *Fourteenth Report* (*Reform of Judicial Administration*), 1959 (New Delhi: Manager of Publications, 1960), Vol. II, pp. 735-744. This practice goes back to British days. It was strongly condemned by the Police Commission, 1902-1903: "The worst offences have arisen from permitting constables and head constables to conduct investigations of offences. No abuse calls more urgently for reform" (p. 36).

for a particularly intractable case. The C.I.D. in Delhi has created a "central team" which rushes to the scene of all major crimes in order to discover, collect, and preserve physical clues.[29] The C.I.D. Special Branch is something of an anomaly to the American observer, and it is apt to make him wonder about the quality of Indian political life. The Special Branch handles political intelligence and surveillance. Its duty, carried out by plainclothes policemen, is to provide a picture of public opinion and the nature and tempo of political activity. The Special Branch is a British legacy. It is understandable that the British should have established such a department. In order to safeguard their own regime it was imperative they keep a finger on the pulse of political activity.[30] But is it necessary today? Should the police be permanently organized to carry out political surveillance? One sometimes reads in the press that a political meeting has been disturbed by the presence of Special Branch operatives taking notes on the proceedings. Policemen make no bones of the fact that the Special Branch watches all political parties, including the ruling Congress party. What distinguishes the Indian practice as compared with that in the United States, for example, is less the fact of surveillance than the obviousness of it. The F.B.I. has long publicized the fact that it has extensive knowledge of subversive political activity based on covert penetration. Since subversiveness is not a clear-cut quality, one must assume that the F.B.I.'s activities cover much more than the one or two most extreme political parties. American police, even local ones, try diligently to remain in touch with the plans of any group that could foment public disorder, confusion, or violence. Even routine public meetings of tepid and unexceptional civic groups will be attended by police officers, if only to keep order.

One might have thought that the government of independent

[29] *Delhi Annual Administration Report, 1957*, p. 5. The C.I.D. does not necessarily do better investigating work than the local staffs. The West Bengal Police Commission noted (pp. 46-47) that its C.I.D. had a ratio of convictions to true cases below the all-India average. It should be said in the C.I.D.'s favor that they dealt mostly with the tougher cases.

[30] In establishing the Special Branch the British were only doing what they had already done at home. The Special Branch of Scotland Yard was created in 1884; its task to "keep watch on any body of people, of whatever political complexion, whose activities seem likely sooner or later to result in open acts of sedition or disorder." Whitaker, *The Police*, p. 73, footnote 1. He is evidently quoting from an official document authorizing the creation of the Special Branch.

India would have viewed the Special Branch as a noxious vestige of colonial control. Evidently it has not. Considering the number of politicians who felt the heavy hand of police detention during the independence struggle and the notoriety of the Special Branch's personal dossiers on leading politicians, the retention of the Branch is really quite remarkable, indicating perhaps the pragmatic cast of mind of the leaders of independence, even in the first full blush of freedom.

Can one say that political liberty has been a casualty of Special Branch retention? Since any government must remain in touch with the swirls and eddies of public opinion, it is doubtful whether the function of surveillance would long have remained inoperative. In fact, hasty abolition of the Special Branch might well have affected public accountability to the detriment of political freedom. The Special Branch is visible; it is publicly discernible; its task is known; its operations recognized. This is certainly preferable to giving a surreptitious mandate to some agency in the bowels of the bureaucracy hiding behind an innocuous name. It is not the fact of observation that is important but the consequences of it in terms of resulting government policy toward political groups. Observation by police is inevitable and necessary; as long as it does not regularly involve invasions of privacy, it may be quite neutral in its political effects.

The C.I.D. is responsible for maintaining files on criminal activity. It prepares the statistical reports issued by each state. It also supervises forensic laboratories, fingerprint, photographic, and handwriting bureaus.

The Central Bureau of Investigation is the central government's C.I.D. agency. It was created April 1, 1963, taking over and expanding the work of the old Delhi Special Police Establishment. The D.S.P.E. became the Investigation and Anticorruption Division of the C.B.I.[31] The C.B.I. has original jurisdiction in certain classes of cases under central government legislation. It is not, however, empowered to intervene in ordinary matters under the criminal codes. Moreover, it must obtain the consent of any state before it can operate within its territory. So far states have been willing to give general consent and the C.B.I. has not

---

[31] The C.B.I. contains six divisions: (a) Investigation and Anticorruption; (b) Technical; (c) Crime and Records and Statistics; (d) Research; (e) Legal and General; and (f) Administrative. The duties of each division are described in the resolution establishing the C.B.I., No. 4/31/61T, Government of India, New Delhi, 1 April 1963.

had to obtain case by case approval. There are no legal reasons why any state cannot withdraw its consent if it wishes.[32] Since one of the C.B.I.'s primary duties is the investigation of corruption in government, the dependence of it on the approval of the separate states renders the accomplishment of this purpose far from certain.

With the exception, then, of sensational crimes attracting widespread public attention or particularly intractable crimes involving activity over a wide area, most crimes are investigated by the staff of individual police stations supervised and assisted by more senior officers from circle or district headquarters.

QUALITY OF INVESTIGATION

The quality of police investigations is frequently made the subject of very critical comment. The Bihar Police Commission, 1961, noted that during "the course of their tours and their examination of witnesses no complaint has been so universally made before the Commission as that regarding the poor quality of police investigation."[33] The Commission accepted the justice of the complaints saying that "there seems hardly any doubt that the standard of investigation has on the whole been very deficient."[34] The West Bengal Police Commission, 1960-1961, referred to "the deterioration noticeable in the standard of investigation."[35] Besides inefficiency, members of the public complained of rudeness, intimidation, suppression of evidence, favoritism and political influence, conniving at false accusations, concoction of evidence, and malicious padding of cases. Police officers themselves are surprisingly acquiescent about the charges. While they may minimize the amount of outright malpractice that exists, they do not hide their own assessment that standards of criminal investigation leave a great deal to be desired. In their turn they produce exhaustive lists of difficulties that honest and conscientious policemen face. A representative sample of the problems cited would include the following items: too few staff of investigating rank, overburdened supervisory staff, jurisdictions of individual police stations far too

[32] Thomas F. McBride, *Report to the Ministry of Home Affairs of the Government of India* (New Delhi: U.S. Agency for International Development, 1965), p. 34.
[33] Bihar Police Commission, p. 103.
[34] *Ibid.*
[35] Page 204.

large, imperfect communications, inferior equipment, reluctance of the general public to cooperate in investigations, the public's almost pathological unwillingness to serve as a witness, the easy repudiation of testimony, the prevalence of groups and factions in criminal cases, the existence of "cooked" testimony among witnesses, the ingrained habit of distrust of the police shown by trial judges, the popularity of making malicious charges against the police, and, finally, the cumbersomeness of accusatorial trial procedures with their interminable delays, multitudinous forms, and accompanying gaggle of unscrupulous lawyers.

As one would expect, the police view and the public view of investigations do not wholly coincide. Nevertheless they are united in their opinion that the caliber can be improved. Considering the comparative figures on clearance rates, this concern, especially on the part of the police, is doubly laudable. They might well have chosen to argue that they were doing much better than anyone had a right to expect. Each of the charges made by the public and the difficulties cited by the police are appropriate to different stages of a criminal investigation. In the ensuing discussion, we shall follow the general procedures of any investigation and seek to determine what the police must do, the circumstances they encounter, and the expedients they feel obliged to adopt.

Police testify that they are crippled at the outset by lack of trained staff to pursue criminal investigations. We have already seen that many investigations are carried out by men below the rank of sub-inspector, and that the qualifications even of sub-inspectors have been seriously questioned. Police complain of the burden of work; there simply are not enough inspectors and sub-inspectors to handle the case load. In police literature it is generally accepted that there are about ten constables and head constables in each police station and three men of investigating rank, that is, inspectors, sub-inspectors, and assistant sub-inspectors. Accepting the figure of 5,890 as the number of police stations in India in the early 1960's[36] and 302,540 as the number of unarmed policemen,[37] then there would be 51.4 policemen per police station. This is not to suggest that all those men are available for station-house work, simply that were they distributed evenly among the station-houses there would be as many as this on

[36] See Chapter 3, p. 78.
[37] Ministry of Home Affairs, *Report*, 1961-1962.

the spot.[38] I have already computed that approximately 33,600 of all police in the same year were officers, meaning I.P.S. as well as men of state services above the rank of head constable. Since the ratio of unarmed to armed police is three to two, there would be 20,100 officers of all kinds available for station-house work. Thus, there would be approximately 3.43 officers of all kinds per police station. Recognizing that there are specialized jobs of many kinds in the police requiring men to be stationed at various headquarters or at non-station-house facilities, I would conclude that there are probably less than three investigating officers for each station, but considerably more than ten constables and head constables. These are averages, of course. In some stations there will be many more than three officers and in others less.

Using figures on cognizable crime for 1963, there were 88 cases of true cognizable crime per station. There were 104 cases of reported cognizable crime. This would mean that there were 25.6 true cases for each unarmed police officer of investigating rank; and 30.1 reported cases. For I.P.S. officers, there were 498 true cases of crime per man.

It is apparent that the supervisory burden on I.P.S. officers is colossal. Since they have extensive administrative functions, one cannot see how they can devote more than passing attention to the investigation of crime. There are, of course, the deputy superintendents of police—the senior rank of the state police services. If there are as many of them as there are I.P.S. officers,[39] the supervisory burden on all officers of deputy superintendent rank and above would still be almost 250 cases per year.

Beyond saying that it seems probable that there are usually between two and three officers of investigating rank in every police station, it is not possible to estimate how many cases are actually borne by the inspectors, sub-inspectors, and assistant sub-inspectors in police stations. A study done in West Bengal showed that during the 1950's the average sub-inspector on station-house duty investigated 87 cases per year: 107 in

[38] In addition to police stations there are police outposts. Even assuming there were half as many outposts as stations, the ratio of constables for each station-outpost would be 34.3.

[39] This is strictly conjecture: I do not have figures distinguishing I.P.S. and state police officers.

town thanas and 77 in rural thanas.[40] The need for more data of this kind is imperative if the staffing needs of police stations with respect to investigation work are to be properly met. There is an appreciable difference among the standards which have recently been suggested by professional observers. The Uttar Pradesh Police Commission recommended 60 cases a year per sub-inspector;[41] the Bihar Police Commission suggested 65 to 70;[42] the West Bengal Police Commission 100 for urban thanas and 85 for rural ones;[43] while a syndicate of I.P.S. officers at the Central Police Training College set the average at 50.[44] If there are about 100 cognizable offenses reported per police station each year—88 of which prove to be true—and there are even two officers of investigating rank in each station, then the case load would be well within what the various police commissions have recommended.[45]

Are case loads of this magnitude conducive to successful investigation? Only fragmentary information is available about how much time is required of a station-house officer to perform other tasks, such as training constables, writing reports, maintaining registers and files, going on patrol, mediating in quarrels, directing traffic, tending equipment, guarding the police lock-up, and investigating noncognizable offenses as well as cognizable offenses under special and local laws, such as the Gambling Act, Suppression of Immoral Traffic in Women and Children, and the various prohibition laws. On the basis of impressionistic evidence, most experts believe that there are indeed too many cases to be investigated by the staff available.[46] Only the West Bengal Police Commission doubted that

[40] See West Bengal Police Commission, p. 31 *infra*, citing a study done by M. A. H. Maswood, special officer to the inspector-general. To my knowledge, this is the only such study ever done in India.

[41] "Causes of Failure of Police Prosecutions," pp. 53-54.

[42] Bihar Police Commission, p. 22.

[43] West Bengal Police Commission, p. 31.

[44] "Causes of Failure of Police Prosecutions," pp. 53-54. The Police Commission, 1902-1903, recommended a case load of 100 per year.

[45] In London where the investigating staff is separate from the enforcement staff, case loads range from 150 to 564 cases a year; the average in 1963 was 284. Sir Ronald Howe, deputy commissioner C.I.D., 1953-1957, has said that more than one case a week per detective is too much to handle properly, and J. Edgar Hoover said to a Congressional subcommittee in 1963 that 20 cases per F.B.I. agent each year was "too high." Cited in Whitaker, p. 45.

[46] Law Commission, *Fourteenth Report*, Vol. II, pp. 736-737, repeats the views of police officers to this effect, and seems to give credence to the testimony.

adequacy in numbers of staff was an important factor. It may be revealing that only the West Bengal Commission sought to gather hard data about the actual work loads in the stations.

"In our opinion the deterioration noticeable in the standard of investigation is not, by and large, to be sought in the excessive number of cases for investigation and inquiry, as often alleged before us, but rather in defective and insufficient training of the investigating officers and lack of adequate supervision by superior officers."[47] So, except for the conclusion that there are not enough senior supervisory officers with time to give to investigation, the issue of case loads and numbers of investigating staff remains open. Although, one must note, the weight of noninvestigative duties is both very heavy and very difficult to assess quantitatively.[48]

Two proposals have been put forward to solve the problem of inadequate staff—whether adequacy is defined as inferiority in numbers or in point of ability. The first is to separate the investigating and enforcement staffs at station-house level, thus allowing some men to devote full time to detective work. Investigations suffer when an officer has to break off to take up some other pressing business. It even happens that several officers in succession take over a case—a situation the Law Commission described as "piecemeal investigations."[49] Furthermore, a higher standard of detective ability can be developed in men specializing in investigation. Separation may also gain greater public cooperation, as the Law Commission has suggested, because investigators are not then contaminated by enforcement duties.[50] But there are disadvantages, too. Investigators may lose the intuitive sense of people and locale that only the beat officers have. Then, too, it is the beat officer who most commonly arrives first at the scene of a crime; he will inevitably handle part of the investigation and it is a mistake to diminish his sense of responsibility toward this part of his duties.[51] In the main, India

[47] Page 204.

[48] Maswood's study in West Bengal also showed that sub-inspectors and assistant sub-inspectors always worked more than ten hours a day and frequently as many as sixteen. Constables, however, worked about eight hours a day. This makes one wonder what the West Bengal Police Commission considered a proper working day since they don't think that inadequacy of investigating staff is the reason for poor detective work.

[49] Law Commission, Vol. II, p. 739.   [50] Page 744.

[51] See O. W. Wilson, *Police Administration* (2nd ed.; New York: McGraw-Hill Book Co., 1963), pp. 282-283, on the desirability of using patrolmen at least as preliminary investigators.

does not have very sophisticated crimes requiring for solution a great deal of specialized knowledge. Crime is largely rural and well within the understanding of policemen raised in the same milieu.[52]

The Law Commission has urged that separation be tried on a trial basis: "We think . . . that the exclusive attention of the investigating officer is essential to the conduct of an efficient investigation and the additional cost involved in the implementation of our proposal is necessary."[53] Similar proposals have been put forward in the past but have never been fairly implemented.[54] The Uttar Pradesh, West Bengal, and Maharashtra police commissions have recommended that separation be tried in major towns, district headquarters, and heavy industrial areas.[55] In the absence of actual experience, debate about the merits of separation will continue to be rather sterile. Once evidence from these experimental efforts has come in, Indian officials will be better able to set national policy. One can only hope that necessary resolution will be found to bring about speedy implementation of the experiments.

The second proposal is to provide more men for discretionary police tasks, such as investigation, by exchanging constables for sub-inspectors in staffing. "It is no doubt true," observed the West Bengal Police Commission, "that the ordinary constable, who is ordinarily illiterate or endowed with the minimum of literacy, is useful generally as the mere physical or mechanical basis of the police force, with little initiative, understanding or imagination."[56] But though they are not entrusted with discretionary tasks, the fact is that they are usually first to arrive on

[52] Report of a Syndicate, "Police Reforms" (Central Police Training College, December, 1962), p. 27.

[53] Vol. II, p. 741.

[54] The Police Reorganization Committee in Uttar Pradesh, 1947-1948, recommended that the plan be tried in Kanpur, Agra, Varanasi, Allahabad, Lucknow, Meerut, and Bareilly. A start was made in 1950 but apparently abandoned. Uttar Pradesh Police Commission, pp. 71-72.

[55] Uttar Pradesh Police Commission, pp. 71-72; West Bengal Police Commission, p. 34; Maharashtra Police Commission, p. 14.

[56] Page 64. Over sixty years ago the Police Commission, 1902-1903, said, "Constables are not a suitable agency for the performance of beat duties ordinarily entrusted to them. . . . The great principle to be borne in mind is that duties requiring the exercise of discretion and judgment should not be entrusted to the lowest class of officers with whom such qualifications cannot be reasonably expected; the duties of constable should not be above his class." Quoted in Report of a Syndicate, "Training of Constables in Modern Set-Up," *Transactions*, April, 1965, p. 54.

the scene of crimes. Because he "is generally ignorant of the fundamentals of his duties" a valuable opportunity to display efficient police work is passed up.[57] Police officers are aware that they may not be getting full value for money invested in constables, though they make up 93 percent of the force. But they have not yet formally gone on record in support of a plan for upgrading them or eliminating them in favor of those who are more useful.[58]

The quality of investigations is generally admitted to be defective, even by policemen themselves. Unfortunately there is remarkably little willingness to experiment with alternative solutions, and even fewer resources available to support an attempt. Of the two proposals suggested for improving investigations, separation of investigation from enforcement staffs is the more acceptable. Although the utility of the present police constable is open to serious question, there is little enthusiasm for reexamining his role in a modern police organization.

IMPROPER INVESTIGATION

"Police methods in India have long been suspect. . . ."[59] This is true to varying extents in almost any country in the world. It should not be surprising that the Indian police have come in for their share of criticism on the score of shaping and twisting evidence in order to secure convictions. The intriguing question is: How much of this in fact goes on? This is not the kind of question which admits of an easy answer. Nor can it be put to policemen themselves with great expectations of obtaining candid replies. Few officers, however, deny altogether that it does go on. Perhaps the most extreme estimate by a police source of the amount of "concoction" that occurs came from an officer at the Central Police Training College:

"This undesirable practice of concoction has become more or less part and parcel of the present-day police working. The majority of the older generation of investigating officers preach that without padding or concoction cases usually do not stand in

[57] Central Police Training College, "Causes of Failure," p. 54.
[58] The only public recommendation to this effect has come from the late Chief of Police of Los Angeles, William H. Parker, who served as consultant to the government of India in 1965 through the auspices of the United States A.I.D. mission.
[59] Jawaharlal Nehru, *Toward Freedom* (Boston: Beacon Press, 1958), p. 168.

court. Hence concoction is resorted to in order to forestall the arguments to defence counsel or to plug loop-holes to meet the requirements of law."[60] Justice Khosla says that "It is known that the police do not scruple to introduce false evidence in order to strengthen what seems to them a weak case."[61]

The survey results show that people in India are willing to believe the worst. They were asked, "When the police present cases in courts, do they twist and/or make up evidence in order to convict people?" Quite a few respondents ventured no opinion. (See Table 12.) As usual this was particularly true among rural respondents in Tumkur district. Of those people who did answer, very few gave the police a clean bill of health. The vast majority thought that they either twisted evi-

TABLE 12

SURVEY QUESTION: When the police present cases in the courts, do they twist and/or make up evidence in order to convict people?

Samples	No opinion (percent)	No (percent)	Twist (percent)	Make up (percent)	Both twist and make up (percent)
Bangalore	49.8	7.2	13.2	10.5	19.3
Tumkur	69.8	9.2	10.7	4.0	6.3
Kanpur residents	25.5	4.6	22.0	32.5	15.4
Kanpur rural migrants	45.4	4.9	17.0	21.6	11.1

[60] O. P. Tandon, "Concoction of Evidence and its Effects" (Central Police Training College, 1964), p. 1.

[61] Murder of the Mahatma, p. 176. The most intemperate statement made in the recent past by a responsible official was that by A. N. Mullah, judge of the Allahabad high court. Passing judgment on a sub-inspector who had fabricated evidence, the judge said: "Criminal cases which are placed before the courts are in a large measure frame-ups and they are supported by fabricated evidence and extorting confessions through third-degree methods and by disregarding the prohibitions contained in the Constitution of India to safeguard the rights of citizens." He went on, ". . . there is not a single lawless group in the whole of the country whose record of crime comes anywhere near the record of that organized unit which is known as the Indian police." The state of Uttar Pradesh appealed to the Supreme Court against the remarks of Judge Mullah. The Supreme Court ordered some of them expunged, observing: "The remarks made by the learned judge in respect of the entire police force of the state were not justified on the facts of the case. To characterize the whole police force of the state as a lawless group is bad enough; to say that its record of crime is the highest in the state is worse and coming as it does from a judge of the high court is sure to bring the whole administration of law and order into disrepute. . . ." Obviously the Indian bench is still deliciously independent, as well as responsible over all.

dence, made it up, or did some of both. Criticism was strongest among northern respondents, and among them strongest among established urban residents.[62]

The forms impropriety takes are innumerable: witnesses are recruited and tutored in the police version of events; witnesses are led in their testimony, being asked if such and such is true, rather than being allowed to volunteer in their own words; incriminating evidence is planted in the house of an accused; false evidence is foisted on an innocent suspect; evidence is created rather than being discovered; cases are lodged against ex-convicts who don't have convincing alibis; and identification parades are rigged.[63]

Why do the police do it? What do they hope to gain? In spite of the constant denials by superior officers that they judge subordinate officers—particularly station-house officers—by the number of convictions they obtain, the fact remains that officers of investigating rank believe that they do. And, indeed, it is difficult to see how it could be otherwise. Suppose that a superior officer does examine the quantity of effort expended by an investigating officer, the quality of his tactics, his finesse in handling members of the public, will he not still unconsciously discount this performance if convictions are obtained in only 10 percent of the cases investigated? Will he be able to resist the thought that efforts, however "genuine," ought to be more productive? So investigating officers feel they must achieve convictions; this is the whole purpose of their labors. They then encounter nagging problems making the achievement of a good record very uncertain. Physical evidence is hard to un-

[62] In Great Britain the survey of public opinion toward the police undertaken in connection with the Royal Commission in 1962 found that 32 percent thought the police might destroy evidence. Among these, 20 percent thought it happened rarely, 7.9 percent fairly often, and 1.9 percent very often. Those knowing personally of cases in which police twisted evidence were 3.4 percent. Half of these involved motoring offenses. *Appendix IV to the Minutes of Evidence*, pp. 17-18.

[63] Nehru in *Toward Freedom*, pp. 83-84, tells a story of how his father was convicted on a charge of belonging to an illegal organization. The most incriminating piece of evidence was a document of the society's which contained Motilal Nehru's signature. Curiously, according to Jawaharlal, the signature was in Hindi and his father hardly ever signed his name in Hindi. The police had difficulty in finding anyone who had ever seen his signature so signed. They finally produced a "tattered gentleman" who was quite illiterate and who held the signature upside down when he examined it in court. This witness pronounced the signature genuine. Stories of this kind, although not always based on first-hand experience, are common among Indian middle and upper classes.

cover and tedious to process; oral testimony is unreliable, if it is forthcoming at all. When police officers believe they have a culprit, how tempting it is to manufacture that one fact or two which will make prosecution ironclad. Many officers contend that the public forces concoction by its very obduracy. In certain classes of offenses—notoriously bootlegging—it is almost impossible to induce witnesses to come forward to attest that incriminating evidence was found where the police say it was. In one area of Mysore, there were 1,500 prohibition offenses in the year; this would require obtaining 3,000 witnesses—an impossibility for the sub-inspector in charge.[64] The solution is to use bogus witnesses, selected from the hangers-on around any police station, the "tattered gentleman" of Nehru's story.

Then officers argue that the courts are overstrict; they demand an impossible standard of evidence. The police are now so hedged about with rules, they say, stemming from courts' suspicion of them, that they are impelled to use improper methods if they are to obtain any convictions at all. Since real life seldom conforms to court requirements, it must be forced a little. Police also believe that they are acting in the public interest when they bring a criminal to bay. They are charged with protecting society; surely they are acting in the spirit of that trust when they secure convictions of notorious bad characters or noted felons who are conclusively guilty. Related to this is the desire to retain the respect of the public. It will be doubly difficult, officers reason, to secure public cooperation if people popularly convicted are allowed to get off. The police will either be labeled grossly inefficient or in cahoots with the guilty party. There are also, inevitably, some officers who out of malice or venality suppress evidence, implicate the innocent, or manufacture facts.[65] Finally, investigating is hard work; it involves endless questioning, painstaking attention to detail, considerable travel, and innumerable procedural technicalities. Investigating officers become tired, they often fail to eat properly, they encounter inclement weather, and they must endure arduous travel conditions. It is much easier to investigate from a chair, allowing others to make perfunctory reconnaissances, then signing their reports before sending them to the superintendent.

[64] K. Balakrisha, "On Witnesses," *The Bulletin of the I.P.S. Association, Mysore State Branch*, Vol. I, no. 3, p. 9.
[65] The subject of police corruption will be discussed in detail in Chapter 11.

For all these reasons the police stoop to bogus prosecutions and phony investigations. Needless to say, they frequently get caught and when they do, courts and general public are alienated—yet these are the very groups upon which police are most dependent and whose good offices are essential if convictions are to be obtained without resort to hanky-panky. For the hard-pressed officer, however, short-run considerations are too often compelling.[66]

While the existence of improper investigations in some quantity is not usually denied by officials, they do usually deny that superior officers, especially men of the I.P.S., have any complicity in such doings. Is this true? Judge Khosla firmly believes that superior officers know what is going on. They may not participate in it themselves, but they wink at it and so are fully as culpable.[67] The redoubtable Judge A. N. Mullah of Uttar Pradesh once roundly chastised supervising officers in connection with a case in which he had discovered the complicity of a deputy superintendent of police:

"On the conclusions we have reached, we have no doubt that Sri Mathura Singh [the deputy superintendent] has fabricated every bit of evidence in this case. Who will now conduct the inquiry against Sri Mathura Singh and if an officer is found to conduct an inquiry against Sri Mathura Singh, what is the guarantee that he will be an improvement even upon Sri Mathura Singh? The police force seems to consist of so many undependable officers that it is almost impossible to investigate their misdeeds. Where the twigs are found to be decayed one hopes that the branches are safe but where the branches have also become rotten one begins to doubt that even the trunk is sound. The rule of law cannot be maintained so long as the so-called guardians of 'law and order' are mostly composed of this class."[68]

[66] An I.P.S. officer has observed: "If the police were to strictly adhere to the provisions of the law, the law itself would be found wanting in several respects, particularly in the matter of arming them with sufficient powers to effectively investigate crime. When, by the employment of several carefully concealed, unlawful, and artful methods, total crime is shown to be 'under control' and percentages of detection high, it is difficult to convince anyone, least of all the legislature, that the law requires amendments or that the strength or equipment of the police require to be increased." Varghese, "Practice and Precepts in Police Work," p. 55.

[67] Khosla, *Murder of the Mahatma*, p. 40.

[68] Ram Singh *v*. State, Respondent, 1959 Cr. L. J. 940, from AIR 1959 Allahabad 518. Judge Mullah found that the magistrate who took the de-

The testimony of I.P.S. officers themselves is inconclusive, contradictory, and, one suspects, untrustworthy. They are impaled on the horns of professional pride. It is awkward for an officer to admit he does not have complete knowledge of what goes on in his establishment. To do so makes him appear inefficient. On the other hand, by appearing to be omniscient, he raises the question as to why I.P.S. officers are not more successful in rooting out these practices. Unless he denies that impropriety exists, except perhaps in an isolated case or so, he must choose between appearing crooked or ineffectual. Superintendents, no less than subordinate officers, are judged by how well they do in criminal investigations. One officer, in an unusually forthright account in a police publication, charged that officers did indeed know what was going on; that though they spoke against improper practices, they rarely followed through; that they were part of the same system as the sub-inspector and were often as culpable.[69] Their culpability, it should be noted, is that of the ostrich, a failure to act on observations. Sometimes officers will admit that a modicum of concocting or padding is necessary if police are not to lose control of the crime situation. Because of public apathy and judicial hostility, police feel forced into compromising expedients; they believe they are more sinned against than sinning.

Supervision over investigations is handled primarily by assistant and deputy superintendents of police. The superintendent intervenes only in the most sensational and important cases. Accountability of an investigating officer is achieved through scrutiny of four sets of written records: (a) station-house registers of complaints received, investigations undertaken, and persons arrested; (b) case diaries; (c) a police report sent to the judge at the completion of investigation outlining essential facts of the case, evidence obtained, and the charge;[70] and (d) statements of witnesses. The superintendent himself rarely has time to plow through this mass of reading; he must rely on his immediate subordinates. Which means that junior officers, some of whom are not I.P.S., are in charge of keeping investigations

---

fendants' statements was also involved: ". . . the magistrate who by his conduct showed that he was no better than a police officer cooperated with Sri Mathura Singh in producing the desired result."

[69] Varghese, entire.

[70] Section 173, Code of Criminal Procedure.

up to the mark.[71] By my own calculations there are 498 true cognizable offenses for each I.P.S. officer every year. Malpractice may come to the superintendent's attention through complaints tendered directly to him or through his own probing when he goes on a tour of police stations. The results in both cases are uncertain. What assurance is there that everyone who has been wronged will complain? When superintendents tour they usually announce their arrival in advance and rarely have time to read carefully case diaries or question investigating officers thoroughly about particular cases.

In short, there is a serious question whether supervision is adequate. Officers may be reluctant to admit how perfunctory their scrutiny is. Moreover, they, too, may adopt the whispered philosophy that a little "assistance" in convicting the guilty is not out of place. Finally, supervising officers may simply give up. The effort required to achieve complete reform would be too great and the rewards too meager to encourage the officer, faced with a pile of smudged and ill-written case diaries, to undertake root-and-branch house-cleaning. Hostility and frustration, he might feel, would be his only reward. A successful officer needs the cooperation of his subordinates. Prudence would dictate that he work within the system, perhaps the better to rectify egregious mistakes of justice. By challenging his subordinates directly, he earns their dislike and the reputation among his own superiors of being a troublemaker.

Impropriety in the conduct of criminal investigations certainly exists, although its proportions can never be gauged accurately. This is one more point at which a serious crisis of confidence afflicts public opinion toward the police. The blame for this situation must be shared by many people: by the politicians who apply spasmodic pressure for results while failing to support reform with enthusiasm or resources; by civilian administrative officers who construe the police role minimally, considering them effective if general order is preserved and public criticism does not become too bitter; by superior police officers who follow a policy of doing what was done in the past rather than reform an entire institution and who pass down-

[71] For some authoritative comments on the lack of supervision in investigations by superior officers see West Bengal Police Commission, p. 205; Maharashtra Police Commission, p. 15; and Report of a Syndicate, "Role of Supervisory Officers in Police Administration," *Transactions*, November, 1964, pp. 33-34.

ward statistical norms for measuring police achievement that
are imposed by secretariat and legislature; by the investigating officers themselves who acquiesce in what they know is
wrong; and by the public that often respects results in terms
of convictions more than adherence to the highest principles
of enforcement procedure. Adjurations directed to others will
produce exactly the results to be seen already. In all probability,
patchwork solutions also will achieve very little. The rules governing investigations, the selection, training, and pay of the men
who carry them out, the amount of manpower to be devoted to
the task, and the supervision required must all be restudied, for
they are all involved.

6 • The Process

CRIMINAL investigation begins when someone comes to the police with information that a crime has been committed. In the case of cognizable offenses the first action of the police is to write down the substance of the report, read it over to the informant, and have him sign it. This is called a First Information Report and it plays a conspicuously large role in subsequent investigation and trial. Except in one or two circumstances, this report (known as an F.I.R.) is not admissible in evidence during trial; it can, however, be used for corroborative purposes—that is, to substantiate the story which emerges during trial about the commission of the crime. Its importance to the police consists in its being the only statement made to them that can be produced during trial to support the informant's testimony. His testimony is more highly regarded if it is borne out by the F.I.R. On the other hand, if there is an item of disagreement, the F.I.R. becomes a weapon to be used against him and to suggest that he does not know what he is talking about. The assumption is that the F.I.R. contains the earliest version of the crime, and hence that it is apt to be the truest, having been made before embellishments or fabrications could be added and before time has clouded memory. The significance of the F.I.R. for prosecution depends upon the position of the informant to the crime: if he is a chance bystander who saw very little, his F.I.R. will not figure in the trial proceedings; if, on the other hand, he is a complainant or a material witness, his earlier statement may be used to support or undermine his entire trial testimony. So great is the importance now attached to the F.I.R. that it has been called the "charter" of the prosecution case.[1] If parts of the F.I.R. are later proved to be false, the suspicion is planted that other elements of the case are also mistaken and that police and/or complainants have fabricated the story in order to punish the accused. If important facts are omitted from the F.I.R. which a reasonable man might think could not have been overlooked by the in-

[1] G. D. Khosla, *The Murder of the Mahatma* (London: Chatto Windus, 1963), p. 181.

formant, the suspicion is planted that the case was made up as it went along. There are cases where victims of robbery have not been able to reclaim stolen property because their descriptions in the F.I.R. do not jibe exactly with what was found; all information in an F.I.R. has been doubted in court because what the complainant says was the murder weapon, medical evidence shows could not have been.[2]

So important has the F.I.R. become that police are now apt to devote as much attention to its preparation as they do to giving chase promptly or to investigation. They have been led to the view that negligence in making out this report is the "most heinous sin a policeman can commit."[3] Policemen have developed two strategies for handling the F.I.R. First, they record as little factual information as possible. Thus, they protect themselves from having the F.I.R. used against testimony later uncovered and presented in court. They "de-fuse" the F.I.R. Or they may record as little information as possible initially so that they may fill in relevant details as investigation proceeds, giving the F.I.R. maximum evidentiary weight. This practice is patently illegal. Second, police officers may demand as much factual information as possible at the outset, even to the extent of asking the informant to go away and obtain more details. In this way they protect themselves against the charge of omitting essential information so that it could be supplied later. This practice, too, is illegal.

As the situation now stands, first information received about a crime affects the evidentiary value of information and material discovered during the course of subsequent investigation. Information given in the heat of the moment, perhaps when police assistance is urgently needed, is allowed to determine the result of trial proceedings. It is no wonder police officers painstakingly provide for solid F.I.R.'s before they venture from the station house. It is no wonder they take liberties with it. The F.I.R., rather than being a means of initiating police action and providing a record of police activity, has become an essential part of both investigation and adjudication.[4] The irony of the

[2] Alakh K. Sinha, *Thirty-Two Years in the Police and After* (by the author, 1952), pp. 182 ff.

[3] *Ibid.*, p. 182.

[4] It is illuminating that an experienced police officer in writing about padding of cases and concoction of evidence by police, devoted more space to the F.I.R. than to any other step in the investigation. Abraham Varghese "Practice and Precepts in Police Work," *Transactions*, November, 1964,

situation is that the importance attached to the F.I.R. in courts of law is a reflection of judicial distrust of the police; but so detailed have stipulations about its use become that it is now a source of contention in itself, reinforcing the very suspicion of the police that its proper use was supposed to reduce. Police want to secure convictions and they take their cues as to what to do from judicial decisions. If corroborative value is attached to the F.I.R. the police will take heed of the fact and use it to the ends of prosecution. This does not mean they will deliberately misuse it; it means only that they will exercise discretion in its proper use so as to conform to the dictates of courts. Rather than redounding to their favor, however, courts have discovered so many instances of misuse they now sometimes treat the F.I.R. as the most reliable signal of police hanky-panky. When the police manipulate an F.I.R. not precisely according to law they may be doing so as much to defend themselves against an overcritical bench as to convict a suspect on too little evidence. Police and bench are caught in a reinforcing system of cause and effect. The result is overattention to petty procedure, a pervasive secretiveness among police—stemming from a feeling that they are damned if they do and damned if they don't—and a failure to bring the guilty more surely to book.

Obtaining Evidence

After the first information is recorded, the investigating officers set forth to gather evidence, record testimony, make an arrest if possible, and establish a case for trial. An investigator is required by law[5] to keep a case diary in which he must record his activities. The diary provides a record of the officer's every move, the exact times of them, and the results. A copy must be sent each day to the superintendent of police. At the conclusion of investigation it is also sent to the presiding judge so he may be able to appraise police methods and tactics. The diary is not admissible in evidence.

The collection of physical evidence is handicapped by lack of

pp. 71-72. Similarly, a group of officers writing about the causes of failure in police prosecutions listed six major points and a number of subsidiary ones connected with making out an F.I.R. of a Syndicate, "Causes of Failure of Police Prosecutions" (Central Police Training College, Mt. Abu; December, 1963), pp. 4-10.

[5] Section 172, Code of Criminal Procedure.

equipment and training. Most police stations are still without even the most primitive forensic equipment, such as a fingerprint kit, a sketch pad for drawing scenes of crimes, or a camera.[6] Complainants are sometimes asked to supply writing paper on which the police can record information and statements. The most that investigating officers can do is to be on the alert for objects which may be or have physical clues, preserve and pack them, and have them sent to a forensic laboratory. Even if officers were better equipped to discover physical evidence, and thus were more alert to it, it is doubtful if they would find very much. Every schoolboy in the United States or Great Britain has been drilled in the necessity of preserving the scene of a crime. Thus has television contributed to good citizenship. Indian people cannot be kept away from the scene of a crime: they walk around it, handle every object in sight, make scuff marks on the dirt floor, spit, and generally make a shambles of the scene. After all, in most cases they have several hours to wait until the police arrive and in the meantime life must go on.

Physical clues cannot be speedily examined in India, but often must be sent a considerable distance to a laboratory. Delhi, for example, has no forensic laboratory; its specimens go as a rule to Punjab. It does not even have its own fingerprint bureau. Many northern states send specimens to the Central Forensic Science Laboratory in Calcutta.[7] West Bengal was the first state to establish its own laboratory; it did so in 1953. Most other states have made modest beginnings, but the efforts are invariably hampered by lack of funds. Fingerprint files, where they exist, are often the old ten-digit system rather than the single-digit system so essential in establishing identity. Sorting fingerprints is done by hand, as is any search that is made through the growing files. Punch cards and sorters are urgently needed if files are ever to be fully exploited in solving crime. All these laboratories and bureaus are inundated with work; it often takes two or three months to obtain the results of an inquiry. Postmortems are performed by a police doctor (if there is one), by the district civil surgeon, or by a raw medical graduate or li-

[6] See comments of the West Bengal Police Commission, p. 227, and Maharashtra Police Commission, p. 10.

[7] For a thorough discussion of forensic facilities in India see Dr. K. V. H. Padamanabhan, "Forensic Science in India," *Indian Police Journal*, July, 1965. The central government maintains three forensic institutions in Calcutta: the Central Detective Training School, the Central Fingerprint Bureau, and the Central Forensic Science Laboratory.

centiate in a hospital. In poisoning cases, for example, the body may have to be brought to district headquarters where the viscera are removed; if the crime is in north India, the viscera are then bottled and sent to Calcutta for processing. A determination that poisoning has occurred, and identification of the agent used, may not be made for several weeks.

The result of a lack of equipment for collecting physical evidence, as well as the lack of training in its use,[8] and the failure to be alert to physical clues, is that investigating officers rely almost exclusively on oral evidence. They are oriented to persons and not to things.

In order to recover physical evidence police must search premises or seize articles from persons. The difficulties they encounter in carrying out searches and seizures are an illuminating illustration of the suspicion with which police evidence is regarded and the problem for the police of securing willing public assistance. Investigating police officers may conduct searches with and without search warrants from a magistrate.[9] Whenever they do they must be accompanied by at least "two respectable inhabitants of the locality."[10] The officer must write up a statement about what is done and what is found, enumerating each item. This is known familiarly all over India as a panchanama. The witnesses are required to sign the statement. The police must be careful that the "panches"—witnesses —have no interest in the case, that they are not related to the accused or hostile to him. Unfortunately for the police, witnesses are extremely hard to obtain. People are afraid of getting involved, and even more of being summoned to court to substantiate what was done.[11] Police officers are uniformly in favor of waiving the requirement that witnesses be from the neighborhood; and several high courts have taken note of the problem and allowed the law to be stretched. The Law Commission, too, favored widening the range of recruitment for wit-

---

[8] Some police officers have noted the curiosity of teaching recruits how to take photographs, fingerprints, and collect blood specimens but then failing to provide them with the equipment to do so. Perhaps, officers suggest, it would be better to train them more extensively in less sophisticated procedures, but ones that they would actually use.

[9] Section 165 and sections 96-99, Code of Criminal Procedure.

[10] Section 103, Code of Criminal Procedure.

[11] People who refuse to cooperate with police in witnessing searches are subject to prosecution under section 187, Indian Penal Code, but this is rarely done.

nesses.[12] Faced with these difficulties some officers have stooped to producing their own witnesses—usually a local vagrant or itinerant vendor, such as a "bidi-wallah" or "pan-wallah,"[13] whom they induce to cooperate by bribing or by threatening with trivial prosecution. These practices are soon discovered by the courts, in turn heightening the suspicion which already abounds in the minds of judges.

It is worth noting that few police officers actually advocate the repeal of the provision requiring search witnesses. The Bihar Police Commission expressed the general view when it took note that frivolous searches intended only to harass do take place from time to time and that the presence of search witnesses was a useful corrective.[14] Furthermore, abolishing search witnesses would make investigations easier but would scarcely reduce the general suspicion of police evidence. At least now the police can be assured that if they conform to the letter of the law a court cannot very well disregard the evidence that is produced.

Respectable witnesses are required too when an investigating officer examines a body to ascertain the cause of death[15] and when the police simply retrieve an object—seizure—that may be in a public place.

Police officers are very defensive, and somewhat bitter, about the need for independent—i.e., non-police—corroboration of police testimony. Their integrity has been impugned and they resent it. Many have stories showing how courts have cavalierly disregarded the testimony of policemen who happened to be alone at the scene of a crime. Whatever the situation actually is, officers believe that the word of an accused, no matter how heinous the crime or patent the guilt, is worth more in the scales of justice than the testimony of any number of police officers, whatever their rank, education, and social standing. Some day, they hope, their word will be accepted at face value and they will be restored to the fellowship of "respectable inhabitants" of the community.

In order to secure convictions the police rely almost exclusively upon oral testimony. An investigating officer, accompanied sometimes by an assistant and always by several constables, will

[12] Vol. II, pp. 755-756.
[13] "Bidis" are home-rolled cigarettes and "pan" refers to the leaves and nuts of the betel tree which are smeared with spicy pastes and then chewed.
[14] Bihar Police Commission, p. 109.
[15] Section 174, Code of Criminal Procedure.

visit the scene of the crime and then begin to sift and winnow testimony. He may spend several days in the area—particularly if the area is some distance from the station house—or he may come back several times. The reliable testimony of witnesses is the keystone of most police cases; at the same time, according to police officers, it is exceedingly difficult to obtain. Besides the delays of the courts and their petty, stultifying legalisms, police officers consistently cite the reluctance of people to cooperate with police in criminal investigations as the greatest handicap to successful prosecution work. They describe the public as indifferent, shy, reluctant, partisan, maliciously interested, hostile, and unresponsive. In words from two generations ago, the people "are not generally actively on the side of law and order; unless they are sufferers from the offense, their attitude is at the very best one of silent neutrality; they are not inclined actively to assist the officers of the law."[16] Officers ruefully repeat stories of traffic accidents or even murders in broad daylight with several hundred people looking on, all jostling and pushing one another for a better view, and how the crowd melts away as if by magic when officers begin to seek witnesses.[17] So great is the reluctance to serve as a police witness that if a witness appears in court voluntarily, without having been served a summons, defense counsel will immediately label him biased.[18] The first question defense counsels ask is whether the witness came in response to a summons; "this practice leads to witnesses insisting upon a summons being served before consenting to give their evidence."[19] Not in all cases are police met with a deafening silence; sometimes they are overrun with witnesses, each more eager than the last to give damaging testimony. This happens in traffic offenses, for example, especially if an unpopular type has run down a victim who claims instantaneous sympathy—such as a child or an old man. But overenthusi-

[16] Police Commission, 1902-1903, p. 22.

[17] One officer told me in all seriousness that he had once dispersed a threatening crowd by pulling out his notebook and making as if to record statements from witnesses. A similar story is current in Scotland, only there the same effect was produced by passing a hat.

[18] Police have full legal powers to summon and examine witnesses. They can compel attendance in court. There has been a running dispute between police and magistrates about who is at fault in not serving summons quickly enough on witnesses to enable them to attend trials on dates specified. The Law Commission believes the fault is mutual. For their recommendations see Vol. II, p. 780.

[19] Law Commission, Vol. I, p. 327.

astic testimony is hardly more of a blessing. What the police require is disinterested testimony. And it is precisely this that most observers concede they are not getting.

In the public opinion surveys, two items bore on the topic of willingness to give evidence to a police officer. Respondents were asked whether they personally would avoid being questioned by police. Note that the stress was not upon whether they would cooperate, but whether they would avoid the police. The survey results conformed to what police expect. While most people said they would not avoid the police, 12 percent in both rural and urban Mysore said they would. There was greater unsureness about whether they would or not in the rural area. In Kanpur, however, about 40 percent of the sample said they *would* avoid being questioned. Established urban residents and rural migrants agreed in their uncooperativeness.

Respondents were also asked to characterize the "attitude of people living in this area toward the police." About 25 percent of the sample in Mysore said others' attitudes were indifferent, suspicious, uncooperative, or hostile, while 60 to 70 percent said people were either friendly or cooperative. The cooperative responses ranged from 28 percent in the urban area to 35 percent in the rural area. In Kanpur in 1965-1966 responses were not as favorable as in the south. More people found their neighbors indifferent, suspicious, uncooperative, or hostile (50 percent among Kanpur residents; 40 percent among migrants). About one-third thought their neighbors were cooperative, which is about the same proportion who perceived cooperation among their neighbors in Bangalore.

If the survey results are taken at face value, then police officers seem to be overstating the difficulty they encounter in making investigations. Although police officers probably *are* overly impressed with the problems involved in doing their job—most conscientious workers are—the survey respondents, it should be noted, were replying in a sterile context; they were not caught up in the emotions of a moment when a crime has been committed and the khaki-clad policeman is seen poking about their street or lane. It is significant, I think, that people were more willing to find an absence of cooperativeness in their neighbors' predispositions than in their own. It would be hasty to conclude that police have been complaining unreasonably, although there may be a greater willingness to render assistance than many policemen believe and hence try to develop. As we shall see, many police officers seem to be aware of this and are urging their subordinates to behave differently in initial contacts so as to gain some of this latent support.

It must also be recognized that the quality of relationship between policeman and prospective witness is a very subjective matter. How does one judge whether a person is cooperative or not? What gradations can be objectified between grudging assistance and enthusiastic cooperation? Cooperation itself is a function of what one party thinks the other is capable of doing. Manner as well as solid oral testimony are involved in measuring cooperation. The best that could ever be done, even if the observer were present at a large random selection of police investigation contacts with the public, would be to make a judgment about the number of people who came forward of their own volition out of an estimation of the number who actually were in a position to know something. Supplementally, one could judge, based again on an assumption of how many actually could give reliable testimony, how many people "held still" for questioning and did not melt into the shadows. It would be possible, then, to make a body count; but note that the body count is only significant in relation to an estimate of how many people potentially could help. And the latter is a matter of speculation.

In short, there are insurmountable methodological and intellectual barriers to making a judgment about the amount of public cooperation. All policemen, whatever the country, think they do not receive enough public cooperation.[20] Whether it is ever possible to make an objective evaluation of public cooperation is doubtful; we will never be able to free ourselves entirely from impression.

Granting then that Indian policemen do encounter difficulties in eliciting reliable testimony, what are the reasons which account for it?

[20] The opinion survey undertaken in connection with the Royal Commission on the Police showed that 87 percent of policemen thought the general public did not help as much as they should when they saw a policeman in difficulties, for instance, in dealing with drunks. Those believing there were other ways the public should be helping the police amounted to 97 percent; 70 percent mentioned reporting suspicious persons and behavior immediately; 21.8 percent said the public should be more prepared to act as witnesses in court cases. Royal Commission on the Police, *Appendix IV to the Minutes of Evidence*, p. 33. The Royal Commission noted the "selfishness" of some people who are not prepared to come forward with information about crimes and accidents (p. 109).

Two of the most frequently heard reasons given for inability of police to get the witnesses they need are (1) that the police manner in conducting investigations is rude, overbearing, and inconsiderate, and (2) that the courts are inhospitable and dilatory. These two reasons comprise the main themes of a dialogue of recrimination between police and courts. The courts pass fierce strictures against the behavior of the police; then police charge the courts with undercutting police attempts at creating more harmonious relations with the public by conducting trials with cavalier disregard for the welfare of witnesses. There is considerable truth in both charges.

Police officers tend to discount the contention that many people are afraid of brutality at the hands of police. To be sure, officers say, members of the public do not want to get involved, but it is not because they have a lively fear for their physical safety. In this day and age, officers point out, it would be extremely risky for a policeman to try to intimidate people into serving as witnesses. People are much too aware of their rights; they are knowledgeable about avenues of redress; and the country is evenly permeated with politicians only too eager to catch the police off base.[21] Mute, resigned, apathetic acceptance of life's conditions and especially of bureaucratic misbehavior is surely giving way. At the same time officers do acknowledge that police are saddled with a reputation for rudeness and lack of sympathy that is too often supported by thoughtless acts of subordinate policemen.[22]

There is still something pertinent in the admonition of the Police Commission, 1902-1903: "Let the police gain by their character and methods the confidence of the community; and their difficulties in gaining information will largely pass away. It must be realized that their success depends on the general support of the community."[23] There is a legacy of suspicion of the police that will only be dissipated through the heroic efforts of younger men conscientiously pursuing a new policy in human contacts. The station-house officer, the circle inspector, and the superintendent must all demonstrate that

[21] For information about public readiness to complain about police behavior, see Chapter 8.

[22] William Wiser and Charlotte Wiser, *Behind Mud Walls* (Berkeley, California: University of California Press, 1963), pp. 103-107, recount several instances of extortion by police officers and village watchmen in a village in southern Uttar Pradesh.

[23] Page 115.

they are available, impartial, efficient, and sympathetic. In short, while reluctance to testify is not wholly of the making of this generation of policemen, it can certainly be affected for the better by their efforts. And every single departure from a higher standard undermines the patient work of an entire police force.

In the recent survey respondents were asked about the demeanor of interrogating officers.[24] A majority of urban and rural people in Mysore said police were courteous and fair. About 15 percent said they were rude and tricky; slightly over one-third were unable to say. Opinion was much less favorable in Kanpur. Almost half of established urban residents thought police were rude and tricky; only 33.6 percent of rural migrants agreed. Almost an equal number of Kanpur residents thought that the police were courteous and fair.

Appearing as a witness in court does cost the citizen time. Then, if there are many delays, he may be called back again and again. Forfeiture of income in a country enjoying high standards of living is bearable; in an underdeveloped country where incomes are very low the loss of several days' wages produces substantial suffering. Even if people are not fully employed every day, as many are not, courts are often a considerable distance away. Government is supposed to reimburse witnesses for travel and maintenance, but the rates are absurdly inadequate and frequently never paid. Police officers complain, too, of the numbers of adjournments obtained by defense counsel. It is generally recognized that counsel, realizing the hardship on witnesses of attending court, sometimes deliberately aggravate the hardship by applying for postponements. Courts simply do not seem to consider that witnesses, after waiting several hours to testify, may have to travel distances of thirty and forty miles to get home. In the end memories fade or witnesses change their stories so as to avoid testifying. And the word circulates that to get embroiled as a witness is like being played as a fish on a long line. Very little regard is had for convenience of witnesses while waiting, whether at police stations or in courts. They squat on verandahs or in the shade of trees in courtyards.[25] Finally, people may be unwilling to fall into the

[24] "When the police come around asking questions about an offense or a crime do they generally act courteously or are they rude and tricky?"

[25] See Law Commission, Vol. II, pp. 777-778. I am a little skeptical of the deterrent effect of not providing better waiting facilities. Police stations

hands of badgering attorneys. "The manner of their cross-examination by the opposing counsel very often borders on the insulting and offensive. This naturally leads to a disinclination on their part to appear in court."[26]

So a combination of police unmannerliness and an insufficient regard by police and courts for the inconvenience to which witnesses are put contributes to the noncooperation shown by the public.

A third factor is the protectiveness of village communities. Villagers do not want outsiders meddling in their affairs and will go to lengths to avoid it.[27] A crime involving villagers is not so much a crime as it is another village event. The law calls it a crime, the villagers think of it as only a particular form of personal interaction. Murder, for example, may be considered as reprisal, it does not require outside intervention; it is the end product of a dispute that should be contained within village society. If someone has been hurt through a criminal act, there seems little point in making another person suffer in the mechanical toils of far-off courts. Better to settle the difference in the village, appeasing the wronged party through payment in money or kind, thus assuring that the fabric of village life will not be permanently rent. Families and small social groups also act like this. They draw together to prevent unhelpful outside intervention. Whether they do so in any specific instance depends upon the nature of the crime and the identity of those involved. Villages do not always protect the criminal. If outsiders, for example, are accused, then intervention by the police may be clamorously demanded.

---

and courts in the United States are notoriously decrepit, dirty, drafty places. (For example, see the article by James Mills, "The Detective," *Life* Magazine, December 3, 1965, p. 90, for a description of the shabby, down-at-the-heels condition of precinct headquarters in central Manhattan.) I would hazard the opinion that relative to standards of life in both countries, waiting facilities in India are better than in most public buildings in the United States. Perhaps the high-born, educated town-man in India needs to be provided a chair and an interior room, but is this true for the majority of Indians? I suspect that provision of ample travel and maintenance allowances would be the most important reform that could be made.

[26] Law Commission, Vol. II, pp. 743-744.

[27] T. S. Epstein, *Economic Development and Social Change in South India* (Bombay: Oxford University Press, 1962), pp. 121-122, describes how a village panchayat was coerced into meeting hastily to settle a long-standing dispute when an aggrieved man and wife, tired of waiting for a meeting that never took place, loaded themselves into a bullock cart and started off to seek help at district headquarters four miles away.

The intimacy of life in India is another factor—a fourth—making people reluctant to stand as witnesses. It is one thing for a man to accuse a stranger of a crime, it is quite another to say it was the neighbor down the street, or the woman who draws water at the well each morning, or the son of a respected elder. Crimes are quickly transposed into personal terms. The law would have the description in terms of victim, accused, witnesses; the community translates it into Ram Singh, Mohan Rao, and the families and friends of one or the other. Giving evidence is choosing sides, and the consequences in terms of personal life in a village may be unsettling and unpleasant. By the same token villagers automatically consider the justice of the event. One man's assault on another may be justified, many villagers reason, because of the victim's ugly behavior previously. The attack is not an isolated event, but part of a skein of happenings extending back in time for months or years. If justice has now been done, intervention by the law may only unbalance the scale of natural justice all over again.[28]

The intimacy of community life makes it harder to get trustworthy evidence as well. Personal scores can so easily be paid off in giving evidence to policemen. Then, if a village is already at odds, people give evidence not in terms of what they know but in terms of what they want to be true or in terms of what they think will be most damaging to the rival party. Witnessing becomes a political act in which considerations of loyalty play a large part. Obtaining disinterested testimony is worst when physical injury is involved, as in assaults or riots. Then there is oral testimony a-plenty, but not a shred of it is any good. The truly impartial man is caught invidiously between opposing forces. Conscience leads him to tell what he knows, but whatever he says one or the other side will be furious with him. The investigating officer, too, has a vested interest in stability and good relations with the village and he will perceive that more is involved than an isolated investigation. He finds himself involved

---

[28] Michael Banton in *The Policeman in the Community* (New York: Basic Books, Inc., 1964), p. 167, has written that people in Scottish country districts are very unwilling to give evidence against neighbors. They argue that they have to live with these people and that to give evidence against them would be an unfriendly act causing serious strain in social relations. Since these doughty folk are also uncompromising citizens they are caught in a dilemma. They sometimes resolve it by giving hints to the police that it just might be worth their while to go to such and such a place.

in a crucial battle of a small war. The crime is lost amid the din of social conflict—the first casualty inevitably is truth.

Fifthly, witnesses may quite simply fear retaliation. An Indian peasant is, as one high-ranking police officer put it, "absolutely vulnerable." The police station is miles away; he works in fields alone and out of sight of others; he travels home in the dusk of evening; his life is so precariously balanced on the edge of misery that it does not take much of a shove to send him head-long into starvation and penury. Thatch huts can be set afire, crops burnt or trampled, cattle stolen or killed, and the witness himself may be beaten senseless or murdered. Dacoits and goon-das take care of their own, or so the villagers believe, and woe betide the innocent man who ventures to speak against them. Bootleggers, too, have a reputation for ruthlessness that makes it difficult for the police to obtain testimony. The police gen-erally realize that if they are to break through the cordon of silence around them, they must demonstrate that they can pro-vide protection.[29] Police must also demonstrate that they are not themselves in league with criminals: that is, they must create a reputation for being incorruptible and impartial. If people think that police support can be had by the highest bidder, then would-be witnesses cannot count on the reliability of police promises. Today the witness enjoys the esteem of the police; to-morrow he is falsely accused of being involved in a crime.[30]

As the survey has shown, Indians do have very serious doubts about the honesty and impartiality of the police. From a third to a half of all respondents think there is a great deal of corrup-tion and favoritism. Almost half of all respondents think that po-lice are either sometimes or often—as opposed to rarely or never —in collusion with known criminals. It is clear that Indians do not have so solid a regard for the rectitude of the police that they may not hesitate before placing their lives and fortunes in police hands through giving evidence against the rich, powerful, or vindictive.

A sixth factor impeding the flow of willing testimony may be the belief that the individual has no duty to assist the state

[29] The Maharashtra Police Commission in its recommendations made a special point of the need to give protection to people who testify against goondas. For example, witnesses should be allowed to remain anonymous as long as possible, being permitted to slip out of police stations unnoticed after filing their statements (p. 12).

[30] The Maharashtra Police Commission suggested that subordinate officers did allow the names of people who gave information against goondas to slip out, for a consideration, of course (p. 12).

in criminal matters. Prevention and investigation of crime are the responsibility of the police. Not that Indians do not abhor crimes of violence, simply that when they occur they become the exclusive concern of the state's agents and not of the ordinary citizen. Many people in the West share this point of view. Some commentators have suggested, however, that this myopia is particularly acute in India because its citizens are submerged in tight little worlds of family and community prerogative: their foremost duties are confined within these circles. Law, courts, and police are not part of the web of fundamental social relations; these agencies belong to "them" and the ordinary citizen need not assist.

When respondents in the survey were asked whether the common man had a duty to help the police catch criminals, the vast majority replied that he did. One may conclude either that they have a well-developed sense of a citizens' responsibility or they have a well-developed sense of what the norm expected of them is. If they are not yet dutiful, they certainly know what duty consists of in the minds of outsiders.

Seventh and lastly, there is a profound human reluctance to get involved in unpleasant situations over which one has little control. Most people think twice before surrendering the opportunity to remain detached, unencumbered, and uncommitted. Crimes involve passions, personalities, and heartaches; the wish to remain free of all such entanglements is entirely too natural.[31]

The reasons put forward to explain why police encounter difficulty in obtaining witnesses fall into two categories: first, there are the "human" reasons, common to all men; second, there are the circumstantial ones—a part of the Indian situation— which presumably could be more easily changed. The police have a crucial pedagogical role to play in affecting all of them, but some much more directly and with greater expectation of success than others. It would be naive to imagine, however, that through their own unaided efforts police will be able to revolutionize public cooperation—although this must not be used as an excuse for inactivity on their part.

[31] Americans have been repeatedly shocked in recent years by stories of incredibly callous disregard shown by onlookers in the United States to crimes committed against others. Stories have been told many times of women's cries for help going unheeded for minutes at a time because those who heard didn't want to get involved. See, for example, the story of Kitty Genovese, New York City, told in *Time* Magazine, May 15, 1964, pp. 50-51. *Time*'s comments: "The Decent Citizen and Taxpayer is apt to feel that taking any kind of action is unwise, unsafe—and unnecessary."

TESTIMONY OF WITNESSES

One of the besetting problems of criminal investigation is holding witnesses during trial proceedings to the testimony they have earlier given to police.

"The percentage of acquittals in criminal cases has reached a high figure; and this is not always due to the police being unable to place adequate evidence before the courts. What often happens is, that the witnesses when they appear to give evidence in courts display a tendency to reduce the effectiveness of their evidence by deposing to a version different from that given by them in their statements to the police. The Inspector-General of Police, Bihar, told us that at least fifty percent of the police cases failed because the witnesses turned completely hostile under the influence brought to bear upon them by the accused and his supporters."[32]

Statements made to police officers and written down by them cannot be introduced as evidence in court.[33] They can only be produced to impugn the credibility of later testimony. In an effort to encourage more stability in testimony, police officers and the Law Commission recommend that statements made to police should be signed by witnesses if they are literate.[34] Some police officers see no reason why illiterates should not make a mark as well, as long as two independent witnesses were present who signed, too, and the witness was then given a copy of his statement.[35] The witness would then be more closely identified with his earlier testimony; it would be more embarrassing personally for him to claim that the earlier version was not correct or the police had recorded his testimony mistakenly.[36]

But holding testimony in line is only a small part of a larger issue—the problem of obtaining truthful testimony at any stage of proceedings. Judges and police officers often say that they are faced with choosing between pairs of liars. And there is a telling folk-saying in northern India: "Speak the truth, you are not

[32] Law Commission, Vol. II, p. 754.

[33] The practice is the same in the United States and Great Britain. This is a hallowed principle of common law. A statement from a witness taken by the police and introduced in court is hearsay evidence.

[34] Vol. II, pp. 753-754. Also, Maharashtra Police Commission, p. 74.

[35] "Police Reforms," pp. 29-31.

[36] To my knowledge the only authoritative group that has recommended that statements be given evidentiary weight, at least to corroborate other testimony, is the U. P. Police Commission (p. 74).

standing in a court of law."[37] The Law Commission, after hearing a great deal of testimony on the subject, said that "the sanctity of the oath has almost disappeared and persons seem prepared readily to make false statements on oath in courts of law."[38] Unfortunately there is no hard data on the incidence of perjury. The law against it is so rarely invoked that figures on perjury indictments are without significance.[39] Judges and police officers may pardonably overstate the case, although the consensus among them is so striking that the saying "where there's smoke there's fire" would seem to apply.[40]

If perjury is a major stumbling block to successful criminal prosecutions, as so many official participants firmly believe, what is the explanation for it? Why should Indian witnesses so glibly dissemble? Police officers themselves cite three primary reasons for either resiling from previous testimony or committing perjury. First: trials drag on for a long time and memories fade; people can easily become confused or begin to substitute the general opinion for what they really perceived. Second: witnesses are induced to testify for one or the other party by being bribed or threatened. The inducement may be quite crude and blatant or it may be only subtle promptings to the effect that a witness should stand by his kinsman or caste-fellow.[41] Third:

---

[37] Khosla, *op.cit.*, p. 10.

[38] Law Commission, *Fourteenth Report*, Chapter 40, para. 1.

[39] The Law Commission made recommendations for making prosecution of perjury easier, Vol. II, p. 831.

[40] It is even more hazardous for foreigners to make an estimation based on comparative impressions. One British observer before independence noted that the English in India had no experience with court actions in their homeland and when they discovered the situation in India, they were so appalled they could not believe the situation was so bad at home. T. C. Arthur, *Reminiscences of an Indian Police Official* (London: Sampson Low, Marston and Co., 1894). Cultural pride substituted for fact. The settled belief among Europeans that Indians were habitual liars was quite false. Englishmen couldn't really judge how many times witnesses failed to understand a question put to them. Moreover, witnesses both in India and England were easily confused; a clever cross-examiner could elicit contradictions surprisingly easily. "Why should he jump to conclusions that the native witness is bent on perjuring himself? Why not make as much allowance for the native as for the Englishman?" (p. 102). "I have been thrown into quite intimate contact with the English agricultural classes, and find them quite as much, if not more, addicted to lying as my old friend Bhow Patel or Bappoo Kunbi in India" (pp. 100-101). These warnings are perceptive and should caution the foreign observer from reasoning from behavior to motives, and especially to the absence of a moral code of a particular kind.

[41] Philip Woodruff has written an excellent novel—*Call the Next Witness* (New York: Harcourt, Brace and Co., 1946)—describing a crime and its investigation in a north Indian village. The book superbly presents the tactics

most witnesses are illiterate and parochial; taken out of their milieu they are like fish out of water, easily flustered, lacking in poise. It is not hard for an insinuating, insulting, haranguing lawyer to lead them into contradictions during cross-examination.

The subject of truth-telling in Indian courts is a complicated one and leads into murky regions of insight, conjecture, and impressionistic observation. Although the subject can only be touched here, let us examine several commonly encountered reasons for falsehood in Indian trials. For the most part these reasons are the hypotheses of observers, usually foreign, and not of Indian police officers. They supplement, or provide deeper reasons for, the causes listed by officers.

First: it is part of the folkways of village life that settlement within the community is more important than judgment in a court of law. In the passion of the moment witnesses may freely depose as to what they saw. But later, as the event recedes in memory, people judge that it is more important that life in the village be sustained as harmoniously as possible; the past is the past, what profit is there in raking up old injuries? Giving testimony in full court is like removing the scab from a newly healed cut.

Second: the court system is alien in intent and procedure, being a British importation, and as a result the mass of Indians do not feel easy with it or bound to it by any sense of trust or loyalty.[42] The alienness of the courts causes them to tell falsehoods for one of three reasons: (a) they are confused; (b) they do not feel it is responsive to justice as they conceive it, so they must overcompensate by injudicious use of testimony;[43] and (c) they employ in courts an entirely different morality from that which they use in more familiar surroundings. Students of village life have commented that villagers try to stretch the truth to their own advantage in panchayat proceedings but they do not indulge in the wholesale prevarication that seems common in formal courts.[44] Professor Bernard S. Cohn, among

---

of officers, their problems, and the impact of prosecution upon a tightly-knit village. Woodruff comments, for example, that the testimony of tenants to either party in a trial is invariably disbelieved.

[42] Curry, *The Indian Police*, p. 192.

[43] Walsh, *Indian Village Crimes*, says that peasants have an abiding conviction that in English courts the truth is never enough. One must always embellish. He makes this point many times.

[44] Panchayats are traditional adjudicating bodies, membership in which was usually hereditary. A new village council structure, known as Panchayati

others, believes that Indians, especially in the nineteenth and early twentieth centuries, thought of the courts as instruments of private purpose. They used them as engines of revenge and punishment in quarrels from the village. They did, in effect, bring a different morality to court than panchayat proceedings. Courts were simply one way of getting back at a rival. There was no value per se in telling the strict truth in a court of law because the court of law did not stand for something important in itself—as it did to the British colonial officers; it was only a tool to be used as best one could.

G. D. Khosla, formerly chief justice of the Punjab, obliquely supports this thesis. Witnesses are not required to swear a religious oath before giving testimony; all they give is an affirmation that what they say is true. There is no element of awe in the situation. Khosla says that he several times took information in private and asked the witness to swear on a holy book. The results were astonishing: witnesses would confess to having lied and in obvious fear would give an entirely new version of the case. By this device the morality of the village was brought into the court; the gap was bridged. He does not know whether it will ever be possible to overcome the scruples of non-Christians in India about swearing a religious oath, but he believes it would work wonders in courts of law.[45]

The making of false charges against rivals is often described as amounting to a national sport. Every policeman can cite instances when the number of accused kept mounting as witness after witness sought to implicate his favorite enemy. The rich, especially, will file suit against an impoverished neighbor thereby impelling him into bankruptcy in order to meet the legal challenge. Sometimes the false charge is used deliberately to muddy the waters of investigation and obtain an acquittal for the accused. By implicating everybody, testimony becomes hopelessly confused and the court is unable to distinguish truth from fabrication. This is a further indication that even today criminal charges are not considered with Anglo-Saxon seriousness; and that behavior in courts does not fall within the prescriptions of day-to-day morality.[46]

Raj, has recently been introduced in India by action of the government. This will be discussed in Chapter 15.

[45] Khosla, *op.cit.*, pp. 10-16.

[46] Philip Woodruff, *The Wild Sweet Witch* (New York: Harcourt, Brace and Co., 1947), pp. 215-216. Other commentators have noted the fortuitous

Third: certainty of guilt often makes facts unimportant. In observation, to re-coin a phrase, belief may be father to the fact. Only the rare individual can distinguish what he perceived from what he thought happened. The next step is to substitute a common opinion strongly held by others for what really took place.[47] The evidence is irrelevant to the verdict. Evidence, indeed, is a means of ensuring that the guilty are punished. Is it not a quibble, people may reason, to talk of perjury and the strict observation of fact when it is "apparent" that the accused is guilty or innocent as the case may be?[48] It is a common failing in criminal cases for witnesses ingeniously to elaborate upon what they know so as to secure what they believe is the proper result. In fact, defense counsel often encourage prosecution witnesses, knowing that sooner or later they cannot fail to tumble into a statement which can easily be proven false. When this happens, counsel seeks to convince the court that the principle *falsus in uno, falsus in omnibus* should be applied. This principle, says Judge Khosla, must be applied very selectively in India; its indiscriminate use has wrecked many a case, allowing the guilty to go free.[49] The prevalence of factional intrigue also makes it difficult to hold tightly to the bare facts. The crime is but an event in a larger context of conflict; it is a new opportunity to score off the other side or to defend one's own from the hostility of the other side. For an individual to insist on recounting only bare facts—and let the chips fall where they may—would take an abnormal amount of courage because it would threaten to cut the witness off from the very basis of his social being.

"call of nature" that figures so prominently in Indian trial. This is very often given as the reason why the witness was up and about in the dead of night and consequently conveniently placed to witness a critical event.

[47] Khosla says, "Many witnesses often feel that they are telling the truth because what they say is true even if it is not true to their personal knowledge." *The Murder of the Mahatma*, p. 17.

[48] Woodruff, *Call the Next Witness*, p. 138, presents the moral problem confronting a Brahman who must decide which side to support in a murder trial. He has been importuned by both sides. Since he doesn't know anything about the circumstances of the case, he will commit perjury whichever way he testifies. He doesn't mind committing perjury as long as he can be confident that the guilty has been punished. If Gopal, the accused, is guilty, then any evidence which convicts him is good evidence; if he isn't, then any evidence which wins his acquittal is good evidence.

[49] Page 23, and other places. This point is one of the recurring themes of the book.

Fourth: perhaps the Indian is not raised so as to revere the truth for its own sake. Long-time residents of Indian villages have noted that the rustic will often tell the stranger what he thinks the stranger wants to hear. It is not the accuracy of what one says that is important but whether it produces a desirable human end—such as propitiating the policeman, or pleasing the stranger, or quieting the questions of a child. Indians seem, also, to be ashamed to admit that they do not know. Rather than confess ignorance, they will pretend to a greater knowledge. The rules governing truth-telling in Indian society have not, to my knowledge, been thoroughly studied. We are given suggestions but little knowledgeable study.[50] An Indian social psychologist once was astonished at the fact that our two-year-old daughter said, "I don't know," in response to a question. "Why," he said, "this would never happen in India!" If a parent does not know something he will make up a story to satisfy the child; the important thing is satisfaction at the moment, not the uncovering of truth. Whether gleanings such as these, part of the burden of current impression carried by many Western observers in India, point to a residue of fact, I do not know. But the problem is fascinating, and urgently requires study.

Treatment of Suspects

The climax of investigation is the arrest of a suspect. Persons arrested must be produced before a magistrate within twenty-four hours. The magistrate decides whether there is sufficient cause to hold the suspect. The need for his continued detention, if charges are not immediately filed, must be reexamined every fifteen days. The suspect may be released if evidence of his complicity continues to be slight or he may be remanded back into custody. The Law Commission found that remands were being granted much too leniently, that police would continually come back to the magistrate pleading that investigation was not complete and that if the suspect were let go the case would be damaged irreparably. In effect, arrest was not the climax of investigation; it was the prologue.[51] The Law Commission rec-

[50] Fragmentary comments on the subject may be found in G. Morris Carstairs, *The Twice-Born* (London: Hogarth Press, 1957), and Leigh Minturn and John T. Hitchcock, *The Rajputs of Khalapur, India* (New York: John Wiley & Sons, 1966).

[51] Law Commission, *Fourteenth Report*, p. 759.

ommended sixty days as the absolute maximum period a person could be held on remands. It also happens that police sometimes lock people up for several days at a time without producing them before a magistrate. Another slippery practice is for police to demand attendance upon them of suspects and witnesses during the course of investigation. This discomfits the suspect and is one way of keeping him in view without resorting to formal arrest.[52]

No issue in police-public relations is more sensitive than the physical treatment of suspects. Use of force to obtain confessions from suspects is known colloquially as "third-degree." But third-degree is only one aspect of a larger problem—the problem of police brutality, whether applied to suspects or to the general public when the police have any objective to accomplish.[53] These aspects are often confused by the public, but they are really very different problems.

Considerable numbers of people in India unhesitatingly say that they believe the police often do beat people up. The proportion varies with the sample from 7 to 37 percent.[54] Rural people are less critical than urban people. Opinion in the north is significantly more critical than it is in the south.

What kind of first-hand observations have the people made about police brutality? In Mysore, 13 percent of the sample had seen a policeman strike a person: 22 percent in Bangalore, only 3 percent in Tumkur. In Kanpur, 43 percent of established urban dwellers had witnessed such a scene; 22 percent of rural migrants. When asked to describe the situations in which beating had occurred, respondents most frequently cited occasions of crowd control, handling persons of doubtful character—such as drunkards, gamblers, and goondas —minor traffic violations in which coolies and rickshaw pullers were manhandled, and arresting suspects in minor criminal cases.

Relatively few people had known a person of their acquaintance to be struck by a policeman, although the figure was strik-

---

[52] As a judge has observed: "Sometimes suspects whom the police officer does not desire to report as under arrest are kept for days together under so-called surveillance which is nothing more than unauthorized confinement or restraint, a system which affords serious opportunity for malpractices." J. Padmagiriswaran, "Bonafides of Investigation and Evaluation of Evidence by Law Courts" (Central Police Training College, 1964), p. 140.

[53] The topic of police use of force in order to control crowds will be taken up in Chapter 10.

[54] The proportions were: Bangalore, 12.2 percent; Tumkur, 7.5 percent; Kanpur residents, 36.5 percent; Kanpur rural migrants, 31 percent.

ingly higher in Kanpur. There, 22 percent of established urban dwellers knew of a friend, relative, or neighbor who had received a blow from a policeman. Only 9 percent of respondents in Bangalore had this experience. Among Tumkur people and Kanpur rural migrants the proportions were 1.3 percent and 12.1 percent, respectively.[55]

Analysis of the survey shows that personal or near-personal observation of police brutality does affect the evaluations people make about police behavior. If the police are interested in transforming the predispositions of people toward them, they must give more attention to the visibility of coercion.

The Indian survey supports the observation of many police officers that while the public condemns police strong-arm methods in the abstract, they are less critical when confronted with real criminal situations and particularly criminal situations in which they have been the injured party. Respondents were asked if the police would be justified in beating a suspect whom they knew to be guilty but would not confess. There was a marked difference between rural and urban responses; there was also a much higher proportion of don't know's in the rural area. In Kanpur, among both residents and migrants, 69 percent said the police would be justified; the proportion in Bangalore was 72 percent and in Tumkur 40 percent. Only about one-fifth of the general public samples said outright that the police were not justified.

At a different point in the interview respondents were asked whether the police "should" use physical force against a suspect who had robbed the respondent in order to get him to confess. Among the general public, the number of people who thought the police should do so gained marginally over the previous question. The proportions were Bangalore, 73 percent; Tumkur, 64 percent; Kanpur residents 76 percent and Kanpur rural migrants, 74 percent. Among rural people in Mysore there

---

[55] Similar questions were asked the public in connection with the Royal Commission on the police. Those who felt the police sometimes used too much force in handling people were 17.8 percent. Of these, 11.6 percent thought it was excusable considering the provocations the police received; 5.5 percent thought it was not excusable. Only 1 percent thought the police often used an unnecessary amount of force; 4.4 percent thought it occurred fairly often; and 11.4 percent thought it was a rare occurrence. Those knowing personally of cases of police using too much force added up to 3.5 percent. The cases most people knew about personally involved police handling of young people, teen-agers outside dance halls, "teddy boys," and students. *Appendix IV to Minutes of Evidence*, p. 8.

was a dramatic change in opinion. When they themselves were victims, they were less willing to be circumspect with guilty parties.

Brutality against suspects is certainly not unknown in India. Every year the press recounts dismissals of officers for inflicting grievous hurt upon suspects and even for torturing suspects to death.[56] Politicians and the press keep up a drum-fire of criticism of the police for mistreating people in their custody. People generally seem prepared to believe the worst. And in a scattering of cases each year they will retaliate directly against the police, often by laying siege to a police station, if they believe an innocent person has been mistreated. They throw brickbats and rocks at the station, may even set fire to it, and demand the immediate suspension of the offending officer. To give only one example, the sweepers of Delhi besieged a police station in Patel Nagar in 1964 and dumped piles of refuse in its courtyard following the death of a sweeper in police custody. The police said the sweeper had thrown himself from the roof of the station house—a height of about thirty feet—the demonstrators were convinced he had been beaten and then thrown off to disguise the wounds. After a day of sporadic clashes in Patel Nagar and a strike by sweepers, the agitation died down, primarily because a full inquiry was promised. The inquiry later exonerated the police, although it did criticize them for allowing a suspect to have access to the roof. It is apparent that the victim was so thoroughly terrified of the police that he did seek to escape by hurling himself off the second-floor roof. The alleged molestation of women in custody is another recurrent theme in spontaneous uprisings against the police. All in all, there is enough hard evidence of gross mistreatment to keep the issue of police brutality alive in the public's mind. The instances may be few relative to the numbers of detentions, but their impact is very great, reinforcing a familiar image of the police.

Police officers generally think that the use of force against suspects and in carrying out other duties is dwindling rapidly. Undoubtedly it still goes on to some degree, but it is not nearly

---

[56] To give one example, *The Times of India*, May 5, 1966, p. 5, reported that three subordinate officers had been sentenced to rigorous imprisonment for eleven, three, and three years, respectively, for torturing to death a suspect believed to possess contraband opium.

so common as it was in the British period.[57] What brutality there is directed against individuals, say police officers, is largely at the hands of older policemen: the new recruits are much more conscious of the rights of citizens and much more aware of the need to win public support.[58] But, as in the United States, men are to be found who believe that respect for the police can only be maintained by the free use of a stick. For them, the importance of restraining criminal activity justifies the use of physical force, even to the extent of beating suspects, just as it excuses resort to padding and concocting evidence. While the indiscriminate use of force as well as the merciless use of force are to be condemned, are we in a position to gainsay the police officer who believes that some judicious use of violence by police is necessary to restrain the depredations of various antisocial elements? Furthermore, how dedicated are most people—whether in India or the United States—to the view that any use of phyiscal force by the police is more serious and more unfortunate than any criminal activity? There are practical as well as moral questions here which must not be lost sight of in a ritualistic, hortatory condemnation of police use of force.

Confessions made before police officers are not admissible in evidence.[59] The Law Commission, which has proposed several changes in law relating to investigations, is strongly against removing this prohibition:

"The large mass of offences in our country are investigated only by the subordinate police officials. The high sense of fairness and justice which might actuate the superior personnel does not permeate the lower ranks. To make a confession

[57] The Police Commission, 1902-1903, said on this point: "The system of investigation which commends itself to the indolent and inefficient police officer is to make life a burden for everyone who is likely to be in any way acquainted with the facts until he tells all he knows, and to extort by all means incriminating statements or confessions from suspects. The evidence before them shows that the practice of working for confessions is exceedingly common" (p. 115).

[58] One straw in the wind comes from the U. P. Police Commission: "We regret to note that the old and crude methods of investigation still continue to persist. Complaints of beating, physical torture, maltreatment and harassment by Police Officers is not wanting. Most of these complaints are concerned with the investigation of cases. In fact the methods of scientific investigation have not yet found an adequate place in the strategy of the Police" (p. 70).

[59] Articles 25, 26, Indian Evidence Act.

made to a subordinate police official admissible in evidence would therefore be fraught with dangerous consequences."[60] They did make one concession: confessions made to officers of the rank of deputy superintendent and above could be admitted in court if the officer himself had conducted the investigation.[61] They stipulated, though, that it should be tried as an experiment only in larger cities where the most able police officers were apt to be found, where the bar would be distinguished, and where a High Court would be immediately available.[62]

PREPARATION FOR TRIAL

There have been no studies of the length of time required to complete the average criminal investigation. It is known, however, that officers are repeatedly urged to be speedy. Many states have set down a time limit for cases of different kinds; cases can, of course, be reopened if need be. If a case involves chemical analysis the limit will almost invariably be exceeded due to arrears in work at laboratories. Most prohibition offenses fall into this category, since they require an analysis of the confiscated liquid to determine if it is fermented spirits.

One factor in the failure of many prosecutions is lack of legal knowledge on the part of investigating officers.[63] A sub-inspector is unable to shape his evidence so as to meet legal rules; he is not alert to the intricacies of procedure and rules of evidence. The problem is a reflection of the arrangements for prosecution in India, as well as the education and training of investigating officers. With some variation among states, police officers

[60] Law Commission, Fourteenth Report, Vol. II, 748.

[61] *Ibid.*, pp. 748-749.

[62] The Uttar Pradesh, Bihar, and Maharashtra Police Commissions supported the opinion of the Law Commission that articles 25 and 26, Indian Evidence Act, should not be repealed. And they supported the suggested experiment, except for the Bihar Police Commission which thought that no distinction in this regard should be made among police officers. Either all should have it or none (Bihar Police Commission, p. 109). The Bihar Police Commission thought that policemen should not rely so much on confession but should devote their energies to producing physical or eyewitness evidence.

Article 27 of the Indian Evidence Act does provide the police with a certain amount of leeway with respect to admissibility of statements made before them. If accused has made a statement which the police use to discover certain facts that help to incriminate him, that portion of the statement can be admitted in evidence as proved. See Law Commission, Vol. II, pp. 749-750.

[63] For comments of the Law Commission, see Vol. II, p. 742.

themselves prosecute cases in magistrates' courts.[64] They may be styled prosecuting inspectors or prosecuting sub-inspectors. If possible they are drawn from the ranks of law graduates, but this does not always happen. Cases before sessions courts are handled by a public prosecutor. He may have a staff of assistant public prosecutors. All are members of the bar. Public prosecutors in the past have been responsible to the police department, and in some places in India still are. There are two important problems with the organization for prosecution. First, it has been difficult to recruit men of good quality. The pay scales are meager and the prestige of being associated with police low. In order to remedy this defect, the Law Commission has suggested that a separate office of public prosecutions be established, directly responsible to state governments. The director of this office would be in charge of all prosecutions in a district. Second, the public prosecutors have not been closely related to the process of investigation. They are contacted only when the investigation is completed and the case ready to go to court. They do not provide advice as to how the investigation should be conducted; they do not help to put the case together; they do not monitor the behavior of investigating officers. They are essentially spectators to the process of investigation.[65] Two changes are going on that should improve the quality of prosecutions. Legal training is being emphasized in recruitment to the rank of inspector and sub-inspector. And police themselves are handling fewer and fewer prosecutions. In some states they have given them up entirely,[66] and prosecution has been entrusted to a full-time professional staff separate from the police department.

Another frustrating problem of criminal investigation is keeping and preparing accurate, legible documentation. At trial the accused must be furnished with copies of the police report to the magistrate, the F.I.R., all documents or relevant extracts of documents upon which prosecution will rely, statements of witnesses intended for use during trial, and incriminating or confessional statements of the accused. The phrase "copies

[64] For criminal cases the court hierarchy is composed of four levels: magistrate courts, sessions courts, High Courts, and Supreme Court. Sessions courts have jurisdiction normally co-terminous with a district. They are the top criminal court in each district. With minor exceptions, they have no original jurisdiction but receive cases from magistrates.

[65] Law Commission, Vol. II, p. 765.

[66] Andhra Pradesh, Madras, Kerala, and Maharashtra.

must be sent" is passed over as standard operating procedure by Westerners but it is laden with significance for Indian officials who know what it means to receive a copy of a case diary, for example, pressed through wrinkled carbon paper with the stub of a blunt pencil by a harried investigating officer with only modest ability in written composition. It is no wonder the Law Commission complained about the delays in furnishing required documents to the accused and the illegibility of them.[67] Police officers are continually distracted from more important work by the need to make out the many voluminous reports, documents, and innumerable registers of the police station. Investigation work is also hampered by the difficulty of utilizing large criminal files maintained in longhand in large, bound ledgers. Modus operandi files, fingerprints, records of arrest, and lists of missing persons or property are all kept this way. Mechanical filing systems and data-processing equipment are desperately needed if criminal investigations are to be properly conducted. The admixture of languages presents an added problem. What languages should reports and registers be kept in? It is easy enough to say that every police station should have a typewriter, but for printing which language? What happens, for example, when trial involves seized documents which are in English and testimony taken in Bengali? One must have two sets of typewriters, and the operators for them, as well as translators who can render a document in one language into another language the court or defendant can understand.[68]

Finally, Indian policemen share the view about lawyers—particularly defense lawyers—that is so common among law enforcement personnel in any country—politely put, they have lit-

[67] Law Commission, Vol. II, p. 761. The Law Commission suggested that the task of preparing copies of materials be transferred to the magistrate's office, relieving the police of essentially secretarial labors.

[68] It is worth noting that even in a modern technological society, such as the United States, police procedures are sometimes distressingly cumbersome and inefficient. The Law Enforcement Task Force appointed by Mayor Lindsay in the city of New York reported in February, 1966, that there were 2,500 forms in use by the police department and strongly criticized the burden of unnecessary paper work. See the *New York Times*, February 7, 1966, p. 1. The Task Force's report frequently used such descriptive adjectives as "unnecessary," "unrealistic," "hyperdetailed," "outmoded." One of O. W. Wilson's first reforms when he took over the Chicago Police Department was to hire clerical help to transcribe reports police officers were required to make.

tle use for them. They believe they are obfuscating, querulous, unscrupulous, self-centered, parasitic, and hidebound. "Scum of the earth" is only one among several earthy phrases used by police officers to describe them. The reasons for this negative view are largely occupational. A policeman's job is to arrest the guilty and see that he is prosecuted with reasonable expectation of conviction; he sees himself standing between society and criminal elements. The defense lawyer represents the opposition in the accusatorial system of justice. His duty is to his client, and to society at large only by making the system work. But while the policeman is paid by society to work in its interest, the lawyer is like a private entrepreneur who sells his services to anyone who can pay the price. It often appears to the police officer that the lawyer is out for himself, society be damned. In any case, there is an appreciable barrier in India separating the investigating police and defense counsel which affects relations between police and the legal community as a whole.[69]

CONCLUSION

Criminal investigation is one of the most important occasions for bringing police and public into contact. The process is not an indivisible whole, but involves many stages with different forms of contact appropriate to each. In summary, these points especially deserve underscoring:

First: Using clearance rates as a measure of police ability, Indian police are appreciably better than their colleagues in the United States or Great Britain.

Second: It seems reasonably clear that investigating officers cannot give enough concentrated attention to detective work because of the distractions of other responsibilities. The solution may be to separate investigating from enforcement work or it may be to increase the number of officers staffing the police stations. However, more study is required in order to determine precisely what investigating officers do with their time, how many cases they handle in a year, and how long it takes to complete them.

[69] Again it is worth referring to American experience. Police officers in New York City, although the view is not unique with them, believe that defense counsel deliberately seek delays until the harassed arresting officer fails to appear—he is required by law to do so every time the accused is produced in court—and then moves for dismissal of the charge on that ground. Mills, "The Detective."

Third: Criminal investigation and prosecution are hampered by a vicious cycle of suspicion and distrust between police, on the one hand, and public and judiciary, on the other. So ingrained is suspicion of police methods that members of the public hesitate to cooperate with them, while the courts seem bent on going to endless lengths to discover evidence of impropriety. The result is a feeling of victimization on the part of the police. In a conscientious desire to do their duty they provide missing evidence an unyielding public will not supply or shape evidence an unsympathetic court will not otherwise accept. These practices, once discovered, set off once again the cycle of suspicion, recrimination, and obduracy.

Fourth: Supervision of criminal investigations by officers of the rank of deputy superintendent of police and assistant superintendent of police or above is far from adequate. Senior police officers are quite unable to devote sufficient time to this critical task. Because public prosecutors do not bear some of this responsibility, as they do in the United States and Great Britain, the courts are in effect carrying almost the whole supervisory burden. It may be that if supervision by qualified senior staff were greater, the courts would feel less compelled to lay down so many procedural rules concerning the conduct of investigations. They might begin to feel less hostile toward police evidence. They would have some assurance that responsible officers of superior attainments were more intimately involved than at present.

Fifth: Public cooperation with the police is grudging and unenthusiastic. However, because the police are convinced the public has this character, they tend to approach members of the public as if they were invariably hostile. Thus, in a classic instance of self-fulfilling prophecy, they fail to uncover and nurture latent sympathy or understanding. The police may give up on the public too quickly, although the limitations of staff and time and the need for action make this practice understandable.

Sixth: The public is hesitant to venture opinions about the quality of police investigating practice, but when they do speak they tend to be critical. It seems reasonable to assume that Indians, like Americans, are willing to believe the worst about their police. Opinions are more critical in the north than in the south and they are more critical among urban residents.

Seventh: Impropriety certainly occurs in some proportion of

criminal investigations, and it seems probable that superior officers, not excluding I.P.S., may be turning a blind eye to it
when the practice is not too blatant and unsubtle. At the same
time, one must always be wary of overestimating the amount of
impropriety, especially where suspicion of the police is endemic. For obvious reasons, there is very little hard evidence
about the proportion of malpractices. The glib public view is
almost undoubtedly overdrawn and exaggerated.

FOUR

THE POLICE AND THE PUBLIC

7 • *Public Contact with the Police*

THE public's contacts with the police constitute a vast and varied area of interaction between citizen and government. The nature of the public's contacts may critically affect political processes. First, the quality of these contacts influences public perceptions of police behavior. They are not the only factor, because myths about the police abound and are passed on from generation to generation. Still, first-hand contacts are the bedrock upon which myths are built. They may reinforce or confute accepted belief. The beliefs that citizens hold about what the police do and how they do it affect not only their predispositions toward the police but their sense of duty to serve the larger society through cooperation with the authorities and their allegiance to the whole network of government. In this respect police contacts are not unique, any authoritative relation with an agency of government may bring similar effects. The police, however, are particularly visible and particularly pervasive. Moreover, they represent the regulatory power of government par excellence. It is not unreasonable to expect that their relations with the public may be a critical indicator of the legitimacy of government. Second, the quality of police-public contacts conditions the manner in which police perform. Since they must restrain, their behavior is compounded of authority and force. Police may produce conformity to laws through actual or threatened physical coercion or through the authority they embody and the respect in which they are held. The flavor of this mixture is in part determined by their own predilections and habitual practices, but it is also determined by the identity of interests between them and the public. In a society with a homogeneous value system, police and public will share beliefs as to the rules that should be enforced and the nature of police regulation. A policeman's actions will be based on the authority of the community and he need rely less on physical power. If he does not share the values of those he must regulate, his relations with the public will be less close—a fact both may perceive—and he will have to rely more heavily on formal sanctions. In a democracy this problem of balance between informal authority and physical force is especially acute, for the police-man "must discipline those whom he serves."[1] If his authority is slight and a cleavage exists between police and public with respect to what should be enforced, the police will have to utilize larger proportions of force, and this in turn may separate people and police even further, frustrating the growth of government as a responsible agency of popular will.

Despite the need to know about the nature of police-public contacts, there has been a surprising lack of attention given to them. Very few scholars or public officials have carefully set about discovering who contacts the police, how contacts are made, the reasons motivating contact, the point within the police at which contact is established, and the nature of official response. The same is true for contacts initiated by the police. If a stereotype of police contacts with the public is to be avoided, it is essential that the texture of police activities be understood. The Indian public opinion survey, carried out during 1965-1966, allows us to make an initial investigation of the topography of this neglected relationship.

The Range of Contacts

The variety of contacts between policeman and citizen is very great. One must distinguish first between contacts made in the line of duty and those made off-duty, when the officer is not acting his role. With respect to off-duty contacts in India, very little is known. There have been no studies of the actual, as well as perceived, social isolation or integration between Indian policemen and the community. Observation of living arrangements among officers and men suggests the following proposition: there is a tendency to social isolation of policemen due to segregation in living accommodations. Officers traditionally live in government colonies, not exclusively with policemen, but among senior government staff. Constables and N.C.O.'s spend substantial amounts of their time in cantonments or barracks near their posts. In the armed police the isolation is even more acute; these men live a garrison life. The evidence of physical isolation in living accommodations is, however, only presumptive of social and psychological isolation. There are

[1] William A. Westley, "Violence and the Police," *The American Journal of Sociology*, July, 1953, p. 35.

in fact two reasons for thinking that isolation in India may not be as severe as might at first be suspected. First, even today after substantial development of police housing colonies, less than 50 percent of the officers and men live in public accommodations. Most of them still must fend for themselves. It is possible that those men not able to obtain government housing tend to cluster together, but if they do it would be fortuitous, subject to the possibilities of the market. Secondly, families are "extended" in India, that is, one living unit is composed of members of several generations as well as relatives outside the immediate family. Then, too, Indian families maintain their ties with family, village, and village caste units even when they move away. Policemen, therefore, have strong ties outside their occupational grouping. It is possible of course that these extended families have a tradition of affiliation with the police; that they are, in effect, hereditary police families. As with living patterns among police in general, no information about this is available. If "police families" do exist and account for a significant proportion of families currently associated with the police, they would tend to offset the integration brought about by extended family ties.

Arguing solely from the basis of housing patterns, there is a presumption then that the policemen of India face greater social isolation than is the case in either the United States or Great Britain. Indian police officers want to encourage this isolation. Many of them are concerned about the temptations, as they call them, that beset lower-ranking policemen forced to support large families on very small salaries and to do so cheek-by-jowl with the very people they are responsible for regulating. Aware also that Indian recruits have so much to learn about professional conduct in a modern social organization, officers want to separate the policeman from traditional influences and to build in him the esprit de corps of an elite group charged with a critical mission. It is difficult to know, without a great deal of further research, whether officers are right in thinking that policemen, especially at the lower ranks, need to be shielded from the touch of society. It is also difficult to know whether an esprit de corps can be built at the expense of traditional links with surrounding society without at the same time cultivating an unprofitable estrangement. But it should be noted that the opinions of police officers are unequivocal on this point: isolation, at least in immediate living arrangements, is both desirable and necessary.[2]

Turning attention to on-duty contacts between police and public, it must be recognized that contacts are not exclusively, and probably not even predominantly, connected with crimes. Policemen are continually called upon to perform a host of services for members of the public that have nothing at all to do with maintaining order and preventing crime. They are simply an available source of information and assistance. They also have many ancillary regulatory tasks. For example, many state police forces in India issue licenses for motor vehicles, firearms, restaurants, hotels, and retail liquor establishments. In many cities the police review and approve films, recommending the parts that should be deleted before showing can be allowed. Policemen are used extensively as process servers, even in cases between private parties. The burden of this work is enormous and recent police commissions have recommended that the police be relieved of this chore.[3] The Indian police are not unique in the extent to which they are loaded with duties extraneous to their primary functions. Policemen around the world complain of this,[4] and with good reason. The fact is that police are on the scene, pervasive, and under the immediate control of government. When something needs doing, the police are ready to hand.

It is one of the peculiarities of police work that the more cordial their relations are with the public the greater becomes the number of extraneous demands made upon them by private citizens. One might indeed propose that a useful test of the rapport between police and public would be the volume of nonenforcement requests made to the police. Although exam-

---

[2] Michael Banton notes in *The Policeman in the Community*, pp. 195-197, in talking about the living arrangements of Scottish policemen, that a policeman's private life is likely to be more contaminated by his public role than that of higher status functionaries in law enforcement. A policeman cannot buy privacy like the judge or the lawyer. He cannot protect himself as successfully against intrusions by his neighbors. It would seem to follow that his public life may then be more contaminated by his private life.

[3] See Uttar Pradesh Police Commission, p. 9, and West Bengal Police Commission, p. 64. The Uttar Pradesh Commission reported that in 1960 the police were given 672,279 summonses to serve. The Commission commented that assuming a constable could serve 1,000 of them a year, a force of 672 constables would be needed to carry out this task alone. The Commission recommended the establishment of a separate process-serving cadre.

[4] For a list of some extraneous duties given to the police in Great Britain, see Ben Whitaker, *The Police* (Penguin Books, 1964), p. 50.

ples abound of such requests being made to policemen in India, there is no measure of whether they are increasing or decreasing and whether they are made by a significant proportion of the populace. This is another area of neglected study that could profitably attract the attention of scholars and officials.

Under the British, the police devoted themselves almost entirely to law and order functions. They deliberately avoided intruding into areas of feeling involving social customs and, to a lesser extent, politics. Their function was construed minimally; they were to maintain intact the vessel of society. With the coming of independence this posture changed radically, with the result that in the last few years police have been asked to shoulder a host of regulatory activities intimately involved with social change. The ambit of criminal law has been enlarged so that law can subserve social renovation. The effect is to bring police into contact with segments of society which were not previously thought of as criminal. This is the case with the enforcement of legislation dealing with prohibition, land distribution, the interstate movement of grain, hoarding of foodstuffs, the purity of gold ornaments, payment of dowries, and profiteering in food-grains. In all these cases the people against whom the police proceed may not be convinced of the evilness of what they do.

If a government is dedicated to social renovation and if persuasion is not instantaneously and generally effective in bringing about required change, laws must be enacted to give effect to new social policy and the police called upon to make behavior congruent with prescription. The police then become a lightning conductor for much of the grievance and frustration that such changes produce. On the one hand, the police require the goodwill of the masses in order to carry out their functions; on the other, they are asked to enjoin acceptance of new ways. There is a serious question whether respect for police functions can be developed while police are called upon to be the striking force of social revolution. The requirements of modernization and of earning the support of the people for a particular institution of government may be incompatible.

One of the most important new areas of contact between the non-criminal violator and the police is that of traffic enforcement. The British Royal Commission on the Police observed that "it is probably as motorists that ordinary men and women most often have dealings with the police."[5] This is not quite the situation in India but the problem is growing. If one were to include cyclists with motorists, traffic enforcement in many large Indian cities may even today constitute the most important form of contact with the public. In Delhi, for example, the number of registered auto vehicles increased from slightly over 12,000 in 1950 to over 50,000 in 1962.[6] The number of registered human-traction vehicles (such as hand-cars and cycles) and animal-drawn vehicles increased during the same period from 108,000 to 170,000.[7] The situation with respect to cycles is undoubtedly much more serious than official figures indicate. While the number of registered cycles in Delhi in 1962 was given as 160,000,[8] the office of the superintendent of traffic estimated the number at about 450,000. This is in a total population of close to 2,500,000 and a male population of 1,300,000. The superintendent of police in Jaipur found that in 1962 the number of people prosecuted for traffic offenses amounted to one out of every ten people in the city.[9] Many of the persons prosecuted were undoubtedly multiple offenders, nonetheless the amount of contact from this source is huge. In Delhi in March, 1964, one of a series of traffic safety campaigns was held, this time to ensure that cycles were properly equipped. On one evening alone police deflated the tires of over four thousand cycles because of improper equipment, most commonly riding without a light.[10] Both the pretext and the punishment seem trivial; one wonders, however, what thoughts about the police were produced in the minds of four thousand individuals trudging home from a day's work in the dusk of a March evening. Would they be angry? Would they be contemptuous of a police force that had such puny tasks to perform? Would they be suffused with injured innocence, convinced once again that police always pick on the little man, allowing the real criminals who know the ropes or have powerful friends to go unchastened? Contacts in India through traffic enforcement are already extensive and, as in the West, they will account more and more for the largest portion of enforcement contacts with the public.

[5] Page 144.
[6] Government of India, Ministry of Home Affairs, *Report of the Committee on Traffic in Delhi*, 1963, p. 6.
[7] *Ibid.*   [8] *Ibid.*
[9] Bhanwanimal, "Traffic Problems in Jaipur City, and Their Solution," *Traffic Safety Week—Jaipur, 1963* (a souvenir booklet).
[10] Office of the Superintendent of Police, Traffic, Delhi.

In sum, the pretexts for contact between police and citizen are undoubtedly growing in number. This is partly due to the changing technological basis of Indian society; it is also due to deliberate government policy. Segregated housing for officers and men, although not a majority of them, suggests social isolation among policemen. Research among the policemen themselves would be required to determine whether the isolation is real.

PUBLIC CONTACTS WITH THE POLICE

If contact with the police is to be measured, it is essential that contact be defined. Being ordered to move along in a crowd is a kind of contact but it hardly possesses the personal immediacy of being questioned in connection with a crime. Going to the police for help in a time of acute personal distress is contact, so too is being cautioned about making an improper turn in a motor vehicle. For the purposes of this analysis "contact" will indicate situations in which a face-to-face relationship was established, where there was more than perfunctory meeting, and in which one of the parties deliberately sought out the other with a purpose in mind. Contact, then, does not include chance and impersonal encounters. In the survey, respondents were asked whether they had ever gone to the police for help; whether, if they had been victims of a crime, they had reported the matter to the police. Since initiative in making contacts is often taken by the police, respondents were asked if they had ever been questioned by the police and whether they knew anyone personally, such as a friend, relative, or neighbor, who had been questioned. The latter question elicited the incidence of "near-personal" contact and was assumed to be almost as significant as first-hand experience. These questions provide a measure of what might be called neutral contact: that is, personal or near-personal confrontation with the police regardless of outcome. Many other questions in the survey elicited information about the quality of people's experiences with the police, such as whether they had been threatened, struck, approached for a bribe, and so forth.

Approximately one-fifth of the urban samples have gone to the police for help at some time or other. The proportion is much less in rural Tumkur, with only 5 percent having gone for help. It is also less among Kanpur rural migrants, indicating that rural people in the north as well tend to seek assistance less often than established urban people. Only about 8 percent of respondents in the cities had gone to the police in connection with a crime committed against them; the proportion in Tumkur was 1.3 percent and among Kanpur rural migrants 2.9 percent. The magnitudes and geographical patterns of responses with respect to being questioned by the police are similar to responses concerning having gone for help. More people have been questioned in cities than in the countryside; slightly more people have been questioned in the north than in the south. There is some overlap between these two items: that is, those who have been questioned by the police are also those who have gone to the police for help. The correlation between these items runs about 0.35 in all samples. Kanpur residents also score more highly than other respondents with respect to whether they have a personal acquaintance who has been questioned by the police, while Kanpur rural migrants have a higher proportion even than Bangalore urban respondents. Clearly, contact with the police is greater in the north than the south, although in both areas urban people appear to have more contact than rural ones. People who have themselves been questioned also have acquaintances who have been questioned.[11]

Making approximate estimations for overlap, it appears that in urban areas as many as one-fourth and perhaps as many as two-fifths of all males have had some personal or near-personal contact with the police. In rural areas, only about one-tenth of all males have had contact. Considering that most Indians live in rural areas and not in major cities, personal or near-personal contact between police and public would not appear to be large.

The data show that contact in urban areas is substantially greater than in rural ones. The explanation for this may be in part that at least two items definitive of socio-economic status, both of which correlate with urban living, are associated with frequency of contact. As income and education rise there is a greater amount of personal and near-personal contact with the police. Or, the lower the income and education of the respondent, the less likely he is to go to the police for help and to be questioned by the police. It seems reasonable that going for help would be more heavily associated with higher income and educational attainments, but it seems peculiar that being questioned by the police would be as well. It should be noted that the effect of higher

[11] The correlations are: for Bangalore, 0.33, N of 600; for Tumkur, 0.24, N of 598; for Kanpur residents, 0.56, N of 798; and for Kanpur rural migrants, 0.41, N of 305.

income or education on these two questionnaire items is not massive. From only 1 to 4 percent of the variance in contact items can be explained by these correlations. One should not make very much of this association as an explanatory hypothesis. One must also remember that income and education may influence the willingness of people to respond forthrightly in a survey interview. People with low income and education may be unwilling to admit even neutral involvement with the police.

At the same time the data show that lower status individuals in cities have greater contact with the police than people placed similarly in the social context in rural areas. (See Table 13.) Contact in cities is greater among all social strata. Urban living itself brings more frequent contacts with police.

One hypothesis underlying the public opinion survey was that contact with police and behavior patterns developed in relation to the police may affect attitudes toward government more generally and toward the rule of law in particular. While the police are instrumental in operationalizing the rule of law in the lives of most people, they are not the only agency which can affect attitudes toward law and government. It would be important to determine the proportion of contacts people have with policemen as opposed to contacts with bank employees, community development workers, clerks in license offices, health officials, and the staff of revenue agencies. The current survey unfortunately throws no light on the subject, since it deals exclusively with the police. Considering the burgeoning activities of welfare and development agencies it seems reasonable to suppose that the proportion of public contacts with the police has fallen relative to those with other agencies. The policeman no longer personifies government to the Indian citizen as much as he did before independence; other examples of government activity are now more readily available. The relative decline in the proportion of contacts with police has been offset to some extent by the expansion of police work itself. As we have seen, the police have not been unaffected by independence and the innovating determination of post-colonial leaders. However, frequency of contacts with officials of different kinds is only part of the story. Not all contacts possess the same value: two favorable experiences with the police may not equal two favorable ones with a postal inspector, nor does a single unpleasant experience at the hands of a sub-inspector have the same emotional impact as one with a health official. One needs to know about the weightage different

TABLE 13

CONTACT WITH POLICE ANALYZED BY EDUCATION AND INCOME

Questionnaire item	Bangalore (percent)	Tumkur (percent)	Kanpur residents (percent)	Kanpur rural migrants (percent)
I. Have you ever gone to the police for help?				
A. Education				
Illiterate	8.0	2.8	14.9	9.9
Literate	13.2	6.4	23.6	6.3
Under matric.	15.8	26.3	30.9	19.4
Matriculate	23.7	22.2	33.3	37.5
Intermediate	20.5	11.1	29.6	20.0
Graduate	27.3	33.3	28.6	33.3
Post-graduate	23.5	0.0	25.0	100.0
B. Monthly Income				
Under Rs. 75	9.1	2.9	12.9	7.7
76-150	13.8	12.0	23.9	12.1
151-300	18.8	6.2	25.6	15.2
301-500	19.2	13.3	30.9	44.0
501-750	33.3	0.0	41.7	0.0
751-1,000	33.3	0.0	33.3	100.0
Over Rs. 1,000	40.0	0.0	25.0	0.0
II. Have you ever been questioned by the police?				
A. Education				
Illiterate	8.0	3.4	24.2	17.0
Literate	8.8	10.9	27.8	13.9
Under matric.	9.2	15.8	34.6	35.5
Matriculate	11.8	44.4	40.0	31.2
Intermediate	19.3	22.2	33.3	20.0
Graduate	18.2	0.0	35.7	33.3
Post-graduate	11.8	0.0	35.7	0.0
B. Monthly Income				
Under Rs. 75	6.1	5.8	23.3	15.4
76-150	10.7	12.0	28.0	19.1
151-300	13.5	0.0	33.8	27.3
301-500	17.0	20.0	34.6	33.3
501-750	14.3	0.0	54.2	0.0
751-1,000	16.7	0.0	33.3	0.0
Over Rs. 1,000	0.0	0.0	0.0	0.0

contacts have with members of the public. Arguing a priori it seems reasonable to assume that contacts with police are potentially more serious than those with almost any other kind of officials —although this clearly depends upon the point at issue in any contact. Policemen deal in punishment and restraint, in security and protection. The threat of their office is palpable, their capacity for disruption very large. If, as a result, police contacts possess greater emotional weight, then even though members of the public are now presented with more non-police examples of official behavior, their contacts with police act like a ponderous flywheel upon the formation of new attitudes toward government, tending to force conformity to their own pulse and rhythm, overlaying and nullifying experiences with other officials.

The survey data show that the public has not had a great deal of experience with the police; they also show that the public does not appear to be reluctant to appeal to the police in situations of personal need or when an unusual, possibly criminal, event has occurred. Respondents were presented with a list of situations and were asked to tell in which of them they would or would not go to the police for help. The circumstances were the following: a child is lost; a person has been injured by an animal or in a fall; a friend is in danger of being attacked by goondas or *badmashes*;[12] a fight between two groups in the area is likely to break out; a house has been robbed of Rs. 100; a house has been robbed of valuables identifiable in the future; a man has been found beaten up; cattle have been stolen; a bicycle has been stolen; a person has been found killed accidentally; a person has been found who looks as if he had been murdered; a landlord is threatening eviction without good reason; a respondent is lost in a strange town or strange part of the country and needs directions. With only a few exceptions, less than 10 percent of the respondents said they would *not* go to the police in a given situation. The most consistent exception was when a person had been injured by an animal or in a fall. Approximately one out of every three respondents said they would not call upon the police in this circumstance. This finding probably does not indicate a reluctance to go to the police; it shows that respondents do not consider an injury a proper police matter. Rural persons in Tumkur were slightly, but consistently, more reluctant to go to the police than urban folk. Approximately 12 percent of them, as against

[12] A badmash is a hooligan or habitual criminal.

5 to 7 percent of urban people, said they would not go to the
police if a fight was likely to break out between two groups, a
house had been robbed of Rs. 100, or a person had been killed
accidentally. In Bangalore and Tumkur about one in four persons
said they would *not* go to the police if a man were found beaten
up. The percentage of Kanpur residents and rural migrants showing a similar reluctance was 9.8 percent and 21.1 percent, respectively. Bangalore and Tumkur respondents were also much
more loath to appeal to the police when a landlord threatened
eviction without good cause. People in Kanpur then, both permanent residents and rural migrants, appear to be more willing to
challenge the landlord by initiating police action. Some reluctance
was shown in every sample about asking police for directions in a
strange locale. The proportions showing hesitancy among Bangalore respondents, Kanpur residents, and Kanpur rural migrants
were under 15 percent in each case (8.8 percent, 14.4 percent,
and 13.1 percent, respectively), but among Tumkur people 27.2
percent said they would not ask directions from policemen if lost
in a strange part of the country. This confirms the view that rural
people tend more to avoid police if they have a choice.

In all the samples factor analysis generated a hesitancy-to-contact factor.[13] That is, unwillingness to appeal to the police for help
tends to show up on several items simultaneously. The factors
are quite clear, although the items that make them up may differ
from sample to sample. Examining the correlations between these
hesitancy-to-contact factors and background variables, one does
not find a significant pattern of association. Neither socio-economic status nor caste and religious affiliation affect willingness
to appeal to the police for help in the enumerated situations. As
we have seen, rural as against urban location does provide some
explanatory evidence.

Two other items in the survey elicited evidence that suggests
a much larger reluctance to go to the police for assistance even
when the personal need was great. Respondents were asked
whether "people, even when they need help, are generally reluctant to go to the police?" Except in Tumkur, at least three out
of five respondents thought that this was true. In Bangalore the
proportion was 64 percent, in Tumkur 29 percent, among Kanpur
residents 79 percent, and among Kanpur rural migrants 68 percent. There is a very large discrepancy between responses to

[13] Manipulation of the data shows that factor loadings of under 0.40 are
not stable. As a rule, I have noted only factor loadings above this threshold.

these items and the former responses with respect to public willingness to go to the police. There are perhaps two explanations
for the difference. First, accuracy of response may be affected
by whether a person is reporting about himself or about others.
Although even here the logic is ambiguous. On the one hand,
people may feel constrained to say that they would not fail to go
to the police in the situations enumerated. They then project their
hesitancy upon others. On the other hand, they may genuinely
misinterpret the amount of reluctance on the part of their neighbors. Second, the self-reporting survey questions are selective.
Hence, it is not inconsistent for the data to show that people
would not contact in *these* situations and yet still be substantially
reluctant to go to the police for help. My own view is that the
second question, about others' reluctance, provided the respondent with an opportunity to project his own hesitancy onto others.
Analysis shows that there is a modest correlation between this
item and responses to questions about police efficiency, treatment
of persons, honesty, and favoritism. With the exception of Tumkur, negative evaluations of the police were coupled with assessments of other people being generally reluctant to go to the police for help. In other words, the more negative a person's attitude
toward the police was, the greater reluctance he found in his
neighbors to go to the police. One's own reluctance to go to the
police for help would be affected by negative evaluations of
them but hardly one's estimation of another's reluctance *unless
projection was taking place.*

A partial bridge between the self-reporting items and the projective question was provided by another question. Respondents
were asked whether they knew of instances when offenses or
crimes had been committed but people had not reported them for
fear of getting involved with the police. Not more than 15 percent said that they did—or were willing to say that they did. If
these findings can be taken at face value, they would tend to show
that at least with respect to crimes, and within the personal knowledge of respondents, people are not much more reluctant to go
to the police than the self-reporting items indicated. Still, there is
a great difference between going unenthusiastically to the police
when a crime has been committed, perhaps because the police
will find out anyhow and silence would prove awkward, and
going immediately and trustingly to the police when a confusing
situation of personal need arises.

The survey items just discussed presented the respondent with rather concrete situations, often criminal, in which an appeal to the police for assistance could be considered natural. Respondents were later presented with another set of hypothetical situations in which there was a large element of discretion—that is, situations in which the individual himself would not be affected by whether he initiated contact with the police. These items allowed for a comparatively unalloyed test of the individual's sense of duty in giving aid to the police voluntarily. Respondents were asked three questions: (1) If you knew the police were coming around here asking questions and looking for information, would you try to avoid being questioned and having contact with them? (2) If a crime had been committed near here and you thought you knew something the police would want to know, would you go to them and tell them or would you wait for them to come around and ask you? and (3) for rural respondents, if there were dacoits camped near here, and you knew about it, would you go and inform the police? and, for urban respondents, if you came to know that a gang of goondas near here was going to commit a crime, would you inform the police? The amount of avoidance shown in answers to these questions was substantial. Generally, northern city dwellers show a greater reluctance to step forward with information than southern urban or rural people. Forty percent of Kanpur residents and rural migrants would avoid the police if they came around asking questions. Only 12 percent of south Indian respondents said they would do the same. When it came to volunteering information about a crime by seeking out the police, 12 percent of the Bangalore sample said they would not do so, but 40 percent of the Tumkur sample, 34.7 percent of the Kanpur resident sample, and 36.6 percent of the Kanpur rural migrant sample said they would not volunteer. These percentages suggest that rural people are less willing to go out of their way to provide information to police than urban people, but that in the north where there is substantial reluctance generally the differential between rural and urban people is less marked. When the threat was an immediate one in the respondent's vicinity, taking the form of a dacoit raid or goonda activity, reluctance to inform the police was shown by far fewer people.

It should be noted that responses to these questions do not indicate just a reluctance to become involved with the police. They also provide information about respondents' sense of civic duty.

It could be that promptings of conscience motivating people to step forward with information simply do not exist among these respondents. Rather than fearing to become involved, it does not occur to them that they should act in this fashion. These threads of motivation may be partially disentangled. All respondents were asked if they thought the common man had a duty to help the police by going to them with information about a crime if he had it. Except in the case of Tumkur, well over nine out of ten people agreed that the common man did have such a duty; and in the Tumkur case 88 percent of the sample agreed. While one may question the sincerity of these protestations, they do indicate that people know what they should be doing or what is expected of them. Unwillingness to step forward to render voluntary assistance to the police, as shown in these responses, is not then the fault of defective conscience but does indicate a powerful avoidance syndrome at work.

Reluctance to contact police is a peculiar attribute. It varies a great deal with circumstances, which is why care must be shown in operationalizing the concept. One might assume, for example, that because people do not relish contact with the police, especially in discretionary situations where they have nothing to gain by contact, they would show some dread of the possibility of more contact. This is not the case at all. Police officers often note, with mixed pride and irritation, that they are inundated with requests to establish new police stations in villages or town areas that do not have them. Villagers have been known to offer free accommodation to staff assigned to them. And they protest vigorously when a station or police outpost is removed to another locale.[14] The survey findings bear this out strikingly. When rural respondents were asked whether they wished a permanent police officer assigned to their village in place of the chowkidar, four out of five said they did. Only 19 percent expressed reservations. Contact, then, presents unpleasant prospects, but it also contains the promise of service. The same individual may be both repelled and attracted by the increased possibilities of contact with the police. Avoidance depends upon circumstances and is not an impregnable attitude carried into all aspects of police-public relationships.

[14] The Police Commission, 1902-1903, noted this as well. See p. 21 of their report.

Conclusion

Five points are worthy of recapitulation with respect to contact between police and public.

1. The range of contacts with the public is increasing, especially with the non-criminal public. At the same time, the frequency of public contacts with the police is probably decreasing relative to contacts with other agencies of government.

2. Defining contacts narrowly as a prolonged face-to-face relation in which one party has singled out the other in order to accomplish a specific purpose, contact between police and public is not very great. Approximately three out of every ten male adults in larger cities have had a personal or near-personal experience through being questioned or going to the police for aid, while only one in ten male adults in rural areas has had a similar experience.

3. Contact with the police, again defined in the more limited sense, tends to rise with education and income, although this relation is not demonstrated conclusively by the data. If generally true, this finding would partially explain the greater frequency of contact encountered in cities than in the countryside.

4. Generally people express a willingness to seek out the police when they encounter a situation which is unusual, criminal, or fraught with danger. Rural people seem to be slightly more hesitant than urban ones. In reporting other people's predispositions, however, without specifying the nature of the situation, two-thirds of the respondents thought that their neighbors hesitated to go to the police even when they needed help.

5. The Indian public is substantially unwilling to volunteer assistance, in the form of information, to the police. They would rather not become involved. Avoidance is significantly more apparent in the north than the south and in rural areas than in urban areas.

8 • *Public Perspectives on the Police*

IN GENERAL, the data obtained from the survey of the Indian public will be utilized to show, first, what the public thinks; second, what processes are involved in that thinking, in the sense of how various attitudes influence others and how experience affects attitudes; and, third, what the distribution of views and experiences is among different social strata and in different locations throughout the country. The present chapter will be devoted to the first of these tasks, namely, to describing the salient features of the public's view of the police. Some of these points will be discussed in greater detail in other chapters, when a particular facet of police activities is under extended scrutiny. The present chapter will also analyze the patterns that exist among attitudes of different kinds. Particular attention will be given to the basis in experience that individuals may have for holding specific opinions. The discussion of social, economic, and locational correlates of these basic patterns will be taken up in the succeeding chapter.

THE PUBLIC'S VIEW

Indians generally agree that the police do a pretty good job in catching criminals. With the exception of the Tumkur sample, about two-thirds of all respondents spoke up for the efficiency of the police in this regard. Only 37 percent of the Tumkur sample spoke favorably. The proportion of outright negative votes against police efficiency was of the same magnitude as in other samples.[1] Less enthusiasm was shown about whether police sincerely tried to help people who came to them in need. While one out of two people in Bangalore thought that the police did sincerely try to help, just over one in three felt this way in the other places. Moreover, the outright negative responses rose appreciably. Nearly one-third of Bangalore respondents answered no to this item,

---

[1] Tumkur, 20.7 percent; Bangalore, 12.7 percent; Kanpur residents, 28.4 percent; and Kanpur rural migrants, 20.9 percent. Eldersveld *et al.* found similar proportions of dissatisfaction in Delhi state. Of rural respondents, 24 percent, and of urban respondents, 36 percent thought the police were doing a poor job. *The Citizen and the Administrator in a Developing Democracy*, p. 30.

as did 50 percent of Kanpur residents and 38 percent among Kanpur rural migrants. The Tumkur negatives hardly increased from the previous item, indicating that rural folk may be more cautious in stating their views. What may be called northern skepticism about the police can be seen even more clearly in the answers to a question asked people who had gone to the police for help at some time or other. They were asked if they were satisified with what the police had done for them. In Bangalore and Tumkur, as many were satisfied as were dissatisfied. In Kanpur, however, nearly twice as many were forthrightly critical of what the police had done.[2]

City dwellers were asked about police efficiency in regulating traffic, especially in reducing the hazards for cyclists, motorists, and pedestrians. Most surprisingly, the police were given very high marks, even in the critical north. Not less than 75 percent in any sample gave the police a vote of confidence. At the same time, an equal proportion said they would like to see the police displaying greater initiative in tackling everyday unpleasant situations. Bangalore respondents, who showed a higher regard for police efficiency on other items than did Kanpur people, were somewhat more reluctant to have the police assume greater initiative. This would seem to indicate that the Kanpur respondents were not anti-police as such but quite genuinely thought police performance defective and were willing to see police activities increase if such a move promised tangible benefits.

Four questions in the survey were designed to show what expectations people had about the treatment that could be expected from the police by persons who came into their hands. The emphasis was upon the possibility of rudeness or physical mistreatment. Once again one can very clearly see that northerners have a more jaundiced view than southerners. Approximately half of all respondents say that police questioning will be conducted in a fair and courteous manner. Sixteen percent of Bangalore respondents and twelve percent of Tumkur respondents think that it will be rude and tricky. In Kanpur, on the other hand, a third of rural migrants and almost half of established urban dwellers think it will be rude and tricky. Asked specifically about whether the police often beat people up, the following proportions said that

[2] Of those people who had gone for help in each sample, the distribution between favorable and unfavorable was as follows: Bangalore, 53.4 percent favorable, 46.6 percent unfavorable; Tumkur, 58.4 percent and 41.6 percent; Kanpur residents, 34.6 percent and 65.2 percent; and Kanpur rural migrants, 41.6 percent and 58.4 percent.

they did: Kanpur residents, 35 percent; Kanpur rural migrants, 31 percent; Bangalore, 12 percent; and Tumkur, 7 percent. In order to determine whether people expected brutality to be shown to criminals or to everyone, respondents were asked whether persons taken to the police station, even those who were not criminals, were often threatened or beaten. Respondents could answer in various ways: by saying that the police threatened and beat everyone, that they threatened and beat only criminals, that respondents had heard other people say that police threatened and beat everyone, or simply that the police didn't threaten and beat anyone very often. Despite the discriminating range of options, a very significant proportion said that the police threatened and beat everyone they took to the police station. The proportions were: Kanpur residents, 49.8 percent; Kanpur rural migrants, 38.9 percent; Bangalore, 23.7 percent; and Tumkur, 19 percent. A substantial proportion of the rest had heard stories to this effect. It is evident, therefore, that the Indian public has very palpable doubts about the physical treatment they will receive at the hands of the police.

Asked to evaluate whether police treatment of people is getting better or worse, most people thought it was getting better. The Tumkur people were the least optimistic, even less so than Kanpur established residents. The proportions who thought police treatment of people was getting better were 72 percent in Bangalore, 54 percent among Kanpur residents, 49 percent among Kanpur rural migrants, and 31 percent among Tumkur respondents. Tumkur residents were also the most forthrightly pessimistic; 21 percent said treatment was getting worse, compared with 8 percent who said this in Bangalore, 15 percent among Kanpur residents, and 10 percent among Kanpur rural migrants.

In almost any country suspicion about the police touches upon the subject of corruption.[3] Respondents were asked how much corruption they thought there was in the police. At least a fourth of every sample, and sometimes as many as half, thought there was a "great deal." Another quarter to a third of each sample thought there was "some." Suspicion was once again most intense in the north. Asked specifically whether a bribe was necessary in order to get the police to do their duty, over a third of all respondents thought so. In Kanpur fully 74 percent of established

[3] See Chapter 11 for a full discussion of this topic.

urban residents thought so and 64 percent of the rural migrants agreed. Most revealing of all, when people were asked whether they would themselves take money with them if they had occasion to go to the police for help, so as to assure obtaining the assistance asked for, the proportions of yes responses were as follows: Kanpur residents, 39 percent; Kanpur rural migrants, 38.6 percent; Tumkur, 26.5 percent; and Bangalore, 11 percent. To be sure, a larger proportion in every sample said forthrightly they would not stoop to bribery, but the size of the proportion indicating they would, since it indicates venality on the subject's part, is so considerable as to allow very little doubt that the Indian public entertains few illusions about the honesty of policemen and of the possibility of extortion.

Perhaps even more indicative of the damaged state of regard for the police in India are the answers to a question about whether respondents thought policemen joined hands with criminals. In Kanpur about one-fourth of all respondents thought that the police often did so. In Tumkur about 10 percent thought so, and in Bangalore 6 percent. Another substantial proportion thought it happened sometimes—as opposed to rarely or never. (Kanpur residents, 40.8 percent; Kanpur rural migrants, 35.3 percent; Bangalore, 30.2 percent; and Tumkur, 13.3 percent.)

The charge of favoritism in the discharge of duties is a common one against policemen. Indeed, unequal treatment by government servants of all kinds is very often suspected and very easily believed by people in many countries. Indians are no exception. Almost a third of Bangalore respondents, one-fourth of Tumkur's, and over one-half of Kanpur's thought the police did show favoritism. Favoritism may mean different things to different people. That it in part means unequal treatment to Indian respondents is borne out by another question which asked if there were groups in society which the police treated worse than others. The yes responses were 15 percent in Bangalore, 1 percent in Tumkur, 40 percent among Kanpur residents, and 36 percent among Kanpur rural migrants. The group that most people had in mind in answering this item was lower-class individuals, especially those who plied a street trade. Respondents singled out the poor generally, then coolies, laborers, rickshaw drivers, beggars, pavement dwellers, and servants. In rural Tumkur the survey showed that some people believe the police take sides among village factions. Holding this opinion were 8 percent of the Tumkur respondents.

Respondents were asked specifically about political control of the police, and were asked to estimate its extent. The numbers of people in each sample who thought there was a great deal of political control were about the same as those who thought the police showed favoritism (Kanpur residents, 57.8 percent; Kanpur rural migrants, 45.4 percent; Bangalore, 39.2 percent—up 10 percent from the favoritism question; and Tumkur, 20.8 percent). Asked pointedly whether the police took sides in elections, a much smaller proportion said they did (Kanpur residents, 21 percent; Kanpur migrants, 14 percent; Bangalore, 13 percent; and Tumkur, 6 percent).

The survey results demonstrate forcefully what many close observers of police-public relations in India have long thought, namely, that the Indian public is deeply suspicious of the activities of the police. A considerable proportion expect the police to be rude, brutal, corrupt, sometimes in collusion with criminals, and very frequently dealing unevenly with their clients.

Toward the end of each interview respondents were asked to name the most important thing the police could do to improve their relations with the public. Although from one-third to three-fourths of respondents, depending on the sample, offered no opinions, among those that did three items cropped up again and again. Foremost, police were urged to be courteous and sympathetic. Then it was suggested that they be honest, not take bribes, and that they more faithfully discharge the duties set them.

It should be noted that people's perceptions of others' predispositions toward the police—or at least what they are willing to attribute to others—are not as negative as what they reveal themselves. Respondents were asked to characterize the attitude of people of the area toward the police, and were provided with the categories "friendly," "cooperative," "indifferent," "suspicious," "uncooperative," and "hostile." The results are summarized in Table 14. Respondents find a good deal less suspicion and more cooperation among their neighbors than they showed themselves to be capable of.

On the basis of the data collected in this survey, the opinion of the Law Commission, 1958, is confirmed: "It must be conceded that in India, the police force as a whole is not, even today, regarded as a friend of the citizen."[4] The Indian people doubt very seriously the honesty, propriety, and integrity of their police. Such a lack of trust would not tend to encourage contact with the police.

[4] Chapter 34, para. 36.

TABLE 14

ATTITUDES OF OTHERS TOWARD THE POLICE

Question Number 103: How would you characterize the attitude of people living in this area (village) toward the police?	Area and Percentage of Residents			
	Bangalore	Tumkur	Kanpur residents	Kanpur rural migrants
Friendly	37.2	28.3	5.4	3.6
Cooperative	27.8	35.5	29.4	30.4
Indifferent	13.0	12.5	20.2	14.0
Suspicious	4.2	10.7	18.2	14.4
Uncooperative	2.8	0.3	9.4	8.8
Hostile	0.8	0.3	0.4	0.03

This situation is not, however, unique to India. Professors Almond and Verba found in their study of attitudes toward administrators in Italy and Mexico that "a general pattern of corruption, discrimination, and unresponsiveness" characterized relations respondents believed existed between bureaucrats, especially the police, and the citizen.[5] Few American observers would expect an overwhelming vote of confidence in the police in their own country. They would be surprised if distrust were very far below the surface. Even in Great Britain, with its paragon police force, all is not entirely well. A survey undertaken on behalf of the Royal Commission on the Police found that as many as 10 percent of the people thought the police took bribes either fairly often or very often, that they used unfair methods to get information, that they distorted evidence in courts, and on occasion used too much force.[6] Suspicion of the police may very well be worldwide. Its magnitude and forms may be critically different from country to country, however, and may reveal a great deal about the relations between rulers and ruled. Precise comparisons need urgently to be made; they must await public opinion data from many nations. So far, the surface has barely been scratched.

Despite the unfavorable opinions widely held about the police and the quantity of unfavorable experiences encountered, few Indians have ever lodged a formal complaint. Kanpur residents were the greatest complainers, although even there the proportion was only 3.6 percent of the total sample. A somewhat larger per-

[5] Gabriel A. Almond and Sidney Verba, *The Civic Culture* (Boston: Little, Brown and Co., 1965), p. 77.

[6] *Appendix IV to the Minutes of Evidence*, p. 16.

centage indicated that they had wanted to complain but had been deterred from doing so because they didn't think it would do any good. The proportions were 9.2 percent in Bangalore; 6.9 percent among Kanpur residents; 3.6 percent among Kanpur rural migrants; and 3.3 percent in Tumkur. The most prevalent cause cited for wanting to complain was unfair treatment and rude behavior. Almost as important were suspected corruption and collusion with criminals. It would appear that Indians not only distrust their police but they don't believe they can do anything about it or that anyone whom they might contact is capable of doing anything about it. Suspicion coupled with apathetic resignation present a bleak picture.

PATTERNS OF EXPERIENCE AND ATTITUDE

The attitudes that people have toward the police are of many kinds and cover a wide variety of behavior. There is no such thing as a person's "attitude toward the police." It is quite possible for an individual to think the police highly efficient yet rude and brutal in method. Or an individual may think the police honest to a fault in matters of money and yet wholly dominated by political control. It is crucial to distinguish among attitudes toward the police. Having done so, one may then seek to discover if certain kinds of attitudes tend to cluster together. For example, if a person doubts police honesty is he more or less likely to feel a keen sense of duty about rendering assistance to the police? If patterns can be discovered among perspectives, it may be possible to determine how attitudes are formed and what would be required to change the basic orientation of an individual toward the police. It is also critically important to determine the effect which experience has upon perspectives. Does the person who has had no contact with the police have attitudes similar to those of the person who has? The public opinion survey was designed with certain patterns in mind, both among attitudes and between attitudes and experience. In this section the data will be analyzed to see whether several rather common hypotheses about experiences and attitudes are serviceable.

The survey was designed to investigate the relationships among four attitudinal sets and two kinds of experience. The attitudinal dimensions were: (1) an individual's sense of security in person and property; (2) his expectations about police behavior; (3) his sense of duty toward the police; and (4) his knowledge of the police. "Police behavior"—point two—is a complicated category involving police treatment of persons, especially physical treatment, and honesty, criminality, and favoritism. Experiences with the police have been separated into two kinds: sheer contact, or neutral contact as it has been referred to earlier, and unpleasant contact in which the respondent was himself witness to an improper police action. For it is important to determine not just whether an unpleasant experience biases a person's evaluation of the police but whether any contact whatsoever has an impact upon perspectives.

The analysis that follows seeks to find patterns of association among different kinds of survey responses, but without reference to background variables. The purpose is to discover what kinds of responses associate together, and perhaps to suggest reasons for this. At the same time it must be recognized that any explanation of patterns of association which overlooks background variables is oversimplified. The reason two variables seem to associate closely together may sometimes be traced to a third factor having to do with education, class conditioning, or occupational perspectives.

In evaluating the propriety of police behavior, do people discriminate among kinds of activities or do they tend to be either positive or negative across the board? If a person thinks that the police mistreat suspects is he more or less likely to believe that police are corrupt or that they are inefficient or in collusion with criminals? Examining police activities under the headings of treatment of individuals, corruption and collusion with criminals, favoritism, and efficiency, the data show that there is a strong tendency for positive (or negative) evaluations to be associated together whatever the aspect of police behavior. In each of the four samples, factor analysis generated a single factor with heavy loadings among many, usually most, of the relevant "evaluation" variables. (See Table 15.) Among Kanpur residents, for example, those persons who believed the police were corrupt or in collusion with criminals were also apt to expect unpleasant treatment from the police in the form of rudeness or physical abuse and to think that police efficiency left much to be desired. In the case of Tumkur, the factor was defined positively: that is, if a person held a favorable view of the police with respect to corruption, he was apt to think the police efficient and that they rarely mistreated people. The data strongly suggest, therefore,

TABLE 15

FACTOR ANALYSIS: THE CLUSTERING OF NEGATIVE EVALUATIONS OF POLICE BEHAVIOR*

Variable number	Questionnaire item	Bangalore factor	Tumkur	Kanpur residents	Kanpur rural migrants
61	Is police questioning courteous and fair or rude and tricky?	—	−0.32	0.34	—
74	Do police beat everyone, even non-criminals, who come to police station?	—	—	0.45	0.35
79	Do police often beat people up?	0.60	0.41	−0.60	−0.69
75	Is bribery necessary to get police to act?	0.69	0.71	−0.52	−0.48
78	Would you take money for bribing if you had to make a request of the police?	0.33	0.73	−0.46	−0.56
86	How much corruption is there in police?	0.80	0.74	−0.69	−0.74
90	How much collusion between police and criminals?	0.71	0.80	−0.64	−0.60
83	Do police show favoritism?	0.67	—	−0.37	−0.45
84	Do police treat some groups worse than others?	0.45	—	—	—
93	Is there much political control of police?	0.48	0.66	—	—
95	Do police take sides in elections?	0.49	—	—	—
96	Do police side with village factions?	—	—	—	—
36	Do police do a good job in traffic regulation?	—	—	—	—
39	Do police do a good job in catching criminals?	—	−0.56	—	—
54	Do police sincerely try to help?	—	−0.61	—	—

* *Note*: The Bangalore and Tumkur factors are defined positively. That is, they represent favorable evaluations of police behavior. The Kanpur factors are defined negatively, representing unfavorable evaluations. This explains the difference in plus and minus signs.

that belief in one kind of malpractice disposes people to believe in malpractices of other kinds.

The survey shows that it is fair to speak of public predispositions in evaluating police behavior generally, just as it is fair to speak of public predispositions in evaluating a particular aspect of police behavior such as honesty, efficiency, or treatment of persons.

Security in one's person and material possessions is one of the most basic requirements of human life. It is highly prized, although like the well that runs dry, usually only after it is lost. Since the police are preeminently charged with ensuring security, it is reasonable to suppose that anxiety about security might color an individual's view of police activity, most certainly with respect to their efficiency. Data presented in Chapter 4 showed that most people do not have pronounced anxieties about their safety; somewhat less than a third of all respondents indicated fear for the safety of themselves or their possessions. The evidence for linkage between security-insecurity and evaluations of police behavior is present but it is not very strong. In none of the samples did the security-insecurity dimensions generated in factor analysis contain significant loadings with any of the evaluative items, not even those items dealing with perceptions of police efficiency.[7] By and large, one would have to conclude that feelings of insecurity do not affect evaluations of the police, not even with respect to how well they do their job—although the Kanpur resident sample is a modest exception. Anxiety about one's safety does not seem to be associated with police performance.

What effect has contact of any kind with the police upon a person's evaluations of police behavior? If a person is thrown together with the police, whether in seeking help or in being questioned, is he more or less likely to regard them favorably than the person who has had no contact? Can one say that the sheer fact of contact produces any effect upon evaluative attitudes? The survey data fail to indicate any significant relation between contact and attitudes. Factor analysis does not generate any factors defined primarily in terms of contact and evaluative variables. A table of correlations among these variables provides barely

[7] In the analysis of Kanpur residents' data, the security factor did have a loading of 0.26 with the item asking whether respondents thought the police did a good job in catching criminals. Here alone, those who were insecure thought the police did a poor job in catching criminals.

meaningful hints that contact with police, either personally or through a personal acquaintance, does dispose people to view police less favorably than otherwise. For example, among Kanpur residents and rural migrants there is an association between going to the police for help and not regarding them as being very efficient in catching criminals (0.28 and 0.21 respectively). There is also a fairly stable—but not very important (0.25 or less)—relation between being questioned and regarding police unfavorably with respect to their treatment of people, their honesty, and their impartiality. There is a persistent hint (0.25 to 0.30) that there is a relation between personal or near-personal contact and belief that there is a good deal of political control of the police. The most likely explanation for this relationship is that people with experience of being questioned suddenly become sensitized to police activities in criminal investigations. Since a considerable segment of Indian public opinion believes political control to be real, it is natural for people to hear police machinations attributed to political influence. Being questioned, or having a friend questioned, is an event of importance in people's lives and would probably become a short-run preoccupation. Their interest would serve to introduce them to rather commonly held explanations of why police do as they do.

Considering the weakness of the correlations, one concludes that there is only a very slight tendency for contact per se to be associated with negative evaluations of police behavior.

People who have gone to the police for help or have been questioned by them are much more likely than others to have witnessed an improper police action of some kind. In the two Kanpur samples, factors were generated combining neutral contact and unpleasant contact items. That is, people who had not had contacts tended not to have seen improper police actions; people who had contacts tended to have seen unpleasant police behavior. This pattern was not as apparent in the south Indian data, although it did exist. In Bangalore particularly there were consistent correlations between having been questioned, or having had a friend questioned, and having seen the police strike someone, threaten someone, or take money. The correlations were between 0.20 and 0.30. One can say, therefore, that people who have had any contact are more likely to have had unpleasant contact.

The proportions of respondents in each sample who have had personal or near-personal experience with an unpleasant police action are shown in Table 16. The most common unpleasant scene

TABLE 16

PROPORTIONS OF PEOPLE IN ALL SAMPLES WHO
HAVE HAD UNPLEASANT CONTACT WITH THE POLICE

Variable number	Questionnaire item	Bangalore % Yes	Tumkur % Yes	Kanpur residents % Yes	Kanpur rural migrants % Yes
77	Do you know people personally who gave money to the police before receiving the help they expected?	7.0	7.5	27.0	14.7
80	Have you ever seen the police strike someone?	22.2	3.2	43.4	22.2
81	Do you know anyone personally who has been threatened by a policeman?	13.5	3.2	24.0	13.1
82	Do you know anyone personally who has been struck by a policeman?	9.3	1.3	22.2	12.1
87	Have you ever seen the police take money?	26.7	6.5	24.0	13.4

witnessed is a policeman striking someone. The next most common is having personally seen the police take money as a bribe. Unpleasant contact is much greater in the north than the south and much greater among urban than rural people. These differences will be analyzed further in the next chapter.

The effect of unpleasant personal experience upon evaluations of the police is less ambiguous than the effect of contact per se: people who have had an unpleasant experience are more likely to hold unfavorable views. It is interesting to note that people with one kind of experience of police impropriety are much more likely to have had another of a different kind of malpractice. The factor analysis shows clearly that if a person has had a negative experience of police intimidation or physical abuse he, or an acquaintance, is more likely to have been witness to the police demanding or taking money in the form of a bribe. (See Table 17.) There are perhaps two reasons for this. First, people who have had negative experiences also have had more contact of any kind with the police. They have had more opportunity to observe, and consequently if malpractices exist they will have been so placed as to see them. Second, it is possible that having witnessed one kind of misconduct raises the individual's suspicions concerning whatever the police do. Being convinced that the police did something improper in one instance, they may be more willing to interpret other behavior in a severe way. Whatever the explanation, the fact remains that people are likely to have experienced

TABLE 17

FACTOR ANALYSIS: NEGATIVE PERSONAL EXPERIENCE WITH POLICE

Variable number	Questionnaire item	Bangalore factor a	Bangalore factor b	Tumkur factor	Kanpur residents factor	Kanpur rural migrants factor
56	Ever gone to the police for help?	—	0.68	—	0.30	0.39
62	Ever been questioned?	—	0.76	—	0.69	0.64
64	Know anyone personally who has been questioned?	—	0.50	—	0.66	0.58
80	Ever seen the police strike somebody?	−0.59	—	−0.41	0.26	—
81	Know anyone personally who has been threatened by the police?	−0.72	—	−0.43	0.79	0.81
82	Know personally anyone who has been struck by police?	−0.73	—	—	0.76	0.78
77	Know personally anyone who had to give money to police before they agreed to act?	—	—	—	0.43	—
87	Ever seen the police take money?	−0.51	—	−0.30	0.55	0.56

either no instances of misconduct or several of different kinds.

Respondents were asked about three kinds of unpleasant personal experiences with the police: their manner of questioning, the use of intimidation or physical abuse, and a bribe transaction. The analysis shows a quite significant relation between experiences of each of these kinds and the corresponding evaluative attitude. That is, if a person experienced rudeness in being questioned, he tends to believe that all police questioning is rude and discourteous. Similarly, if a person has not experienced police intimidation, he tends to doubt that police engage in intimidation. In all samples the relation between holding an unfavorable view of the manner of police questioning is very significantly related to having experienced rude treatment either personally or by a personal acquaintance (correlations between 0.57 and 0.75). People who have personal experience of police threats or beating are more disposed than those who have not to believe that the police frequently beat people (correlations about 0.30). The relation between experience of this kind and a belief that police beat even non-criminals taken to the police station is less evident. Similarly, people who have seen the police take money are more willing to believe in a substantial amount of corruption in the police, to believe that bribery is necessary, and to take money to a police station when they have occasion to make a request (correlations from 0.13 to 0.32 depending on the sample). Respondents were also asked if they knew of instances when people known personally to them had been asked for a gratuity by the police before taking action. The correlations between this item and attitudes about corruption were either insignificant or too fragmentary to base any conclusions upon.

The survey findings bear out the expectations of common sense that people will generalize from their own personal experience. If their experience has been bad, they will interpret unfavorably. They are more likely to have favorable opinions about the police if they have not personally been a witness to police misconduct. It also follows that a single instance of police misconduct may bias a whole range of attitudes toward the police. We have already seen that evaluations of police behavior of various kinds—such as mistreatment, dishonesty, partiality, and inefficiency—tend to cluster together. Thus, if a person is given cause to doubt the police in one area of activity, he is not only likely to generalize from that one instance to others but from that one kind of experience to others involving other forms of misconduct. When it comes to creating opinions about a group of individuals or an organization, a single unhappy experience will offset a large number of favorable ones.

The factor analysis shows that items dealing with a respondent's willingness to cooperate with the police do tend to cluster in their variation. Although the duty items are sometimes mixed with others, they had significant loadings on the same factor. For example, a person who would not avoid the police if they came around asking questions is not likely to refrain from going to the police with information about a crime if he has it. One might cynically say that a respondent who says the common man has a duty to help the police is at least intelligent enough to see that he must say he would inform the police about the presence of a dacoit band or a possible goonda affray.

It should be noted that what precisely these items measure is not clear. On the one hand, they may be measuring an individual's sense of duty or, on the other, they may be measuring his willingness to have anything to do with the police. This was discussed in the previous chapter, where we also saw that there was a substantial reluctance to volunteer information to the police about criminal events.

Granting that a posture of willingness to help the police is defined in the data, to what extent is it associated with certain kinds of experience with the police and with evaluative attitudes of police behavior? The analysis fails to show any significant relation between duty items and neutral contact. Willingness to contact or sense of duty is independent of contact with the police. What is more, it does not appear to be related to unpleasant experience with the police either.[8] This latter finding is somewhat surprising. One might have thought that a person who had seen the police strike someone or who had a friend threatened would be more reluctant to volunteer help to the police than those who had not.

Having found that actual experience with the police is unassociated with whether an individual is likely to assist the police as a normal citizen might, it is worthwhile determining whether there may be a relation between willingness to assist and an individual's general evaluation of police behavior. One might hypothesize that a person expecting the police to maltreat people, to be corrupt, or to be in collusion with criminals would not willingly become involved with them. On the other hand, one might argue with equal plausibility than an undeveloped sense of duty with respect to agencies of social regulation is associated with a deep suspiciousness toward these agencies, and hence rather than negative evaluations underlying a spoken unwillingness to assist, they are simply part of a general lack of identification with, indeed a suspicion of, these impersonal agencies. The direction of cause and effect, if any, is unclear.

The statistical analysis did not show any significant relation between evaluations of police behavior—with respect to efficiency, treatment of persons, corruption, collusion, and favoritism—and the readiness of respondents to assist the police. One would have to conclude that the survey has failed to show persuasive evidence that people who evaluate police behavior unfavorably are apt to be more unwilling to lend assistance to the police. It must be stressed once again that what people say they will do and what they will in fact do may be very different.

[8] Significant correlations were scattered and were generally not greater than 0.15.

An interview situation may easily put an individual on his mettle.

People may differ a great deal with respect to their cognitive knowledge of the police and their personal acquaintance with members of it. Public relations experts sometimes suggest that if people could get to know government functionaries, could penetrate through the role to the personality behind it, their feelings would be much more generous toward them. It has also been suggested that negative feelings toward government personnel go hand in hand with meager knowledge about them. The person, therefore, who reacts in a reflexively hostile or suspicious manner to the police is also likely to be a person who possesses little knowledge of them, especially the kind of knowledge required to approach them and to make demands upon them successfully. These hypotheses may also be turned around. Unfavorable evaluations of the police may contribute to the failure to develop personal contacts with the police or to develop knowledge of them and of the manner in which one might approach them for one's own ends. Several items in the survey did provide an indication both of people's personal recognition of policemen and their cognitive knowledge of elementary facts about them.

The measures of personal recognition of policemen and knowledge about them might be contaminated by a respondent's having been himself in the police or having a close relation on the force. Respondents were asked about both these matters. Out of a total of 2,400 male respondents only twelve had been members of the police. The percentage in any sample was never larger than 1 percent.[9] The number of respondents with a relation in the police was never more than 9 percent (Kanpur residents) and generally under 7 percent. Neither variable was significantly loaded on recognition or knowledge factors. Nor were there significant and stable correlations between these items and respondents' evaluation of police efficiency, treatment of people, honesty, and evenhandedness. If personal recognition of policemen and cognitive knowledge about them is significantly related to other important variables in this survey, the relationship is unalloyed with police occupational involvement.

The factor of personal recognition of policemen was defined by two questions: Would you recognize on sight some of the policemen of this area? and, Do you know any policemen by name?

[9] It was exactly 1 percent in Bangalore and among Kanpur residents. It was 0.33 percent in Tumkur and 0.33 percent among Kanpur rural migrants.

Elementary knowledge of the police was provided in these questions: What is the salary of a police constable? What is the title of the top police officer of the district? and, In which town is the office of the top district police officer located?

Generally more than half the respondents in each sample said they would not recognize any policemen of their area on sight: Bangalore, 57.5 percent; Tumkur, 61.7 percent; Kanpur residents, 47.6 percent; Kanpur rural migrants, 59.2 percent. One might have expected recognition of policemen to be greater in rural than urban areas. The visit of a policeman is surely more notable and the personnel less varied in villages than in cities. The data show, however, slightly less recognition in Tumkur than elsewhere. Similarly Kanpur rural migrants recognize fewer policemen than their established urban brethren. The vast majority of respondents know no policeman by name. Once again the proportion of negative responses was largest in the rural area and among rural migrants. Ten percent of Tumkur respondents knew a policeman by name; about 20 percent in Bangalore and Kanpur did. Kanpur rural migrants knew more policemen by name than Tumkur respondents but less than established urban dwellers.

A surprisingly large number of people were able to give the salary of a police constable correctly (34.8 percent in Bangalore; 5.2 percent in Tumkur; 26.4 percent among Kanpur residents; and 21.9 percent among Kanpur rural migrants). What is even more surprising, in every sample fewer people knew the title of the top police officer of the district than knew the salary of a constable. In Bangalore, 96.3 percent did not know his title, in Tumkur 84.5 percent, among Kanpur residents 59.8 percent, and among Kanpur rural migrants, 68 percent.[10] In effect, there is more confusion about the title of the superintendent of police than about the economic straits of the lowest ranking police officer. Not only was ignorance about his title very great, but very few people knew in which town his office was. In south India four out of five respondents did not know where to go and to whom to go at district level to appeal against the actions of a local police official. This finding casts serious doubt on the adequacy of any departmental grievance machinery. Contrary to the opinions of many superintendents, who believe people will bring complaints freely to them, the mass of the people may not even know the superintendent exists, let alone where to go to contact him. Among Kan-

---

[10] The Bangalore figure is suspiciously out of line. One suspects an interviewing error.

pur residents, by contrast, only one in five respondents did not know the location of the top officer's office. A very large percentage—more than half—did not know his title, however. Kanpur rural migrants were less knowledgeable than their established urban neighbors but not as unaware as people in Bangalore. Three out of five of them did not know the superintendent's title; and two out of five did not know where his office was. It is hard to believe that people failing to possess even elementary information of this kind will be very confident about their ability to approach higher authority for redress of grievance at the hands of local officers.

A low score in recognizing policemen is strongly associated with an absence of personal or near-personal experience with the police. In every sample except Tumkur one factor shows up that is defined in terms of no recognition and no personal contact of any sort. (See Table 18.)

Turning attention to the relation between recognition and knowledge, on the one hand, and general evaluations of the police, on the other, analysis shows that involvement with the police —whether personal or cognitive—tends to be associated slightly with unfavorable views. That is, the person who does recognize some policemen on sight, who does know some by name, and who does know a policeman's salary, the title of the district's top officer, or the location of the top officer's office, this person is more likely to hold unfavorable views of the police. The correlations are weak, however, generally not over 0.25. Therefore, it would be rash to conclude that unfavorable judgments are importantly determined by familiarity with policemen and by accurate knowledge of them. Nonetheless, if there is some relation between judgments and recognition-knowledge, the data show that familiarity breeds contempt and unfavorable views of the police are more apt to be found with an individual who has accurate knowledge of the police.

Part of the explanation for the association between unfavorable evaluations and recognition is that people who recognize policemen are more apt to have had contact with the police, both neutral and unpleasant contact. The correlations fluctuate around 0.25. We have already seen that contact, especially unpleasant contact, biases evaluations against the police. People who have had contact are, therefore, both more likely to have unfavorable views and more likely to recognize policemen of their area. Cor-

TABLE 18

FACTOR ANALYSIS: NO CONTACT AND NO RECOGNITION

Variable number		Bangalore factor #6	Tumkur	Kanpur residents factor #1	Kanpur rural migrants factor #2
56	Have you ever gone to the police for help?	—		0.30	0.39
62	Have you ever been questioned by the police?	—		0.69	0.64
64	Do you know anyone personally who has been questioned by the police?	—		0.66	0.58
77	Do you know personally anyone who gave money to police before they were willing to respond?	—		0.43	—
80	Have you ever seen a policeman strike someone?	−0.59		0.26	—
81	Do you know personally anyone threatened by a policeman?	−0.72		0.79	0.81
82	Do you know personally anyone struck by a policeman?	−0.73		0.76	0.78
83	Do the police show favoritism?			0.22	—
84	Do police treat some groups worse than others?	−0.54		—	—
87	Have you ever seen the police take money?	−0.51		0.55	0.56
105	Ever participated in a demonstration?	−0.56		—	—
121	Would you recognize some policemen of this area on sight?	−0.33		0.50	0.39
122	Do you know any policemen by name?	−0.57		0.52	0.45

relations between knowledge and contact are for the most part insignificant or very unimportant.

Analysis revealed an interesting relationship between knowledge and sense of duty. Accurate knowledge tends to be associated with a high sense of duty. The man who is more willing voluntarily to assist the police is more likely to know something about them. Among Kanpur residents, for example, a factor was generated which was defined in terms of a very low sense of duty and lack of correct knowledge about the police. Inspection of the correlation matrix shows a similar tendency for Tumkur and Kanpur migrants. The Bangalore correlations are either insignificant or mixed. The data suggest, therefore, that a low sense of moral involvement with the police is associated with low cognitive involvement as well. Can one go so far as to say that a person who is disengaged from an issue morally will probably be so cognitively as well? Certainly people fail to attend to matters they feel are of no concern to them. Which, however, is primary—knowledge or moral involvement? Does knowledge follow after moral attention or does moral involvement follow a rise in knowledge? This fascinating and perplexing issue cannot be resolved here. Suffice it to say that the Indian data do show an association.

There is, of course, another explanation. Both duty and knowledge are positively associated with education and income. Rather than the two dimensions interrelating, they may both be responding to another set of independent variables.

CONCLUSION

The survey data reveal a profound public distrust of the police, especially with respect to their honesty and their impartiality. The familiar observation of public officials, scholars, and policemen themselves that the police are suspected of many kinds of improprieties is clearly borne out. People's evaluations of police behavior tend to be favorable or unfavorable across the board. If they suspect police honesty, they suspect the manner in which police treat people. If they think the police engage in favoritism, they are likely to believe the police are corrupt. The data also show that unfavorable evaluations of police behavior are associated with personal or near-personal experiences. Moreover, because unpleasant experiences are associated slightly with contact of any kind, contact is somewhat more likely than not to affect evaluations of the police negatively. The survey data show what many public officials know intuitively, namely, that one unpleasant experience with a government agency or employee may bias an individual against a whole gamut of behavior; it will predispose him not to give officials the benefit of the doubt.

The data fail to show that unpleasant experiences with the police affect a person's willingness to assist them in preventing crime. These results may be flawed, however, because the survey items on which the conclusion is based were projective, indicating not what people do but what they say they will do. People may pretend to a higher standard of rectitude than they ever reach in practice. The data also fail to show that negative evaluations of police behavior are associated with a lowered sense of duty. Even people who are very critical of the police are apt to articulate a high standard of duty with respect to being willing to assist them as a citizen might.

Less than half the public recognizes policemen personally; they do not recognize them on sight nor do they know their names. Contrary to expectations, impersonality is greater in the rural areas. Lack of knowledge of the police, especially about the title of the district's top police officer, is enormous. In south India, for example, four out of five people did not know in which town his office was located. In the north, respondents' orientation was better—only one out of five did not know where the office was. The data cast serious doubt on the ability of people to appeal to senior district officers over the heads of local policemen who may be guilty of improper actions.

The data show a strong no-contact, no-recognition dimension. For the majority of people the police are faceless and nameless creatures with whom they have never had any contact. Their opinions, it follows, must be wholly derived from the community's storehouse of common knowledge.

People who recognize policemen by face or name tend to share more negative opinions of police behavior than do those who do not. The relation is particularly strong with respect to a belief in police partiality. Familiarity may well breed contempt. People who recognize policemen personally are also more likely to have had contact with police. This contact is also more likely than not to have predisposed them against the police. The evidence linking knowledge and evaluations is fragmentary and mixed; there is only a suggestion that people who know more about the police tend to have more favorable views of them, unlike the effect of recognition. The data also suggest, although not conclusively, that a low sense of moral involvement with police affairs is associated with low cognitive involvement. People who know very little about the police are not apt to have a high sense of a citizen's obligation to render them assistance.

$\mathcal{9}$ • *Determinants of Public Perspectives*

IN THE previous chapter we discovered what patterns of association existed among experiences and attitudes for respondents of the various samples. It was found to be possible to speculate with some profit about the reasons for some of these associations. The analysis was limited, however, because the distribution of experiences and attitudes among different social strata had not been taken into account. The present chapter will remedy that defect. The analysis will attempt to discover the relations between crucial social variables—such as age, education, occupation, income, caste, and religion—and responses about the police. It will also attempt to measure the extent of differences in responses among the four samples and to determine whether location or social background makes the difference.

SOCIAL PLACEMENT AND PUBLIC PERSPECTIVES

Tables 19-22 present a social profile of respondents in each sample with respect to age, education, occupation, income, caste, and religion.[1] There is a serious omission with respect to caste. Caste data were not obtained for the two southern samples. Conclusions about the effects of caste will be limited therefore to the north Indian urban situation.

[1] The representativeness of the samples, using 1961 census data as the basis for comparison, was remarkable. For example, the Bangalore sample produced exactly the same proportion of Hindus, Muslims, and Christians as the 1961 Census. In Tumkur the survey sample showed the same relative proportions as the Census but slightly understated the proportion of Muslims (1.67 percent survey as opposed to 4.3 percent Census). The proportion of literates in the survey samples in Kanpur and Bangalore agreed with the 1961 Census. The proportions of Hindus and Muslims in the Kanpur samples agreed almost exactly with the Census. That is, the rural migrant proportions reflected the religious composition of rural Uttar Pradesh, while the urban residents' sample reflected the Kanpur Census totals. Similarly with the proportion of scheduled castes in the Kanpur samples: they agreed very closely with the 1961 Census. For example, the Census shows that 19.8 percent of Kanpur district's males belonged to scheduled castes; the survey produced a figure for Kanpur city of 24.3 percent. The Census proportion for Uttar Pradesh as a whole, among males, was 20 percent. On the basis of the Census and survey items amenable to comparison, analysis creates a strong presumption in favor of the representativeness of the survey samples.

Analysis reveals important differences in the composition of the samples.[2] For example, between Bangalore and Tumkur—the rural and urban samples in the south—there are significant differences with respect to age, education, occupation, income, and religion.[3] The differences are especially marked for education, oc-

TABLE 19

BANGALORE: SAMPLE COMPOSITION BY AGE, EDUCATION, OCCUPATION, INCOME, AND RELIGION

I.	Age	*Percentage*
	Under 20	0.67
	21-30	25.0
	31-40	31.0
	41-50	24.7
	Over 50	18.5
II.	*Education*	
	Illiterate	18.8
	Literate	26.5
	Under-matriculate	12.7
	Matriculate	15.5
	Intermediate	13.8
	Graduate	9.2
	Post-graduate	2.8
III.	*Occupation*	
	Professions, owner cultivators, government officials, and businessmen	9.3
	Retail traders, students, self-employed	18.2
	Artisans, skilled workers	47.5
	Unskilled workers, non-owner cultivators, agricultural laborers	15.5
	Retired, unemployed	8.3
IV.	*Income*	
	Under Rs. 75	11.0
	75-150	37.5
	151-300	32.0
	301-500	7.8
	501-750	3.5
	751-1,000	1.0
	Over 1,000	0.83
V.	*Religion*	
	Hindu	83.7
	Muslim	10.8
	Christian	4.7
	Sikh	0.0

[2] In order to test for significant differences I have employed a t-test supplemented by a chi-square test for proportions for dichotomous variables.
[3] These are all significant at the 1 percent level.

cupation, and income, as one might have expected. People in Bangalore tend to be more highly educated and to have higher incomes than people in Tumkur. Similarly, one finds a higher proportion of respondents who are government servants, business executives, and members of professions in the Bangalore sample. Comparing the urban north and the urban south (Kanpur and Bangalore) one finds significant differences at the 1 percent level

TABLE 20

TUMKUR: SAMPLE COMPOSITION BY AGE, EDUCATION, OCCUPATION, INCOME, AND RELIGION

I.	Age	Percentage
	Under 20	0.0
	21-30	15.3
	31-40	24.2
	41-50	30.3
	Over 50	30.2
II.	Education	
	Illiterate	59.3
	Literate	33.7
	Under-matriculate	3.2
	Matriculate	1.5
	Intermediate	1.5
	Graduate	0.5
	Post-graduate	0.2
III.	Occupation	
	Professions, owner cultivators, government officials and businessmen	86.0
	Retail traders, students, self-employed	0.7
	Artisans, skilled workers	2.3
	Unskilled workers, non-owner cultivators, agricultural laborers	11.0
	Retired, unemployed	0.0
IV.	Income	
	Under Rs. 75	69.0
	75-150	20.8
	151-300	2.7
	301-500	2.5
	501-750	0.0
	751-1,000	0.0
	Over 1,000	1.2
V.	Religion	
	Hindu	96.3
	Muslim	1.7
	Christian	0.0
	Sikh	0.0

TABLE 21

KANPUR RESIDENTS: COMPOSITION BY AGE, EDUCATION,
OCCUPATION, INCOME, CASTE, AND RELIGION

		Percentage
I.	*Age*	
	Under 20	0.5
	21-30	33.2
	31-40	28.2
	41-50	17.4
	Over 50	18.8
II.	*Education*	
	Illiterate	26.9
	Literate	20.1
	Under-matriculate	20.2
	Matriculate	9.4
	Intermediate	3.4
	Graduate	5.2
	Post-graduate	3.5
III.	*Occupation*	
	Professions, owner cultivators, government officials, and businessmen	4.5
	Retail traders, students, self-employed	27.1
	Artisans, skilled workers	49.0
	Unskilled workers, non-owner cultivators, agricultural laborers	12.8
	Retired, unemployed	5.1
IV.	*Income*	
	Under Rs. 75	14.5
	75-150	51.9
	151-300	16.6
	301-500	6.9
	501-750	3.0
	751-1,000	1.1
	Over 1,000	0.5
V.	*Caste*	
	Scheduled castes	20.5
	Jat, Ahir, Yadav	2.2
	Rajput	6.1
	Vaish (Banya, Gupta, Aggarwal, Marwari)	7.4
	Kayastha/Khatri	13.6
	Brahmin	17.8
VI.	*Religion*	
	Hindu	69.4
	Muslim	27.6
	Christian	1.0
	Sikh	1.2

TABLE 22

KANPUR RURAL MIGRANTS: COMPOSITION BY AGE, EDUCATION,
OCCUPATION, INCOME, CASTE, AND RELIGION

		Percentage
I.	*Age*	
	Under 20	0.33
	21-30	37.2
	31-40	28.1
	41-50	15.4
	Over 50	17.6
II.	*Education*	
	Illiterate	54.2
	Literate	25.8
	Under-matriculate	10.1
	Matriculate	5.2
	Intermediate	1.6
	Graduate	1.0
	Post-graduate	0.3
III.	*Occupation*	
	Professions, owner cultivators, government officials, and businessmen	2.6
	Retail traders, students, self-employed	12.1
	Artisans, skilled workers	45.8
	Unskilled workers, non-owner cultivators, agricultural laborers	37.6
	Retired, unemployed	2.0
IV.	*Income*	
	Under Rs. 75	31.0
	75-150	51.3
	151-300	10.8
	301-500	2.9
	501-750	0.3
	751-1,000	0.3
	Over 1,000	0.3
V.	*Caste*	
	Scheduled castes	37.9
	Jat, Ahir, Yadav	5.6
	Rajput	4.9
	Vaish (Banya, Gupta, Aggarwal, Marwari)	6.2
	Kayastha/Khatri	8.2
	Brahmin	19.0
VI.	*Religion*	
	Hindu	84.9
	Muslim	12.4
	Christian	0.3
	Sikh	2.3

for education, income, and religion. The samples are not different with respect to age and occupation. Educational levels are lower in Kanpur than in Bangalore, as are income levels. The proportion of Muslims is significantly larger in Kanpur, while the Christian population is greater in Bangalore. Comparing the samples within Kanpur—established urban residents and rural migrants—there are significant differences in social composition with respect to education, occupation, income, caste, and religion.[4] Educational attainments, incomes, and occupational status are all higher among Kanpur residents than among rural migrants. Lower castes bulk larger among rural migrants than among urban residents, suggesting that the lure of the cities is greatest among lower caste individuals unhappy with their lot in a rural setting. Hindus and Muslims migrate to Kanpur in proportion to their numbers in rural Uttar Pradesh. However, because Kanpur is more Muslim than the surrounding rural areas, the proportion of Hindus among migrants is greater than among the resident urban population.

Whether or not an individual has had contact of some kind with the police seems to be a function of education, income, and to a lesser extent occupation. Analysis of the survey data showed that in all samples the higher the education the more apt the respondent was to have gone to the police for help, to have been questioned by them, or to have had a personal acquaintance questioned. It is also true that people with more education are more apt to have witnessed the police strike someone or to have had a friend threatened or struck. The association between unpleasant contact and education is probably a matter of logical dependency with neutral contact. The greater contact there is with the police, the greater the likelihood of seeing something disagreeable. It should be noted that although the relation between education and contact is clear, it is not terribly strong. The correlations are never over 0.30, meaning that less than 10 percent of the variation in the contact items can be associated with changes in education.

[4] These are all significant at the 1 percent level. It is instructive to note that the differences between the two Kanpur samples were less great than between the rural-urban samples in the south but greater than the differences between the urban north and the urban south. Extent of difference is measured by the number of characteristics which are significantly different. This would indicate that rural-urban differentials are greater than north-south differentials whether among rural or urban groups. People in cities north and south tend to be more similar to one another than they are to people in surrounding rural areas and to the people who move from those areas to the cities.

The evidence does suggest, however, that more highly educated people are both more apt to call upon the police for assistance as well as more likely to be contacted by the police in turn when information is required.

Another interpretation is possible as well. It may be that more highly educated people are less reluctant to admit to contact with the police. This might especially be the case when it comes to answering whether they have had some unpleasant contact with police. There is little question that the higher the education of respondents, as well as the higher the income and occupational status, the more willing they are to venture opinions and answer questions. The proportion of "Don't know" responses is greater among lower classes. By and large the proportions of "Don't know's" for each education or income category are the same between samples. When there is a difference, rural respondents tend to be the more unknowing. Rural residence intensifies the reticence of lower status respondents. The presentation of opinions and factual answers is more likely the higher the education and income of the respondent. The possibility cannot be dismissed, therefore, that the somewhat greater contact shown among educated people may not be a real difference but simply indicates a greater degree of forthrightness. This important caveat is relevant throughout the discussion whenever class is found correlative with presence of an experience or the holding of an attitude.

In all samples, although to a lesser extent in Tumkur, higher incomes and contact with police, both neutral and unpleasant, are associated. The very poor have less contact than others. The correlation is, once again, quite plain but not very important. It accounts for hardly more than 5 percent of the variance in the contact items. Occupational status is also positively associated with contact, at the same levels of importance.

There is no indication that age is associated with contact with police, whether contact is neutral or pleasant. Nor, moreover, do the data show any relation between the religion of respondents and contact. Whether one is a Hindu or a Muslim or a Christian or a Sikh makes no difference as far as the amount of contact they experience with police is concerned. Caste, however, may be related although the association does not appear to be great. The Kanpur data—both resident and migrant—show that the higher the caste the greater the amount of neutral contact. At the same time it should be observed that caste is strongly correlated with both education and income.[5] Thus contact with the police is related both to caste and class, at least in the north, but neither may be wholly independent variables.

Factor analysis generated a strong "willingness-to-contact" factor in all samples. This factor was composed of responses to hypothetical questions dealing with situations in which the respondent would or would not go to the police for assistance. The evidence for linkage between this factor and parameters of social change is weak. In all the samples loadings were either very small or not statistically significant. Respondents, regardless of social position, appear to share the same norms about when help is to be expected from the police.

One of the most important contributions a survey of Indian opinion could make about the police would be to explore whether evaluations of police behavior vary with social position. That is, do unfavorable evaluations of how police treat people or of their honesty and their impartiality change with social class, caste, or religion? The factor analysis has already shown that in each sample, evaluations of several aspects of police behavior tend to cluster together. Quite unambiguous factors were generated which were defined in terms of respondents' views of police efficiency, treatment of persons, honesty, or favoritism. The conclusion was that attitudes tend to be consistent with one another; that an individual is unlikely to have a favorable view of the manner in which police handle questioning and an unfavorable view of their honesty, and so forth. Policemen themselves accept almost as an axiom that people of higher class tend to view police more unfavorably than others. This is the stock explanation of why opinion about police seems to be more vociferously negative in urban areas. The educated man with high income who may often belong to a profession is commonly considered to be the most critical. Is this in fact the case?

The data indicate that it may be, but that the significance of social position has been overrated. Examining the results of the factor analysis, one finds significant loadings for variables of social placement on evaluative factors only in the case of Bangalore. But even these loadings, though statistically significant, are very slight, accounting for about 4 percent of factor variance. The data show that negative evaluations tend to be associated with

---

[5] Among residents caste correlates with education 0.41 (N of 539) and with income 0.37 (N of 510); among rural migrants, with education 0.41 (N of 245) and with income 0.30 (N of 243).

youth, higher incomes, advanced occupations, and greater education. Unfortunately, only one sample shows consistent
associations.[6]

*The conclusion is that age, education, occupation, income,
caste, or religion are not associated importantly with the attitudes
people hold about police efficiency, treatment of persons, honesty,
or evenhandedness.* If one also accepts the plausible view that
people of higher social position are conscious of their rights,
poised in their relations with authority, and forthright in their
opinions, then the failure to discover a consistent and important
pattern of relationship is doubly surprising. The survey casts serious doubts on the proposition that the most advanced segments
of Indian society tend to view the police with the most jaundiced
eye.

Respondents were given several opportunities to show what
their reading was of other people's attitudes toward the police.
The presumption was that though people might be reluctant to
reveal their own views, they would not be reluctant to tell what
others around them were thinking. Accordingly, respondents were
asked at different times (1) if they thought others were reluctant
to go to the police even when they needed help, (2) if they knew
of instances when offenses had been committed but were unreported because of fear of involvement and (3) whether they
would characterize the attitude of people living in their areas as
friendly, cooperative, indifferent, suspicious, uncooperative, or
hostile. Analysis of the answers to these items fails to produce
more than fragmentary evidence of an association between evaluations of the police and social position. Age, caste, and religion
show no meaningful correlations whatsoever. Education, occupation, and income do show some small correlations but they are
fragmentary. Except for Tumkur the correlations are consistent,
hinting that the higher the education, occupational status, or
income the more likely the respondent is to believe people reluctant to appeal for help that is needed and to know of instances
when offenses were not reported for fear of getting involved. So
slight are these correlations that one cannot conclude that background plays an important role in structuring opinion. Whether
a respondent is giving information about his own attitudes or

---

[6] Inspecting the correlation matrix upon which the factor analysis was
based, one finds some hints of association but very little persuasive evidence
of consistent linkage. What feeble correlations there are support accepted
opinion, namely, that the higher the class the lower the evaluation of police
activity.

about those of others, social class and caste do not affect the results.

The readiness of people to lend assistance to the forces of law enforcement may importantly affect the success that these forces have in fulfilling their function and the manner in which they proceed. In a developing nation especially, where the pre-eminent goal of government policy is raising education and income levels, discovery of a relation between these parameters and duty might have an important bearing on the pattern of civil government in the future. In the two Kanpur samples, factor analysis defined a dimension having to do with respondents' articulated sense of duty. The only important background loading was for education, and it was only 0.20 for Kanpur residents and 0.18 for rural migrants. Correlation analysis shows, too, that of all the background factors education is more consistently associated. One must conclude that education and worldly progress are not likely to contribute to the development of a more substantial sense of duty.

Social placement seems definitely to be related to personal recognition and knowledge of the police. Education and income are the most highly correlative elements. Personal recognition and knowledge both increase with education and income. The correlations among these items are the highest that the survey generated between background and survey items.[7] As one would expect, the relation is especially strong between education and knowledge of the police. Kanpur data also show that caste status is related to recognition-knowledge. Low-caste people are less likely to be familiar with policemen or to know much about them. The results support a common expectation: familiarity with the personnel of government and knowledge of government agencies increases with social status.

Summing up the results of analysis, can one say that variables dealing with social position play an important role in structuring public opinion or public experiences? The answer would have to be no. While there are some hints, the patterns are not so distinct as to indicate that social placement can be counted on to affect attitudes and experiences markedly. The exception to this generalization is the effect education has upon recognition and knowledge of the police. Neither age nor religion account for any differences whatsoever. Caste, education, income, and oc-

---

[7] About the 0.30 level generally.

cupation may have effects but they are slight. They cannot be considered important independent variables. Caste may be faintly related to frequency of contact; it is also marginally related to a high sense of duty and to amounts of recognition and knowledge. Education is related to contact, sense of duty, and recognition-knowledge. So is income. Occupational status—an awkward variable since the same scale had to be used for both rural and urban areas—may be related to contact but is only marginally related to sense of duty. The most important conclusion is that social placement does not appear to affect an individual's evaluation of the quality or rectitude of police behavior. This is contrary to accepted opinion. The potential importance of this finding will be discussed in the next section when an attempt is made to explain differences in experience and attitude among the four samples.

The Effects of Environment

The survey operation was designed to provide information that would be useful in testing two hypotheses about the structure of attitudes toward the police: (1) that important differences in attitudes, as well as experiences, exist between rural and urban areas, and (2) that length of urban residence affects attitudes held or experiences encountered. The rural-urban contrast that was made was a south Indian one, involving two areas in Mysore —urban Bangalore and rural Tumkur district. The effect of urban experience upon attitudes was tested in a north Indian city—the city of Kanpur.[8] Out of 400 migrants, 306 of them proved to be from rural areas, neither from major cities nor even large towns. If the sampling was representative, about 52.9 percent of all Kanpur inhabitants have come from outside the city and about 25 percent of all Kanpur inhabitants have migrated to Kanpur from rural areas.[9]

[8] See Appendix A for a discussion of sampling techniques in each area.

[9] A survey of Kanpur in the mid-1950's produced somewhat different results. There, 70 percent of all heads of families were found to be migrants. D. N. Majumdar, *Social Contours of an Industrial City* (Bombay: Asia Publishing House, 1960), p. 69. It is possible, of course, that the rate of migration is greater among heads of households than among all males generally. A more likely explanation for the discrepancy is that migration has declined since 1950. There is evidence for this. Majumdar, *ibid.*; Donald J. Bogue and K. C. Zachariah, "Urbanization and Migration in India," *India's Urban Future*, ed. Roy Turner (Berkeley: University of California Press, 1962), p. 31; and *U.S. Army Area Handbook for India* (Washing-

In the discussion that follows I shall seek to describe the important differences in attitude and experience between rural and urban people and among people with varying lengths of urban experience and to attempt to discover whether significant differences are the result of different social characteristics of each population or unique locational factors having to do with environment. Samples will be compared with respect to the following characteristics: perceptions of personal security; contact with the police; evaluations of police efficiency, police treatment of persons, police honesty, and impartiality; citizens' sense of duty in assisting the police; personal recognition of policemen; and elementary knowledge about the police.

Rural and urban people differ significantly about whether they think it safe to keep valuables in their homes, to travel at night in the immediate area, and to have a firearm for protection. Respondents did not differ between samples in their overall assessments of the security of their areas or with respect to how safe they thought travel at night was outside their immediate vicinity. Urban residents were more fearful than rural people about the safety of money and jewelry kept in their homes. Urban people were also more anxious to possess a firearm. Urban people were more secure, however, traveling about their immediate vicinity at night. Police officials seem to be right then when they deplore the lack of the "banking habit" among rural people, suggesting that were this habit to develop, theft in rural areas would be less of a problem. It would appear that not only many rural people distrust banking institutions but they do not perceive their need to the same extent as urban folk. Anxiety in urban areas attaches to possessions, possibly to physical injury, but is not connected with freedom of movement in the immediate vicinity. Rural people are concerned about movement at night, reflecting that such movement at night is much less common in a rural locale.

The question which then arises is whether these differences are

---

ton: Government Printing Office, 1964), p. 81. However, that migration had declined so substantially as to produce a difference of 25 percent in ten years seems unlikely, though not impossible. Results from the earlier survey agree with mine about the proportion of migrants that come from rural areas. They found 76 percent had come from rural areas, I found 75 percent. In short, it would seem that the proportion of migrants to total urban population has declined in the decade 1955-1965 but that the proportion of migrants from rural areas to total migrants has remained the same. It would follow that the rural component of Kanpur's population has also declined during this period.

due to location, that is, the results perhaps of environment—or environment-specific attitudes—or due to differences in the social composition of each sample. For example, we have already seen that incomes are higher in the urban area, and it could be that people in the urban area are more fearful about keeping valuables in their houses because they have more of them, because they have more to lose. This does not in fact seem to be the case. If level of income were a controlling factor, one would expect that in both urban and rural areas a higher proportion of upper income people would be anxious about the safety of valuables kept in their homes. Moreover, they would be anxious to the same degree in each sample. If, on the other hand, location was a controlling factor, one would find that the same income groups in each sample differed from one another in the extent of their anxiety. Analysis shows that people in the highest income group—earning over Rs. 1,000 per month—in Bangalore are substantially more anxious about the safety of valuables in their houses than are their counterparts in Tumkur. Indeed, in all but one of the seven income groups this is the case. Fewer even of the very lowest-income individuals expressed confidence about the security of valuables at home in Bangalore than in Tumkur. The conclusion would be that urban people are less secure in their personal property precisely because they are in an urban environment and not because they differ from rural folk in social background and especially in income.

Between rural migrants and residents in an urban area (Kanpur) there were meaningful differences in responses on all security items, although on three of the seven items the level of significance approaches 5 percent. Analyzing all migrants—whatever the size of the community they came from—the data show that the larger the community the greater the respondent's security anxiety. The Kanpur data conform with south Indian results, namely, that urban people are more fearful than rural ones. The data do not show how quickly rural migrants to urban communities take on the fears of their urban brethren. Although a question was asked about how long the migrant had lived in Kanpur, there are no meaningful correlations between this item and any of the security questions. It would appear that rural migrants never become quite as anxious as their urban counterparts. The children of rural migrants, however, raised entirely in the city, will have all the fears and trepidations of established urban residents. It should be reiterated that less than 20 percent of any sample express anxiety on the security questions. The vast majority of Indians, wherever they live, are not particularly fearful for the safety of their persons or property.

The survey results show very clearly that urban people have more contact with the police than rural people. They go for help more often, they have more personal experience with being questioned, and they have more often been witness to the police abusing someone or accepting money as a gratuity. The rate of neutral contact with the police is about twice as high in Bangalore as in Tumkur. There is a greater difference between rural and urban areas with respect to unpleasant contact than neutral contact. About four times as many urban people as rural people have had personal experience with an unpleasant police action. It is quite possible of course that this differential is due to greater reluctance to admit of such experiences among rural respondents. Urban residents have significantly more contact of all kinds with the police than rural migrants. The data also show that the size of the community from which migrants have come is correlative with the amount of contact they have had with police. Clearly, urban living produces much more contact with police, both in terms of neutral contacts and having seen the police do something unpleasant or improper.

Since contact is not greatly associated with social background, the greater frequency of contact in cities and among lifetime urban residents must be a function of location and not of differences in social background. This conclusion is borne out by inspection of the amount of contact experienced by people in the same income and educational categories in rural and urban areas. (See Table 23.) As with perceptions of security, contact is a function of urban situation. Unfortunately caste data were not available for the south, thus preventing a test of the effect of that variable. Data on the religion of respondents were gathered, and analysis shows that religion is not a determinant of the amount of contact. People of the same religion responded substantially differently between the rural and urban area. Caste data for Kanpur residents and rural migrants do show that caste members responded to contact items very differently. (See Table 24.) Environment, not social background, conditions the amount of contact people experience.

Turning to the evaluations people make of police activity, the survey shows quite substantial differences between urban and rural areas. Generally Bangalore respondents were much more

TABLE 23

RESPONSES TO CONTACT QUESTIONS DISTRIBUTED BY EDUCATION, INCOME AND RELIGION

	56				62				64			
	Bangalore		Tumkur		Bangalore		Tumkur		Bangalore		Tumkur	
	Yes	No	Yes	No	Yes	No	Yes	No	Yes	No	Yes	No
	%	%	%	%	%	%	%	%	%	%	%	%
Education												
Illiterate	7.9	92.0	2.8	96.6	8.0	92.0	3.4	96.6	6.2	93.8	4.5	95.5
Literate	13.2	86.8	6.4	93.0	8.8	91.2	10.9	89.1	8.8	91.2	6.9	92.1
Under-matriculate	15.8	82.9	26.3	73.7	9.2	90.8	15.8	84.2	6.6	93.4	10.5	89.5
Matriculate	23.7	76.3	22.2	77.8	11.8	88.2	44.4	55.6	8.6	91.4	22.2	77.8
Intermediate	20.5	79.5	11.1	88.9	19.3	80.7	22.2	77.8	12.0	88.0	0	100.0
Graduate	27.3	72.7	33.3	66.7	18.2	81.8	0	100.0	14.6	85.4	0	100.0
Post-graduate	23.5	76.5	0	100.0	11.8	88.2	0	100.0	23.5	76.5	0	100.0
Income												
Rs. 75	9.1	90.9	2.9	96.6	6.1	93.9	5.8	94.2	3.0	97.0	3.9	95.9
75-150	13.8	86.2	12.0	87.2	10.7	89.3	12.0	88.0	7.1	92.9	11.2	88.0
151-300	18.8	80.7	6.2	93.8	13.5	86.5	0	100.0	12.0	88.0	12.5	87.5
301-500	19.2	80.8	13.3	86.7	17.0	83.0	20.0	80.0	14.9	85.1	13.3	86.7
501-750	33.3	66.7	0	0	14.3	85.7	0	0	23.8	76.2	0	0
751-1,000	33.3	66.7	0	0	16.7	83.3	0	0	16.7	83.3	0	0
Over 1,000	40.0	60.0	0	100.0	0	100.0	0	100.0	0	100.0	0	100.0
Religion												
Hindu	17.2	82.6	5.4	94.2	12.2	87.8	7.1	92.9	10.0	89.9	5.8	93.9
Muslim	15.4	84.6	0	90.0	9.2	90.8	10.0	90.0	7.7	92.3	0	100.0

KEY: 56   Have you ever gone to the police for help?
       62   Have you ever been questioned by the police?
       64   Do you know anyone personally who has been questioned by the police?

TABLE 23 (Cont'd)

Education	80 Bangalore Yes	80 Bangalore No	80 Tumkur Yes	80 Tumkur No	81 Bangalore Yes	81 Bangalore No	81 Tumkur Yes	81 Tumkur No	82 Bangalore Yes	82 Bangalore No	82 Tumkur Yes	82 Tumkur No
	%	%	%	%	%	%	%	%	%	%	%	%
Illiterate	18.6	81.4	2.2	97.5	8.9	91.2	2.5	97.2	6.2	98.8	1.1	98.9
Literate	16.4	83.0	3.5	96.5	10.0	90.0	4.0	96.0	6.9	93.1	1.5	98.5
Under-matriculate	15.8	81.6	15.8	84.2	9.2	90.8	0	100.0	7.9	92.1	0	100.0
Matriculate	28.0	72.0	0	100.0	15.0	85.0	11.1	88.9	10.8	89.3	0	100.0
Intermediate	25.3	74.7	0	100.0	18.0	82.0	11.1	88.9	15.7	84.3	11.1	88.9
Graduate	32.7	67.3	33.3	66.7	23.6	76.4	0	100.0	14.6	85.4	0	100.0
Post-graduate	41.2	58.8	0	100.0	23.5	76.5	0	100.0	5.9	94.1	0	100.0
Income												
Rs. 75	10.6	89.4	1.9	97.8	7.6	92.4	2.7	97.1	1.5	98.5	1.2	98.8
75-150	18.2	80.4	5.6	94.4	9.3	90.7	4.0	96.0	7.1	92.9	1.6	98.4
151-300	27.6	72.4	12.5	87.5	16.7	83.3	0	100.0	13.5	86.5	0	100.0
301-500	25.5	74.5	6.7	93.3	14.9	85.1	0	100.0	8.5	91.5	0	100.0
501-750	33.3	66.7	0	0	38.1	61.9	0	0	14.3	85.7	0	0
751-1,000	66.7	33.3	0	0	50.0	50.0	0	0	50.0	50.0	0	0
Over 1,000	20.0	80.0	0	100.0	0	100.0	14.3	85.7	0	100.0	14.3	85.7
Religion												
Hindu	21.9	77.5	3.2	96.6	12.6	87.4	3.22	96.6	8.7	91.3	1.4	98.6
Muslim	26.2	73.8	0	100.0	16.9	83.1	0	100.0	9.2	90.8	0	100.0

KEY: 80   Have you ever seen a policeman strike someone?
       81   Know anyone personally who has been threatened by a policeman?
       82   Know anyone personally who has been struck by a policeman?

TABLE 24

Responses to Contact Questions Distributed by Caste in the Kanpur Samples

Caste	56		62		64		80		81		82	
	Resi-dents	Mi-grants	Resi-dents	Mi-grants	Resi-dents	Mi-grants	Resi-dents	Mi-grants	Resi-dents	Mi-grants	Resi-dents	Mi-grants
	%	%	%	%	%	%	%	%	%	%	%	%
Scheduled castes	22.5	11.0	26.2	18.0	20.1	16.3	43.9	18.0	23.8	12.8	22.6	11.0
Jat, Ahir, Yadav	38.9	5.9	22.2	5.9	38.9	5.9	44.4	11.8	22.2	5.9	22.2	0.0
Rajput	18.4	0.0	28.6	13.3	26.5	20.0	40.8	33.3	18.4	13.3	20.4	20.0
Vaish	20.4	21.0	25.4	15.8	35.6	10.5	49.2	31.6	20.3	15.8	15.2	5.3
Kayastha/Khatri	27.5	8.0	33.0	16.0	36.7	16.0	46.8	32.0	28.4	8.0	26.6	4.0
Brahmin	34.5	19.0	45.1	29.3	33.1	22.4	40.1	27.6	31.7	17.2	28.2	22.4

harsh in their judgments of the police than respondents in Tumkur. At the same time, they gave the police higher marks for ability to catch criminals than did respondents in Tumkur. They also were more likely to think that police treatment of people was improving. It should be noted that the samples did not differ concerning the manner of questioning or the extent of police collusion with criminals. Urban residents were markedly less charitable in their judgments about police corruption, the need to bribe, favoritism and discrimination, political control of the police, and police taking sides at election times. Urban residents were also much more willing to say they would yield to the necessity for bribery and would themselves ensure the assistance needed by taking money to the police station if they had need to go. The urban residents found much greater reluctance among their neighbors to go to the police in time of need; they also knew of more offenses that were not reported for fear of getting involved.

Differences on evaluative items between urban residents and rural migrants were less marked than between rural-urban people. In only four of the seventeen items did significant differences at the 1 percent level show up between residents and migrants. Three more were significant at the 2 to 3 percent level. In each of these instances the residents were more negative. They were more doubtful about the sincerity of police responses, they found the manner of questioning more often rude and tricky, they thought non-criminals were more often beaten, and they believed corruption in the police to be more extensive.

Why should urban people be less favorable in their judgments than rural people? One reason is that they have had more unpleasant contact with the police, and unpleasant contact produces negative evaluations. Are there other factors at work as well? Social background does not seem to make a difference. It has already been shown that age, education, occupation, income, caste, and religion are not importantly associated with the evaluations people make. Therefore, one cannot argue that because urban respondents as a group rank higher on the scales of education, income, and occupation, urban evaluations tend to be harsher. Examining the responses of people in the same categories for age, education, income, and religion, one finds urban people consistently answer differently than their rural counterparts. It may be that environment itself makes a critical difference. While the greater amount of contact with police in cities is undoubtedly a factor, there may be an urban climate of opinion toward the police which is much less favorable than the climate of opinion found in rural areas. Readiness not only to think unfavorably but readiness to articulate the disdain may well be a characteristic feature of urban life.

If this hypothesis is correct, one would expect length of urban residence to affect evaluative judgments. The longer the rural migrant was in the city, the less charitable would become his opinions. This does not happen to be the case. There are statistically significant correlations between length of urban residence and only four of the evaluative items. In these four cases, the expected relationship is reversed. That is, it is the most recently arrived migrants who have the harshest opinions. The correlations are not great—being around 0.25, or accounting for about 4 percent of the variance—but they are consistent. I cannot explain this anomaly, and cite the facts so as to indicate the complexity of the phenomenon. It is quite clear that urban residents make harsher judgments than rural people or rural migrants. But the way in which migrants are socialized to the urban environment remains obscure.[10]

With respect to sense of duty the survey shows a marked difference between rural and urban areas. Bangalore residents are much quicker to recognize the principle that the common man has a duty to give information to the police. Bangalore residents also appear vastly more willing to go unprompted to the police with information about a crime that has been committed. At the same time, the data show no difference between samples with respect

[10] My findings differ somewhat from those of Eldersveld *et al.* We agree (a) that hostility—as they call it—toward administration is greater in rural areas and (b) that lower status groups are more reluctant to venture an oral evaluation of official performance. *The Citizen and the Administrator in a Developing Society*, pp. 37-38. But we disagree about the effect that high social position has upon evaluative attitudes. They found that ". . . in the urban areas, among upper caste members and the educated, one finds the greatest hostility to administrators, while among rural illiterates one finds the least hostility" (pp. 136-137). "The suggestion implicit in these findings is that improvement in social status is accompanied by increased hostility toward the administrative system, that there is a tendency to criticize public authority as a person moved from his traditional depressed social status toward more enlightenment, higher income, and more exposure to 'modernization' influence" (p. 58). Certainly my study, strictly limited to the police, does not show that social status alone is the critical factor. Environment—perhaps what they refer to as "modernization" influence— seems to be. With respect to the police, I find that urbanization will bring a higher level of articulated hostility and criticism, but not that improvement in living standards or social status will do so.

whether respondents would avoid the police if they came around asking questions. Rural people, in comparison with urban respondents, will not go out of their way to help the police but neither will they go out of their way to avoid contact initiated by the police.

Between urban residents and migrants from rural areas there were no significant differences with respect to sense of duty. Since this contrast was made in the north and the rural-urban contrast was made in the south, the lack of difference between residents and rural migrants may indicate that views about duty are more homogeneous in the north between rural and urban areas.

With respect to personal recognition of policemen as well as knowledge about the police, urban people score higher than rural people on both counts, as do established urban dwellers in comparison to rural migrants. There is one exception. A much larger proportion of rural residents know the title of the top police officer of the district. Since urban living is associated with impersonality, it is curious that more urban respondents than rural ones recognized police of their area on sight and knew some of them by name. It may in fact be that the policeman is an occasional, almost faceless intruder in most villages while in the city he is a regular feature of the landscape, like the postal clerk, the chemist, or the *pan* vendor. At the same time, it has already been demonstrated that both income and education are correlative with recognition and knowledge. At least in part, therefore, recognition and knowledge are greater in cities because of the difference in social composition of the population.

Summing up the analysis, one may say that with respect to experience of the police and attitudes toward them there are substantial differences between rural hinterlands and major urban centers. Differences are less great between established urban residents and rural migrants. Length of residence in a particular urban area is not nearly as important as the kind of community environment the migrant comes from. Migrants from villages are more different from urban residents in their attitudes than migrants from other large cities or even medium-size towns. They are closer to sharing the rural point of view. With respect to the evaluative judgments people make of the police there does seem to be an "urban attitude," an attitude characterized by suspicion. This attitude is not correlated with social background; it would appear to be something learned from urban experience. In part it is a product of increased contact with the police, especially negative contact, which urban people encounter. Sense of duty, personal recognition of policemen, and knowledge about them are all higher in the city, a fact which is explainable in terms of higher educational attainments and income levels in the city. Urban folk are less secure in their personal property than rural people. This disposition seems to be an urban attachment but, unlike the tendency to negative judgments about the police, is probably not learned in the urban environment. It is a latent attitude activated by contact with the urban milieu. Either everyone knows that cities are more hostile or cities immediately appear more hostile, for rural people migrating to cities adopt the anxieties of their urban brethren upon initial contact.

Many people, and certainly many policemen, believe that southerners are quite different from northerners in their attitudes toward the police. Southerners are often described as more docile, less pugnacious, easier to get on with, and less disputatious. Many policemen say they are much less suspicious of the police as well as more cooperative. The survey data allow these propositions to be tested, although only with respect to northern and southern urban environments.

Thirty-eight items in the survey pertain to the following crucial aspects of experience or attitude: sense of security, contact with the police, police efficiency, police treatment of people, police corruption, collusion, favoritism, respondent's assessment of neighbors' attitudes, sense of duty, personal recognition of policemen, and knowledge of police. Thirty-three of these items are significantly different at better than the 1 percent level between the northern and southern cities. Of the remaining five items, two are significantly different at the 4 percent level and three are not significantly different at all. It would certainly appear that accepted opinion about north-south differences is in close touch with reality. Bangalore and Kanpur opinion is different on every one of the police evaluation items. It is consistently much more negative among Kanpur respondents. Kanpur respondents find the police less efficient than Bangalore respondents, more abusive and brutal, less honest, more apt to be in collusion with criminals, more guilty of discriminatory treatment, and more apt to be under political control. Kanpur people have also had more experience with the police; they have not only contacted the police and been contacted by them more often, they have also been witnesses more often to unpleasant aspects of police activity. Since unpleasant contact is correlative with unfavorable explanations, the greater contact among Kanpur people probably provides one reason for the substantially less favorable evaluations there. The sense of obligation to help the police and willingness to do so is much less developed in Kanpur than Bangalore. Indeed, between Bangalore and Kanpur samples thirty-eight items were compared; of the six that showed the greatest amount of difference, four of them dealt with duty questions. By a large margin Kanpur respondents are more likely to avoid the police when they come around questioning; they are less willing to inform on goondas; they are more likely to take money to the police station in order to obtain the service they desire; and they are more reluctant to volunteer information to the police about a crime. Even for the question asking whether the common man had a duty to help the police—a quite abstract matter—Kanpur residents showed much lower standards than Bangalore's. The two items which showed greatest discrepancy between the samples dealt with cognitive knowledge—the title of the district's top police officer and the location of his office. Very few Bangalore respondents knew his title. I would not expect so great a difference to be apparent on the title item. Possibly a systematic interview error produced the strange Bangalore figure. Kanpur residents were also better informed about the town in which the top officer's office was located. Almost four times as many Kanpur residents as Bangalore's could give the correct answer.

The results for perceptions of security-insecurity between north and south are mixed. Anxiety about keeping valuables in one's home is common to both communities in the same proportions. Bangalore residents are more fearful about traveling at night in their immediate vicinity; Kanpur residents are more fearful about traveling at night outside their immediate vicinity. The desire for firearms is, somewhat surprisingly, more intense in Bangalore. From these data it would be difficult to draw a persuasive generalization about differences in security perceptions between urban areas in north and south India.

A pattern is to be discerned among the various sets of attitudes found in the Kanpur data. The data suggest an engine of reinforcement at work. Profound suspicion of the police is coupled with a great reluctance to help the police. Perhaps suspicion breeds reluctance. Finding uncooperative people, the police redouble their efforts in other directions, even to dealing with unsavory elements or utilizing more coercive methods, such as striking suspects in public so as to set an example for would-be miscreants. These efforts in turn feed the suspicions of the public. They become even more unwilling to interpret police actions in a favorable light. Public suspicion occasions noncooperation; non-cooperation occasions, on the part of the police, a falling back upon less desirable methods for accomplishing their purposes; police impropriety reinforces public suspicion. The survey data cannot demonstrate conclusively the existence of this vicious circle. Many police officials believe strongly that it is not a figment of theory but is an ineluctable fact in many parts of India.

OTHER FORMATIVE INFLUENCES

The survey analysis has delineated major patterns among attitudes toward the police; it has shown what the opinions are and who holds them. It has also suggested some probable causes of these attitudes. For example, the data show quite clearly that unpleasant experience with the police tends to affect attitudes toward the police in all aspects of police behavior. Moreover, the analysis has shown that urban living tends to multiply the number of these experiences. But there are many other reasons why a police force may be disliked, shunned, and treated with suspicion. These reasons may not emerge from a survey research effort. Widely held views of why people mistrust police are undoubtedly correct in some cases but they are also mixed with rank conjecture, improper generalizations, and inherited myths. Police officials themselves are not unaware of the state of esteem for them, and they are often as eloquent as anyone when citing their own faults as reasons for their low estate. But they also point out that the situation is not entirely of their own contrivance. Let us turn now to consideration of some of the factors most commonly cited as contributory causes of this state of affairs.

It should be first recognized that law enforcement is not an easy commodity to sell in any country. While many kinds of police activity are supportive of individuals directly, and will be appreciated as such, other activities wear the garb of restraint. Police are seen as an enforcement agency. People may understand the necessity for a restraining authority at least as a matter of abstract principle but they may not enjoy its application to them or to others with whom they identify. By the nature of their task, police cannot expect universal enthusiasm, consistent regard, or passionate impartiality to be shown toward them. In a democracy, furthermore, where police authority rests upon the consent of the governed and where indeed a special point is made of securing public cooperation, police are called upon to constrain the very people they are responsible to. How much sophistication is required for the citizen to understand that his public servant must also at times be his master? On the other side, how much sophistication is required for the policeman to understand that though he speaks with society's authoritative voice he is at the same time responsible to that society?

In India inherited prejudice and particular historical experiences are often cited as reasons for the low regard in which police are held. Throughout Indian history, police have been thought of as repressive, abusive, venal, and unfair. In his excellent study of the India of two millennia ago, A. L. Basham has noted that one of the most valued privileges a king could give a brahman village was immunity from entry by the police, who were often "fierce and oppressive."[11] Countless anthropologists and other commentators on rural life have pointed to the extreme reluctance of villagers to have anything to do with the police, except in those rare instances when they seek to manipulate the police for the furtherance of their own purposes.[12] Suspicion of the police is described as an inherited attitude, as much a part of upbringing as regard for ritual or deference to elders. The practice of threatening children with the police is still reported from many parts of the country. Ghosts and policemen are standard bogies of the very young.[13]

[11] *The Wonder That Was India* (Bombay: Orient Longmans Limited, 1963), p. 103.

[12] Major-General Fendall Currie, *Below the Surface* (London: Archibald Constable and Co., 1900), p. 144, cites the words of a rustic at the latter part of the nineteenth century: "Better for a man to die than to go to law and fall into the hands of a native policeman." And Charlotte and William Wiser, *Behind Mud Walls* (Berkeley: University of California Press, 1963), p. 220, quote contemporary peasants as follows: "We are free of the rent collectors now, but we still have the land recorder, the police, and other minor officers of the government to blame. . . . Sometimes we cannot escape their avarice. When we see a police constable or a deputy's assistant in the village we know that someone is going to be threatened and will have to part with some of his money."

[13] See Leigh Minturn and John T. Hitchcock, *The Rajputs of Khalapur, India* (New York: John Wiley and Sons, 1966), p. 348. This practice is not unique to India. A sociologist friend of mine who spent a great deal of time studying a police control room in a large American midwestern community heard mothers call the police to ask them to say a stern word to their child over the phone and to say that if the child wasn't good they would come and get him. My informant believes that this is done mostly by lower class parents.

It appears that Indians do not use the familiar, derogatory nicknames for the police so commonly encountered in the United States and Great Britain. People all over India said that police were just "police," not "flatfoot," "cop," "copper," or "the man." "Copper" seems to be growing in popularity with some sections of the young; this reflects the influence of foreign motion pictures and not a widespread practice of articulating disdain. In Bihar and Uttar Pradesh during the British period police were referred to as "lal pugree," red turban. The term seems to have been almost strictly descriptive and did not have the bite of denigration.

In America and Great Britain bits of folk wisdom about the police are not hard to find. For example, in the United States every schoolchild has heard the sally, "Does your father work or is he a cop?" Such phrases have not been generally reported in India and my own explorations have been unavailing. One police official quoted a Hindi saying to the effect, "A policeman doesn't even care about his father." The nature and currency of such expressions would show something about the biases of the common man.

If inherited opinion has always been suspicious of the police, the independence struggle did nothing to improve it. In fact, it probably added the element of contempt. Police were quickly made the butt of anti-British propaganda; they were ridiculed, held up as stooges of the colonial power, sometimes spat upon, often insulted, and exhorted to desert the service and join ranks with patriotic Indians. Gandhi called off a satyagraha campaign in 1923 after a police station was burned to the ground with half a dozen policemen besieged inside. Nonviolent civil disobedience taught the virtue of disregarding commands of governing authority; in enforcing flaunted rules the police became the instrument of what was regarded as oppression. Nehru has described his feelings toward them in these words: "It was not a question of hatred or anger, for they carried no weight whatever and we could ignore them. But deep within us was contempt for their weakness and opportunism and betrayal of national honour and self-respect."[14] It is doubtful if many others were as detached, objective, and charitable as Nehru. He was probably nearer the mark about the effect of those years when he commented in connection with his own daughter, "I am afraid those early impressions are likely to color her future views about the police force

[14] *Toward Freedom* (Boston: Beacon Press, 1958), p. 74.

generally."[15] During the years of the independence struggle the police became an effigy, and like an effigy attracted the temper of an entire movement. Redemption of the police image has been materially hindered by the memories of those years that have been firmly implanted in the children of that age, now the opinion-leaders of this one.

Articulated attitudes taken together make up a climate of opinion; a climate of opinion generates congruent views. In this cycle the press plays a crucial role, at least in a society like India's where press freedom has been so firmly established. As in many Western countries, stories about crime and police activities are the stock-in-trade of much of the Indian press. While the great national dailies rarely discuss the police, at least not in episodic detail, the local press, which is almost exclusively an indigenous language press, gives full play to crime, criminal investigations, and police misconduct. Most of the recent state police commissions commented on the importance of good press relations and some of them urged creation of special police press officers. Policemen feel the press staring over their shoulders; they are concerned about the damage that may be done through publication of slanted, unfair, or incorrect stories. In discussing the press with police officers, the term "sensationalism" frequently crops up. One gets the impression that officers steel themselves against its tone and innuendo while trying to find a way of placating its most fiery protagonists. The press certainly acts to reinforce accepted, and generally unfavorable, views. The real question is whether accepted views are by and large correct. If they are, then sensationalism is indistinguishable from candid description; the press cannot be faulted for what it says.

Politicians, too, are megaphones through which opinions are broadcast, confirming or confuting popular belief. They create the climate of opinion that helps to determine whether suspicion and antipathy flourish. Relations between police and politicians will be discussed at length in Chapter 14.

To understand the position of the police in the public mind it is not enough to find out what the police are doing. Their actions take on meaning within the context of inherited perceptions and beliefs, within the group memory of significant events, and as in-

[15] *Ibid.*, p. 91. For an eloquent description of what it was like to be subjected to a lathi-charge by police during the independence struggle, an account suffused with muted passion, see Nehru's account, *ibid.*, 135-138. One would doubt that such experiences would ever be entirely forgotten.

terpreted by public agencies of opinion-formation. Environment interprets. It may negate heroic efforts to present a better image or it may render innocuous the inevitable faults of zealous officials. Police activities provide the bedrock upon which opinion is founded; the edifice of opinion, however, is built in an important measure by non-police hands. In the Indian case one cannot say that the social environment is charitably disposed toward the police.

CONCLUSION

From the public opinion survey several conclusions have been drawn about the effect upon attitudes and experiences of social position and environment.

1. By and large Indians do not appear to be very concerned about the safety of their persons and property, at least not in the areas studied. The urban respondents tended to be more concerned about the safety of their physical possessions than were rural people. They also had a greater desire to own a firearm. Rural people, on the other hand, while worrying less about possessions, showed greater anxiety about traveling at night. These differences between urban and rural people are a function of location and not of social class.

2. Contact with the police is much greater in cities than rural communities. Going to police for help and being contacted by the police in turn occur twice as often in cities. Moreover, urban people are three times as likely to have had personal experience with an unpleasant or improper police action, such as seeing them accept a bribe or strike someone in public. Contact is slightly affected by education and income. The association is not overwhelming, accounting for not more than 10 percent of contact variance.

3. In an attempt to discover when people would go to the police for assistance, respondents were presented with a series of hypothetical situations and asked what they would do. There were differences in responses between urban and rural respondents, but these did not correlate with class differentials. Norms regulating recourse to the police appear to be similar across class line, while differing with environment. Another set of questions, involving class-specific situations, might produce different answers.

4. The judgments people make about the efficiency or propriety of police behavior differ very much with location, especially

between urban and rural areas, but hardly at all with social class. In two samples some slight association was shown between social position and several evaluative items. Nonetheless, the data do not support the common belief that the higher the class the more unfavorable are judgments about the police. Considering that class does correlate with willingness to respond in an interview situation, the lack of association between class and judgments is doubly significant. Unfavorable judgments are markedly greater in the cities, however. Perception of this fact may have led people to conclude that class was the underlying determinant. Class composition of urban populations is skewed upward relative to rural populations. The survey data suggest that the harsher judgments of urban people are a product, first, of significantly higher rates of contact with the police and, second, an urban-specific climate of opinion.

5. An individual's willingness to render assistance to the police is unaffected by social position. Urban people are slightly more willing to give help—or at least to say they will give help—but this does not appear to be a function of class.

6. Social placement, involving caste status too, is associated with the amount of personal recognition of policemen and knowledge about them that people have. The higher the class and caste, the more likely people are to know some policemen by name, to recognize some on sight, and to know the salary of a constable, the title of the district's top officer, and the location of his office. The survey shows that police are much more anonymous in rural areas than cities. In cities they are everyday fixtures of life, as well as being known more thoroughly through greater amounts of contact. In rural areas they are seldom seen at all and rarely recognized.

7. As police officers have long contended, experience with and opinions about the police are very different between south and north India. Southerners have less contact with the police; they are less critical in their judgments; and they have less familiarity with policemen.

10 • *The Maintenance of Public Order*

THE maintenance of public order in India presents a unique problem partly because of the many forms the challenge assumes but even more because of the extent and constancy of it. It is fair to say that the tenuousness of social peace in India is one of the foremost factors conditioning police activity. Moreover, it has impelled law and order into the forefront of political attention. This is both because politicians seek to utilize the fragility of domestic peace for their own ends and also because they contest with government the duty as well as the tactics of government in meeting the challenge. In order to understand the importance of the law and order question in political life it is essential to assess the magnitude of social violence and the forms and genesis of it. These topics will be discussed respectively in sections one and two. Then, having the nature of the problem well in hand, it will be possible to evaluate, first, the police response and, second, its effects upon political activity and debate. These topics will comprise sections three and four.

THE MAGNITUDE OF VIOLENCE

Public violence committed by groups in India is frequent, often massive, and permeates every corner of the nation. The brutality and horror of partition have often been noted, although this may be dismissed by some as a peculiar situation consequent upon becoming an independent nation. Similarly with the Telingana uprising in 1948 in the former princely state of Hyderabad and the violence of the Communist-inspired general strike and industrial dislocation of 1948-1951. These were unique situations, not indicative of a generalized state of affairs, and there were only a handful of participants. Even setting these events to one side, however, no history of political life since independence can fail to note a depressing series of outrages against public order. The following illustrations will suffice to make the point: the struggle for establishment of linguistic states beginning in 1952 and continuing through the fall of 1955; the subsequent unrest in what is now Maharashtra and Gujarat through 1958 and in the Punjab until 1966 over the proper division of those areas between different language groups; food riots in Calcutta in 1959 and in Kerala in 1966; anti-Brahman and pro-Dravidistan activity of the Dravida Munnetra Kazhagam in 1960-1961 in Madras; resistance to establishment of Hindi as the national language in several southern states, 1964 and 1965; on the labor front a teachers' strike in Calcutta in 1954, a firing incident at Gorakhpur in 1952, the Kharagpur disturbances in 1956, TISCO strike in Jamshedpur in 1958, and government employees' general strike in 1960; food price agitation in the north led by the Praja Socialist party in 1958; language riots in Assam in 1960; Hindu-Muslim violence in Calcutta in 1964, and in the three-cornered area of Bihar-Orissa-Madhya Pradesh in 1964; and a constant drumfire of student protests resulting in the closing at one time or another of most of India's major universities. And, what does not meet the eye, for every instance of actual violence there were numerous situations poised unsteadily on the knife-edge of disorder.

But these situations are only the most dramatic, the most extensive, and the most harmful. Beneath the surface of publicity are a continual series of sporadic clashes involving small groups championing local causes and grievances, many of which never involve challenges against government but are essentially private struggles. The Indian press almost daily recounts clashes between groups of villagers somewhere in India where the police were forced to arrest individuals on both sides and may have had to resort to the firing of tear gas or bullets in order to restore order.

Reliable data on the frequency of group violence are scarce. The picture must be built of bits and pieces. There were 28,114 cases of riot in 1963.[1] Rioting is defined as the use of violence by a group of five or more persons.[2] There has been a gradual increase in the incidence of rioting since 1953 when all-India figures were first produced. The figure in that year was 20,529. The peak year between 1953 and 1963 was 1962, when there were 29,096 cases. Rioting ranks third among types of serious crimes occurring each year. In 1963 there were 6.1 riots for every 100,000 people.[3] In the same year 159,851 persons were arrested for rioting; 32,179 persons were convicted. The statistics on rioting are somewhat misleading. Many of these riots are quite minor affairs, really only

[1] The last year for which crime figures are available at the time of writing. *Crime in India.*

[2] See section 146, read with section 141, of the Indian Penal Code.

[3] The incidence per 100,000 for theft was 46.1; for housebreaking, 30. Next after riot was cattle theft, 5.1 per 100,000.

brawls. Others are spurious cases. Two or three men may fight and, when the police come, implicate a number of witnesses so as to discredit their testimony and spread the blame. The police then record a riot case, not a case of assault or an affray. If a dispute between two men involves a touchy subject of family pride or prerogative, such as water rights in a rice field, relatives and friends will be rung in so as to defend the honor of family, clan, or caste. So riot statistics provide a general indication of group violence, but they do not reveal either the intensity or seriousness of violent disputes.

Unfortunately, no careful study has been made of the incidence, extent, and consequences of various kinds of violent clashes. The Bihar Police Commission spoke for most official observers when it noted, "Street riots are not uncommon."[4] Figures on police firings provide only a partial clue, because most of them involve other forms of criminal activity. For example, the West Bengal Police Commission reported that between 1947 and 1960 there were 400 firings in the state, 110 of them in Calcutta.[5] But most of these had to do with dacoities, smuggling, looting, hooliganism, arson, and attempts at rescuing arrested persons. Thus, while the seriousness of the situation is generally recognized, there is very little hard data to document what most people considered obvious.[6]

One measure of the visibility of public violence, and by inference the incidence of serious riots, can be found in a survey of the daily press. Several years ago I undertook such a survey for the mid and late 1950's. I found that in 1955 the *Times of India* reported serious riots at the rate of about 70 a year; the number of individuals killed about 120. Police fired about 14 times into crowds in order to restore order. In 1958, the *Times of India* reported about 80 riots, 30 people killed, and almost 900 injured in riots. The police fired 20 times. In 1957, the *Statesman* reported approximately 60 riots, 18 persons killed, over 1,000 persons arrested, and 60 police firings.[7] Here, then, is an indication of the

---

[4] Page 91.   [5] Page 219.

[6] Rudolph J. Rummel of Northwestern University in 1963 sought to construct an index of conflict within and between nations. He found that India ranked in the top group with respect to riots and demonstrations. Along the domestic dimension of "turmoil," India was ranked third from the top, behind France and Argentina. With respect to revolutionary activity, it was third behind Argentina and China. With respect to subversive activity, it was eighth. *Dimensions of Conflict Behavior Within and Between Nations* (Northwestern University, monograph, June, 1963).

[7] See my "Violent Agitation and the Democratic Process in India" (unpublished Ph.D. dissertation, Princeton University, 1961), pp. 15-16.

quantity of serious riot. Although each of the years surveyed is distinguished by one or another special agitation, this is true of any year in India. I see no reason why a newspaper survey of 1968 would not show a situation at least as serious.

Public violence may range through an indefinite number of gradations of gravity. At one end of the continuum are the brawls already mentioned. At the other are instances of mob depravity extending over several days and resulting in scores of deaths and incalculable property damage. In the language disturbances in the Brahmaputra valley, Assam in 1960, 39 persons were killed, 487 persons were injured, and upward of 5,000 huts and dwellings were burned.[8] During the general strike of central government employees in 1960, there were 120 cases of sabotage on the railways; 244 cases of rioting, assault, and intimidation were reported. Police used lathis or tear gas against crowds 24 times; they resorted to firearms 5 times. Five persons died in police firings.[9] In the food riots that swept Calcutta in September, 1959, 39 persons were killed in four days of rioting.[10] By all odds the greatest amount of human agony results from violence with a communal basis.[11] The "Great Calcutta Killing," August, 1946, took an estimated 5,000 lives.[12] Authorities generally agree that during the three months immediately following partition, August 15, 1947, in excess of one-half million people lost their lives. While these events are now twenty years old, they indicate the explosive possibilities of communal unrest. In Calcutta, during five days of rioting in January,

[8] *Lok Sabha Delegation Report*, August, 1960, p. 12. There is some discrepancy between the figures in this report and the findings of Government of Assam's *Report of the Commission of Inquiry into the Goreshwar Disturbances* (Shillong: Assam Government Press, 1961), p. 5. But the general magnitude of destruction is fairly indicated by the Lok Sabha report.

[9] S. S. Khera, *District Administration in India* (Bombay: Asia Publishing House, 1964), p. 144.

[10] Statement by Chief Minister B. C. Roy, quoted in the *Times of India*, September 9, 1959, p. 7.

[11] The word "communal" needs some explanation. Some observers use it to refer to relations between any communities, whatever their nature—tribe, caste, language group, or religion. Among Indians generally, however, "communal" has a more restricted meaning; it refers to relations between religious groups and especially to relations between Muslims and Hindus. If one asks a police officer how the communal situation is, he will invariably respond by talking about Hindus and Muslims. I shall use the word in the more restricted way, not only because it conforms to Indian usage but because the more serious law and order problems of a communal kind do involve relations between Hindus and Muslims.

[12] Richard D. Lambert, "Hindu-Muslim Riots" (unpublished Ph.D. dissertation, University of Pennsylvania, 1951), p. 173. Officials actually collected 3,173 corpses.

1964, over 40 people were killed. In rioting in and around Jamshed-pur in southern Bihar, March, 1964, 164 persons were killed before order was restored.[13] Considering that the violence extended through a very large area of southern Bihar, northeast Madhya Pradesh, and northern Orissa, it is certain that several hundred people must have paid the supreme price of communal intoler-ance. The point is that Indian authorities have had sufficient ex-perience, some of it quite recent, with the ferocity of mob violence and public disorder so that they cannot dismiss any clash out of hand. An avalanche of violence may be dislodged by the most trivial incident.

Without hard data it is virtually impossible to determine the trend with respect to public violence. A person's perception de-pends upon his point of view; some areas experience quiet, rela-tive to their past, others break out in horrid acts of brutality. Al-though no single issue has succeeded in galvanizing public protest and sparking violence as the State's Reorganization Plan did in the mid-fifties, nonetheless few people would conclude that the situation has generally improved. Things may not be worse, but they are certainly not better. The president of India said in his Independence Day speech in 1966: "If we look around, we see on all sides growing lawlessness. Strikes, demonstrations, agita-tions for trivial reasons are increasing."[14] Some officials of the Min-istry of Home Affairs thought the violence of 1965 and 1966 more serious than previous disorder for two reasons: (a) it was more widespread than violence in the mid-fifties, and (b) the causes were more endemic and could not be resolved at a stroke, as for example, the food situation or the communal disharmony in the north which is firmly rooted in India's brittle relations with Pakistan.

In lieu of an objective count, one is left with impressionistic as-sessments of quantity of violence. Although the lack of hard data is to be deplored, the fact is that statistical counts may be beside the point. The significance of disorder lies in its effects, not ex-clusively in its sheer occurrence. Subjective magnitude is of greater political significance than statistical totals. The effects of public disorder with respect to police and politics may be summarized in three statements: (a) apart from limitation of

[13] Chief Minister of Bihar, quoted in the *Times of India*, March 26, 1964, p. 4.

[14] Quoted in Sundar Rajan, "The Congress Party After Nehru," *The Reporter*, October 20, 1966, p. 35.

finances, the possibility of widespread public disorder is the most important factor affecting the nature of the police establishment; (b) so common are breakdowns in law and order that the occurrence and handling of them has become one of the catalyzing issues of political debate; and (c) the habit of agitational politics, imbued with the potentiality of uncontrolled public outbreaks, has become deeply ingrained in contemporary political life and provides a clear confrontation between the forces of risk and the forces of order. These effects will be explored in greater detail in the sections that follow.

THE ANATOMY OF DISORDER

In the welter of disorder to which India is subjected, three very broad categories of public violence may be discerned. I shall call them the violence of remonstrance, the violence of confrontation, and the violence of frustration. One of the major difficulties in analyzing violence is that, once started, separate incidents of violence often look very much alike. It is during the growth of violence that different sets of characteristics may be discovered. This is partly because observation may be more precise before violence than after. One can ask a demonstrator or a striker what political party he belongs to or may elicit information about his social class, but rioters can hardly be halted in mid-stride in order to uncover information required for scholarly analysis. The loss of differentiating characteristics after ignition of mob violence is also a function of the scale of the uprising and its duration. In India, for example, a dispute over land between a Hindu and Muslim may result in a brawl which in turn grows into a small riot among partisans known personally to one another, which in turn triggers an orgy of communal violence extending impersonally over a vast area and involving many classes from both rural and urban areas. If the riot had been stopped during the first fifteen minutes, it would have exhibited one set of characteristics but after four days it would have become something much different. To be sure, there is not complete discontinuity between events leading up to violence and those following. But the longer violence lasts and the greater its scale, the greater the discontinuities are. Furthermore, the characteristics of different violent incidents are more apt to converge the longer the violence lasts and the wider its spread. In short, incidents of public violence are more successfully compared with respect to events preceding and immediately following the actual outbreak of violent actions. The characteristics differentiating the violence of remonstrance, the violence of confrontation, and the violence of frustration pertain, therefore, to this period.

The three categories of violence will be compared with respect to nine aspects: (1) occasion, (2) target, (3) catalytic agent, (4) organization, (5) duration of growth, (6) visibility of growth, (7) manner of growth, (8) participants, and (9) location. I need hardly say that the three categories are generalizations, not every violent event in India fits neatly within only one category. A chart summarizing the attributes of each major form of violence under the proper headings has been included for reference.[15]

I. *The Violence of Remonstrance*

The occasion for violence in this case is activity designed to bring a point of view to the attention of "the authorities," in most cases government or some agency of government. Violence is a result of a process of public remonstration and the heightening of a sense of open contention. While the violence itself may not be organized, the events leading up to it are. The participants are likely to be members of formal groups possessing the leadership and organizational capacity to articulate a grievance, to mobilize human and financial resources, and to command a following. By and large that means that the politics of remonstrance result from an occasion created by modern social forces. Remonstration with authorities, in a public manner, is a technique of the modern political sector in India; it is not indulged in by traditional groups, which tend to work informally and whose horizons are usually limited to a small geographical area and to informal political mechanisms. By the same token, the violence of remonstrance is more an urban than a rural phenomenon. It does seem to be true, however, that forms of public protest are becoming more common in India's rural hinterland, partly due to the increased penetration of modern organizational forces, particularly political parties, and partly because of the increased awareness on the part of rural people of the importance to them of government action directed from remote state and national centers. The prelude to the violence of remonstrance is visible; it has a clear beginning in terms of a publicly taken decision or action. Violence is not spontaneous; it comes after a quite prolonged period of public activity.

[15] See p. 255.

The Anatomy of Violence

	(1) Occasion	(2) Target	(3) Catalytic agent	(4) Organization	(5) Duration of growth	(6) Visibility of growth	(7) Manner of growth	(8) Participants	(9) Location
I.	The Violence of Remonstrance	Authority	Police	Organized	Prolonged	Clear	Definable	Modern social and political groups	Urban
II.	The Violence of Confrontation	Private groups	Another private group	Loose and informal	Indeterminable	Not visible	Indefinable	Informal, traditional groups	Primarily rural
III.	The Violence of Frustration	Society	Impersonal experience	None	Short, abrupt, instantaneous	Clear	Indefinable	Anyone	Urban

Since the target of activity is authority, the catalyst for violence is almost always some action by the police. Or at least so it appears to the remonstrators. In a typical pattern, there is a crescendo of obstructive or disorderly activity by people already in the streets. The police respond: they may arrest leaders, disperse a crowd, prohibit further meetings, or manhandle a demonstrator. The crowd, or elements within it, retaliate directly against the police, and violence engulfs the mob. Brickbats, bottles, paving stones rain like a monsoon shower; destruction is vented on public and private property. If hooligan elements—the unemployed dregs of any metropolitan area—quickly intervene the violence may be extreme, widespread, and long-lasting.

Public remonstrance in India assumes five common forms: (a) demonstrations, including rallies and processions; (b) *satyagraha,* which I think may be separated into obstruction and the courting of arrest—i.e., a passive and an active form; (c) strikes; (d) *hartals,* and (e) fasts. These forms may be arranged according to the following diagram:

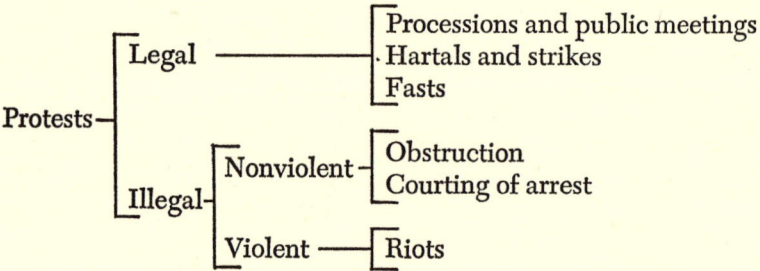

Some of those forms require an explanation. Satyagraha is the technique of protest developed by Mahatma Gandhi during the struggle for independence. In a satyagraha people nonviolently defy the law, willingly bearing its exactions in order to demonstrate the injustice of a law or of a policy behind a law. It focuses attention and dramatizes an opposing point of view. It also, Gandhi believed, may work a change in the heart of an opponent by presenting him with examples of sublime sacrifice, the dedication of men and women bearing pain and trouble for the sake of something they believe supremely important. The currency of protest has been considerably cheapened since Gandhi's time. Today "satyagraha" is used to describe any sacrifice made publicly as a protest. Fasts, for example, are described as satyagrahas. I have distinguished an active and passive form of satyagraha because satyagrahis[16] show a marked difference in the manner of their defiance. In its active form—the courting of arrest—participants announce their intention to commit an unlawful act. They may break into food warehouses in an attempt to distribute food to needy people or march into an area where an order bans the meeting together of five or more people. The purpose is to break the law, to be arrested, and to go noisily to jail. In the passive form—obstruction—participants are willing to break the law and to suffer the consequences but they don't go out of their way to do so. Their first objective is simply to create an obstruction, to slow down or stop some kind of activity, and thus compel the attention of authority. They may squat in the middle of a public thoroughfare or directly outside the door to a government office; they may even jam onto railroad tracks and bring train travel to a halt. In most cases there is some law that can be brought to bear against the obstructors, and if the stoppage persists it is applied. But going to jail is not essential to the demonstrators. The difference between the two forms, then, has to do with the amount of defiance against the law itself.

Strikes, like public meetings, parades, and satyagrahas bring about the formation of groups of people whose sole purpose is the ventilation of a grievance. They produce the elements necessary for violence out of remonstrance—critical mass of people, sense of injustice, and idleness.[17] A related form of protest is the hartal. It is the voluntary cessation of business and commercial activity in support of the demands of others. Through a hartal a community demonstrates its solidarity with certain protesters. Unfortunately, not all hartals are voluntary. Groups announcing a hartal will sometimes organize squads of young men whose job it is to tour the affected area and enforce cessation of activity. There have been numerous complaints in recent years from workers, business and professional people who have been intimidated into "voluntary" support for a hartal.[18]

Next to nonviolent civil disobedience, fasting as a means of protest strikes the Western mind as being most uniquely Indian. Fasts

[16] Those who resort to satyagraha are known as satyagrahis.

[17] One of the most peculiar strikes ever to take place in India, indicating the readiness of people to protest however they can, involved "professional" blood donors in Bombay. They refused to give blood until the price per unit rose to match recent increases in the cost of living. Four thousand donors joined the strike. *Hindustan Times*, September 21, 1963, p. 5.

[18] For example, see the *Statesman*, June 7, 1957, p. 6, and the *New York Times*, March 15, 1966, p. 9.

may be undertaken by single individuals or groups of persons. Fasts are not illegal and are certainly nonviolent. They serve as a pretext for violence, however, through the sympathy they arouse in onlookers. Particularly as the health of the faster declines —an event followed closely and reported assiduously by the daily press—public sympathy grows. The fast then sparks demonstrations of support and, if these are large enough, they cause a police response of containment that brings about the necessary confrontation between crowds and the mobilized forces of government. Fasts may be undertaken for stated periods of time, a day or a week, or "unto death." The latter, particularly if the faster is well known and shows the courage of his conviction, will rivet attention as almost no other act in India can. Potti Sriramlu died of a fast in 1952 in an attempt to wring from the government agreement to redraw state boundaries in accordance with language distribution. He succeeded. Master Tara Singh of the Sikh Akali Dal began a fast unto death for a Punjabi-speaking state in 1961; upon assurances from the government that the matter would be studied, he was finally persuaded to stop. There are even instances of people fasting against one another: that is, one group will undertake a counterfast to offset the example of the first.[19] Fasting touches a responsive cord in the Indian breast. Although it first gained worldwide attention during the independence struggle, it has been used as a tool of protest for centuries. The custom was for aggrieved persons to fast at the door of their oppressor's house. He, in turn, was then required to undertake a counterfast as a token of his innocence, if such was the case.[20] Fasting is a customary weapon of women in household disputes. One observer has said: "Fasts are almost instinctive in children and women of all age groups to record their protests on any domestic issue."[21]

The number of demonstrations, strikes, hartals, satyagrahas, and fasts held each year is almost beyond numbering. Public protest is a habit. Unfortunately, so is satyagraha. There seems to be little, if any, stigma attached to going to jail as long as the individual appears to be sacrificing for a cause beyond himself. In major cities, demonstrations, parades, rallies are daily affairs. Shouting demonstrators, shepherded along by bored policemen, may be

[19] See P. P. Mahurkar, "Problem of Hunger Strike," *Transactions*, April, 1965, pp. 92-93. There was one such in Kerala in February, 1966.

[20] Cox, *Police and Crime in India*, Chapter 5.

[21] Mahurkar, p. 69. See also William L. Rose, *Values, Ideology and Behavior of Emerging Indian Elites* (New Delhi: U.S. A.I.D. Mission, August, 1964), p. 23.

seen almost any day along the maidan in Bombay, in Dalhousie
Square in Calcutta, or along Parliament Street in Delhi. Demonstrators are as much a part of the scene around legislative buildings as cornices and arches. In fact, public demonstrations, not
avoiding lawbreaking, have become a stock-in-trade of political
parties. A peripatetic demonstration is worth several rallies; and
a head-on meeting between police and demonstrators, with
attendant publicity, is worth a hundred. Politics feeds upon
drama; since the requirements of drama are higher in India than
in the West, it is more imperative for the Indian political party
to get out into the streets than it would be for a Western party.
There is another side to the story, however. Public demonstrations
cannot be called too often or overused. There is a point of di-
minishing returns. They must be held in reserve for the important
issue, the big organizational effort, the critical political moment.
Followers get tired of endless processions; they become cynical
when the results are slight. The shrewd political leader must
choose with great care the moment to agitate. Nevertheless, the
number of groups and the number of possible grievances are so
great that there never seems to be a lull. The potentiality of violence from remonstrance is never far removed.

II. *The Violence of Confrontation*

The occasion for violence in this case is the confrontation between two groups of private citizens brought into enmity over
some issue. The target of attention, on both sides, is another group
of individuals, not authority generally or some agency of government in particular. Communal rioting is of this nature. Perhaps the
Hindus play music in front of a Muslim mosque or the Muslims
slaughter a cow on a holy day. Tension mounts until some incident unleashes the fury of inherited antagonism, distrust, and
fear. The catalyst is never the act of police, but an act of the other
side. There is little organization prior to violence; only the informal cooperation of friends, relatives, caste-fellows, and religious
cohorts. By and large the violence of confrontation occurs between
traditional groups. The major exception to this is the case of
strikers confronting employers. If the strikers challenge police
primarily, then the resulting violence would be violence of remonstrance. If, on the other hand, they fight among themselves—
as rival unions or factions of unions—or fight the forces of employers, then the violence falls into the second category. Violence
of confrontation is not apt to be the culmination of a series of

discrete steps publicly visible. The buildup to violence will be sub-
terranean. The time span of fomentation will be difficult to discern
too. For example, a great deal of rural violence involves disputes
over the boundaries of landholdings. Memories of villagers are
long where personal and family status is concerned. The formation
of competing parties, psychologically prepared to carry their dispute even to the point of violence, is not a matter of a few days
or weeks. The counterpart in some urban areas of India is land-
lord-tenant disputes, with both sides lining up friends and hired
henchmen. The problem is especially acute in Delhi, where one
police officer estimated that perhaps 90 percent of all riots were
from this cause. Because violence from confrontation is as varied as
the issues that can estrange man from man, the manner of the
growth of violence is indefinable. Unlike the violence of remonstrance, one cannot say that the movement culminating in violence
of confrontation exhibits specific forms. Most violence from confrontation probably occurs in rural areas. Partisanship is stronger
there; relations between individuals are more personal, thus contributing to long-standing feelings of jealousy, suspicion, and animosity. Violence from confrontation is not likely to spread over a
wide area. It may be brutal and degrading, but because it is predicated upon issues between individuals it is not likely to be generalizable. The exception to this is communal violence, which
spreads like a prairie fire. For this reason, and because communal
memories touch such a well-spring of passion, communal violence
is undoubtedly the most serious form of the violence of
confrontation.

III. *The Violence of Frustration*

The third major form of violence is the result of frustration. It
involves the seemingly senseless hitting out of individuals at anything at hand. The target is circumstances. The catalyst is
usually an impersonal occurrence, not one that singles out the
would-be rioters specifically as in the case of police action against
a demonstration or confrontation between opposing private
groups. But the impersonal event is perceived as an unendurable
irritant and the result is a spontaneous eruption of passion. Com-
muters on trams or trains have sometimes smashed vehicles,
burned trams, stopped trains, and beaten official personnel because there was a breakdown on the line or their train was shunt-

ed to one side to allow a faster train to pass.[22] Student violence
has been of this kind when they were denied a privilege or favor,
such as attending cinemas at reduced prices or using some mode
of transportation free of charge. In recent years riots have begun
around food shops, especially the government's fair price shops,
when stocks of food were low and shopkeepers refused to sell or
to open their shops. In Calcutta in 1958, the fire brigade advertised
for candidates for one hundred firemen's jobs at a salary of Rs. 55
per month. When from ten to twelve thousand persons showed
up for interviews, the authorities closed recruitment for the day.
The crowd exploded, wreaking destruction over the area.[23]
The genesis of violence of this kind is usually clear to see but it is
almost instantaneous. Because it is so quick, the forms of outbreak are indefinable. The participants may be anyone. While the
upper classes may be exempt from it, the middle classes certainly
are not. In fact, there is considerable evidence that the worst
violence in the past twenty years has erupted from middle class
grievances. Commuter violence is of this kind, as was the violence
occasioned by a secondary school teachers' strike in Calcutta
in 1954.[24] After the prolonged violence in Ahmedabad in 1958
over the "Martyrs' Memorial" during the agitation for separation of Gujarat and Maharashtra, a judicial inquiry found that
the worst area was a middle class ward. "It is in evidence
that most of the persons residing [there] are of the better and
more educated classes and are usually to be found in the forefront of all political activity." "They are exceptionally adept in
the gentle art of rioting, and within their own ward they
cannot be subdued by any force short of firing."[25] In the communal violence of Calcutta, January, 1964, middle class and
lower-middle class persons played a prominent part.[26] While there
is a great deal to be known about class and participation in social

[22] For example, see the *Statesman*, June 8, 1956, p. 1, for a description of
such an incident near Bombay.
[23] Myron Weiner, *The Politics of Scarcity* (Bombay: Asia Publishing
House, 1962), Chapter 5.
[24] *Ibid.*
[25] Government of Bombay, *Report of the Commission of Inquiry (Shri
Justice S. P. Kotval) on the Cases of Police Firing at Ahmedabad on the
12th, 13th and 14th August 1958* (Bombay: Government Printing, Publications and Stationery, 1959), pp. 47-48.
[26] See Patrick Wilson, "Letter from Calcutta: Fire-Balls in the Air," *The
Economic Weekly*, January 25, 1964, pp. 111-112. Friends of mine who
had done refugee work during the riots made the same observation.

violence, the impressionistic evidence from the United States as well indicates that it is not the very poor, the very uneducated, and the very backward that are responsible for violence; it is apt to be the status-conscious, striving classes. The violence of frustration is primarily an urban phenomenon. The violence of frustration is action searching for a cause. Whatever the pretext, the violence is out of proportion to the irritant. Much of the urban violence among Negroes in the summers of recent years in the United States has this characteristic. Police action accounted for the spark, but the violence was not directed exclusively against the police; it was directed against the world. In India, whether violence comes from remonstrance or confrontation, much of its momentum comes from frustration as the circle of participants widens. The rickshaw drivers, hooligans, street urchins, and unemployed young men join not because they identify with the initial cause but because violence appeals to their personal predicament.

The Police Response

The prevalence, as well as the seriousness, of violence affects the police in several ways. First, it has determined recruitment, training, organization, and disposition of forces. Indian police are divided between armed and unarmed branches; this division is founded upon the need to prevent and cope with outbreaks of violence. Were it not for the prevalence of violence, there would be no reason to maintain from two-fifths to one-half of all police as quasi-soldiers not engaged in ordinary police work but saved for law and order operations. Second, the prevalence of violence affects the efficiency with which all police work is performed. Officers complain continually, and with good reason, that they must be preoccupied with law and order work. They may not actually be coping with violent crowds, but they are making tours and providing for arrangements required if violence is to be prevented. Any crowd worries an officer. Knowing from bitter experience the volatility of surging throngs, he cannot afford to be complacent. An officer's career depends upon his alertness to violence. Third, violence exposes police to the teeth of political debate. It undermines their authority and undercuts their resolve because it makes their every action the subject of intense discussion about its correctness and adequacy. As we shall see later, Indians are not united in their opposition to lawbreaking and even to violence. Police are uncertain and sometimes hesitant in their handling of lawbreakers. Demonstrators test the undefined boundary of propriety in public remonstrance; they press the police, seeking to make them appear the aggressors because they know full well that prominent voices will be raised loudly against police brutality. The handling of violence is without question the most contentious area of police activity. All in all, the prevalence of violence, next to limitation of finances, is the most important formative factor shaping the police of contemporary India.

The first requirement for coping effectively with public disorder is adequate intelligence. Violence resulting from remonstrance is discernible in advance; it does not occur without prior warning. At the very least crowds will have formed and been active. The police will have an opportunity to assess the leadership, personnel, and temperment of the gathering. Violence of confrontation is more difficult to prevent. Especially in the case of communal violence, it may spring into being very quickly. Furthermore, the violence of confrontation takes place farther from police resources; it is scattered all over India in remote villages and hamlets. The police may not hear of a riot over land, for example, for several hours. In rainy seasons they may not be able to intervene for several days due to impassable roads. The violence of frustration is almost totally unpredictable.

Police officers list three groups as most troublesome and that most bear watching. They are students, industrial labor, and leftist political parties. When such groups agitate, knowledgeable police officers take precautions. Certain groups are noted for participating in riots, such as rickshaw drivers and the unemployed and dispossessed. These groups often form the cannon fodder of political parades and demonstrations. Usually, however, these groups do not perform their violence where they live, which is often in *bustee* areas of shacks and mud hovels. They go where the action is or where they are directed, usually to a prominent thoroughfare or customary agitation point. Geography of residence becomes important to the police only in anticipating communal troubles. Certain areas of towns have a reputation for being the scene of communal disturbances. For example, the area immediately around Jamma Masjid in Delhi is closely watched by the police.

The job of regulating crowds and monitoring them for incipient violence is arduous and continual. India is an outdoor society, its public events occur in the open and draw immense throngs. Processions are constant. Streets of towns almost daily sound to the blare of musical instruments or the driving beat of drums. A visit of a V.I.P. may draw thousands of people; in the case of President Eisenhower's visit to New Delhi in 1959 it was estimated that a million persons turned out to hear him speak. Major religious festivals or annual fairs draw millions. Furthermore, certain religious festivals—such as Dussehra, Bakr-Id, Moharrum, and Holi—are traditional occasions for communal tension. During them the police hold their breath. Intelligence units are stretched too thinly to cope with so vast a problem of crowd control. The police often feel like fire watchers in a dry season, when the forests are like tinder and one careless act by a single individual may cause a holocaust beyond hope of containing.

The police have an impressive armory of laws that they may use to head off public violence. Any assembly or procession in a public thoroughfare may be regulated by the police. The police may specify time and route of a demonstration. If violence is considered possible, leaders may be required to apply for a license.[27] If rules are violated or a license is not taken out when required, the assembly or procession becomes unlawful and the police may disperse it as well as arrest its members, an offense punishable by imprisonment up to two years.[28] Against individuals the police find most useful provisions of law which allow them (a) to require security for good behavior, in lieu of which a person may be detained;[29] (b) to arrest preventively persons believed to be about to commit a cognizable offense (rioting or joining an unlawful assembly is a cognizable offense);[30] and (c) to pass orders regulating the conduct of individuals or of persons generally within prescribed areas.[31] There are also broad provisions allowing the police to arrest persons who show no visible means of livelihood and who cannot give a good account of their presence in a certain place.[32] Such persons may also be required to post a bond and if they cannot do so, or pending their doing so, they may be detained.[33] Both provisions, like vagrancy laws in the United States, allow police, with magisterial cooperation, to remove from

[27] Section 30, Indian Police Act.
[28] Section 145, Indian Penal Code.
[29] Sections 106 and 117, Code of Criminal Procedure.
[30] Section 151, Code of Criminal Procedure.
[31] Section 144, Code of Criminal Procedure.
[32] Section 55, Code of Criminal Procedure.
[33] Section 109, with section 117, Code of Criminal Procedure.

the streets persons known to enjoy participation in violence. The preventive sections requiring the posting of bond have been known to be used as a means of harassment. The innocent are sometimes penalized, as well as the truly contentious. In disputes involving land and water boundaries—a very common form of dispute—when a breach of the peace is believed imminent, police may obtain an order prohibiting controversial actions with respect to the right in question until a magisterial inquiry has been made.[34]

All of these measures require the cooperation of the judiciary. When they accept the imminence of public disorder, the police are able to move against individuals as fast as their resources and the political climate will allow.

Preventive powers against individuals are provided in two other, rather notorious, pieces of legislation. The Preventive Detention Act of 1950 allows persons to be detained for periods up to one year if their actions are considered to be prejudicial to the defense of India, the security of the state, the maintenance of public order, or the maintenance of supplies of services essential to the community.[35] Because it takes some time to produce an order against an individual, the police do not find the P.D.A. much use in an emergency. It is a weapon of long-range utility, and has been used by the police to detain hard-core elements habitually engaging in fomenting or abetting public violence. The act was originally intended to be used against communal agitators, spies, saboteurs, and persons of violent political persuasion. Increasingly, however, hard-pressed police officials have sought to widen its use, so that they may detain antisocial criminal elements against whom it is very difficult to obtain convictions on specific charges. Whether the use of the act against these criminal elements is in accord with the rationale of the act is a matter of dispute. Since the declaration of a state of emergency in November, 1962, following the Chinese invasion, police officers have also had at hand the even more stringent and expeditious provisions of the Defence of India Rules. Without judicial intervention of any kind, or even the scrutiny of an independent advisory board as in the case of the Preventive Deten-

[34] Section 145, Code of Criminal Procedure.

[35] Section 3 (a). For the story of its workings, its provisions, and its political history, see my "The Indian Experience with Preventive Detention," *Pacific Affairs*, Summer, 1962, pp. 99-115, and "The Policy of Preventive Detention, 1950-1963," *The Indian Journal of Public Administration*, April-June, 1964, pp. 235-256.

tion Act, government may detain people for an unlimited time in order to safeguard, among other things, public safety and the maintenance of public order.[36] These powers were used against several leaders of political parties with a communal bias during the mob violence of March, 1964, in Bihar, Orissa, and Madhya Pradesh.

When orders are passed regulating the conduct of individuals or of all persons frequenting a specific area, they are issued under Section 144 of the Code of Crime Procedure. A "144" is designed to prohibit specific actions at the very brink of an emergency. At places where agitations are common, permanent "144's" may be in effect, that is, constantly renewed at the end of the two-month expiration period. This is true, for example, of the space immediately in front of Writer's Building, Dalhousie Square, Calcutta. The public is probably most aware of "144's" being used to prevent the assembly of five or more people when the authorities consider the danger of violence to be substantial. Orders under Section 144 are also often used to prevent the carrying of weapons in designated areas.[37] Orders must be issued by a magistrate. The timing of their issuance can be very delicate. If used indiscriminately or at the wrong moment, they may exacerbate the situation by serving as a red flag to demonstrators. The "144" becomes a provocative action that may set off the explosion feared.

Once the crowds are massed and milling, a different set of tactics is required; the crowd must be coped with directly. This does not always involve the employment of physical force. Detachments of police may circulate through the crowd keeping it moving, never allowing it to coalesce and form a united front. Or cordons of policemen with linked arms may prevent the crowd from obtaining its physical target and the crowd may be herded away from the scene of possible trouble, until it loses interest and

[36] Section 30, rules under the Defence of India Act, 1962.

[37] A prohibitory order was once issued in Bombay by the commissioner of police against "(a) the carrying of arms, cudgels, swords, spears, bludgeons, guns, knives, sticks or lathis or any other article which is capable of being used for causing physical violence; (b) the carrying of any corrosive substance or of explosives; (c) the carrying, collection and preparation of stones or other missiles or instruments or means of casting or impelling missiles; (d) the exhibition of persons or corpses or figures or effigies thereof; (e) the public utterance of cries, singing of songs, playing of music; and (f) the use of gestures or mimetic representations and preparations, exhibition or dissemination of pictures, symbols, placards or any other object or thing which may cause a breach of the public peace or public safety." *Times of India*, November 13, 1955, p. 3. As the *New Yorker* might say: "For the man who has anything, better stay indoors."

goes home. Or perhaps the mere presence of potential force, such as armed policemen in nearby streets or a troop of mounted police on the fringes of the crowd, may serve to deter provocative actions.

When a decision is taken to use force against a crowd, it most commonly comes in one of three forms: tear gas (tear smoke, as the Indians say), batons, and guns. Police regulations lay down that police should employ the minimum effective force. They are not to overreact. This means that tear gas should be used first, before policemen are ordered to charge pell-mell into a crowd, striking out with batons to scatter it. Some states even require this order in the use of forceful methods. However, it is more common for tear gas to be employed after batons for two reasons. Tear gas is expensive and batons are more readily at hand. Tear gas is kept at district headquarters or with the tear gas squad of the armed police, while the majority of policemen are equipped with batons of some kind. Batons come in several forms. First, there is a cane, the model being the one employed in Bombay which is from three to three-and-a-half feet long and one inch in diameter, fashioned out of bamboo. Second, there are various kinds of lathis. A lathi is a heavier bamboo stick, two inches in diameter, coming in various lengths. Minimally it is about two feet eight inches long, but in many northern states particularly it may be as much as four or five feet long and tipped with metal. This hefty stick is a formidable weapon. There is some feeling that canes should be employed before lathis, since lathis do greater damage, but whether this is possible depends upon the equipment available. In many states riot police as a matter of course carry only the heavier lathi.[38] When the batons are used, police move against the crowd in a line striking so as to drive off the agitators. This is referred to as a cane- or lathi-charge. Police may be directed to strike only between shoulders or ankles, thus minimizing serious injury. A blow from a lathi on the head may cripple or kill. The number of men used in a charge of course affects its severity; when eight or ten are used it is considered mild, thirty or forty is severe.

High-pressure fire hoses are hardly ever used against crowds, due largely to lack of fire-fighting equipment and water at sufficient pressure. Dogs have not yet been introduced into crowd-

[38] The West Bengal Police Commission, for instance, recommended the use of the Bombay baton (p. 216 ff.).

control work. Horses are occasionally used, and are considered very effective.

Force is ordered against a crowd by a district magistrate or by any police officer above the rank of station-house officer. The senior officer present assumes responsibility.[39] When junior officers use force they immediately inform the nearest district magistrate. The most delicate decision a police officer, or magistrate, must make is when to bring force to bear and in what quantity. Enough force must be employed to remove the threat but not enough so as to be unnecessarily provocative or to inflict unwarranted injury. It requires niceness of judgment, courage of conviction, and an intuitive knowledge of the psychology of crowds. Mistakes are inevitably made, and differences of opinion about what was required in a particular situation are legion. The Bihar and Kerala Police Commissions recommended that armed squads be kept out of sight initially, that there was a tendency for officers to expose them too quickly to the view of the crowd.[40] Many officers believe, however, that their presence has an immediate deterrent effect; armed police demonstrate the capacity of the police and the potential price of foolishness. Officers have been criticized both for responding too late, having allowed the situation to get out of hand, and for employing force too quickly and unnecessarily. An officer is faced with an agonizing evaluation: is *this* crowd likely to get tired and go home if they are allowed to blow off steam, even at the cost of a little lawbreaking, or is it likely to catch fire, leniency being a provocation, and grow out of hand? The answer is: some crowds will do one thing and others another. There are probably as many stories of successful instances of giving an unruly crowd its head and letting it run out of steam as there are successful instances of applying overwhelming force early and nipping violence in the bud. Officers are haunted by the imponderable question of what might have been.

The final deterrent is to order firearms to be directed against the rioters. As with lesser violence, any station-house officer or above may order it. And again as with lesser violence, if at all possible the crowd should be warned of the course the police intend to take. They should be ordered to disperse as an unlawful assembly and warned of the consequence of failing to do so. Rules

[39] Sections 127, 128, Code of Criminal Procedure.
[40] Kerala Police Commission, pp. 62 ff.; Bihar Police Commission, pp. 139-141.

for police firing are strict and similar all over India. Fire is to be directed against individuals in the crowd, especially the leaders or specific sections of the crowd. In most cases the officer-in-charge calls out an armed policeman and directs each shot he fires. Rarely do groups of policemen fire. Controlled or directed fire serves to safeguard innocent spectators. Nothing is more damaging to police reputation than to discover after a firing that a young boy, mother, or old man, standing in an upstairs window or caught against a building at the fringes of a mob, has been struck down by a police bullet. Firing is always to kill; it is to be low and never over the heads of a crowd. Officers comment that armed policemen don't like to fire into crowds, except perhaps when they are in serious danger, and although they pretend to shoot to kill they often fire in the air. Buckshot is not to be used, nor are blank cartridges. The strict injunctions about making firing effective is to ensure that the crowd will not believe the police weak-kneed and hesitant and thus be emboldened to further violence. Since firing is the last resort, it must deter.

Whenever force is employed, a cry immediately goes up for a judicial inquiry into its circumstances and justifiability. There are always departmental inquiries, but these are distrusted by politicians as self-serving; only judicial, and hence independent, inquiries are trusted. Independent inquiries are not ordered automatically, although Mahatma Gandhi advocated this before independence. A resolution to this effect was voted down at the Congress party convention at Avadi in 1955.[41] Most judicial inquiries into police firings have supported the actions taken by police. But there have been several cases in which firing was labeled clearly unjustifiable and excessive.[42] Because of the unfavorable publicity and the threat of a judicial inquiry, most officers are exceedingly loath to order a firing. Some of the judicial reports document a paralysis in decision-making between district magistrate and superintendent. No one wants to take the onus upon himself, so that endless meetings, consultations, and phone calls take place, sometimes involving officials at the state capital, be-

[41] *Times of India*, January 24, 1955, p. 6, editorial.
[42] For example: inquiry by Mr. Justice Das, Chief Justice of Patna High Court, into firings at Patna and Nawadah, 1955; Mr. Justice Khanna's report on firing at Kalka, May 29, 1959; one instance of firing, out of a total of nine, during the Ahmedabad disturbances of August, 1958. The latter commission of inquiry also found that two incidents of firing had been suppressed.

fore action is taken.[43] When strong action is required, superintendent and district magistrate lean heavily on one another. There are those that say that paralysis is already so deep that law and order are being jeopardized by police inactivity. Decisions to use force must be made on the spot and in the heat of action. The calm judge sitting miles away weeks later in the cool of his chambers cannot be allowed to second-guess operational officers. Morale would suffer even more, the paralysis would consume the body. The Uttar Pradesh Police Commission used this argument as their basis for rejecting the proposal that judicial inquiries be automatic.

No one can understand the problem of crowd-control without appreciating the conditions of an Indian riot. Oftentimes the danger to the police is extreme. In urban riots massed gangs of young men will make forays out of narrow alleys, hurling rocks, bricks, and sometimes homemade gasoline bombs. The byways surrounding major streets in older parts of Indian cities are a maze of twisting alleys and narrow tunnels. Police are powerless within them. Barricades may be put up at major intersections by rioters who pelt the police from behind them with debris of all kinds. The roofs of buildings, seeming to arch over narrow streets, provide an unlimited field of fire to the rioter. Police are dreadfully exposed below. In some of the more organized riots squads of former army men will be formed who advance before the crowd, pushing pails of water on small carts into which they throw tear gas canisters lobbed at them by police. There are instances of these experienced men shrouding the canisters with wet cloths and then throwing them back at police. Violence, whether urban or rural, springs up at widely scattered points; the police spend their time hastening from one place to the next but frequently too late. Furthermore, the police must cope with a host of nonenforcement duties. They must establish aid stations and carry the wounded, on both sides, from the field of fire. They must see that food shops open under protection so that the populace may buy their daily rations. They have to provide alternative water supplies or supervise cordons around major fires. Electricians must be kept at hand to repair damaged power lines. Telephone switchboards go dead, leaving the police radio network as the only means of communication in a distraught city or enflamed rural district.

When the police are overwhelmed or are unable to cope the

[43] See, for example, the report of the commission of inquiry into the Ahmedabad disturbances, 1958.

army may be brought in. This happened in Calcutta in January, 1964, for example. Armed forces are called in by the civil authorities and have discretion in the use of force as the police do.

Indian police officers are remarkably experienced in confronting riotous crowds, certainly far more than officers in any Western country. Most officers who have had an independent command have faced a disorderly crowd at one time or another. Few of them have ever ordered a firing, but many of them have used lathis or tear gas. Considering that I.P.S. officers commonly achieve superintendent rank in their early thirties, experience with harrowing decisions comes fast. In many ways confronting and successfully handling a riotous mob are the initiation rites for I.P.S. officers as well as I.A.S. district officers. This is the way they win their spurs. They display a considerable pride in the techniques they have employed, in the imagination displayed, and the expedients devised to avoid violence. Older police officials and I.A.S. administrators are fond of reminiscing about the situations they confronted and the difficult decisions they had to make. Even the most senior officers—I.A.S. and I.P.S. alike—responsible now for vast territories and thousands of men, will unbend and show a proud nostalgia for those days in the past when they stood between order and massive violence in a remote country district.

The techniques that officers devise to avoid violence are often ingenious, and a few stories should be told. Many officers tell of deliberately being away from headquarters "on tour" when demonstrators arrive. With no target, the agitators often quickly grow tired and disperse. Others will give a demonstration its head and take no containing action at all. This may infuriate and ultimately frustrate the agitation leaders whose real purpose is to gain publicity and provoke a dramatic, though nonviolent, encounter between government and citizenry. Shouting and squatting in the hot sun before a collector's compound can be tiresome work. Students have been given holidays when they left classes for the streets, particularly if the end of term was approaching. Demonstrating is fine when classes can be missed, but loses its appeal when students are free anyhow. When informal food rationing came to one city, an agitation developed when shops ran out of food. The senior police official opened the police food warehouses to the demonstrators and sold food on a quota basis to each person. One of the most elaborate schemes to frustrate an agitation came in Punjab in 1958. A statewide agitation was organized protesting the level of taxation. In several days over twenty thousand persons were arrested. Then the agitators mobilized women and brought them out into the streets. The chief minister responded by chartering buses, bundled the women into them, and took them for an excursion to Bhakra Nangal dam. They were given free teas and food and put up overnight. The government used the opportunity to show the women what their taxes were doing. The women went home and the agitation died out.

THE POLITICAL EFFECTS

The existence of violence in public life, and particularly violence with an organized agitational basis, has two immediate consequences: (a) it thrusts the police into the limelight of public attention in an invidious role and (b) it polarizes political debate between those who support and those who criticize order-sustaining policies. Let us examine each of these in turn.

Public Reaction to Crowd-Control

A priori one might suppose that the notoriety police earn through using force against crowds would estrange the public from them. An image of succoring servant is difficult to maintain when people are manhandled, struck with batons, or shot at. Is this in fact true? In the survey people were asked to describe the manner in which police usually handle public demonstrations. At least a fifth of all urban respondents—all samples except Tumkur—said crowds were handled "firmly but properly." An equally large group replied that crowd-control was "very haphazard." A very small minority of people, never larger than 12 percent in the urban samples, said handling was done either "too firmly and harshly" or "with too much force." In all samples there were a substantial number of "don't knows." This was especially true in the rural area, where responses were meaningless due to failure to respond among 91 percent of the sample. Kanpur rural migrants had a no-response rate of 54 percent. Even among established residents in Kanpur the no-response rate was a third of the total sample. Since urban people are not generally reticent in answering questions about the propriety of police behavior, the large proportion of "don't know" responses would seem to indicate a lack of knowledge. People simply do not have ready-formed opinions on this subject. This is even more true in rural areas, where experience with crowd-control is very slight. Among those who do hold opinions, the worst that people say is that control is haphazard. Very few people have a strongly critical attitude.

Respondents were also asked if they thought the police resorted to too many firings. The proportion of "don't knows" declined markedly. Even in rural Tumkur only 22 percent failed to give an answer. The overwhelming majority of respondents did not think the police fired too often. Not more than 3 percent in any sample criticized the police on this score. It would seem, therefore, that when people criticize the police for using too much force, they do not generally have in mind firings.

One of the most interesting findings of the survey is that personal experience with police violence against a crowd does not predispose people to evaluate police crowd-control activities negatively. As one would expect, many more people have seen lathis used than have seen a firing. (See Table 25.) People with per-

TABLE 25

PERSONAL EXPERIENCE WITH CROWD-CONTROL

Mysore: (a) Have you ever seen the police use lathis or canes on a crowd?
         (b) Have you ever seen a police firing?

	Rural		Urban	
	(a)	(b)	(a)	(b)
Percentage yes	3.3	0.8	45.3	14.8
Percentage no	96.7	99.2	54.7	85.2

Kanpur: (a) Have you ever seen the police use lathis or canes on a crowd?
         (b) Have you ever seen a police firing?

	Residents		Rural migrants	
	(a)	(b)	(a)	(b)
Percentage yes	32.4	15.1	18.0	8.5
Percentage no	67.5	84.9	82.0	91.2

sonal experience of the use of force by the police are much greater in number in urban than in rural areas. On one of the personal experience items, namely, having seen the police use lathis or canes, experience is greater in the south than the north. Experience with crowd-control is much less extensive in rural areas and among rural migrants. Among urban respondents, at least a third have seen the police use canes or lathis; and, quite surprisingly, one out of six have seen a police firing. Examining the correlations between personal experience of use of force by police and personal evaluations of police crowd-control activity, one finds very few significant correlations and only in the case of Tumkur respondents are any of them important. Only among Tumkur respondents can one say that having seen a firing or the use of batons predisposes people to a harsh judgment about police handling of crowds. Among those segments of the population with the greatest amount of experience with crowd-control activities—city dwellers—there is no important relationship.

Nor do the data show an important association between having witnessed police using force against a crowd and any other evaluation of police behavior. Generally, then, first-hand experience with forceful crowd-control measures affects judgments neither about crowd-control activities nor other types of police activity.

It would appear that when police use force against a crowd as many onlookers are quietly in favor of it as are against it. The fact that first-hand experience does not predispose people to make unfavorable judgments about crowd-control activities probably indicates that in the minds of these witnesses the police were justified in their resort to lathis, canes, or firearms. Violence or the threat of violence may be acutely disturbing to onlookers. When police action comes, it may bring relief from anxiety. The police might take heart, then, both in the fact that their actions have not alienated the survey's witnesses and that when police act forthrightly, although not intemperately, to restore order they may earn the unarticulated thanks of many people.

The survey also shows that the police have more latent support among the populace in handling demonstrators than they might have thought. Respondents were asked whether demonstrators who break the law should be arrested straightaway or tolerated. In rural Mysore, where 77 percent offered no opinion on this item, the tolerant view was supported five to one. But in urban areas, both north and south, the firmer line was supported. In Bangalore, 55 percent replied that demonstrators who break the law should be arrested right away, as against 34 percent who wanted them treated tolerantly. In Kanpur, the figures were similar: 53.8 percent for immediate arrest, 27 percent for toleration. Rural migrants agreed with their urban brethren.

Though the police would seem to have substantial latent support for a firm line against lawbreaking by agitators it should be noted that a third of respondents resented such a policy. A third of the public—if these findings are generalizable—is a lot of people; they could be most troublesome and noisy in support of satyagrahis. So the police still have reason for showing care in their treatment of lawbreaking demonstrators. But the often-expressed view that most Indians automatically support agitation does not seem to be correct.

Indians may be getting a bit tired of demonstrations and may have begun to suspect their legitimacy. Reactions of urban residents in Kanpur were distributed equally among those who thought demonstrations were used too often, those who thought they were not used too often, and those who had no opinion. In Bangalore, where a third had no opinion, almost twice as many people believed demonstrations were used too often than said they were not overused. In rural Mysore, where results again were marred by a very high "don't know" response, respondents were not as critical of demonstrations. By and large, they supported them.

As a general rule, the public continues to believe that demonstrations are a useful way of compelling official attention. For example, when they were asked whether demonstrations were useful in getting the authorities to do the right thing or correct some wrongs, approximately half of the urban samples said they were useful. Rural residents and rural migrants were not so convinced. They tended to duck the question. In Tumkur more people spoke against them than for them. Among Kanpur rural migrants 35 percent spoke for their usefulness, 24 percent against. Demonstrations against officialdom both occur more often in urban areas and attract a larger measure of support in principle. At the same time, established urban people are also more cynical about the frequency of their use in practice.

Few people proportionately have ever participated in a demonstration. Hardly any rural people have done so, or will admit to having done so (Less than 1 percent). In urban areas, about one out of six people have participated in a demonstration. Participation by urban residents in demonstrations occurred for the most part within the last three years or over eight years ago. What this shows is that the respondents are not recording participation in the independence struggle, although there must be some of that. We shall see in fact that by and large age does not correlate with participation. Participation by Indians is as likely to occur today as at any time in the past. Inspection of the correlations between participation and social background is uninstructive. The statistically significant correlations occur only in the Bangalore and Tumkur data, and they are very slight. In the north—

Kanpur—participation is not affected at all by age, education, income, occupation, or caste. In Tumkur and Bangalore more highly educated people have a slightly higher participation rate. In Bangalore income is directly proportional to more frequent participation as well. Finally, in Bangalore older people are less likely to have participated in a demonstration than younger ones. Once again, all these correlations are too slight and fragmentary to base firm conclusions upon.

In summary, the survey data show that urban dwellers, as opposed to rural people, have participated more in demonstrations, have more experience with police crowd-control activities, and favor demonstrations more in principle as a way of shaping official policy. At the same time, they are growing cynical about the frequency with which demonstrations are launched. They tend to support a tougher line against lawbreaking demonstrators by the police. Most surprisingly, having been a witness to the police using force against a crowd does not affect judgments about the propriety of police crowd-control activities. A man who has seen the police fire into a crowd is as likely to support police crowd-control policies as the man who has not. Despite the tremendous hue and cry raised by interested parties and politicians whenever the police use force against a crowd, the people with first-hand experience of it tend to be unaffected by it in terms of their judgments about police behavior.

Partisanship and Crowd-Control

The second major consequence of violence and of the need to restrain it is that law and order have become the subject of an emotional, vituperative public debate. Police actions are broadcast from the housetops. Whether stigmatized or defended, police notoriety increases. The effect of this upon public attitudes is unmeasurable. It seems reasonable to expect that the swirl of debate tarnishes police prestige and reduces the sanctity of their charge. Even more fundamentally, the debate involves the question of responsibility for preserving stability and order. When violence comes from remonstration or from confrontation in which one of the parties has wider political support—as in the cases of a strike or communalism—politicians stride forward to excuse or justify its occurrence. Violence is explained by them in terms of government's being heartless and unfeeling; violence, it is suggested, is the natural outlet for grievances unassuaged. There will be ritualistic regret that violence should ever have broken out but the message that comes across so clearly in these recriminations is that violence is justifiable or, at the least, the result of callous represssion by the police.[44] When violence occurs there is a flurry of legislative maneuvers in Delhi or state capitals with the object of challenging the government and producing resolutions in support of demonstrators so brutally mistreated. Protest marches and rallies will be held. Legislators will walk out in high dudgeon at the callousness of government. In some instances, fights have broken out on the floor of legislative chambers and members have been manhandled. Even during the horror of communal disorder, spokesmen are to be found portraying the unendurable suffering of one of the communities—usually the Hindus—and arguing that violence is an inevitable, necessary, and understandable response to brutality visited upon members of that community by the other. During the gruesome events of January and March, 1964, in eastern India, only a few plaintiff voices could be heard saying that communal violence is never justified, that India must first put her own communal house in order, that Hindus must show forbearance in spite of what may be going on in Pakistan. Much more loudly, however, were the solemn avowals by some political figures that exchange of population was the only solution. Thinly disguised threats are also made. Government is told that unless compassion is shown to the injured and immediate action taken to remedy their grievance, or if provocations by the other community continue, the cycle of disorder will be renewed, justifiably. Violence, especially that of remonstrance, quickly becomes an issue in itself, eclipsing earlier causes. The stakes become higher, the emotion greater, and the reciprocating engine of recrimination-hostility grinds on.

The issue of law and order becomes a battleground for the supporter of government and the opposition. The opposition reflexively gives aid and comfort to the violent who in their terms

[44] Remarking on the charge of police brutality (*zulum*), Prime Minister Nehru said in the Lok Sabha, 1956: "There is no doubt reference to police *zulum*. It is a constant factor that is brought in everywhere because it is expected that everybody will immediately accept any charge of misbehavior by the police. The poor police is so used to being kicked and cuffed like that and always condemned. It is easy to make a charge against the police. . . . It is becoming intolerable always for this poor policeman to be condemned for trying to do his duty in the most difficult of circumstances. Let us punish the policeman when he is guilty or anybody else when he is guilty. But the stone-thrower becomes a hero and is taken out in procession— maybe—and the poor policeman who gets the stone on his head is a person who is guilty of *zulum* and atrocities." *Lok Sabha Debates*, col. 9822.

are the violated; the supporters of government must negotiate the difficult task of giving sympathy to the injured while blaming them for the incident. Too often those individuals who abhor violence, whatever the pretext, find themselves lumped with the partisans of government and perhaps of the policy that served to precipitate disorder. On the other hand, not all supporters of government stand beside the police when violence occurs. Indeed, the police are expendable in the sense that they can be freely condemned without jeopardizing one's alliance with government. Law and order is a partisan issue in the narrow sense. It is a permanent *casus belli* at the core of Indian politics.

Debate about law and order is also a debate over the place of agitational politics in modern life. There are many observers who believe that Gandhi's example of nonviolent civil disobedience has become a terribly pernicious, possibly destructive, legacy to modern India. Agitational politics has become the stock-in-trade of groups large and small, organized and unorganized. Congressmen are not an exception. Law is not considered sacred in itself; it may be freely broken without a qualm of conscience if the cause is just. Satyagraha is a word to conjure with, and it hides any miscreant under the umbrella of self-sacrifice. Civil disobedience is used whenever a point of opposition is to be made against government—people expect it, politicians thrive on it. It doesn't matter that other remedies exist. Nor does it matter that freely elected representatives have by majority vote determined otherwise. Agitational politics has become a customary coercive force supplementing, sometimes supplanting, the orderly processes of parliamentary government.

In order to understand the politics of policymaking in India it is necessary to use two eyes, one for observing legislative machinations, the other to study the accompanying activities outdoors. It is standard procedure for parties to convene noisy rallies immediately outside legislative premises during important debates. Legislators move easily between their audiences, haranguing their followers outside one moment, invoking the image of the crowd indoors the next. Political groups use agitation to dramatize issues, to fix attention upon themselves, to mobilize a political following, and to frighten government. Politicians admit that nothing contributes more to an individual's or a party's status than the judicious use of agitations. Among opposition parties the decision to launch a major agitation is made by the national leadership. They insure that the effort is properly timed and well supported. Individual politicians and local groups may undertake agitations protesting matters of strictly local importance whenever they want. It has become a politician's normal gambit to announce that government is repressive and unsympathetic and that as a result he must command attention by taking "direct" action. A politician, of whatever party, who shrinks from agitation and from selective defiance of law is at a tactical disadvantage to any opponent.

For all the hurly-burly and frenetic activity of Indian politics, it would be a mistake to conclude that India was quivering on the edge of political collapse. Because of their frequency, agitations are much less significant than they would be in most Western nations. A politician in India demonstrates as habitually as a politician in the United States writes letters and with as much effect. This is precisely the problem. There is so much noise of public protest that it is often difficult to hear the important, the real, the heartfelt calls for attention. To attract attention against such a background, one must raise the pitch of protest perilously high. Government and political leaders alike have become slightly deaf; this is the consequence of prolonged exposure to protests and the requisite of stability amidst public agitation. In many instances, too, defiance of law and massive confrontations between police and protesters are not as uncontrolled as they appear. Many agitations are really ritualistic trials of strength, and both sides know it. Although laws may be broken, police and protesters are aware of what is going to happen; their conduct is bound by norms built up in years of experience with demonstrations. For example, it is quite common for authorities to declare Section 144 in effect, then for agitation leaders to announce publicly, sometimes in letters to the superintendent or collector, that the order will be violated at a specific time and place. Opposing forces meet as scheduled amid an ear-splitting din; volunteer lawbreakers cross the police cordon, the magic circle of authority, and are hauled away in police vans. It is almost like a game, with leaders on both sides working together to provide the rank and file with an exciting outing. The point of protest is made, the leadership of particular individuals is confirmed, and police authority maintained.

Not all agitations are conducted in as civilized a form. In some of them agitation leaders are undoubtedly guilty of provoking violence. It is difficult to make a judgment about complicity because leadership is of many kinds—it covers notable public figures at the very top and ward heelers at the bottom. Moreover, violence can be provoked while talking nonviolence, and it is impossible for an outsider—perhaps even for the spokesman in question—to know what is really intended. The deliberate planning of violence seems to be rare. However, violence has so many uses, especially when it can be laid at the door of the police and through them the government, that politicians undoubtedly organize activities designed to push to the brink. In the Ahmedabad disturbances of 1958 and the Assamese in 1960, judicial inquiries exonerated political parties of explicit complicity, but criticized them severely for contributing to a climate of opinion in which violence was almost inevitable.[45] Also, parties may be guilty of indirect complicity by not exerting themselves as they could in order to prevent violence. They choose not to organize to prevent violence, although they have not organized to create it.[46]

Conclusion

The prevalence of violence and agitational politics presents a democratic government with a very complex decision: it must measure the requirements of law and order against the requirements of democratic political development. It is easy enough to advocate that government pursue a firm policy against lawbreaking agitators. Certainly, with respect to the violence of confrontation or the violence of frustration, few people would argue that they should be tolerated. But with the violence that flows from remonstrance, the choice is much more tendentious. It may be a mistake to allow remonstration too free rein; it may also be a mistake to choke it off too precipitously and firmly. Government must learn to choose the lesser of evils, and this is not easy. Let us examine the gains and losses which might flow from a strict control of agitational activities.

A policy of control could be justified in terms of the following

[45] See the Ahmedabad inquiry report, pp. 2-3, and the report on the Goreshwar disturbances, pp. 15-16.

[46] See the comments of Myron Weiner, *Politics of Scarcity*, Chapter 5. Gene D. Overstreet and Marshall Windmiller, *Communism in India* (Berkeley: University of California Press, 1959), p. 322, note the efforts made by the C.P.I. to restrain popular agitations, even though they could have been seriously embarrassing to government. They cite the Goan satyagraha scheduled for 1956; agitation for Bombay state in 1956; and the agitation against the merger of Bihar and West Bengal in 1956. In each of these instances the C.P.I. deliberately refrained from exploiting potentially explosive situations.

objectives: (a) lessening the cost to the nation imposed by destruction of human life and property and the disruption of stable social processes; (b) preserving the legitimacy of the government in power, because no government can afford to have its rules flaunted cavalierly and at will; (c) defending the primacy of majority rule by frustrating the coercive tactics of aggrieved minorities; (d) protecting the sanctity of the rule of law; (e) offsetting the intrusion of Gresham's Law into political activity by placing disorderly and disruptive politics firmly beyond the pale; and (f) reinforcing the sense of social discipline which is so essential to sustained economic growth.

These objectives are all worthwhile. It is generally less recognized that a policy designed to achieve them, while meritorious in itself, may bring unfortunate consequences. What are these? (1) A stricter policy of control can stopper a socially useful response. Social protest may be necessary as a safety valve in a rapidly changing society accustoming itself to new processes and structures. Were people to be held too firmly in line, they might react by an even greater revulsion against the existing system of law enforcement. (2) Consensus between ruler and ruled may be predicated upon the appearance of a dialogue between them. If people do not wholly trust the new political mechanisms of ballot boxes and legislatures, political agitation may be a necessary supplement. With the streets clear, the mass of the people would find it easier to believe in the haughty isolation of its rulers. (3) The first results of augmented control might be to intensify the spirit of martyrdom left over from Gandhian politics. Rather than deterring would-be agitators, repression would provide them with a more impressive cause upon which to lavish their dedication. (4) Tightening of control may pass the torch of democratic principle to the non-democratic opposition. They would be able to appear as the only true champions of democracy; to argue that they had known all along that the Congress party represented reactionary forces of oligarchy, privilege, and authority. (5) It might further alienate the people from the police and courts. A sympathetic regard for law and its instruments can hardly be built upon the widespread experience of repression. (6) It is important for the leadership in government itself, particularly when its hold upon parliament has been so strong, to avoid reinforcing elitist isolation. It is a moot question whether coercive public protest in India provides new insight for government leaders into the intensity and extent of grievances or whether it unnecessarily supplements an adequate picture. If leaders are somewhat isolated, perhaps only by the tyranny of daily tasks, then agitations may widen their perceptions. (7) It is very easy for hard-pressed planners to become enthralled with economic development to the neglect of less tangible, less material, gains. By subordinating agitational politics to the demands of economic order, the importance of free political modes may be neglected as a whole. The preservation of stressful political forms is perhaps an indication that open politics continues to be valued for itself. And (8) where the habits of democracy are as yet unformed—perhaps in any country they are never beyond relapsing—any departure from the free interplay of political forces becomes a precedent more difficult to set aside later than it would be in a more established polity. This is partly because the elitist habit is more deeply rooted but also because other and particularly modern countervailing forces are less strongly entrenched.[47]

Here, then, are possible gains and losses that may flow from a policy of stricter control of agitational politics. The control of public agitation is clearly not a simple matter. Decisions affecting it require a firm grasp of political principles as well as a sensitive awareness of the potentialities of human situations. The balance between freedom and control, permissiveness and authoritarianism, public agitation and public resignation, violence and order is always a delicate one to maintain. Policy is a truce between competing claimants; it is always uneasy. Neither academicians nor state officials should ever be beguiled into thinking that the balance could ever be otherwise.

[47] An earlier version of the arguments for and against a stricter policy of control of public protest appeared as "The Pedagogy of Democracy: Coercive Public Protest in India," *The American Political Science Review*, September, 1962, pp. 663-672.

11 • *Corruption and the Police*

JUST as it is impossible not to taste the honey or the poison that finds itself at the tip of the tongue, so it is impossible for a government servant not to eat up, at least, a bit of the king's revenue. Just as fish moving under water cannot possibly be found out either as drinking or not drinking water, so government servants employed in the government work cannot be found out (while) taking money (for themselves).[1]

In democracies, we are often told, people are ruled by law and not by men; this means that government makes demands on individuals in conformity with written enactments publicly promulgated and that demands are made on the basis of public policy, resulting from a free public debate, and not the whims of officials operating from ad hoc and personal considerations. Justice is accomplished if laws are fair and right and if they are administered as enacted. The first task is the responsibility of lawmakers, the second of law-enforcers; both are essential to justice. The police, the primary enforcing instrument of criminal law, serve all men by serving the law. This noble conception is undermined when the actions of police, or any government servant, are affected by considerations other than duty to the law—when their actions in the name of the law are modified by interests other than those enjoined by public policy. The effects of failing to act in conformity with the law can be serious. If faith in the rule of law is to be built and maintained, then it must be administered in accord with its spirit and not made the captive of personal consideration. Furthermore, in order for the rule of law to be effectuated, public cooperation is essential. Adherence to the dictates of law must be regarded as important in itself; individual conscience must be molded so as to reject and abhor lawbreaking. The cost of malpractice by police, and especially of partiality, is that the evenhandedness of public justice is destroyed and the sympathetic regard of the public for law, and its minions, is imperiled.

Corruption in the police has become a byword in India, as in-

[1] *Kautilya's Arthasastra*, trans. by R. Shamasastry (7th ed.; Mysore: Mysore Printing and Publishing House, 1961), p. 70.

deed it has for government servants generally. Along with brutality, corruption is the issue most prejudicial to the image of the police. Considering the importance of impartial law enforcement, not only for itself but for the wider interest of anchoring respect for the rule of law, it is important that the myths and realities of corruption among the police be thoroughly explored.

Corruption has been defined as "inducement (as of a public official) by means of improper considerations (as bribery) to commit a violation of duty."[2] A bribe is defined as "price, reward, gift or favor bestowed or promised with a view to pervert the judgment or corrupt the conduct esp. of a person in a position of trust (as public official)."[3] Bribery and corruption are intimately linked together, but they are not inseparable as common parlance would often have it. A person bribed is a person corrupt; but a man may be corrupt who does not take bribes.[4] Corruption, then, while being tied particularly to the act of bribery is a general term covering misuse of authority as the result of considerations of personal gain, which need not be monetary. This point has been well made in a recent Indian government report on corruption: "In its widest connotation, corruption includes improper and selfish exercise of power and influence attached to a public office or to a special position one occupies in public life."[5]

The Public's View of Police Corruption

The survey results leave no doubt that suspicion of police honesty is widely felt. In Bangalore 33.2 percent of respondents thought there was a "great deal" of corruption in the police. Only 3.5 percent said there was none. (See Table 26.) In rural Mysore, 24.5 percent thought there was a great deal. Rural respondents show themselves, once again, less willing to give opinions generally and somewhat less critical of the police. In Kanpur, 55.1 percent of the residents and 40.5 percent of rural migrants thought there

[2] *Webster's Third New International Dictionary*, 1961.

[3] *Ibid.*

[4] In this respect there has been a change in the relation between bribery and corruption from the second edition of *Webster's New International Dictionary*, 1958. In the earlier edition the definition of corruption explicitly mentioned bribery and the definition of bribery explicitly mentioned corruption.

[5] Government of India, Ministry of Home Affairs, *Report of the Committee on Prevention of Corruption*, 1964, p. 5, known as the Santhanam Committee, after its chairman.

TABLE 26

CORRUPTION IN POLICE

Is there corruption in the police?	Mysore		Kanpur	
	Rural (percent)	Urban (percent)	Residents (percent)	Rural migrants (percent)
Great deal	24.5	33.2	55.1	40.5
Some	21.2	30.5	28.4	25.5
Little	4.7	5.2	3.0	4.2
No	6.7	3.5	1.6	3.2
Don't know	43.0	27.7	11.8	26.5

was a great deal of corruption in the police. Thus, people in the north are more critical on this score than people in the south.

People were asked about the necessity of bribing the police in a specific situation, namely, when they wanted help or police cooperation. Forty-six percent of respondents in Bangalore and 37 percent in rural Mysore thought that police would have to be bribed before they would do their duty and help people; 78 percent of established urban dwellers and 64 percent of rural migrants thought money was required. As one would expect, respondents' personal knowledge of the police taking money before they were willing to help was meager. In Mysore, only about 11 percent of rural and urban dwellers knew of instances when the police had taken money before helping. In about 60 percent of those cases the people involved were known personally to the respondent. In Kanpur, many more people knew of such instances —37 percent among established urban dwellers, 20 percent among rural migrants. Between 60 and 75 percent of them knew the people involved personally. Still, the results show that about 7 percent of people in Mysore and 20 to 25 percent in Kanpur think they know of personal instances of the police demanding money before helping.

In order to obtain a personal indication of the necessity people attached to bribing policemen to obtain results, respondents were asked a hypothetical question: "If you wanted help from the police for some reason, and you had to go to the police station, would you take money with you so as to be sure of getting the help you need?" Among the general public, the lowest proportion from the various samples that admitted they would stoop to bribing was 12 percent. This was in Bangalore. In rural Mysore 27 percent said they would take money as a precaution, compared to forty percent of established urban dwellers and 38 percent of rural migrants. So convinced is the general public of the venality of the police that, even in order to obtain assistance in the normal course of duty, one-fifth of all respondents would provide themselves with money so as to be in a position to grease a palm.

We have already seen that between 7 percent (rural areas) and 25 percent (urban areas) of respondents knew someone personally who gave money to a policeman in order to obtain action. Respondents were also asked if they had themselves ever seen a policeman accept money.[6] In rural areas of Mysore about 6 percent of the respondents have witnessed what they thought was a bribe changing hands. In Bangalore and Kanpur, about 25 percent had themselves seen bribery occur.

In sum, the Indian public not only believes that there is a good deal of corruption in the police—and a majority believes there is more than "a little"—but about one out of five has seen it and a similar proportion has taken the lesson to heart and would take money with them in their dealings with the police in order to secure action.[7]

What effect has personal experience with police corruption upon an individual's evaluations of police corruption and his own willingness to engage in it? Knowing of instances when help wasn't forthcoming until money was paid and having seen the police accept money are both consistently associated with believing there is a lot of police corruption and believing that bribery is necessary in order to obtain needed assistance. It should be noted, however, that the correlations, while significant, are not very large—they account for never more than about 10 percent of the variance. There is a slightly more important correlation between being willing personally to bribe, on the one hand, and having seen police accept money or knowing of instances when they didn't help until bribed, on the other. One could conclude that personal experience or knowledge of police corruption leads to

[6] This does not of course mean that a bribe was actually passed, but it does indicate that the respondent thought it had been.

[7] Eldersveld et al., in their Delhi state survey, found that expectations of corruption for *all* government officials was very high. A majority of respondents thought that at least half of all officials were corrupt. *The Citizen and the Administrator in a Developing Democracy*, p. 29. They also found that "officials are inclined to minimize the extent of corruption, while a majority of the public is ready to charge officials with corruption" (p. 141). I have found a similar tendency to discount corruption among I.P.S. officers.

greater readiness to engage in it oneself as a protective measure. But one could argue with equal plausibility that people who are willing to bribe are precisely the people who are likely to have personal experience of it. Who, then, is being misled, and by whom—police by public or public by the police?

Personal experience or knowledge of police corruption is not associated with social status. There are no significant correlations that replicate from sample to sample. One must conclude that social status, caste, and religion do not affect experience with police corruption or the willingness to bribe.[8]

The importance of corruption in framing the public image of the police is shown by two others items. Respondents were asked if the police showed favoritism and if so, for what reasons. In every sample, wealth was listed first as the factor that had greatest weight with police. Indeed, almost twice as many people traced favoritism to wealth than to the next most important cause, which was either political position or something generally referred to as "influence." Respondents were also asked what "would be the most important thing the police could do to improve their relation with the people?" Becoming less corrupt or more honest was given as the fourth most important action the police might take by respondents in rural Mysore; it was listed third by people in Bangalore. Among Kanpur residents it was listed second. These responses show again that corruption is not quite so important in the minds of people in south India as it is in the north. Improvements in courtesy and sympathy were listed first in all samples as the improvements that would most improve relations with the public.

Indians have no illusions about the morality of their policemen. Dishonesty is readily associated with the police and colors

[8] In another survey, Karl Deutsch and Bruce Russett found that 12 per cent of their sample (which was of 1,980 persons) thought that they could obtain favorable treatment from officials by giving a bribe. "The fairly common acceptance of this need for bribery is a striking aspect of our report." Indian Institute of Public Opinion, *Monthly Public Opinion Surveys*, Nos. 112, 113, January, February, 1965, p. 47. This conclusion conforms to my own. They also found, however, that the higher the education level of respondents the greater was the expectation of the need to bribe. They concluded that it was among persons with no formal educational level that the need to bribe was most discounted. I did not find this relationship in my data. Sampling and interviewing in my study and theirs was carried out by the same organization, the Indian Institute of Public Opinion. The samples were different, however. Corruption is bound to be a delicate subject for interview work, and clearly much more needs to be done before we can stand on solid empirical ground.

their image of the police in striking hues. Indian people may not, however, be unique in their suspiciousness about police honesty. The Royal Commission on the police in Great Britain in 1962 found that 42.4 percent thought there was some truth in the suggestion that police sometimes take bribes, although it should be noted that a slightly larger proportion (46.9 percent) thought it most unlikely. Only 1.2 percent of the total sample thought they took bribes very often; 32.7 percent thought it was very rare.[9] A national survey done for the President's Commission on Law Enforcement and Criminal Justice in the United States found that 58 percent of the population thought the police were almost all honest; 30 percent thought most were honest but a few were corrupt; and 3 percent thought that almost all were corrupt.[10]

Suspicions about police honesty seem to be tenaciously rooted in several countries, but the depth of suspicion is certainly greater in India than in the United States or Great Britain on the basis of information at hand.

AN ANALYSIS OF POLICE CORRUPTION

There are many impressionistic assessments of the amount of police corruption. It is almost impossible to penetrate below the level of rumor. Figures on dismissals or charges laid against officers reflect not just the extent of corruption but the enthusiasm and ability of investigating agencies.[11] Corruption in the police, and among government servants generally, is certainly a staple topic of conversation. As Morris-Jones has said, "Corruption—the fact itself but, even more important, the talk about it—occupies a great place in Indian politics."[12] The amount of corruption is easy to exaggerate and people seem to delight in dwelling on its extent or in recounting particularly gross instances of it.[13]

[9] Royal Commission on the Police, *Appendix IV to the Minutes of Evidence*, p. 116.

[10] President's Commission on Law Enforcement and Criminal Justice, *Field Surveys II, Criminal Victimization in the United States: A Report of a National Survey* (Washington, D.C.; U.S. Government Printing Office, 1967), p. 53. The study was carried out by the National Opinion Research Center.

[11] See comments of the Santhanam Committee report, p. 14. The same point can be made about figures on numbers of complaints received by official agencies.

[12] *Government and Politics in India*, p. 62.

[13] President Mohammed Ayub Khan, upon taking power in 1958, made it an offense to spread rumors of official corruption without first having brought the matter to the attention of authorities responsible for investiga-

There is general agreement among police commissions and police officers that there is a vast amount of petty corruption among the subordinate ranks but relatively little among I.P.S. officers. "There is no denying the fact that corruption exists in the police force, and *the majority of the subordinate ranks are corrupt.*"[14] Referring to the severe strictures made against the police by the Police Commission in 1902-1903, the Uttar Pradesh Police Commission observed that " . . . the Police Department is no better today. There is little doubt that corruption is rampant in the non-gazetted ranks of the Police Force. Imputations of corruption against gazetted ranks are not wanting, but they are not so pervading in their character. We do not think that corruption has assumed a serious shape among the higher ranks of the police, namely gazetted officers. . . ."[15] The Bihar Police Commission also testified to the permanence of corruption: "There is complete unanimity among witnesses on the point that corruption . . . survives as an inveterate disease defying all administrative measures that have been adopted from time to time to tackle this problem."[16] While the incidence of corruption is greater in the subordinate ranks, it is generally agreed that the most notorious, injurious, and serious instances of corruption are found among assistant sub-inspectors and sub-inspectors. Their powers and hence their opportunities are greater than those of men of lower rank.[17]

Nor is the judiciary in India immune from the temptation of corruption. As the Santhanam Committee reported: ". . . we were informed by responsible persons including Vigilance and Special Police Establishment Officers that corruption exists in the lower ranks of the judiciary all over India and in some places it has spread to the higher ranks also."[18] The Law Commission in 1958

---

tion. Henry Frank Goodnow, *The Civil Service of Pakistan: Bureaucracy of a New Nation* (New Haven: Yale University Press, 1964), n. p. 237.

[14] West Bengal Police Commission, p. 20 (emphasis added).

[15] Uttar Pradesh Police Commission, 139.

[16] Page 212.

[17] It is worth noting that Americans have little to be proud of in this respect. John Coatman, *Police* (London: Oxford University Press, 1959), p. 164, says that among the United States, France, and Great Britain, the United States enjoys with all authorities the most unfavorable reputation with respect to police corruption. Great Britain is considered the best; France occupies an intermediate position. The links between organized crime and the police in the United States are unprecedented in these other countries. To be sure, even Great Britain has had its police scandals, as for example the Brighton case in 1958. But it has never had the wholesale corruption that has been discovered in Chicago, Philadelphia, and Boston.

[18] Page 108.

noted that "there is . . . in some states an absence of the tradition of impartiality and integrity in the criminal judiciary as has been the general characteristic of the civil judiciary."[19] The Commission commented, too, that corruption among the staff of courts is substantial and has existed for a very long time.[20]

The forms of corruption are almost infinite. Police may exact a cost for doing something, for not doing something, for doing something properly, for misdoing something, for maintaining goodwill, and for seeing that something is done speedily. When any activity combines human agency by one party and considerations of gain from that activity by another, the possibility for corruption exists. The nature of an officer's duties, which are correlative with rank, determine the form of corruption in which he might be involved. For example, a superior officer may receive a lavish gift upon the marriage of his daughter in return for an official favor; a head constable, on the other hand, may extort money from hawkers who do not have the necessary permit.[21]

Perhaps the most repugnant form of corruption concerns misconduct in enforcing the criminal law. There are two basic forms of this—applying the law improperly or refraining from applying it at all. There are innumerable ways in which an investigating officer can bias an investigation so as to turn guilt from one party onto another. He may misrecord information, trump up a case against an innocent accused, lose evidence, or commit some mistake of procedure that renders the whole case suspect. Partiality of policemen is commonly charged in disputes over land in rural areas. Land is life in India, and the police have the power to place one of the parties in the wrong and shore up the case for the party that provides the largest gratuity. Police may delay the serving of summons, purposely fail to appear to testify in a criminal trial, submit inaccurate reports when an individual is ordered to post a surety under the preventive sections of the Code of Criminal Procedure, not give a faithful version of statements of witnesses, or even sell case diaries to the defense. The Uttar Pradesh Police Commission noted that policemen were refusing bail to accused in bailable offenses unless a bribe was given. The accused had no idea they were entitled to bail and gave

---

[19] Law Commission, Vol. I, p. 217.

[20] *Ibid.*, p. 224.

[21] The West Bengal Police Commission, pp. 257-258, presents many examples of the kinds of corrupt practices appropriate to different ranks of police.

money to the police to do what the law required anyhow.[22] An officer may also accept money in return for inaction; the briber buys abeyance of the law. Failure to prosecute for offenses committed is almost impossible to detect. Unless the crime was witnessed the only parties to it are the bribed and the briber, and neither is likely to complain about the transaction. Corruption of this kind most frequently involves offenses in which the police have great discretion and in which the public is not continually interested or does not feel morally involved. Prohibition, gambling, and prostitution are common examples. The interstate movement of grain is prohibited in India without a permit and, like prohibition, provides a rich opportunity for police to earn money on the side. Traffic offenses are another lucrative harvesting ground. In some police stations payment of "protection" money to the police is institutionalized. Monthly payments are expected from houses of prostitution or gambling establishments. Police stations alongside arterial roads collect a small payment as a matter of course from every truck that passes. Refusal is met with a threat to prosecute the driver for having a defective vehicle— which most of them have—or to unload the entire vehicle so that it may be searched for smuggled goods or have its weight checked.[23] The money from these "*mamools*," as they are known, is distributed among the staff of the station house. A monthly increment of this sort can become a critical item in many a policeman's budget. So far in India the payment of protection to the police for not prosecuting is done on a small-time basis. It involves the local police, or a single officer, and a single private individual operating just over the margin of the law. Massive collusion between police, even of high rank, and organized criminal interests extending over vast territories and involving very substantial payments is not yet a feature of police corruption. It can be expected to grow in the future, centering upon illicit distillation of liquor, drug smuggling, and prostitution.

Officers may misuse their authority to obtain illicit returns. Usually this involves threatening to take some action unless a payment is made. Power to put up cases under the preventive sections of the Code of Criminal Procedure, under which an accused must post a bond, allows the police considerable scope for extortion. Perhaps a peasant has gotten in a brawl with another

[22] Page 75.
[23] Abraham Varghese, I.P.S., "Practice and Precepts in Police Work," *Transactions*, November, 1964, pp. 76-77.

man; the local station-house officer or head constable can threaten to represent the man as a chronic brawler or suggest to the magistrate that there is a possibility of breach of the peace between the two men, in both of which cases the man could be compelled to post a bond. The peasant, knowing that he couldn't post a bond of even ten rupees and having been suitably impressed by the policeman with the rigors of jail, meekly agrees to give the officer five rupees. People dependent upon the use of public thoroughfares for their livelihood are frequent targets of the police extortioner. Hawkers, sidewalk vendors, the roving cane-juice vendor may all be required to pay a rupee or two every so often so that they may be allowed to pursue their occupations where they wish. They know they are vulnerable; a rupee is easy to part with when measured against the trouble a thwarted officer could cause.

Supervising officers contribute to the corruption of their subordinates by the manner in which they provide for supplies when on tour. Because touring allowances, especially for inspectors and sub-inspectors, are low, subordinates are required to provide meals, beds, teas, and cigarettes for the touring officer. They cannot raise the money from their own pay, so they must solicit funds from local concessionaires or through malpractices, such as taking a small fee for doing any job promptly. A report from Maharashtra stated that "*sarbarai*," or hospitality, "is far too prevalent than is admitted [*sic*]. Had all district officers not been susceptible to this, it would long since have disappeared. . . . Now-a-days, hardly any Circle Inspector pays for his meals. Most of the Mamlatdars follow suit. Unless the District Officers show some courage in stamping out this evil, very little can be achieved."[24] The subordinate officer is compelled to contract an obligation to local suppliers or to engage in petty corruption. He is caught between the devil and the deep blue sea: he can affront his superior or join the ranks of the venal. Since his own livelihood may be at stake, an uncommonly high standard of morality can hardly be expected of him.

[24] Government of Bombay, *Report of the Officer on Special Duty on the Reorganization of District Revenue Offices* (Bombay: Government Central Press, 1958), pp. 96-97. The Maharashtra Police Commission concurred, strongly urging that touring officers take along their own cook and provisions. Rates for daily travel allowance should be increased. There is no excuse, in their opinion, for camp supplies to be obtained free of charge (p. 21). The West Bengal Police Commission was as concerned about the evil and as adamant that it be stamped out (p. 261).

Undoubtedly, the most ubiquitous form of corruption has to do with thwarting or facilitating routine requests. " 'Speed money' is reported to have become a fairly common type of corrupt practice particularly in matters relating to grant of licenses, permits, etc. Generally the bribe giver does not wish, in these cases, to get anything done unlawfully but wants to speed up the process of the movement of files and communications relating to decisions. Certain sections of the staff concerned are reported to have got into the habit of not doing anything in the matter until they are suitably persuaded."[25] Expert witnesses for the Bihar Police Commission testified that police corruption was largely in the submission and procedural apparatus rather than in decision-making.[26] A fee will be expected with any request and at separate stages of submission. The sums involved are not large, but they are required constantly. The burden upon poor people must be acute. The machine of justice, supposedly established to act automatically in the interest of the public, is fueled individually. Superior officers unwittingly provide an occasion for it. Whenever access to them must be obtained through subordinates a screen of petty exactions may be erected.

Police officers do not believe that location—rural or urban—appreciably affects the incidence of corruption. In cities the opportunities are greater and the scale of payments may be larger. But supervision is also more intense and urban people are more willing to complain about corruption. In rural areas, by contrast, the individual policeman is more on his own and the people more acquiescent, but the scope for corrupt practices is more limited and the scale of exactions cannot be so high. The rural station-house officer, particularly, is master of all he surveys, unlike his city counterpart. But "big money," regularly forthcoming, is not his lot. Due to offsetting factors, then, the incidence of corruption may not vary between remote county districts and congested modern towns.

THE ERADICATION OF CORRUPTION

Government authorities are very concerned about corruption and have created an elaborate structure of investigating agencies to control it. Within the central government, each ministry, department, and public undertaking has a vigilance unit—sometimes ex-

[25] Santhanam Committee report, pp. 9-10.
[26] Pages 212-213.

tensive, sometimes only a single officer—to receive and investigate complaints of corruption. Acting on the recommendation of the Santhanam Committee, the central government established a Central Vigilance Commission in February, 1964, to serve as watchdog for the anticorruption effort. The Commission is autonomous, like the Public Service Commission. Apart from separate vigilance units, investigations for the central government are handled by the Investigation and Anticorruption Division (formerly the Delhi Special Police Establishment) of the Central Bureau of Investigation. In the states the pattern is repeated: each department or public undertaking has a vigilance unit and there is a central anticorruption department of some sort. Many states also have district anticorruption committees, under the direction of the collector, whose membership is made up of all department heads.

The larger share of anticorruption work is handled by the separate departments. For the most part, then, charges of police corruption are received by police officers, investigated by police officers, and judged by police officers. Most police forces now have a special unit within the C.I.D. to handle cases of police corruption. Officers in each district may be deputed to handle anticorruption work for the force.

The task of eliminating, or at least reducing, corruption among the police is handicapped by two factors: (a) lack of information about instances of corruption, and (b) cumbersome procedures for assessing guilt and awarding punishment. The superintendent, and his staff, must bear primary responsibility for investigating corruption. The superintendent of police has the power to discipline subordinates, his staff is best equipped to conduct inquiries, and he is most strategically located to obtain information and to remain in personal touch with happenings in his geographical area. Many officers will admit that they cannot begin to know about all the episodes of misconduct that go on in their charge. Their duties are simply too numerous. As we saw in the case of brutality, it is difficult for I.P.S. officers to admit they have less than perfect knowledge of the activities of their force. If they know all, they must say they have successfully eradicated corruption or admit their impotence or possibly their condonation of it. If, on the other hand, they admit they don't know everything, they run the risk of appearing to be inefficient officers. Officers are probably right to stress the impact which a dedicated superintendent of police can have on the moral tone of his establishment; a vigorous example by the superintendent of giving no quarter to the corrupt officer cannot fail to curb many abuses. But the success of personal example cannot be fully tested and a superintendent is rash indeed who believes that because no instances come to his attention corruption does not exist. Most district officials will admit that a great deal of petty, pervasive corruption is never reported.

Information about corruption comes from several sources: the briber; a third party to a bribe; the press; subordinate officers, especially supervisory staff; and through personal inspection and attention. The superintendent's own ability to unearth corruption is limited because of the range of his responsibilities and by the decreasing number of prolonged tours he makes. Superintendents are dependent upon the reports of assistants or on complaints sent directly to them. When suspicion of dishonesty arises, close scrutiny must be made of a policeman's actions before a solid indication of corruption can be found. Blatant misconduct, particularly in important matters such as criminal investigations of serious crimes or breaches of the peace, will come to light. But for much of it, plausible excuses can be easily devised. There is a real but indefinable gap between the I.P.S. cadre and the lower ranks, especially constables and head constables. They differ in social strata, styles of life, nature of duties, and quality of training. Furthermore, the spirit of the clan affects lower ranks: because they must live and work with one another, even the innocent constable will hesitate to inform on his confreres. Next to the superintendent, the station-house officer is the most important post for reducing corruption. If the station-house officer is himself tainted, it is doubtful if his own subordinates will inform and he enjoys considerable opportunity to lead inspecting officers by the nose when they come on their well-publicized tours. But information from the public is only somewhat more obtainable. Members of the public are likely to complain if they have a well-developed sense of duty and if they are a wronged party. Too many people acquiesce in bribe-giving. Rather than complain, they would rather put up with a petty exaction. Prudence in accomplishing important tasks seems to require it.[27] In other cases, there is no

[27] William and Charlotte Wiser, in *Behind Mud Walls* (Berkeley: University of California Press, 1963), Chapter 9, especially pp. 124-125, describe graphically the suspicious, impotent world of an Indian villager. The villager feels surrounded by hostile forces trying to put something over on him. There is no one he can trust; certainly no one outside his village. Since he has no confidence that anyone will stand up for him, it is better to soften the rigors of his hostile environment by giving a bribe.

wronged party. Both briber and bribed are pleased with the transaction, and no one else is the wiser. Then, too, people may be afraid to complain. Complaints about the police are invesigated by the police. Even if a citizen has faith in the superintendent or the collector, these exalted officials come and go, the station-house officer is there for a long time. The man on the spot, with authority backed up by force and the threat of jail, can suppress evidence and intimidate witnesses well out of sight of the superintendent in his remote district headquarters. Although from time to time someone suggests that investigation apparatus for police malpractices be made independent of that force, there is little momentum behind the proposal.[28] That the public may be apprehensive about complaining directly to the police seems to have been perceived by the West Bengal and Maharashtra Police Commissions. The West Bengal Commission recommended that a sealed box for complaints be put in the district office of the public relations office, to be opened only by the collector.[29] The Maharashtra Commission recommended that departmental inquiries on charges of corruption in the police should be handled by a special officer appointed by government.[30]

Even when complaints do come to responsible officers they are often found to be false and malicious. The experience in Uttar Pradesh was that 22 to 26 percent of complaints coming to the "Deputy Superintendent, Complaints" between 1956 and 1959 were true. This does not mean that all the rest were false; it simply means that the police were unable to substantiate them.[31] I.P.S. officers are eloquent in their irritation over the number of false complaints they receive. And they cite instances of innocent officers being charged by individuals precisely because they had the courage to resist a blandishment. If the police cannot be won over, the next tactic is to discredit them so that they cannot help one's opponent.

Many officers feel they must tread softly in the handling of complaints about corruption. They are aware, for example, that

---

[28] It was suggested, for example, in John Mathai, I.P.S., "A Scheme for Reorganization of the Police Force" (Central Police Training College, 1963), p. 7. Politicians are very skeptical about departmental investigations. They often complain in the legislatures that police protect their own. They sometimes press for the creation of a special investigation officer, or agency, apart from the police service. So far, this demand has been resisted.

[29] Page 260.

[30] Page 6.

[31] Uttar Pradesh Police Commission, pp. 141-142.

morale in a force may be destroyed if subordinates are not defended by superiors from malicious charges. Considering the prevalence of such charges, the concern is not unfounded. Then, too,
officers feel compelled to support subordinates when they make
inadvertent mistakes. Given the educational level and ability of
many of the lower ranks, innocent errors abound. The conscientious superintendent defends the innocent inept and tries to distinguish his case from that of a venal officer. Much less excusable
is the practice of hiding corruption because it will reflect poorly
either on the department as a whole or on the superior himself.[32]
An officer may reason that if public confidence in the police is to
be built, less noise should be made about the inevitable cases of
corruption. The West Bengal Police Commission commented that
". . . this perhaps happens more in the police department than elsewhere."[33] Unfortunately, there is a reinforcing relation between
lack of information and failure to proceed vigorously to make use
of information to punish the guilty. If superintendents, for whatever reason, shield the miscreant—at least try to hide corruption from public view and keep it in the bosom of the police family—people lose confidence in superior officers' independence and
their willingness to champion the cause of the public against
their own force. The public hesitates to come forward; they lump
all policemen together as colleagues in corruption. The public
image of the force declines, morale suffers, and the superintendent
must be doubly conscious of the need to defend his few honest
men and to salvage some favorable image for the force by muting
criticism of corrupt officers. Somehow the process of reinforcement
must be turned around; for the process is logically reversible. Vigorous public prosecution of corruption can raise the morale of the
honest men, deter the malicious complainer who often has dirty
hands himself, and encourage the public to trust certain classes
of police officers. Information will become more plentiful and the
corrupt, rather than the innocent, go on the defensive. The possibility is there; the problem is how to bring about a new climate
of opinion and action, and so to use the cycle of reinforcement
between information about corruption and anticorruption action
for the benefit of society.

Some officers in every state have a reputation for being amenable to corruption or at least to conniving at it in subordinates.
A much larger number may actually know of corruption, or have

---

[32] See comment of the Maharashtra Police Commission, p. 22.
[33] Page 262.

strong suspicions, and while they personally disapprove of it, do not have the stomach for a thorough housecleaning. They are individually innocent, but nonetheless contribute to its perpetuation. An unusual amount of courage is required to use the full resources of one's office to eliminate widespread and customary abuses. The individual officer feels very alone; he fears for his promotion, for his reputation, and for the willing cooperation of his subordinates in line of duty. But, by failing to stand up individually, officers forego an opportunity to encourage their colleagues to stand a bit taller together. The answer to this dilemma is for strong leadership to be applied from the top, both from I.P.S. and I.A.S. staff. Reform will more assuredly percolate down than it will well up from below—although this truth is too often used as an excuse for acquiescence. Finally, many officers sympathize with the lot of the policeman who is required to undertake hazardous and distasteful duty and to work long hours for a pittance. The officers know that policemen cannot support their families on what they are given. Therefore, they condone the small bribe that makes life just bearable.

The second problem handicapping the elimination of corruption involves the cumbersome procedures set down for evaluating guilt and awarding punishment. Departmental proceedings, by which most corrupt policemen are punished, are only slightly less involved and ponderous than those of the courts. Although procedures vary somewhat from state to state, they must all conform to Articles 310 and 311 of the Constitution of India. The key regulatory phrase is, "No such person as aforesaid shall be dismissed or removed or reduced in rank until he has been given a reasonable opportunity of showing cause against the action proposed to be taken in regard to him." The courts thereby gain purchase on disciplinary proceedings and have laid down many rules defining "reasonable opportunity." In most states the Indian Evidence Act applies, lawyers are permitted, the accused may file a written statement against the charges, he has a right to challenge all evidence and to cross-examine witnesses, and he may move the courts to overturn a departmental decision.[34] Many police departments complain of the burden of work caused by having to meet the demands of prerogative writs taken out by subordinate policemen concerning punishments and promotions. Departmental proceedings drag on for months, and although the officer may be

---

[34] Santhanam Committee report, pp. 34-35.

suspended there is no assurance at all that the courts will not order his reinstatement with a huge award for arrears in pay. The Bihar Police Commission noted that 25 percent of cases for departmental punishment took two months for processing; over 30 percent took from six months to two years.[35] Disciplinary proceedings are neither sure nor swift. The Santhanam Committee strongly recommended simplifying departmental proceedings. The "protection given to the Services in India . . . is greater than that available in the most advanced countries."[36] The Committee called this protection one of the "major contributory factors for the growth of corruption."[37] Furthermore, corruption is a notoriously difficult charge to prove. Elaborate traps are required to catch an official in the act of soliciting or receiving a bribe. When the police do plant a bogus briber, they must find respectable non-police witnesses to observe the planning of the trap, the distribution of the marked money to the operatives, and the discovery of the money on or near the suspect. An invisible dye that turns hands red is often used to mark money; corrupt officials are literally caught red-handed. All of the problems of obtaining witnesses that cripple the prosecution of criminal work crop up once again in anticorruption cases.

A full departmental inquiry or court prosecution is not the only way of moving against corrupt officers. When a reasonable suspicion of corruption against a man exists, the superintendent may warn him in no uncertain terms about the gravity of corruption and the superintendent's own suspicions. The superintendent may also enter adverse remarks about the man's honesty in his personal file; in most states copies of adverse remarks must be given to each man once a year. The message usually comes across. If intimations of misconduct persist, the superintendent may try to rig an entrapment. When it proves impossible to substantiate corruption charges sufficiently to file a criminal case or begin departmental proceedings, some superintendents have sought to punish the officer, as a severe warning, on some other ground. Faults can often be found in the actions of even the most exemplary policeman if one looks hard enough. While his corruption may not be punished, other mistakes or instances of misconduct can be, with resulting loss of pay or privileges. The prosecuting officer must be

[35] Page 183.
[36] Pages 10-11. The Committee compared the United States, Great Britain, and Australia.
[37] *Ibid.*

careful, however, that he does not expose himself to the charge of false punishment.

Basically, then, there are two areas where attention must be given if bribery is to be curtailed. The public must be encouraged to report the bribe solicitation or payment and must be willing to trade inconvenience as a witness for honesty in public life; and rules for dismissals and punishment must be weighted more heavily on the side of purging government service of the dishonest official and less on the side of iron-clad job security. The latter reform can be made by government on its own initiative. Such a reform might begin the process of reconstructing the climate of opinion among members of the public concerning the usefulness of reporting bribery.

The Causes of Corruption

There is no single cause for corruption in the police. Many factors converge to produce this unhappy state of affairs. By the same token, no single reform is likely to prove sufficient to the need. The battle must be fought on several fronts at the same time. Among the reasons most persistently and authoritatively advanced to explain corruption in the police are the following:

1. Corruption is not unique to the police but permeates society generally. Because the malaise is nationwide there are few examples serving to strengthen the resolve of the uncorrupted to resist temptation.

2. Bribery is a traditional practice of hoary antiquity. No stigma attaches to it; for an officer to make a small sum on a transaction is considered his due, by his fellow officers and the public alike. As the Bihar Police Commission observed: "The tradition of corruption in the police is deep-seated and certain forms of corruption have come to be accepted by society as harmless."[38] But the whole idea of corruption does not cause the same revulsion that it may in the West, although it was not always that way even in the West. These ruminations by a character in a modern Indian novel—a businessman—may be typical: "Bribery and corruption! These were foreign words, it seemed to him, and the ideas behind them were also foreign. Here in India, he thought, one did not know such words. Giving presents and gratitude to government

[38] Pages 213-214.

officers was an indispensable courtesy and a respectable, civilized way of carrying on business."[39]

Indeed, the practice of bribing may be so common that the rejection of a bribe by an official may cause the briber to wonder if the official hasn't already been won over to the other side or is being purposely malicious. Some observers have noted that the safest way to retain the respect of competing parties is to take money from both sides and then proceed firmly according to merit. Certain services are supposed to have set rates, as do certain kinds of licenses. Everyone pays them, without protest and as unthinkingly as a man puts money in a parking meter. He would feel insecure if he did not do so.[40]

3. The bonds of family and immediate social groups are stronger than those of state or nation; there is a common expectation that official position will be used to the benefit of those groups. Family culture, rather than reinforcing a morality of anticorruption, presses upon the officeholder to use his position for the common good.

4. Administrative procedures are too detailed, intricate, and cumbersome. Papers are passed endlessly from official to official. Access is rigidly rationed through a system of intermediaries. Every multiplication of steps in the process of decision-making or implementation increases the opportunities for corruption. In the end, the supplicant realizes that his only hope of beating the labyrinth is to enlist the cooperation of as many officials and underlings as possible. If procedures were simpler, opportunities for venality would be fewer and responsibility for action could be more quickly ascertained.

5. The Indian masses are illiterate, uneducated, and unknowledgeable about the world of rights, rules, and regulations. They have no idea what should be done on their behalf or what they have a right to demand. They are incredibly easy to bamboozle. If a man says five rupees is required for a stamp before a document can be passed on, how are they to know this is untrue, that

[39] R. Prawer Jhabvala, *The Nature of Passion* (New York: W. W. Norton and Co., 1956), p. 46.

[40] See, for example, Myron Weiner, "India: Two Political Cultures," *Political Culture and Political Development*, eds. Lucian W. Pye and Sidney Verba (Princeton: Princeton University Press, 1965) and my own discussion of the functional value of corruption in "The Effects of Corruption in Developing Nations," *Western Political Quarterly*, December, 1966, pp. 719-732.

the stamp is not required? They are uncertain, fearful of the men who control processes of government. An indication of this is the enormous growth in the number of intermediaries—touts, they are often called—who, for a price, intercede to accomplish even the simplest item of business for the unlettered villager.

6. The policeman himself is subject to endless temptations. His work brings him into contact with the dregs of society, those whose moral standards are at rock-bottom. Moreover, he contacts people who have a vested interest in getting away with something. Given the prevailing climate of corruption, the policeman need not make opportunities, they are constantly being proffered to him routinely. One reason police officials give for having lower ranks live in police colonies, set apart from the general public, is that it isolates them from bad influences. With their low pay, they could not afford housing that would not put them side by side with the criminal elements they are supposed to regulate.

7. Even the lowest-ranking police officer has enormous powers. When greed or necessity is combined with power to harass, corruption is the ready result.

8. Since the public is prepared to believe the worst about a police officer, why not be hung for a sheep as a goat. No one will believe him if he persists in his honesty; they will treat him as if venality were his badge of office. In that case, many of them must reason, it might as well be.

Given causes such as these, it is apparent that corruption will not yield to a single and simple solution and it will be a long time giving way, whatever reforms are enacted. Reform is the work of generations, not of a year or a five-year plan.

There is another cause, however, that deserves particular attention in explaining the incidence of corruption among the police. This cause is usually cited at the top of the list of factors contributing to police dishonesty. It is the meagerness of police wages. The scale of wages is significant not only for its effect upon honest practices, but because it shows the place of the police in the thinking of government. As in most countries, police are accepted as being necessary but they are also considered to make a limited contribution to society. Their contribution is essentially defensive: they are doing a proper and adequate job if conditions of law and order are not too bad. As long as criminality is not too rampant and as long as police practices are not too terribly bad, there is no need to invest more money in them. Police are not considered as playing a larger, positive role in the formation and maintenance of habits of mind essential to a political community of a particular kind. When questions of allocating increased funds to police arise, the formative role of the police[41] is denied, ignored, or discounted. In an underdeveloped country, such as India, where financial resources are agonizingly scarce, containment of crime must be considered even more restrictively. The police are, in the parlance of development, a "non-plan" department. Whether the effects of this kind of reasoning are unfortunate in the Indian case I shall examine in a concluding chapter.[42] One thing is certain: substantial improvement in police honesty cannot be expected while salaries are held to their present level.

Corruption in the police is not exclusively a problem of its lowest wage earners but it is certainly more prevalent among them. Accordingly, discussion will focus upon their standard of life and assume that, while middle class striving may be intense and frustrating, the I.P.S. officer should not plead economic necessity to justify his dishonesty. Rates of pay for non-gazetted ranks are determined by the states individually, so, in describing rates of remuneration for all India, generalizations are unavoidable. Base pay for constables, including "dearness allowance" for rises in cost of living, begins at about Rs. 60 and may be as high as Rs. 75. During their career, total emoluments grow to a monthly salary of Rs. 105 to Rs. 120. Sub-inspectors receive from two to two and one-half as much to begin with—thus, from Rs. 120 to Rs. 150. Head constables earn generally less than half again as much as constables. Rates of pay are lower in the states than with the central government. A police constable earns the lowest acceptable salary for the most unskilled central government employee.[43] Thus the peon who opens the door or carries messages in a central government office in New Delhi makes about the same salary as the constable in Patna who arrests a man during patrol duty at night. A study made in 1958 notes that a postal department clerk earned almost twice as much as a constable. Minimum salaries for the lowest clerk in the State Bank of India, the Life Insurance Corporation, or Air India were twice as much as the starting salary of a constable.[44] Unskilled labor in industrial

[41] As explained in Chapter 1.   [42] See Chapter 16.
[43] See Chapter 3, "The Indian Police Today," p. 58.
[44] Government of Bombay, *Report of the Officer on Special Duty on the Reorganization of District Revenue Offices*, p. 81.

plants earn a monthly wage of approximately one hundred rupees.[45] A constable should not be thought of as unskilled labor, particularly if one considers his training and the responsibility of his duties. Even the new scales of pay recommended by recent police commissions leave the starting pay of constables below that of unskilled labor. In short, if one assumes that the average constable's family consists of five people, then the lowest ranking police officer in India supports a family below the level of the national per capita annual income (about Rs. 370).

Comparisons among occupational groups tell only part of the story. Perhaps there *are* inequalities in income distribution, but nonetheless a constable's salary could still be quite sufficient for his needs. The Central Pay Commission, 1958, computed a minimum adequate wage for central government employees. Making every attempt to construe needs as minimally as possible, they found that a family of the equivalent of three adult consuming units would need Rs. 82.50 per month to live.[46] Food consumption, strictly vegetarian and without milk, amounting to 2,600 calories per adult per day, accounted for Rs. 52. This caloric intake is what the Nutrition Advisory Committee of the Indian Council of Medical Research considered adequate for a man engaged in light or sedentary work.[47] Even assuming the family gets free housing—which is not the rule—the family has thirty rupees, or one rupee per day, left over for clothes, medical care, furniture, household utensils, and other expenditures. Speaking of the adequacy of this rate of pay for the lowest paid central government employee—peons—the Commission said: "Without wishing to underestimate the importance of social effects of low wages, we think that from the restricted angle of the efficiency of the employee it would be reasonable to take the view that the present minimum remuneration is not perceptibly inadequate."[48]

[45] The all-India wage for unskilled labor in 1958 was about Rs. 70; for all factory labor the unskilled wage was about Rs. 100. Central Pay Commission, pp. 59-60. See also, M. M. Singh, "Minimum Wage for a Policeman," *Transactions*, October, 1962, p. 17; Central Police Training College, Report of a Syndicate, "The Police Forces of India—Their Strength and Cost," *Transactions*, October, 1963, p. 13; *United Nations Statistical Year Book*, 1965, p. 524, gave figures for all industrial labor (including salaried employees) of Rs. 122.9 per month in 1963; Bihar Police Commission, p. 216.

[46] Their recommendations were based on scales set up by the Fifteenth Indian Labour Conference, 1957. The Central Pay Commission then cut these requirements down, arriving at its present figure. See pp. 62-68.

[47] Central Pay Commission, p. 66.

[48] *Ibid.*, pp. 61-62.

Prices have risen considerably since 1957. Between 1956-1957 and 1963-1964 the working class consumer price index rose by 30 percent. Moreover, by the end of 1964 it had risen 50 percent.[49] Today, therefore, a minimum adequate wage for a person engaged in light or sedentary work would come to about Rs. 120. The average wage for all constables in India is less than that by a third. There can be no doubt, as most police officers maintain, that a constable cannot perform adequately and support his family even minimally on the wage that he is paid.

Sub-inspectors are paid from half again to two times as much as the minimum adequate wage at current prices. At the same time, they are required to be university graduates. They bring to their job a set of expectations about standards of life to which they are entitled that must exceed by twice a barely minimum salary. One can understand that although they may be able to keep body and soul together on this salary, they are bound to feel dissatisfied and frustrated. Yet these are the men who for the most part are in charge of police stations and are responsible in the first instance for the supervision of the bulk of the police.

Housing and welfare schemes make some contribution to the alleviation of this situation, but it is not substantial. Nor are allowances in lieu of housing nearly adequate. Due to the limitations on resources, the lower ranks of the Indian police by and large must make do on their salary supplemented by dearness allowance.

But police work is not ordinary work. It is arduous, often dirty and unpleasant, and sometimes dangerous. Indian policemen are always subject to call; they may be routed out for special duty at any time. Night work is a standard feature of their life. They are not paid for overtime work. They often work holidays and during special festivals, times during which civilians are released from work to spend with their families. Dirty jobs fall their way, such as removing decomposed bodies—human or animal—from wells or roads. They are expected to risk their lives to prevent robberies or dacoities. And, finally, the responsibility thrust upon them is enormous. India is no exception to a general rule: of no other occupation is so much demanded with so little recognition and recompense.

Low pay is certainly not a new problem; it has been the bane of police administration for more than one hundred years. Sir

[49] *India, A Reference Annual, 1965*, p. 163.

John Shore once wrote that ". . . the subordinate police in India were paid so low as almost to justify corruption."[50] And a British officer of the 1920's said that a sub-inspector's salary "barely suffices to secure a good cook in Bombay or an indifferent chauffeur."[51] But despite many strong recommendations for higher pay and trenchant documentation of the plight of the lower ranks, the situation today falls far short of a desirable state of affairs. The recommendations for higher pay will continue to issue like water from a spring—all the recent police commissions have commented on the need—but they will provide scant refreshment in place of the substantial increases that stringent financial conditions as well as higher priority needs seem to preclude.

Raises in pay and allowances are certainly not sufficient conditions for achieving honesty among the police. Many rich people have very low moral standards and take and give bribes shamelessly. But raises in pay would erode the sympathy which the straitened conditions of the lower ranks elicit. Improvement in the standard of livelihood would remove the virtue in necessity upon which a great deal of toleration of corruption rests.[52]

[50] Quoted in Bihar Police Commission, p. 169.

[51] T. C. Arthur, *Reminiscences of an Indian Police Official* (London: Sampson Low, Marston and Co., 1894), p. 111.

[52] The question this discussion indirectly raises is the relation between amounts of corruption and standards of life of police in different countries. There are no studies, to my knowledge, that seek to compare relative standards of remuneration and occupational status of the police with their reputation for honesty. As I have noted, there are more causes for misconduct than economic need. But it would be interesting and possibly important to determine for many countries (a) the place of the police in each country's occupational structure with respect to pay and status and (b) whether rank on a livelihood-status scale correlates at all with the incidence of corrupt practices.

12 • *University Students and the Police*

In developing nations university students constitute a group that plays an unusually important role both in the conduct of day-to-day politics and in determining the character of social development. University students more than almost any other set of individuals are forced to mediate in their daily lives the conflicts of tradition and modernity. They constitute the leading edge of self-conscious change. Because an intellectual class is generally not large in these countries, students contribute disproportionately to informed public opinion. From their ranks will come tomorrow's politicians, administrators, journalists, judges, doctors, scientists, and teachers. Moreover, university students are generally restive. They are conscious of being part of a unique social stratum; they are also conscious that students in the recent past, especially during struggles for national independence, played a conspicuous part in practical politics. They demand rights commensurate with their conception of their potential importance and they seek to act as the intellectual, at least idealistic, conscience of their countries. Politics for them is not an avocation to be assumed after graduation; it is an imperative of academic standing. In many countries, and certainly in India, agitational activities by students have challenged university authorities again and again and have often shattered the peace of surrounding communities and the nation as a whole. "Student indiscipline," as it is known in India, has become a byword. Police authorities treat university students with great circumspection. When police officials are asked about especially critical groups to watch in order to prevent a breakdown of law and order, they invariably specify university students.

University students, then, both because of their potential importance in development and their contemporary activism, are deserving of particular study and attention. The basic question to ask in a study of the police and political development is, To what extent are the experiences of university students with the police and their attitudes toward them different from those of the general public? If students are unique, is this a function of being a student or of more general factors at work in the society at large which are simply more heavily concentrated among university students? And, finally, if they are different, what does this bode for the future? Is their uniqueness of experience and attitude specific to the university environment and hence something that may be shed in the next of life's stages? Or is it likely to have persistent effects, bending this generation much differently than their parents' or the succeeding intellectual generation.

NATURE OF THE SAMPLE

The survey of student opinion was based on four samples, each sample coincidental with one university.[1] Twelve hundred interviews were conducted. Both male and female students were included. No attempt was made to construct an all-India sample.[2] The universities were chosen so as to represent the major university types: large and small, unitary and affiliating, center and state administered, and in north and south India. The characteristics of each university sample are shown in Table 27.

Do the four universities differ from one another with respect to the background of students attending them? In what ways is the typical student from Allahabad different from the typical student from Osmania, Delhi, or Bangalore? The highest concentration of women students is in Delhi and Bangalore universities. In

[1] Details of sampling procedure will be found in Appendix A.

[2] The data can only be considered representative of particular universities. Running the risk of a certain amount of distortion, I shall occasionally refer to findings based on the combined university samples, thus treating the four samples together as if they represented the totality of student opinion and experience. This will be done when statistical analysis has shown no significant differences in responses among the samples.

From official sources information is available with which to judge whether the student samples are representative of Indian students generally. See University Grants Commission, *University Development in India, 1964-1965*. The survey was made in 1965-1966. Women made up 20.3 percent of all students enrolled in 1964-1965; the survey proportion was 28.5 percent. Nineteen percent of all students lived in university hostels according to official figures; the survey percentage was 28.5 percent. Thus the sample slightly overrepresents women and people living in university residences. The sample proportions are remarkably similar to all-India figures with respect to nature of studies undertaken. In 1964-1965, 54 percent of all university students were in arts, commerce, and law; the survey proportion was 48.9 percent. Four percent were in medicine; the survey's proportion was 7.2 percent. Thirty-six percent were in science and engineering; the survey's proportion was 43.7 percent. These comparisons indicate that the samples are quite representative with respect to nature of studies being pursued by students. This is a factor many observers consider exceedingly important in affecting student behavior.

TABLE 27

DATA ON UNIVERSITIES CHOSEN FOR SAMPLING

| University | Enrollment | | | Type | Location | Central or state |
	Teaching depts.	Affiliated	Total			
Delhi	6,249	24,182	30,431	Federal	North	Central
Allahabad	6,970	3,018	9,988	Unitary	North	State
Osmania	12,482	17,640	30,122	Affiliating	South	State
Bangalore	1,050	17,034	18,084	Affiliating	South	State

SOURCE: Government of India, University Grants Commission, *University Development in India, 1964-1965*, Tables III and VII.

those schools about two out of five students are female. Figures given by the University Grants Commission for 1964-1965 put the proportion at Delhi at 37.8 percent, as compared with 41.7 percent in the survey.[3] At Delhi the proportion of women was rising slightly each year—between 1960-1961 and 1964-1965 at about the rate of 3 percent per year. The Osmania student sample is one-quarter women, compared with 17.3 percent officially. The Allahabad sample had the smallest proportion of women—11 percent compared with 15.5 percent officially. Most students sampled were in the age group below twenty years old. The rest were between twenty-one and thirty. Only a fractional percentage was older than thirty. Moving from youngest to oldest student sample, the universities were in order Delhi, Allahabad, Osmania, and Bangalore. For example, the proportion twenty years old and under is 89 percent in Delhi; in Bangalore the proportion is 51 percent.

Comparing the universities with respect to course of study adopted by students, the data show that the proportion of students in arts, commerce, and law together is greater in Delhi and Allahabad, while the proportion in science and engineering is greater in Bangalore and Osmania. Once again survey findings agree satisfactorily with official statistics.[4] Delhi has the highest concentration of arts, commerce, and law students, 74 percent, as opposed to 78 percent officially. Allahabad has 60 percent, as opposed to 63.6 percent officially. The proportions for Osmania and Bangalore are 30.7 percent and 31 percent, opposed to 38.9 percent and 27.1 percent officially. The northern schools, which also

[3] University Grants Commission, pp. 29-30.
[4] *Ibid.*, Table XVII, pp. 41-43.

have the youngest students, tend to stress arts, commerce, and law in comparison to the southern schools' stress on science and engineering.[5]

Some indication of the excellence of the students at each university can be obtained by examining the class of their school-leaving certificates. In American parlance this would be similar to examining their class standing. There are three divisions among school-leaving certificates. Delhi has the highest proportion of threes—the lowest division—and the smallest proportion of first. Allahabad and Osmania rank together and are better than Delhi. The highest proportion of firsts and lowest of thirds is at Bangalore. The data support the often-repeated proposition that better brains go into science and engineering than go into arts, commerce, and law.

The proportion of degree-holders interviewed—that is, people with at least a B.A. degree and doing post-graduate work—did not differ significantly among the universities.

Turning to criteria of social class, the data show that proportionately more students at Delhi University come from families of high educational attainments and high incomes than at the other schools. (See Table 28.) What is more, Delhi University ranks highest in proportion of students coming from an urban environment. Bangalore ranks next with respect to these criteria, followed by Allahabad and Osmania together. Delhi students, then, tend to be more well-to-do, to be more urbanized, and to come from more educated families than is true of students at the other three schools. Allahabad and Osmania have student bodies that come from less well-educated families, lower incomes, and rural environments. For example, only 4 percent of Delhi students come from families where the father is illiterate; the proportion for Osmania is 19 percent and for Allahabad 14 percent. Among Delhi students, only 5 percent come from rural villages; in Allahabad 44 percent do and in Osmania 35 percent.

[5] For purposes of statistical analysis, curricula have been grouped together along a continuum of increasing technological and scientific involvement. Thus students in arts, commerce, and law have been put together in the same category. Many people believe that courses of study become more demanding in the same progression. Arts is the easiest, physical sciences the most difficult. The prospects for employment also become much brighter as one moves from arts-commerce-law to science-engineering. Finally, there is a common supposition that curriculum is an important variable in determining the participation of students in agitations and demonstrations. Students in arts, commerce, and law are believed to be the most active; students in science and engineering the least. For all these reasons, then, the various curricula have been ordered in this fashion.

TABLE 28
EDUCATION OF FATHER, INCOME, LOCATION OF HOME

	Delhi (percent)	Allahabad (percent)	Osmania (percent)	Bangalore (percent)
Education of family				
Post-graduate	12.3	13.0	9.7	8.0
Graduate	33.0	16.7	21.7	37.0
Intermediate	5.3	7.7	10.0	11.3
Matriculate	26.3	18.7	12.3	28.7
Under-matriculate	13.3	16.0	6.3	3.0
Literate	2.7	13.0	15.3	6.0
Illiterate	4.3	13.7	19.0	4.0
Income				
Over Rs. 1,000	21.7	5.3	18.3	19.0
751-1,000	15.0	6.0	4.7	9.7
501-750	10.7	7.3	8.3	6.7
301-500	24.7	10.7	12.7	20.7
151-300	16.7	25.3	20.0	21.7
75-100	3.7	23.0	22.0	17.0
Under Rs. 75	0.7	17.0	8.3	3.3
Location of home				
Rural	4.7	43.7	35.3	8.0
Town	5.0	24.3	41.0	18.3
City	90.3	32.0	23.7	73.0

The vast majority of students in all samples come from families of literate fathers. Indeed, most of the students come from families where the father was at least a matriculate. The proportions with matriculate fathers are Delhi, 77 percent; Allahabad, 56 percent; Osmania, 54 percent; and Bangalore, 85 percent.[6] At Delhi and Bangalore a majority of students come from families whose incomes are over Rs. 300 per month. At Osmania and Allahabad the income floor for the majority is only over Rs. 150 per month. Allahabad has the poorest students. The vast majority of students are town people; this is especially true in Delhi and Bangalore. In fact, except at Osmania, one-third of all students surveyed came from large-city backgrounds.

Due to a survey error, caste data were available only for the northern universities. At Delhi and Allahabad a majority of students sampled came from upper caste backgrounds. They were Brahmans, Kayastha, or Khatri. The proportion at Delhi was

[6] Margaret L. Cormack, *She Who Rides a Peacock* (New York: Praeger, 1961), p. 20, estimated that 60 percent of all Indian university students came from families which had never sent anyone to an institution of higher learning. My survey found a lower proportion of "new students."

70.4 percent and at Allahabad 67.4 percent. Scheduled castes made up 5 percent of the students at Allahabad and 1 percent at Delhi. Delhi is more caste homogeneous than Allahabad; it has proportionately fewer Brahmans and fewer scheduled castes as well. Allahabad also has more Jat, Ahirs, and Yadavs than does Delhi. These are low but not scheduled castes.

As one would expect, Delhi and Allahabad contain proportionately more Hindus; Bangalore and Osmania, especially the latter, more Muslims. Sikh students are concentrated in the north and more so in Delhi than in Allahabad.

Putting the bits and pieces together, the most modern and urbanized students are in Delhi and Bangalore universities. The most able, however, appear to be in Osmania and Bangalore. Osmania and Bangalore also have a heavier concentration of students in the sciences. It would appear from the north Indian data that more modern students are also more caste homogeneous, that is, representing a lower proportion of castes belonging to the ends of the caste continuum. One would expect then that Bangalore, like Delhi, has proportionately fewer of both Brahmins and scheduled castes. The two northern universities have both the highest and the lowest proportions of students living in, Allahabad, 38 percent, and Delhi, 8 percent. In the southern group, Osmania had 11 percent living in university hostels, Bangalore had 13 percent.[7] The religious composition of the student bodies reflects the distribution of religions in the surrounding regions. More Sikhs in the north; more Muslims in Hyderabad; and more Christians in the south.

The survey data provide a unique opportunity to explore the relation between social class and choice of curricula. Do students from more modern, higher status groups tend to gravitate more to arts, commerce, and law or toward science and engineering? The answer is that there is no effect. In none of the four samples is the proportion of students in arts, commerce, and law as opposed to science and engineering affected significantly by caste, location of home, and father's education and income. (See Table 29.) Within each sample the proportion of students from families with high caste status, incomes, and education that chose arts, commerce, and law was the same as from among families of low caste status, income, and education. There were, however, major differences in proportions between samples, that is, in different parts

[7] University Grants Commission, pp. 96-97.

TABLE 29

The Distribution of Students in Curricula
According to Social Background

A. Delhi University		Variable 9	
	Arts, commerce, law (percent)	Medicine (percent)	Science, engineering (percent)
Variable 14: Father's education			
Post-graduate	73.0	5.4	18.9
Graduate	65.7	6.1	28.3
Intermediate	81.2	6.2	6.2
Matriculate	73.4	2.5	24.0
Under-matriculate	85.0	2.5	12.5
Literate	75.0	12.5	12.5
Illiterate	84.6	0.0	7.7
Variable 15: Father's income			
Rs. 1,000, and over	73.9	1.5	21.5
751-1,000	60.0	20.0	20.0
501-750	71.9	3.1	25.0
301-500	77.0	1.4	20.3
151-300	74.0	0.0	26.0
75-150	72.7	9.1	18.2
Under Rs. 75	100.0	0.0	0.0
Variable 13: Caste			
Brahmin	66.0	6.0	24.0
Kayastha-Khatri	78.3	3.1	18.6
Vaish	70.4	0.0	27.3
Rajput	50.0	0.0	50.0
Jat, Ahir, Yadav	100.0	0.0	0.0
Scheduled caste	0.0	33.3	66.7
Variable 16: Location of home			
Rural	64.3	7.1	28.6
Town	40.0	0.0	53.3
City	76.0	4.4	18.8

of the country. In Delhi and Allahabad all castes and classes sent
the larger proportion of their offspring into arts, commerce, and
law. In Osmania and Bangalore, on the other hand, all classes—
we don't know about castes—sent the larger proportion of their
offspring into science and engineering. If a school has a majority
of its students in science and engineering a majority of the
students of every class and caste will choose science and engineering. Caste and class simply do not affect whether a student chooses science as opposed to arts, or medicine as opposed
to law, or commerce as opposed to engineering. Nor does it mat-

TABLE 29 (cont'd)

B. *Allahabad University*

	Arts, commerce, law (percent)	Medicine (percent)	Science, engineering (percent)
Variable 14: Father's education			
Post-graduate	71.8	0.0	28.2
Graduate	52.0	0.0	48.0
Intermediate	21.7	0.0	78.3
Matriculate	57.1	0.0	42.9
Under-matriculate	62.5	0.0	37.5
Literate	66.7	0.0	33.3
Illiterate	78.0	0.0	22.0
Variable 15: Father's income			
Rs. 1,000, and over	68.8	0.0	31.2
751-1,000	72.2	0.0	27.8
501-750	59.1	0.0	40.9
301-500	43.8	0.0	56.2
151-300	50.0	0.0	50.0
75-150	63.8	0.0	36.2
Under Rs. 75	78.4	0.0	21.6
Variable 13: Caste			
Brahmin	69.5	0.0	30.5
Kayastha-Khatri	53.3	0.0	46.7
Vaish	52.8	0.0	47.2
Rajput	50.0	0.0	50.0
Jat, Ahir, Yadav	77.8	0.0	22.2
Scheduled caste	73.3	0.0	26.7
Variable 16: Location of home			
Rural	62.6	0.0	37.4
Town	46.6	0.0	53.4
City	66.7	0.0	33.3

ter if a student is from an urban or rural environment. Students from rural areas are as likely to go into science as students from a major urban center. The reasons for the choices students make with respect to their course of study must be found elsewhere than in the influence of caste, class, or home location.

One explanation for this finding would be that choice of curricula is determined not by social antecedents but by influences peculiar to the setting of higher education. When students become immersed in higher education, they begin to respond to forces that are a part of its environment, certainly with respect to choices that deal in its own terms, while the parochial influences of family, class, and childhood environment begin to dissolve. This would suggest that when one participates in higher

TABLE 29 (cont'd)

C. *Osmania University*

	Arts, commerce, law (percent)	Medicine (percent)	Science, engineering (percent)
Variable 14: Father's education			
Post-graduate	31.0	20.7	48.3
Graduate	30.8	12.3	56.9
Intermediate	20.0	13.3	66.7
Matriculate	29.7	10.8	59.5
Under-matriculate	26.3	5.3	68.4
Literate	37.0	21.7	41.3
Illiterate	26.3	12.3	61.4
Variable 15: Father's income			
Rs. 1,000, and over	40.0	12.7	47.3
751-1,000	35.7	21.4	42.9
501-750	20.0	20.0	60.0
301-500	18.4	18.4	63.2
151-300	38.3	6.7	55.0
75-150	24.2	21.2	54.6
Under Rs. 75	24.0	8.0	68.0
Variable 13: Caste			
Brahmin	—	—	—
Kayastha-Khatri	—	—	—
Vaish	—	—	—
Rajput	—	—	—
Jat, Ahir, Yadav	—	—	—
Scheduled caste	—	—	—
Variable 16: Location of home			
Rural	23.6	17.0	59.4
Town	33.3	13.0	53.7
City	36.6	11.3	52.1

education one becomes a part of another subculture, a subculture that demands and restrains on its own. The choice of curriculum a student makes is the product of interaction between the individual student and the immediate university environment and not between individual student and his family environment. The implication would be that government in India can affect the composition of skills being learned and knowledge acquired without recourse to changing fundamental social conditions but merely by manipulating rules, structures, and norms within university communities. The course of study an Indian student chooses is a function of what universities do and not what that student is or where he comes from.

TABLE 29 (cont'd)

D. *Bangalore University*

	Arts, commerce, law (percent)	Medicine (percent)	Science, engineering (percent)
Variable 14: Father's education			
Post-graduate	25.0	12.5	62.5
Graduate	30.6	9.0	60.4
Intermediate	38.2	0.0	61.8
Matriculate	30.2	12.8	57.0
Under-matriculate	22.2	33.3	44.4
Literate	27.8	11.1	61.1
Illiterate	33.3	25.0	41.7
Variable 15: Father's income			
Rs. 1,000, and over	36.8	26.3	36.8
751-1,000	34.5	13.8	51.7
501-750	30.0	10.0	60.0
301-500	37.1	4.8	58.1
151-300	23.1	3.1	73.8
75-150	29.4	7.8	62.8
Under Rs. 75	20.0	0.0	80.0
Variable 13: Caste			
Brahmin	—	—	—
Kayastha-Khatri	—	—	—
Vaish	—	—	—
Rajput	—	—	—
Jat, Ahir, Yadav	—	—	—
Scheduled caste	—	—	—
Variable 16: Location of home			
Rural	29.2	29.2	41.7
Town	30.9	16.4	52.7
City	31.5	6.4	62.1

SENSE OF SECURITY AND CONTACT WITH THE POLICE

By far the vast majority of university students feel no marked sense of anxiety about their safety in the university area. The greatest insecurity was expressed by Delhi students—14 percent saying that they did not generally feel that in the university area there was safety for the student. At Allahabad and Osmania anxiety was expressed by half as many and in Bangalore by only a third as many. Nor did students who lived outside the university, in a private dwelling of some kind, express a greater fear for their safety in these surroundings than all students did within the university precincts. Even in Delhi, only 8.7 percent of the students sampled said they felt a lack of security in their living area, that they felt they could be easily robbed or hurt there. Delhi students as a whole, regardless of where they lived, were most concerned about security within the university campus. Students who lived "out" were less anxious about their safety outside the university than all students were about their safety within it. Students who lived in university hostels were asked a special series of questions. They were asked whether they thought it was safe to keep valuables in their rooms. Most of them did; the percentage that did not ranged between 5 percent (Delhi) to 11 percent (Osmania). This is analogous to the question asked the general public about the safety of personal property in their homes. Eighteen percent of the public said that it was not. It is probably true that students have less of value to worry about. Asked specifically about thievery in the residence halls, there was little indication of concern. Three percent or less said there was a lot of it. Twenty percent or less said there was little, and the rest said there was none. The students were asked to characterize discipline generally in the residence halls. Most said it was good, although about 40 percent of the residents described it as "so-so." Ten percent or less said it was bad. Osmania students showed the greatest concern. There about half said it was so-so, while another 12 percent said it was bad. Only about 40 percent said it was good.

Students were asked to estimate the amount of criminal activity engaged in by other students. Their responses indicate a surprising extent of criminal action by students, at least in the eyes of their peers. While about 3 percent of all students said that many engaged in it, 20 percent of all students thought that "some" engaged in it, as opposed to a few or none. "Some" and "a few" might have been considered synonymous except that "some" lay between "many" and "a few" in the categories provided. I am inclined to believe that the choice of "some" indicates something substantial.

Students had personally been victims of a crime with greater frequency than people in the general public rural sample but less often than people in the general public urban sample. Of the combined student sample, 3 percent had been the victims of a crime; for the urban samples the figure was 10 percent and for the rural sample 1.3 percent.

On the basis of this data, one could not say that students are beset by nagging fears for their safety. There is an indication, however, that there is room for improvement at Delhi University. Nor does it appear that hostel living creates many anxieties about the safety of person or property. At the same time, student indiscipline of a criminal kind—perhaps not directed at other students —may not be negligible. At least this seems to be the opinion of students themselves.

Partly because of the incidence of student indiscipline and partly because security conditions within certain universities have from time to time been cause for concern, suggestions have been made that the universities develop their own security forces or that local police be allowed to play a larger role on the campuses. The latter policy would represent a considerable break with traditional police-university relations. University campuses are hallowed ground; local police intrude upon them only with the permission of university authorities or in situations of extreme disorder or serious criminal activity.[8] The survey asked students about their willingness both to have universities develop their own police systems and to have the local police play a larger role in curbing crime within the university. These two questions provide a measure of student anxiety about their security as well as of the extent to which they prize freedom from police authority in the university setting. As might be expected, students were more favorably disposed to the development of university security forces than they were to greater intrusion by the local police. About 35 percent of all students were in favor of the development of university security forces. Almost half of Delhi respondents approved the measure. This may reflect the greater apprehension about safety found among Delhi students. Bangalore students were least receptive, only 20 percent being in favor. About 30 percent of Osmania and Allahabad students approved the development of university security forces. With respect to local police playing a larger role, only 20 percent overall were in favor. Considering the sanctity the campus enjoys in student minds, this figure is surprisingly large. Once again Delhi students were the most receptive, 30 percent being in favor. On the other hand, only 7 percent of Allahabad students were in favor. This may reflect the more abrasive relations that have existed in the recent past between Allahabad students and police. About 20 percent of the students at Osmania and Bangalore were in favor.

Since most students, even at Delhi, are against either proposal,

[8] Seymour M. Lipset has commented about the special position of universities in underdeveloped countries: "In many societies the university is responsible for student conduct and the corporate autonomy of the university is often a symbol, as well as a bulwark, of the immunity of the students from external authority on their dependent condition." "University Students and Politics in Underdeveloped Countries," *Minerva*, Autumn, 1964, p. 30.

the chances of obtaining student approval or even acquiescence would not seem to be great. At the same time, if the issue of security arrangements was carefully handled and not simply sprung on the students as a fait accompli, it might be that over a period of time new security procedures could be introduced that would win the appreciation of students. The key, however, would be careful preparation and gradual implementation.

University students have generally had less contact with the police than members of the urban public but more than rural people. Throughout the total student sample 13 percent have gone to the police for help at some time or other. The range of proportions was from 18 percent in Bangalore to 8 percent in Allahabad. About 20 percent of urban people in the general public sample had gone to the police for help, while only 5 percent of rural people had. Ten percent of the student sample had been questioned. Once again these figures were greater than among rural people but less than among the urban public. Significantly, Allahabad students, who are the most rural in their origins, had the lowest percentages under each heading. The data confirm a finding stated earlier that urban living tends to increase police contact.

Evaluating the treatment they received in their contacts, students were more complementary than critical. Three to four times as many students thought they were treated courteously and sympathetically than rudely and unsympathetically. This conforms to survey findings for the general public, except in Kanpur where as many were displeased as pleased. With respect to being questioned or having had a friend questioned, opinion tended to be complementary in the majority of cases. At the same time, students are not strangers to certain unpleasant actions of the police, especially having seen someone struck or witnessing money being paid over to them. Almost one in three said they had seen the police accept money. The proportions were 44 percent in Osmania, 35 percent in Bangalore, 17 percent in Delhi, and 16 percent in Allahabad. Experience with seeing someone struck was more uniform: 41 percent in Osmania, 36 percent in Allahabad, 36 percent in Delhi, and 30 percent in Bangalore. Much fewer knew someone personally who had been struck or threatened. Asked about the occasion for the physical abuse they witnessed, most students cited what they thought had been the beating of suspects, mentioning black-marketeers, thieves, or smugglers. It is of course not clear whether they saw sustained abuse or simply the cuffing of a suspect in a public place either while he was being apprehended or in transit. Next, students cited crowd-control activities of the police, as during agitations and demonstrations or in keeping order at cinemas or festivals, as the occasion for the physical abuse they had witnessed. Finally, they cited police handling of undesirable, antisocial persons, such as goondas, drunkards, gamblers, and people of doubtful character. The lesson from this data is that university students have personally witnessed physical abuse by the police. Most of it seems to occur in public places. Unless the need is imperative, police should be advised to curb these activities especially in public places. We shall see later that experiences such as these do affect the judgments students—and the general public—make about police behavior.

Background characteristics do not affect neutral contact with the police—with one exception. The Delhi data suggest that females tend to have somewhat less contact with the police in the form of having gone to them for help, being questioned, or having a friend questioned. The association, however, is not strong, being about 0.20 in a sample of three hundred. And it is only in Delhi that this relation shows up. Similarly, there is no meaningful relation between background and experience with unpleasant police behavior. There is a suggestion on several items that women have had less experience. This is especially true with respect to seeing the police take money. By and large, however, experience with the police is not affected by social background. The pattern among the general public was different. There the higher the social class the greater was the likelihood of contact, although the association was not terribly strong, the correlation being less than 0.30.

There is hardly any relation between neutral contact and unpleasant contact. That is, people who have had some contact with the police are not necessarily likely to have been a witness to some unpleasant police action. There are significant but slight correlations between a respondent's having had a friend questioned and having had a friend threatened or struck by the police. It would appear, therefore, that friends of students are apt to describe their experience of being questioned in terms unfavorable to the police. Of course it may be that in questioning, police are in the habit of threatening or cuffing. This seems not to be the case since there is no consistent linkage between the respondent's own questioning and his having been struck. In sum, there may be a tendency for students to exaggerate the difficulty of their experience with police to the detriment of police reputation. It should be stressed, however, that the tendency to exaggeration, if any, has little effect, accounting for only about 5 to 10 percent of the variance in the unpleasant experience variables.

Students, like the general public, were asked to specify whether they would or would not go to the police for help. As with the general public, they were least inclined to go to the police if someone was injured by an animal or in a fall. About 50 percent of the total sample said they would not go in this situation. The police are not generally thought of as being helpful in situations of medical emergency. The next item of greatest reluctance concerned finding a man who had been beaten up. Whether students didn't want to get involved or didn't think police could be helpful in healing the man is not clear. Sixteen percent said that they would not ask police for directions if they were lost in a strange town. On the other hand, students overwhelmingly would have recourse to the police if a child was lost. Ninety-three percent held this view. Ninety percent said they would go to the police if a person had been killed accidentally or if a person was found who looked as if he had been murdered. For the other items, such as being robbed of various amounts or anticipating a fight or an attack by goondas, the percentage who would go to the police was never less than 70 percent. In sum, students seem to be willing to go to the police when it cannot be avoided, when the police are likely to find out anyhow, or when the situation is neutral from a criminal standpoint but urgent, as when a child is lost. But they do not reflexively think of the police when a medical emergency arises or even when they need personal assistance in a city.

Hesitancy to contact is not related to social position or locality. Only in the Delhi and Allahabad data is there a suggestion that the lower the income of the family the greater the reluctance to appeal to the police. This finding does tally with the general public results.

EVALUATIONS OF THE POLICE

Students are generally about as critical of the police as northern urban residents. They have strong doubts about police behavior, particularly about corruption and favoritism. Students are much more critical than the rural public. In other words, Indian university students are as uncharitable in their judgments about the police as the most negative section of the public. They partake of the cynicism of India's urban communities. This may be because they are as forthright as urban people or because they are genuinely as disenchanted with the police. At the same time, there is a tendency for southern university students to be somewhat more favorably disposed than northern ones, although this is not true on all issues, certainly not with respect to favoritism and political control.

University students do not see the police as being implacably hostile to them as students. Asked to evaluate the attitude of police toward them, not more than 25 percent said police were suspicious, uncooperative, or hostile. About a third in each sample said police were cooperative. About a fourth said indifferent. And from 8 percent to 24 percent said they were friendly. Students evaluated the police most favorably in Delhi and Bangalore. Allahabad students were the most negative; Osmania students were less critical than Allahabad's but not as well disposed as Delhi's and Bangalore's. Students do not, then, appear to feel especially victimized by the police.

They do not rate the police highly, however, with respect to general willingness to help. Asked if they thought the police sincerely try to help people who come to them, exactly one-half of all respondents said they did *not*. With the exception of Bangalore, more students spoke against the police than spoke for them. Allahabad students were overwhelmingly critical, 74 percent saying they did not think the police sincerely tried to help people.

Students, like the urban public in the north, are strongly inclined to view the police as rude, abusive, and violent. Depending on the sample, from a third to two-thirds of all respondents thought that when police came around asking questions they were generally rude and tricky and not courteous and fair. Moreover, from 15 to 50 percent believe that police "often" beat people up. At least two-thirds of the respondents believe that police "sometimes" beat people up. Asked especially whether people who are taken to the station house, even those who are not criminals, are often threatened and beaten, approximately 50 percent said that the police in this situation threatened and beat everyone. Being a criminal is not a critical factor. For each of these items, Allahabad students were by far the most critical, followed by Delhi and Osmania. Bangalore students were the most charitable.

Students are not quite as willing to justify physical abuse of suspects by the police as the general public. Still, a majority of them did say that the police would be justified in beating an individual to obtain a confession if they knew he was guilty and didn't have sufficient evidence to convict him. Allahabad students were least willing to countenance this kind of behavior. Perhaps because Allahabad students were so extremely suspicious of the police, they realized the cost of allowing police this license. Students' willingness to justify recourse to coercion increased in all samples by about 10 percent when they themselves were the projected victims of the offense. That is, when asked if police were justified in beating in order to obtain a confession from a suspect who had robbed the student, more than half—and in Bangalore two-thirds—said that they would be justified.

The police are undoubtedly right when they assert that the public has very ambiguous feelings about police use of force. Although they may criticize the police for it, they are often insistent in demanding it, especially when they are themselves involved. The data also suggest that physical coercion is not as frowned upon in India as in the United States or Great Britain. Indians may accept it not only as common police practice but as necessary police practice. It would probably be wrong to think that because belief in police coercion is so widespread police are universally despised because of it. To be sure, the prospect of brutality must affect ready cooperation with the police. But the public, and students, may not be able to see a feasible alternative. Their reaction to police coercion may not be anger and disgust but a mental shrug. Many people may even question whether the police are doing their duty if they forswear physical abuse.

Students seriously doubt the honesty of police investigations. Asked whether police twist and/or make up evidence in order to obtain convictions, the vast majority—85 percent and above—said that they did.

Belief in the venality of the police is very widespread among students. From a third in Bangalore to three-fourths in Allahabad believe there is a "great deal" of corruption in the police. What is more, about two-thirds in each sample believe it is necessary to bribe in order to get the police to do their duty and to help people. Students are not quite as willing as the urban general public to put belief into practice—or at least not as willing to admit they would do so. Not more than 22 percent in any sample

admitted they would take money with them as a precaution-
ary measure if they had to go to a police station with a request.
By contrast, 11.7 percent of Bangalore city respondents would take
money, 26.5 percent of Tumkur's, 39.0 percent of Kanpur residents, and 38.6 percent of Kanpur rural migrants.

About a third of all students think they know of instances
when police refused to give assistance until money was paid.
However, like the general public, very few knew personally the
people involved. On the other hand, somewhat over a fourth of all
students had seen police accept money. The proportion was
greatest in Osmania, 44 percent; next highest in Bangalore, 35 percent; and least highest in Delhi and Allahabad, 17.3 percent and
16.3 percent, respectively. Belief in corruption is nurtured by and
large by rumor. The amount of first-hand experience students
think they have of it is certainly great enough to keep the rumor
mills grinding productively for a long time to come.

Students are less inclined to believe that police "often" join
hands with criminals than that they are corrupt, although more
than half of them believe collusion occurs either "often" or "sometimes." Delhi and Allahabad students are the most suspicious; 20
percent believe police often join hands with criminals. Fifty percent believe collusion occurs sometimes. Osmania students are the
least suspicious, only 4 percent believing collusion occurs often;
30 percent saying "sometimes." At Bangalore, 7 percent said
"often," 50 percent sometimes.

University students do not see the police as being impartial
or free from political control. There were major differences between universities. The split was along north-south geographical
lines. About 60 percent of Delhi and Allahabad students thought
that there was favoritism in police work. Respondents could have
chosen to say "sometimes" rather than a flat yes or no. Since
60 percent did not choose the lesser category, it is clear then
that they have substantial doubts about police impartiality in the
north. At Osmania and Bangalore the proportion was half as great.
Very few people, however, gave the police a clean bill of health.
Among rural students—a small proportion of the total sample—
more of them said the police took sides among factions in their villages than said they did not. At Allahabad, for example, which
had the largest proportion of rural students, three times as many
said the police took sides among factions as said they did not.
In the south the responses were more evenly balanced. Whatever
the truth is about favoritism in the faction game of village India,

the fact remains that behavior of the police will be judged from a factional perspective. Where emotions are engaged in intravillage contention, the police will be damned if they do and damned if they don't.

Students both north and south think there is a "great deal" of political control of the police. Sixty percent of the combined sample hold this view. The greatest difference in opinion is between Delhi and Allahabad, 53.3 percent and 66 percent, respectively. Many but not most students say they have heard stories of politicians of the area being able to stop an investigation or get the police to go after someone. From 14 to 30 percent think that the police take sides at election time. Public opinion, among students and the man-in-the-street, is certainly not yet disposed to view the police as everyman's champion of the right.

Students assess one another's predispositions toward the police in a mellow light. As in their evaluations of police predispositions toward them, the largest group think that students are generally cooperative.[9] The next largest group is indifferent. Not more than 25 percent perceive other students as suspicious, uncooperative, or hostile. Among these three categories, uncooperative is the dominant negative attitude attributed. Close to one-fifth perceive other students as "friendly" toward the police. It must be said once again that the meaningfulness of a question of this kind is open to serious question. Nonoperational, omnibus attitudes tell us very little about what respondents will do in real situations, whether in terms of verbal or physical behavior.

Do students perceive the behavior of the police in the way they treat people as getting better or worse? After all, India is going through a time of great change; it is important to determine whether police are seen as part of changing society, and whether the change is healthy. The data were very different at each university. Delhi and Bangalore students thought that treatment of persons by the police was improving. Sixty-six percent shared this opinion at Bangalore, 51 percent in Delhi. Only 11 percent and 15 percent at Bangalore and Delhi, respectively, thought things were becoming worse. At Allahabad and Osmania, on the other hand, perceptions of a negative trend were much greater. Thirty-nine percent at Allahabad thought behavior was getting worse, as against 25 percent who thought it was improving. At Osmania the favorable and unfavorable perceptions balanced, 32 percent

---

[9] Delhi, 29.0 percent; Allahabad, 29.3 percent; Osmania, 28.0 percent; Bangalore, 40.0 percent.

in each case. In short, students do not feel that police are rigidly unchanging; they are aware that change is possible, and many more students perceive a change for the better than a change for the worse.

Students were asked what they thought of the people who entered the police. Compared to the army, did they think that a higher, similar, or lower type joined the police? A majority in every sample said recruits to the army were superior. At the same time, students were not universally negative about careers in the police. They were asked whether they thought being in the police would be a good or bad job. At least half of all respondents in every sample thought being in the police would be a good job.[10] Allahabad students, as might have been expected, were the most negative. Very few students spoke outright against a career in the police.[11] It would seem, therefore, that while the army has pride of place, the police force is not beyond the pale. A caveat is in order, however, because these items may not be properly comparable. Indians distinguish between officers and "men" in the police. It may have been that respondents had "men" in mind when asked about the quality of recruits and officers in mind when asked about their own career evaluations. It would not be inconsistent for individuals to think that recruits to non-officer posts were inferior in the police and yet still find becoming an officer in the Indian Police Service an attractive prospect. Any future survey might usefully obtain more accurate information about the status of a career in the police at different rank levels and with people of various classes and communities.

Students are uniformly of the opinion that police are underpaid. Like members of the general public, they would presumably not be opposed to higher wage rates for policemen, especially, one would think, if it were coupled with a well-publicized program for the elimination of corruption.

Having established a general picture of the kind of judgments students make of the police, what factors account for these opinions? Of particular importance is the question what effect contact has upon the evaluations students make. We have already seen in the case of the general public that there is no association between contact per se and evaluations of the police. Unpleasant experi-

[10] Delhi, 55 percent; Allahabad, 61 percent; Osmania, 50 percent; Bangalore, 66 percent.
[11] Delhi, 21.3 percent; Allahabad, 30.7 percent; Osmania, 15 percent; Bangalore, 5.3 percent.

ence with the police, however, does correlate with negative evaluations of them. Not only does unpleasant experience of some kind associate with negative judgments on the same topic but any unpleasant contact is likely to be associated with negative evaluations across the board. What is the pattern among students?

In every sample at least one factor was generated that was defined in terms of the evaluative judgments students make of the police. That is, there was a strong tendency in every sample for answers to the evaluative items to cluster together. This indicates that students tend to hold favorable or unfavorable views across a range of police behavior. Examining the association of contact variables—neutral and unpleasant—with these factors, one finds that the neutral items are not significantly associated with the making of judgments, while the unpleasant contact items certainly are. The conclusion to be drawn is that contact as such is without effect on attitudes; what is important in attitude formation is the personal reading of the pleasantness of that contact. And since, as we have already seen, unpleasant contact among students is not associated with contact as such, increased contact with the police is likely to be neutral in its effects upon attitudes. One cannot say that those students who have had more contact with the police are more likely or less likely to hold unfavorable opinions about them.

Several unpleasant contact items are strongly associated with evaluative judgments. People who have been well treated when they went to the police for help or people who have had a friend questioned courteously and fairly or people who have not seen the police strike someone or have not seen the police take money, all these are much more likely to hold favorable opinions about police behavior.[12] The converse is also true. Four other items are associated with the kind of judgments students hold, although less strongly than the former. They are whether an individual was himself questioned courteously and fairly; whether an individual knew personally someone who had to give money to the police before help was rendered; and whether an individual knew someone personally who had been threatened or struck by the police. There can be no question then that eyewitness or near-eyewitness experiences teach a powerful lesson. An unpleasant experience ramifies; it touches the opinions of others through word of mouth and it touches the whole range of opinions people hold

[12] The loadings of contact items on the evaluative factors in each sample ranged from 0.15 through 0.57. The association was strongest in Bangalore.

about the police. An unhappy experience with the police is not quickly swallowed up in daily preoccupations; it echoes for years and may even become magnified in its influence by warping the readings people are then inclined to make of innocuous encounters with police.

Although there were very significant differences in evaluations among students at the different universities, these cannot be explained in terms of different social composition of the samples or in terms of curriculum choices or place of residence at the university. Examining the correlations between background variables and the well-defined evaluation factors generated in each sample, one finds only sex showing a consistent loading in each sample. The loadings are not high, usually less than 0.30 although as much as 0.42 in the case of Bangalore. The factor loading of sex on an evaluative factor generated from the combined student population was 0.28. The Delhi loadings were contradictory, however, so one must be cautious in assessing the effect of sex. If there is a consistent influence at all, it seems to be in the direction of creating more favorable judgments, but the effect is not large, accounting for only about 10 percent of the variance in the evaluative factor. There is a hint in the data from the combined sample that higher performance in secondary school and city residence tend to be associated with more favorable views of the police. It must be stressed that the correlations are very small and were only found in the combined sample. In general, social and university background do not affect judgments made about the police, with the modest exception of being female, which tends to mute critical judgments.

The marked differences in evaluations between universities must be explained in terms of greater negative contact or of specific environmental influences. There is no consistent relation between the ranking of universities with respect to an item of evaluation and with respect to having had personal experience with police misbehavior of the same type. For example, more Delhi and Allahabad students think there is a good deal of corruption in the police than do students at Osmania and Bangalore. Yet more students at Osmania and Bangalore have seen the police take money. Another example, three times as many Allahabad students think the police often beat people than do students at Osmania, yet 6 percent more students at Osmania than Allahabad have seen someone struck, 12 percent more know someone who has been threatened by them, and 9 percent more know someone who has been struck by them. One cannot, therefore, explain the differences between universities concerning evaluations on the basis of unpleasant experience differentials, although it is true within each university that negative evaluations tend to be associated with unpleasant experiences. What this means is that each university community is uniquely different from the others as far as inculcating certain predispositions toward the police. At each university first-hand unpleasant contact is influential, but it is influential to varying degrees depending on the general climate of opinion. Evaluations of the police are to some extent environment-specific. There seem to be propensities within different universities and the incoming student is socialized to them. A similar finding was discovered among the general public, with urban communities having the more critical climate of opinion. It is surprising, however, that universities, which one would have thought were more homogeneous with respect to one another than urban as opposed to rural settings, would show such unique traits. The survey evidence clearly shows that judgments about the police are affected by subcultural environments, although within each subcultural unpleasant experience is biasing against the police.

STUDENTS AND PUBLIC DISORDER

The problem of "student indiscipline," as it is popularly referred to in India, has plagued authorities and worried educators for many years. The phrase "student indiscipline" refers to collective and public acts of defiance and disorder. It involves strikes, mass obstruction of offices or streets, public demonstrations, riotous behavior, intimidation of shopkeepers, and clashes with the police. The causes of these collective disturbances are almost invariably local; they do not usually involve issues of national importance. Sometimes, although rarely, a wave of sympathetic agitations sweeps the universities, particularly if students at another school have been hurt or killed by the police in a firing. More commonly the causes are matters of strictly local concern, such as an increase in fees, failure to establish adequate facilities of some kind, too stiff examinations, unexpectedly severe examination results, a rise in the price of cinema tickets, rivalry in a student union election, opposition to the dismissal of a faculty member, recognition of certain kinds of degrees (Ayurvedic or

Unani), and appointment or removal of a vice-chancellor.[13] Unrest has been more common and more serious in the north and northeast of India, especially in Uttar Pradesh and West Bengal. Several universities have been closed indefinitely. Banaras Hindu University was closed in 1958 and a formal commission appointed to investigate the breakdown of order. Lucknow University was closed four times between 1958 and 1960. The police are extremely sensitive to the possibility of student disorders. They are the group most commonly cited by police officers as bearing careful watching and most delicate handling.[14] It would be fair to say that university authorities and police officials throughout India run, if not scared, certainly apprehensive about the possibility of uncontrollable student disorder.

The survey operation among the four universities was directed to explore three topics: (1) the student's experience with public demonstrations, (2) his predispositions toward them, and (3) his judgment of the manner in which the police handle them. Because the survey also collected information about the student's place in the community, both within the university and without, it should be possible to determine what social variables are associated with participation, predispositions, and judgments. It is interesting to note at the outset that students showed little hesitation in answering these items. The "don't know" responses were never higher than 15 percent, and even that was rare.

By and large, university students consider demonstrations and agitations useful, necessary, and proper.[15] (See Table 30.) At Al-

[13] The University Grants Commission has kept a record for several years of the incidence of student indiscipline, its effects, and occasions. The roster of indiscipline is submitted to the U.G.C. at each of its regular meetings.

[14] See, for example, the comments of the Uttar Pradesh Police Commission, pp. 147-148.

[15] The conclusions about usefulness, necessity, and propriety are based on three questions. Students were first asked whether they thought public demonstrations were a useful way of getting authorities to do the right thing or to correct some wrong. Then they were asked specifically about the university situation. Did they think student agitations were necessary in order to get university authorities to notice student needs and grievances? Lastly, they were asked if strikes were a proper means of exerting pressure on university authorities. Although each question is slightly different in emphasis, they allow us to define the student's predisposition toward agitations within the university. If a student considers agitations necessary against college or university authorities, he certainly must consider them useful. And if he considers *strikes* a proper means of exerting pressure within the collegiate community, it is proper to infer that he would consider *agitations and demonstrations* useful as well. There is a technical difference between a demonstration and an agitation, although it is generally passed over in com-

lahabad, Osmania, and Bangalore the preponderance were of this persuasion. In fact, with the exception of Osmania students on the question of the propriety of strikes, a majority of students at every school thought demonstrations useful, necessary, and proper. And at Osmania the responses were 48 percent for their propriety and 35 percent against—nearly a majority. Only at Delhi did a majority of students sampled consistently doubt the usefulness, necessity, and propriety of student agitations. Tests for significance show that Delhi is unique. On all three items the responses from Allahabad, Osmania, and Bangalore are not significantly different from one another, but all are different from Delhi.

Among the general public about 50 percent of urban dwellers, roughly similar to student proportions, thought demonstrations useful, while only 6 percent of rural residents agreed.

Students are more discriminating in their judgments than many people may expect. While predisposed in favor of public demonstrations, most students thought them utilized too often and too frivolously. Almost half of all students sampled at Delhi, Osmania, and Bangalore held this opinion. Only among Allahabad students did more individuals speak up for them than spoke against them, and even there those who thought them frivolously used amounted to 41 percent of the whole. Students were not so cynical in their reading of the genuineness of *student* demonstrations at their own universities. They were asked whether those were founded on real and serious grievances or rather on artificial concerns not reflecting widespread student opinion. Only at Delhi was the genuineness of student demonstrations doubted by more students than defended them (43 percent doubting and 29 percent defending). Students at Allahabad and Bangalore were most convinced of the genuineness of the causes—68 percent giving a vote of confidence. At Osmania 58 percent agreed. Indian students would appear to be condescending toward public protest in the community at large but to feel for the most part that demonstra-

---

mon speech, and these both differ from a strike. My impression is that a strike is considered by students a much more serious tactic to employ than agitation or demonstration. Public demonstrations and agitations usually precede a strike, not the other way around. To march and shout slogans, even to offer token satyagraha, is one thing; to boycott classes and withdraw from the life of the university is quite another. If my premise is correct, it is not unfair to assume that a person approving the propriety of strikes will also approve the propriety of demonstrations and agitations. Thus the three questions do establish that, excepting Delhi, Indian students sampled judge demonstrations and agitations to be useful, necessary, and proper.

TABLE 30

Attitude Toward Demonstrations
(PERCENTAGES)

University	97		98		99		103		109		102			104	
	Useful	Not	Yes	No	Yes	No	Real	Artificial	Yes	No	Reluctant	Indifferent	Eager		
Delhi	41.7	53.0	41.3	52.0	32.0	52.0	29.0	43.0	50.3	35.0	10.0	23.3	62.7	No	24.0
														Rarely	22.7
														Some	12.3
														Frequent	23.0
														Yes	18.0
														No	15.3
Allahabad	69.3	28.0	63.3	35.7	56.7	39.0	68.0	18.3	41.0	55.3	12.3	26.7	58.3	Rarely	5.3
														Some	21.0
														Frequent	18.3
														Yes	40.0
														No	29.0
Osmania	63.0	20.7	66.0	22.3	48.3	35.3	57.7	20.7	48.0	23.3	6.3	24.7	51.7	Rarely	20.7
														Some	27.3
														Frequent	9.7
														Yes	13.0
														No	13.0
Bangalore	56.3	25.7	57.3	25.7	57.3	26.7	67.3	16.0	48.0	11.0	9.7	15.7	53.0	Rarely	39.0
														Some	20.3
														Frequent	17.7
														Yes	10.0
														No	20.3
Combined	57.7	31.9	56.9	34.2	45.2	39.4	55.4	24.5	46.8	31.2	9.6	22.6	56.5	Rarely	21.9
														Some	20.2
														Frequent	17.2
														Yes	20.2

tions in their own universities are required and founded upon accurately perceived and widely felt grievances.

The students were more critical of demonstrations as a common tactic of protest than were members of the public generally. In the general public survey the proportions who thought demonstrations were used too frequently were 42 percent in Bangalore city, 33 percent among Kanpur residents, 28 percent among Kanpur immigrants, and 3 percent in Tumkur. Excepting the marginal Tumkur responses, these proportions are 10 to 20 percent below student opinion. A telling contrast might have been obtained if the general public had been asked the same question about *student* demonstrations. Possibly each group, preoccupied with its own concerns, is unable to empathize with the protests of the other, writing them off hurriedly as due to "politics"—adolescent student politics, on the one hand, and self-centered party politics on the other.

Students were asked to assess whether their colleagues were reluctant, indifferent, or eager to participate in demonstrations. A majority in each sample said they were eager. About a fifth said others were indifferent and about one-tenth found them reluctant. There were no significant differences among universities.

While many students are predisposed to view demonstrations favorably, very few have joined one. Participation in demonstrations and strikes is a minority activity. Not more than 25 percent of all students sampled had participated in a strike or demonstration. (See Table 31.) The proportion was significantly higher at Osmania, for there 23 percent had been in a strike. Since most students sampled had been at the university less than two

KEY TO TABLE 30:

97   Do you think that public demonstrations are a useful way of getting the authorities to do the right thing?

98   Are student agitations necessary in order to get the college/university authorities to take notice of student grievances and needs?

99   Are student strikes a proper means of putting pressure on university/college authorities?

103   In your opinion, are student demonstrations at this university founded on real and serious grievances or are many of them artificial and not based on widespread student concerns?

109   Are demonstrations used too often, too frivolously, these days?

102   Are students generally eager, indifferent, or reluctant to participate in demonstrations?

104   Are there attempts among students to organize demonstrations from time to time? Yes, frequently, sometimes, rarely, never.

TABLE 31

EXPERIENCE WITH CROWD-CONTROL

		Delhi	Allahabad	Osmania	Bangalore	Combined
100	Neither	80.7	80.7	62.7	77.3	75.5
	Demonstration	12.3	9.3	4.7	8.7	8.8
	Strike	6.0	7.0	23.3	8.3	11.2
	Both	1.0	3.0	9.3	5.0	4.6
106	Yes	40.0	33.7	66.3	49.0	47.3
	No	59.7	66.0	33.3	50.3	52.4
107	Yes	4.7	16.0	14.7	10.3	11.4
	No	95.0	84.0	85.3	89.0	88.5

KEY: 100   Have you ever participated in a demonstration or a strike?
        106   Have you ever seen lathis or canes used against a crowd?
        107   Have you ever seen a police firing?

years, the survey's findings about participation are bounded by the years 1964-1965. If the survey had been a year earlier or later, the proportions might have been quite different. It is apparent, for example, that Osmania did experience a dramatic strike during those years and that consequently the proportion of participants at Osmania is higher than at other schools.

Among the general public 20 percent or less had participated in a demonstration. One cannot say, then, that a larger proportion of students than public have participated in a public agitation. The students sampled, at least for the years 1964-1966, were not a unique part of the population as far as participating in demonstrations was concerned. Their participation rate was the same as the public's as a whole. This evidence supports the view that demonstrational politics is not peculiar to students but is part of a society-wide pattern of political behavior.

The overall rate of participation is not negligible in absolute terms. If the sample is representative, eight thousand students at the four universities have been in a demonstration. Moreover, students have concentrated their activity in a relatively short span of years; the public has distributed its activity over a longer span of life. There is no question, then, that in terms of number of incidents, numbers involved, and potential seriousness of encounters, student agitations must be a first-order preoccupation of government and university officials.

One of the critical questions about which there has been a good deal of speculation is which students are the most active in agitations. Perhaps the most popular theory is that students in nonscientific courses are most given to public agitation. Students in arts, commerce, and law are more active and more disorderly than students in engineering or the physical sciences. The survey shows little evidence to support this conclusion. The only item of background consistently associated with participation was sex: female students were less likely to have participated than males. This is hardly an earthshaking finding. The correlation was even then not particularly high; it accounts for not more than 10 percent of the variation in participation. No other background variable consistently produces a significant correlation with participation. The worth of this finding is of course limited by the amount of agitation experienced by students during their particular years at the university. If the two years previous to the survey were unusually quiet, then we still might not know which students were most participation-prone. However, even among Osmania students there is no correlation between participation and curricula. What is more, an analysis by background of *predispositions* toward agitations does not show consistent linkage either. Among Delhi and Bangalore students, being female is associated with not being supportive of demonstrations. But even this not very strong relation fails to show up in Allahabad and Osmania. The only significant correlation between course of study and predisposition is found in the Allahabad data. There a correlation of 0.23 (N of 289) links being in a scientific discipline with thinking demonstrations are used too often and frivolously. Lumping all students together, a correlation of 0.14 (N of 961) was found between course of study and whether students considered university agitations to be founded on real or artificial issues.

As one would expect there is a clear correlation between participation and being predisposed to favor agitation. In each sample, analysis generated a factor defined in terms of support for agitational activity—that is, whether it was considered useful, necessary, and proper. A supportive predisposition correlated with participation in Delhi, Allahabad, Osmania, and Bangalore, respectively, by 0.24, 0.39, 0.33, and 0.19.

The evidence of the survey suggests that the importance of course of study in contributing to agitational activity has been seriously overestimated. Among the students sampled, the greatest amount of participation was found in Osmania which has only 30.7 percent of its students in arts, commerce, and law. Fifty-five percent of its students are in science and engineering and 14 percent in medicine, a fact confirmed by U.G.C. figures. Among the Osmania students there is no correlation whatsoever between course of study and participation in its recent strike. The only background variables significantly, though not very importantly, associated with participation at Osmania are place of residence (whether on campus or off), sex, and education of the student's father. People tended to participate more who lived in a university hostel, who were male, and whose father was not so well educated.[16] In other words, even at a university where there has been a recent agitation, course of study was not an important determinant.

Although further study is quite evidently needed, I suggest that the incidence of agitation is a function of living arrangements,[17] university regulatory policies, and specific climates of opinion. Demonstrations require a critical mass of people. These can be most readily created among the residents of university hostels. Large, unitary, residential universities—such as Allahabad—may be more agitation-prone than schools which affiliate and scatter their students over a wide area, either in private residences or small colleges. Furthermore, students and administrators together create a climate of opinion concerning agitations. We have seen in the case of certain attitudinal predispositions that location is uniquely associated. The same kind of individual in one environment may hold one opinion, in another environment a different one. Some universities may perhaps develop a habit of agitation; public protest becomes the thing to do, and all incoming students assimilate the values of agitational behavior. Universities in the north, particularly in Uttar Pradesh, may be the scene of agitations so often not because they have a higher proportion of arts, commerce, and law students—this is a coincidence—but because the environment is attuned to agitation. Although transforming the climate of opinion will be uphill work, there is no reason to think it cannot be done; that concerted action by responsible stu-

---

[16] The correlations were, respectively, 0.18 (N of 300), 0.34 (N of 300), and 0.22 (N of 283).

[17] Living arrangements were found to be correlative with income of the parents and the location of the student's home—that is, whether city, town, or rural. Hostel residents are more likely than non-hostel residents to be from rural areas and to have relatively well-to-do parents. Living arrangements do not correlate with course of study (except in Allahabad), caste, or religion. The correlation values for income were on the order of 0.20; for location of home, 0.30.

dents, a determined administration, and a neutral authority-structure outside the university cannot bring about the required change. If basic attributes of social class and university curricula are not associated with participation in demonstrations or a predisposition toward them, then a particular incidence of student indiscipline is not inevitable. Rather, the incidence can be affected by appropriate environment-molding policies.

What effect upon a student's predispositions toward agitational politics has his interest in political activity? Does being an office-holder in some university group predispose him toward or away from participation in demonstrations? The survey data show a slight correlation between office-holding in a student organization and participation in strikes or demonstrations. For the student sample as a whole the correlation is 0.12 (N of 1,200). Similarly, the greater a student's expressed interest in student politics the greater is his participation. Once again, however, the association is slight, 0.10 (N of 1,146). There are no consistent or meaningful correlations between office-holding or interest in student politics, on the one hand, and predispositions toward demonstrations on the other. Students who have no interest or participation in student politics are as likely to judge agitational activity as useful, necessary, and proper as those who have. Student politics does not especially select for leaders who are strongly in favor of agitations. Any leader is likely to engage in demonstrations; it is the normal tactic of protest. And students as a whole will support the demonstration if they think it is justified. Office-holders will, by virtue of their position, be somewhat more active in demonstrations than others. One would suppose that student office-holders will be more active in any kind of university organizational activity than the rank and file. Demonstrations seem to be a normal outgrowth of Indian student organizations, just as petitions, letter-writing, or holding social functions would be in the United States.

About 6 percent of all students sampled hold some kind of office in a student organization. There are no significant differences among the samples. Apathy toward student politics is shown by about half of all students. Asked whether they had no, a little, some, or a lot of interest in student politics, about half said that they had little or none. From 5 percent (Bangalore) to 15 percent (Delhi) said they had a lot. About 33 percent said they had some. There seems to be no association between social origins and either office-holding or interest in student politics. The survey data provide no insight into the cause of active political interest among students or willingness to engage in radical political activity such as an agitation. All that can be said is that among respondents at Delhi, Allahabad, Osmania, and Bangalore, students from all social classes and home environments participate to an equal extent in student organizations and manifest an equal interest in student politics.

Among students as a whole in the combined sample about one-third think the police are too harsh or employ too much force in handling public demonstrations. An equal proportion believe that police handling is firm and proper. About a fifth judge it to be haphazard. The most severe opinion is held by students at Allahabad, as with other items pertaining to evaluations. Students are most favorably disposed at Delhi and Bangalore. Osmania students are less severe in their judgments than Allahabad's but not as charitable as Delhi's or Bangalore's. Student opinion is much more critical than the general public's. Only about 12 percent of the general public thought police were too harsh and used too much force. With respect to the frequency of firings, very few students think they are used too often. In every sample, 39 percent or better gave the police a clear vote of confidence on this score. This was not markedly different from the general public. Moreover, a substantial proportion of student opinion is willing, in principle at least, to support police arrests of demonstrators who break the law. They were asked if, when demonstrators or strikers break the law, the authorities should arrest them right away or be considerate and tolerate them. Except in Bangalore, half of all students thought they should be arrested right away. In Bangalore only one-third supported an immediate punitive response. One cannot dismiss the opinions of the remaining half or two-thirds, as the case may be. To say that almost half of all students are willing to condone lawbreaking by demonstrators is very meaningful indeed in terms of public sympathy. Police and magistrates are undoubtedly wise in hesitating to act too precipitously in arresting lawbreaking demonstrators.

Evaluation of police handling of demonstrations is not affected by background, with one slight exception. At Allahabad and Osmania there is a tendency for arts, commerce, and law students to be more tolerant of lawbreaking by demonstrators. The correlations were 0.27 (N of 298) and 0.19 (N of 280), respectively. For the student sample as a whole, the same relation is just barely discernible—the correlation being 0.09 (N of 1,074). There is very slight evidence, therefore, that arts, commerce, and law students are more permissive in the latitude they allow demonstrators, but the relationship is not nearly as marked as many observers would have expected. What is even more surprising is that there is no consistent and important relation between participation in demonstrations or witnessing police handling demonstrations and evaluations of police handling. Students were asked not only about their participation in public protests but about whether they had ever seen the police use lathis or canes against a crowd and whether they had ever seen a firing. The survey data show that first-hand experience of this sort has absolutely no effect on whether the respondent judges police handling of demonstrators as proper or with too much force. Even those who have seen the police use lathis or canes against a crowd are not more likely to judge the police severely. As with the item about firings, only at Osmania University was there a significant, although slight, association between seeing a firing and judging that the police fire too often.[18] In Allahabad and Bangalore there was a tendency, again slight, for students who had participated in public protests to think the police fired too often. The correlations were 0.16 (N of 300) and 0.31 (N of 298), respectively.

The number of students who have seen lathis or canes used or have seen a firing was not small. From a third to two-thirds of the respondents, depending upon the sample, had seen lathis or canes used. (See Table 31.) The highest proportion was at Osmania, the smallest at Allahabad. This is more evidence of the importance of the time period being studied. Surely in other years Allahabad would have ranked much higher. Of all students interviewed, 47 percent had seen lathis or canes employed. The proportion is substantially higher than among even the urban general public. Yet it had no effect on their judgments about police handling of crowds. About 11 percent of all students interviewed had seen a police firing. This is about the same proportion as among the urban public.

In short, the student community has had rather general experience with police use of force; a very significant minority have even been treated to the shattering experience of a police firing. Still, witnessing police use force does not influence their evaluations of the propriety of police tactics in controlling demonstrations. The police are quite wrong in concluding that employ-

---

[18] The correlation was 0.16, N of 300.

ment of force against crowds is a teaching experience of the first order. As with the general public, support for police in the maintenance of public order may be impervious even to first-hand experience. I have suggested elsewhere[19] that the potential violence of crowds and of demonstrators may be more alarming to bystanders, students or public, than the force employed by the police in restoring order. If so, this speaks well for the restraint generally shown by the police. It also indicates a residuum of support among the public that the police might profitably exploit and build upon in addressing themselves to the vexing problem of public protests and disorders.

This conclusion gains credence when we observe that there are only a few, scattered, and very slight correlations among the student samples with respect to evaluations of police handling of demonstrations, on the one hand, and predispositions toward demonstrations, on the other. In other words, believing that demonstrations are useful, necessary, or proper does not lead students to judge police handling of them more severely. Their predispositions are without effect. Students may support, mostly passively, public demonstrations, but they will not for this reason automatically condemn the police for their tactics in maintaining order.

DUTY, FAMILIARITY, AND KNOWLEDGE

Students, like the general public, agreed in nine out of ten cases that the common man has a duty to go to the police with information about a crime if he has it. On the other items pertaining to duty, which ask for behavioral decisions in specific situations, the students show themselves to have a slightly higher sense of duty than the public. Asked about situations in which the respondent had a choice about contacting the police, Delhi students were consistently less prone to solicit contact than others. They were as negative as established urban residents in Kanpur. In the combined student sample 16 percent said they would avoid the police if they were coming around asking questions. Greatest avoidance was in Delhi, 26 percent, least in Osmania, 12 percent. To the question whether they would inform the police about a gang of goondas in their vicinity that was going to commit a crime, 15 percent said they would not. The negative high was 24 percent in Delhi, followed closely by Osmania at 23 percent, and with the

[19] See Chapter 10.

low of 4 percent in Allahabad. Finally, students were asked whether if a crime had been committed in their neighborhood and they knew something the police would want to know would they volunteer information or wait to be contacted. The vast majority said they would volunteer. Twenty-six percent said they would not: high of 42 percent negative responses in Delhi, low of 14 percent in Bangalore.

One would not expect the sense of duty among students to be markedly different from the general public unless a factor peculiar to the university environment or peculiar to educated people was at work. Analysis of the general public data has already shown that age is not correlative with duty. Only education was associated with duty, although on the order of 0.30, explaining about 10 percent of the variance in sense of duty. Although there are significant differences among student samples, there is no great divide between urban general public and university students. University life does not breed a particularly low sense of duty relative to the public in general.

Among students the amount of personal recognition of policemen and knowledge about them was of the same order of magnitude as among the urban public. Once again there were major differences among universities. Except for Bangalore, about twothirds of all students recognized no policemen on sight. At Bangalore, only 36 percent showed such a lack of recognition. A much larger proportion of students at Bangalore knew one or two policemen than was the case at other schools. Two out of every ten students knew some policemen by name. Only Delhi and Bangalore showed a significant difference on this item: at Delhi 16 percent knew some policemen by name, at Bangalore 25 percent. The data show that there is not a total abyss between police and students. Police are not entirely impersonal figures, although one would hesitate to say that recognition is very deep or meaningful. With respect to elementary knowledge of the police, from 8 to 42 percent knew the salary of a police constable. The extremes were Bangalore and Allahabad, respectively. The title of the top police officer of the district was known by less than half of all student respondents taken together. At Bangalore only 29 percent knew. The high was at Allahabad, where 59 percent knew. A healthy majority of all students knew in what town the chief officer's office was located; Allahabad students ranked first, with 88 percent, Delhi students next, 65 percent, Bangalore students third, 61 percent, and Osmania students last, only 52 percent. Most students, therefore, know where the focal point of district police administration is, though they could not call the top officer by his correct title. This is a bit surprising, since one would have thought the district superintendent to be a fixture of local folklore. The general public was equally uninformed. One wonders whether the collector is any better known by his title.

In the analysis of the general public data, the question was asked whether contact with the police—both neutral and unpleasant—affected the sense of duty a person articulated. The answer was that contact was without effect. The same pattern crops up again in the student data. The public posture a person adopts, at least in an interview situation, with respect to his willingness to provide assistance to the police is uninfluenced by personal experience with the police. Nor is there a consistent meaningful pattern between articulated sense of duty and the evaluations a student makes about the police. Once again the finding conforms to general public analysis.

Among the general public, sense of duty was quite significantly associated with education, to a lesser extent with income, caste, and occupation.[20] As status declined, so did sense of duty. This relation was not discovered in the student data. Sense of duty cannot be linked among students to sex, course of study, location of home, or social status. It would appear that students show a sense of duty that is caste- and class-homogeneous. It differs between students at different universities but it is of a piece within any university. This leads to the conclusion that there is a common pattern of socialization with respect to duty at each university. Another very plausible hypothesis is that there is a common pattern of socialization all right, but it applies to the way one responds to an interviewer on subjects of a certain kind.

Personal recognition of policemen and knowledge about the police proved to be very different dimensions for the general public. The same is true for students. Statistical analysis failed to generate any factors combining scores on both. A person may know policemen by name but know little about their salary or where the office of the district superintendent is. Factor analysis indicates that recognition and knowledge together are not sufficiently associated to define a factor between them.

Contact with the police does improve recognition of the police

[20] These findings were especially strong in Kanpur.

but not overwhelmingly and not in every sample. In Allahabad, Osmania, and Bangalore, students who know someone personally who has been threatened or struck are more likely to recognize some of the policemen of their area on sight. It would appear that having been sensitized to the potential danger of a policeman, students take more note of them. Similarly, at least at Allahabad and Osmania, students who know someone personally who has been threatened or struck are more likely to know a policeman by name. Among the general public, contact played a larger role in structuring recognition than it does among students. There is no association at all between knowledge of the police and contact with them. First-hand experience with the police does not have cognitive effects.

The evaluations students make about police behavior are unaffected by their familiarity with the police or their knowledge of them. They are as likely to be poorly disposed toward them if they know some by name than if they did not. In two samples, Allahabad and Osmania, there is a hint that belief in favoritism or outside political control are associated with knowing a policeman by name. This same curious relation was found more strongly among the general public. It could be that familiarity breeds contempt or that contempt breeds recognition. In any case, the association, does not show up consistently and is slight when it does.[21]

Recognition of policemen by students is not affected by social background. Among the general public there was an association. Education was especially highly correlative, as was income and caste to a lesser extent. University students, of course, are educationally homogeneous; and one would not expect the educational background of their fathers to be binding. Students also seem to take on the recognition patterns of urban people. That is, they are more familiar with police than are people from rural areas. Among the general public there was a clear discrepancy on the recognition items between rural and urban respondents. Relation between background and knowledge for students is in the same direction as with the general public but less strong. By and large there are very few correlations among all the student samples between criteria of background and knowledge of the police. Where they do exist, they point in the direction of social status—both caste and class—and a city home environment improving knowledge of the police.

[21] Being on the order of 0.25.

In summary, duty, familiarity, and knowledge of the police among students are in the same proportions, maybe slightly less, than among the general public. Patterns of association between these variables and others, whether of experience or background, are even less easy to discover than was the case in analysis of the general public. By virtue of being within major universities students are "citified" and educated. Since these were the most important correlates among the general public with duty, familiarity, and knowledge it is not surprising that student findings about these aspects cannot be further analyzed in terms of social background and experience.

CONCLUSION

Indian university students are certainly not well disposed toward the police. They are cynical and suspicious. They are inclined to doubt police honesty, impartiality, and freedom from political control. They show themselves to be quite willing to believe the worst in respect to the manner police treat people. Police are thought of by many, if not most, students as rude, discourteous, and given to physical abuse. Students are very far from conceiving the police as an agency possessing integrity, dedication, and a sincere desire to help the citizen in distress.

By the time a student has matriculated he has adopted and learned to exhibit forthrightly the distrust toward police shown by India's urban public generally. Like the educated everywhere, he shows little reticence about judging the police unfavorably. Whether the more educated are genuinely more disenchanted or simply allow the massive distrust of all citizens to show through is not clear. What is clear is that India's future opinion-leaders have learned at an early and impressionable age to view police with deep suspicion and perhaps hostility. The cloud is not, of course, without its silver lining; there are many students who are not ill-disposed toward police. At the same time, the proportion of students with unfavorable views is so massive that minimization becomes difficult. Evidence from the survey of the general public shows that these attitudes will persist, even if students return to rural areas. A critically important social group has thus been conditioned as negatively toward the police as many intellectuals and politicians of the independence struggle were in their time.

The lesson that should be drawn from these findings is that government, and police especially, should make a particular effort at rehabilitating the attitudes of this seminal group. Students should not be allowed to persist in their evaluations. This means of course that the obvious causes of their distrust must be eliminated. Too many students have been first-hand witnesses to money being passed to policemen, to abuse of disadvantaged and helpless individuals in the streets, to the use of physical force against prisoners under guard, or to palpable unconcern with the plight of people who come to them for help. It also means that the favorable side of police activity must be brought home to this group particularly. Government might seriously consider special programs designed to acquaint students with police work and to demonstrate to them both the difficulties and the achievements of modern police operations. In other words, their education about the police should not be left to chance encounters in public places; haphazardness must be replaced, at least in part, by a well-conceived educational program.

The police should realize that their honest efforts, even those which are superficially distasteful, are capable of being understood by university students. Students are capable of discriminating judgments. They do not react in a reflexively hostile fashion to the employment of lathis or even guns against unruly crowds. They seem to accept these events as necessary. This indicates that students will give the police a fair hearing provided the police are in fact justified in what they do and that the police make clear their own responsibilities toward the community. In situations of public disorder the requirements for reestablishing elementary conditions of order are usually obvious, and students apparently draw conclusions about what is needed which are similar to those reached by the police.

Opinions about the police appear to vary substantially from locale to locale. Unless more subtle background variables are involved in conditioning attitudes toward the police than we yet know, the survey shows that opinions are not locked in any unyielding mold. Climates of opinion appear to some extent to be specific to environment. A person brought from a rural village to an urban community will soon adopt the attitudes of the new setting. Moreover, mobility in status also encourages flexibility in attitudes. Officials must stop thinking that hostility toward police is an inherited characteristic, impervious to social surroundings. There may be very subtle sociological or psychological variables in Indian culture that predispose people negatively toward the police. If these exist, they may render attempts at attitude remodeling unavailing. The survey has shown, however, that major parameters of social position are not unyielding barriers to attitude change. As people move physically or socially, their views change. This is an opportunity upon which the government must seize, and especially within the student community.

FIVE

ADMINISTRATORS, POLITICIANS, AND PANCHAYATI RAJ

13 • *The Police and Civil Administration*

POLICE are not exclusively responsible for the administration of law and order. The responsibility belongs to government generally; the police are simply government's agency for this purpose. The structural as well as the informal relations between the police and the rest of government affect the efficiency with which this critical task is carried out. Moreover, these relations determine the nature of police accountability, which is another way of saying they affect the autonomy of police power. Also, whether these relations are harmonious or not may affect the legitimacy of government by forcing people to choose between police and other instrumentalities of government as being correct embodiments of political authority. The relations of police with the larger system of administration is not then a narrow, technical matter of structure and organization; they are potentially of great political significance.

THE SUPERINTENDENT AND THE COLLECTOR: A QUESTION OF EFFICIENCY

Indian administrative structure presents notable problems of description largely because of the existence of a federal system. Since, however, police and law and order are state subjects under the constitution, administrative arrangements that most directly concern the police are those created by states and accountable to state legislatures.

The apex of state administrative authority is the chief minister. He presides over a cabinet of appointed ministers, all of whom are accountable to an elected legislative assembly. The ministers preside over departments responsible for the performance of different specialized tasks. Below the secretariat offices at the state capital are several tiers of structure. Most tasks are performed by administrators placed at the level of district, subdivision, *taluka*, and village. The structure becomes attenuated at the bottom reaches; not every village has government officials stationed in it. The hierarchy of district-subdivision-taluka-village has remained intact for over two millennia and was used by Moghuls and British for the organizing of their imperial responsibilities. The major level for coordination of administration, below the state secretariat, are the districts. Below district level, various departments have set up special administrative units departing from the primeval system. For example, the police are organized in terms of circles and police stations. Economic development activities are organized in terms of blocks, talukas, and villages. The curiosity of the system is that while above and below the district there are functionally specific lines of command and accountability, at the district level there is a single executive officer with overall responsibility for the direction and coordination of all tasks within the district. This is the collector. In effect, he is chief minister for a district, although he is a permanent civil servant. It is as if Indian administrative structure had an hourglass figure. The collector is the pinched waist.

One of the most persistent problems of Indian administration has been how to associate the generalist collector reporting to the chief secretary with functional specialists reporting to a number of different ministries. In the police case, for example, the chief district police officer is the superintendent. The hierarchy to which he is accountable extends upward through a range deputy inspector-general of police to the state inspector-general of police. The inspector-general reports to the home secretary and in turn to the home minister. To complicate the situation even more, the collector belongs to the Indian Administrative Service. And so, too, does the home secretary. Thus the police establishment is accountable at two different levels to a civilian administrative official of the I.A.S. cadre.

As government's functions have expanded, especially since independence, the collector has become increasingly burdened. In British days his duties took in revenue collection, law and order, and the administration of justice. Today, governmental responsibilities include community development, health and welfare, agricultural extension, cooperatives and marketing arrangements, establishment of programs of rural savings, and the creation of representative political institutions under Panchayati Raj. One solution to the problems of coordination and of overburdening is to remove certain tasks from the collector's purview and to have functionally specific chains of command from Delhi to state to district and so on. There is a tendency to move in this direction, especially with respect to development functions.

From the days of the British the collector has retained formal responsibility for the maintenance of law and order. The Police Commission of 1861 established the principle that police in each district were to be under the "general control and direction" of the collector. Since the collector was responsible for law and order, he had to have authority to direct the police. The police, however, were to be autonomous throughout each state with respect to their own internal administration. Hence the creation of the post of inspector-general. The superintendent was responsible to the collector for what the police did affecting law and order; he was at the same time responsible to his uniformed superiors for the internal management of the police establishment. In short, he was subject to a system of dual control. The collector, however, was chief district officer in his own right for every department except police. The relation between superintendent and collector was special. They were not exactly superior-subordinate, but not quite equals either. In the rubric that has developed, the superintendent was a "colleague" of the collector but not a "subordinate." The Police Commission of 1902-1903 reaffirmed the principles governing this relation but noted that friction had been encountered.[1] The relationship was inordinately difficult to define in hard and fast terms. It was amorphous and in practice reflected the opinions and personality of different collectors. Some collectors did think of their superintendents as colleagues; others conveniently forgot and treated them as narrow-minded advisors fit only for a limited charge. A national police commission meeting today would make the same observations about the quality of the relationship. Beneath the coherence of descriptive terminology there exists a wide variety of operational solutions and these in turn have created a considerable amount of animosity, confusion, and inexpediency in the utilization of the police.

The difficulties do not of course arise in the larger cities which have commissioners of police. The commissioner is his own collector and communicates directly with the Home Department. He not only directs the internal administration of the force but bears full responsibility for law and order as well.

The ambiguity in the relationship between superintendent and collector has led to a proposal that responsibility for law and order be transferred from the collector to the superintendent. The collector should confine himself to non-enforcement tasks. There would thus be a unified command structure for law and order in

[1] See Police Commission, 1902-1903, p. 115, and Bihar Police Commission, pp. 147-152.

each state. The proposal does not, it should be noted, abolish accountability to civilian authority; it merely concentrates it at one level—that of inspector-general—and eliminates dual entry of civilian direction. Behind this proposal, which enjoys great popularity among police officers, especially younger ones, lie many specific irritants that police officers cite in their relationship with the collector. Generally they object to the diminution of their status implied in having to be responsible to him. Specifically, they complain about the practice of requiring collectors to write confidential reports on character, fitness, and performance of superintendents which are forwarded to police superiors; they complain that collectors inspect police stations without the approval of the superintendent; that superintendents must inform collectors in advance of their movements away from headquarters; that the collector must countersign the superintendent's travel allowance; that the collector must approve the postings of station-house officers, as well as dismissals, promotions, and transfers of others; that the superintendent must submit to the collector police plans and dispositions for emergencies; that organization of work units in the force, the abolition of a station, or the expenditure of certain categories of funds all involve prior notification of the collector.[2] Not all these practices exist in every state. And even within states there is appreciable variation in practice. Nonetheless, this is a representative list of the kind of subordination to the collector that ruffles the feathers of a great number of police officers.

In support of the proposal that law and order should become the exclusive responsibility of the senior professional police officer in every district, subject to direction by the state police hierarchy, four broad arguments are generally made.

First: in spite of what the regulations require, collectors do not exercise active control over law and order administration. They are far too busy nowadays to give the kind of continual personal attention that they once did. Collectors become involved in law and order affairs only when an emergency arises, when crowds are actually milling in the street or communal violence has broken out. The rest of the time they are submerged in a multitude of development tasks, because this is now the area of maxi-

[2] See, for example, West Bengal Police Commission, p. 199, for five complaints made by police about the relation. The Police Commission dismissed all but one. See also Syndicate of I.P.S. Officers, "Control of Police," December, 1963, Central Police Training College, Mt. Abu.

mum governmental concern. Rather than pretending to a thoroughness of control that he does not exercise and competence he has no time to develop, let the collector be honest about his burdens and eliminate the petty, formal checks that are his only real contact with law and order administration. It is time to abolish spasmodic accountability and allow the professionals to assume undivided responsibility.

In support of the contention that superintendents enjoy de facto primacy except in extreme situations, some observers have noted that the I.A.S. staff in state secretariats increasingly communicate directly with the inspector-general about law and order problems and no longer work as much through the collector.[3] It may also be true, as some have suggested, that the standard for collectors has declined in the past twenty years. The post of collector no longer enjoys the prestige among the I.A.S. it once did. Consequently the single-mindedness, the dedication, the paternalistic regard, and perhaps even the expertise of collectors have suffered a decline. The height of an I.A.S. officer's ambition before independence was to possess his own district. Postings to a secretariat were considered distractions from the main purpose. The pattern today is more and more for young officers to move directly into secretariat work, after perhaps serving briefly as a subdivisional officer. They stay in secretariat posts, or perhaps in public economic undertakings, for the rest of their careers.[4] Because the luster of district service has worn off, collectors tend to be young I.A.S. officers or older appointees from state civil services. The middle rank of I.A.S. officers are loath to give up their higher status secretariat posts. As a result, training of probationary I.A.S. officers serving in subdivisions is not in the hands of as experienced and far-sighted men as it used to be. The young I.A.S. collector's acquaintance with law and order problems is probably less extensive than that of his superintendent.

Second: law and order work requires special knowledge, expertise, and training; it cannot be directed by an amateur, no matter

[3] See comments of the West Bengal Police Commission, pp. 197-201.
[4] Ralph Braibanti, "Reflections on Bureaucratic Corruption," *Public Administration*, Winter, 1962, p. 63, says, "It does appear to be true that the dominant interest of the I.A.S. has shifted rather sharply away from district administration to corporate management and economic planning." And Braibanti notes that in his interviews with I.A.S. probationers in 1959, 1961, and 1962, everyone replied without hesitation that "the assignment desired more than any other is one in corporate management, secretariat, or economic planning."

how gifted. The superintendent is better informed, better trained, and much more sensitive to the nuances of law and order administration. Superior ability is in part a function of time devoted single-mindedly to this range of problems. Moreover, the superintendent sits at the listening end of an organization designed to collect information pertaining to law and order. The collector, on the other hand, can only keep in touch with the criminal situation, as well as with the disposition of forces and equipment, through the superintendent. The collector cannot possibly supplement police information from his own sources or even bring to bear a substantially independent point of view.[5]

Third: police performance would improve if police were conscious of the fact that they were standing on their own feet as sole custodians of law and order throughout the country. They would be put on their mettle and would not be able to hide behind the skirts of the collector. Public accountability, too, would be more surely secured because politicians would have a single man to hold responsible for police inaction, inadvertence, or malpractice. As it is now, accountability is strained through a layer of I.A.S. officials.[6] Proponents point out that the London police force, one of the most respected in the world, has just this system of exclusive police responsibility. Moreover, the most efficient police in the subcontinent are to be found in cities that have the commissioner system.

Four: the superintendent is in a better position to monitor the activities of the police from the point of view of securing public respect than is the collector. Collectors pride themselves on their intuitive feel for public opinion in their districts; in fact, they are fooling themselves. They are prisoners of their multifarious duties and a vast bureaucratic machine. Their attention to public opinion about the police is spasmodic. In British days a collector toured extensively and held public meetings wherever he went. This is no longer true. Touring has declined markedly, and with

[5] The dependence of collector on superintendent is very clearly seen in the case of taking out preventive orders under the Code of Criminal Procedure, sections 107-110. These powers belong to the collector, except in commissioner towns. But the collector is invariably forced to obtain a recommendation for action from the police. They alone know whether preventive action is required. Even police officers not in favor of transferring all responsibility for law and order to the superintendent will agree that preventive sections of the Code could be administered more effectively by the superintendent.

[6] For a forceful presentation of this point of view, see the swinging note of dissent to the West Bengal Police Commission by H. N. Sircar, pp. 273-280.

it the ability of the collector to step outside his channels of command.[7] An energetic superintendent, required to make inspections and constantly called forth to deal with delicate situations of investigation or control, is in a much better position to solicit complaints and to hear of the mistakes of his far-flung force.

The proposal that collectors be stripped of their authority in matters of law and order is far too controversial not to be opposed. The fraternity of the I.A.S. has drawn together to oppose any move in this direction. They press three counterarguments.

First: law and order administration is but one aspect of governmental direction; it cannot be separated felicitously from the rest and carried out by men with a narrow police view. The collector, because of his vantage point and contacts with other aspects of district life, is able to see law and order problems as one part of general human needs and responses. He can better understand their genesis and can more aptly prescribe a cure. A superintendent is a specialist, although a necessary and talented one, and he cannot see the world in the round. The British perceived the unity of district problems and created the generalist post of collector; events of the past twenty years, or half century, have not lessened the need for a single administrator with a synoptic view of district problems. Even today with the headlong thrust of government into economic development, unity of direction must be preserved. Rapid social change and problems of law and order often have an organic connection; only the collector is situated to perceive these subtle connections.

Second: though opinion may be changing for the better, police are still widely and deeply distrusted. The collector is a visible promise to the public that independent civilian control over the police still exists, and at a level they can contact. If the collector was taken from the arena of law and order administration, the public view might be reinforced that the police are a closed corporation from which there is no appeal, except through political auspices at a distant state capital.

The survey sheds some light on this aspect of the controversy. Respondents were asked if they had ever complained to anyone

[7] See Government of Bombay, *Report of the Officer on Special Duty on Reorganization of District Revenue Offices* (Bombay: Government Central Press, 1958), pp. 103-104. "Touring in general is on the decline." Officers, he says, cover more ground now, but they are in less close touch with the people of their districts. This is a function of fast jeep transportation. "The paper work is considered routine, and the individual work has become old-fashioned. This happens in an era of jeeps, tours and opinion-finding."

in an official position about the behavior of the police. Of the Bangalore sample, 3 percent had done so, while only 0.5 percent—or three individuals—had done so in the rural sample. In Kanpur, more than twice as many established residents as rural migrants had made a complaint, but the absolute number was still not large. Four percent of residents and 1.6 percent of rural migrants had done so. Asked to specify to whom they had made their complaint, not one respondent in either Bangalore or Tumkur had contacted the collector. Instead they complained most to a superintendent, an inspector, or a politician. Kanpur complainants, those who were established residents, did use the collector. Complainants distributed their contacts equally among the superintendent, a police inspector, the collector, or the police station. Migrants used the superintendent or the police station. It is quite clear, therefore, that people tend to enlist the support of police officials primarily in making complaints.

Another item asked all respondents was who they would complain to if they ever wanted to make a complaint about the police? Here the totals were more substantial, although about a third of all respondents were unable to give a specific answer. The collector was unmentioned by any respondents in Bangalore, Tumkur, or among Kanpur rural migrants. He was cited only by Kanpur residents. By and large, respondents indicated they would contact another police official in order to curb police misbehavior. Moreover, it is apparent that people think of an official closest to them, a person associated with their area. For example, rural respondents in Mysore overwhelmingly would appeal to a police patel or village police officer; Kanpur migrants would appeal to a police station and then to an inspector. Rural people also would make more use of politicians than would city folk.

Generally, therefore, the collector does not appear to provide a major avenue of redress for the mass of the people. Whether people have much confidence in redress through the police or not, they nonetheless are more inclined to make a complaint to them than to other officials or to politicians. In rural areas, especially, the collector seems to be ignored, appeals being made to police officers closest at hand or to politicians.

University students, too, single out police officials. In Delhi, Osmania, and Bangalore never more than 2 percent of respondents cited the collectors. Instructively, it was at Allahabad, where distrust of the police was greatest among the students, that 17 percent said they would appeal to the collector. Although it should be noted that 50 percent even there would appeal to the superintendent. Very few students would contact a politician. The majority of students think first of filing a complaint somewhere in the police hierarchy.

Based on survey knowledge, both north and south, about whom people have contacted and would contact if a complaint is made against the police, collectors do not enjoy the prestige they think. People do not think of the collector as a ready source of impartiality but, instead, do not consider him much at all. In Kanpur it does seem that with length of stay in the city the collector becomes more important in people's minds. While they would still go first to a police official—especially the superintendent—they would go next to the collector. Based on these data, the conclusion must be that civilian review of police activities is not widely prized in India. Or, more accurately, that the civilian review which is represented in the person of the collector is not generally considered as an important avenue of redress.

Third: law and order are contentious areas of responsibility; decisions taken involve bodily injury and bloodshed. Not only are two heads better than one but shared responsibility between the expert in violence and the civilian generalist may strengthen the voice of decision when unpleasant but necessary choices must be made. Police officers may hesitate to prescribe a bitter ounce of prevention when they are alone on the job. The collector serves as a shield of civilian legitimacy, and his opinion carries more weight than the superintendent's with senior officials and politicians in state capitals. I.A.S. officials and senior I.P.S. men alike think that when force must be applied superintendents very much appreciate having collectors at hand to share the decision. The collector is also useful to police officials in lending weight to recommendations about needed reforms in police administration in the districts. A superintendent's plea for a hundred more men or an improved but costly radio network may be dismissed by politicians and secretariat officials as the result of professional ambition; supported by a collector's recommendation it becomes much less easy to disregard. In short, if the superintendent were on his own he would find himself both more exposed and less well supported. The result would be a failure of nerve and the less certain improvement of police administration.

It seems clear that both I.A.S. and I.P.S. men perceive problems in the relationship between collector and superintendent. Not surprisingly, both sides advocate different solutions; and in each case advocacy serves the status interests of their respective services. Currently the weight of official opinion is against reducing the authority of the collector in matters of law and order. The I.A.S. fraternity is dead set against it. Among police, the proposal finds strongest support among younger officers, especially those recruited in the last ten or fifteen years. The clamor for change can be expected to swell in the future as the old guard departs, those whose opinions were formed under the British or immediately after independence, and the young officers begin to assume top command positions.[8]

In passing, mention should be made of two other proposals affecting the relations between police and I.A.S. administration. Both of them would make the police more sensitive to considerations of general administrative and political need. They would bind the police organization more harmoniously into the larger administrative framework. The first is the recurrent proposal for a unified civil service. Probationers would elect to specialize in one or two functional areas. Superintendent and collector would be part of the same service, distinguished only by the amount of expertise they had in particular matters.[9] The second proposal would open the closed-club of the police to outside influence. This could be accomplished, for example, by abolishing the post of inspector-general or by placing a joint secretary, Home Department, between the inspector-general and the home secretary.[10] Alternatively, the post of inspector-general could be filled by someone from outside the uniformed service, perhaps an I.A.S. officer.[11] These suggestions are not being pushed vigorously, but they do indicate that the problem of I.P.S.-I.A.S. relations is being considered from many perspectives.

[8] The recent police commissions were unanimously in favor of retaining the existing system, although they all made minor recommendations designed to make relations between collector and superintendent more tranquil. The personnel of the commissions was drawn from police, I.A.S., politicians, and public. At the time of writing, the Punjab report had not been released. Maharashtra, West Bengal, Uttar Pradesh, and Bihar spoke for the existing system and against strong representations from I.P.S. Associations.

[9] S. P. Jagota, "Training of Public Servants in India," in Ralph Braibanti and Joseph J. Spengler (eds.), *Administrative and Economic Development in India* (Durham, North Carolina: Duke University Press, 1963), pp. 91-93. This proposal was advocated by Asok Chanda and Paul Appleby in the early 1950's.

[10] Proposed by V. S. Bakhle in a note of dissent to the Maharashtra Police Commission, p. 33.

[11] Suggested as worth trying by the West Bengal Police Commission, p. 148.

THE SUPERINTENDENT AND THE COLLECTOR:
A QUESTION OF COMPATIBILITY

Because of the peculiarities of their formal relationship, collector and superintendent are thrown into intimate but ambiguous contact. There is always the chance that one will overstep what the other thinks is appropriate behavior within the rules of their minuet. They are aware of the necessity of working together and of the importance of harmonious relations. But it would be too much to expect that they are always in agreement. The superintendent may resent the collector's suggesting that a certain station-house officer has behaved very badly and ought to be investigated. The collector, on the other hand, may feel that his superintendent is too protective of the personnel under his command and is not ready to weed and prune as complaints to the collector warrant. A collector suddenly perceives the need for a movement of armed police in order to restrain potentially dangerous events. The superintendent, feeling the move is unnecessary, interprets the suggestion as a command and goes away believing he has been treated as a subordinate and not as a colleague. The opportunity for misunderstanding is all the greater because of the importance of service identity in India. Morris-Jones has observed that "to the bureaucrat it is more important to know to which service one belongs than to remember what level of government one served."[12] A superintendent thinks of himself first as an I.P.S. officer, second as the member of a district command team. The collector, too, nurtures a profound sense of pride in his service and talks paternalistically of "his district." Role ambiguity, service esprit de corps, and stubborn human pride not infrequently scar the working relationship between collector and superintendent. Every state has had instances when relations so deteriorated that one or the other officer had to be transferred. Bitterness communicates itself to staffs, to the public, and to politicians. Self-servers seek to ingratiate themselves with superintendent or collector by probing the sense of hurt, inventing or magnifying slights. Even the local press may choose sides, writing articles about the overbearing actions of collector or superintendent. Fortunately, stress between collector and superintendent is usually kept within the official family; public hostility is rare. Still, both sides are thoroughly sensitized to the problems of their relationship and offi-

---

[12] *Government and Politics in India*, p. 23.

cers of both I.A.S. and I.P.S. can tell stories of real or fancied difficulties and latent or actual animosity.

Discussion of proper arrangements for the administration of law and order are not held in an antiseptic atmosphere of dedication to the public good. The exercise is charged with the electricity of status. I.P.S. officers are undoubtedly the more sensitive of the two; they are the least secure psychologically. They often have a chip on their shoulders and dare an I.A.S. officer to knock it off. They are painfully aware that the qualifications for I.P.S. are not as high as for the I.A.S.; they are also aware that in the past the I.A.S. (then the I.C.S.) was far and away the senior service and police officers were often not university graduates. I.P.S. officers project their uneasiness about status onto I.A.S. officers; they believe as a matter of faith that I.A.S. officers look at them with disdain and condescension. And indeed their defensiveness is not entirely without foundation. I.A.S. officers know they did better on the recruitment examination than I.P.S. officers. Moreover, paramount authority in districts and secretariats is theirs; the police report to them; they are the "steel frame" of Indian government. In short, differences between the two services are perceived, based perhaps on minute differentials that may seem trivial, but nonetheless they encase human relationship in a durable, resistant jacket, and it takes a supreme effort of will on the part of new recruits not to adopt the customary forms habitual to both sides.

Tension between collector and superintendent is not new; its antecedents go back to British times. Philip Woodruff has made a list of the qualities a good superintendent had to have and concluded by saying that "he must be something of a diplomat to live beside the district magistrate."[13] "Altogether, it was an arrangement peculiarly English which worked on the whole very well. When there was pettiness or spite on one side, things were difficult, but usually there was enough generosity on the other side to make up for it."

The problem may be aggravated by age differences between collector and superintendent. At least I.P.S. officers often cite this as a contributory factor, a view which is echoed by I.A.S. officers. Peculiarly, though, there is no consensus among officers about whether an older collector or an older superintendent creates the more uneasy situation. One suspects that informants have erected a theory of age on the warrant of their own personal experi-

[13] *The Men Who Ruled India,* Vol. II: *The Guardians,* p. 53.

ence. When the superintendent is older he may resent the supervision of a young collector. Having to obtain approval for travel expenditures or the timing of tours made away from headquarters may be very disagreeable for him. The collector, too, may feel the gap between them. He may be falsely deferential, too obviously condescending, or he may be tactlessly abrupt in an effort to demonstrate sureness in command. The fresh ideas of a young collector may be resented by the superintendent as being too book-bound and theoretical, not matured through practical experience in the field. But the shoe is sometimes on the other foot. Police officers often comment on the difficulties a young, imaginative superintendent has with an older collector who is not of the I.A.S. but has been promoted from a state civil service. The directly recruited I.A.S. officer goes straight to the secretariat leaving collector posts to be filled by promoted deputy collectors and *Mamlatdars*.[14] In some parts of India, over half and even as many as three-fourths of collector posts are filled by officers promoted from inferior services.[15] A proud I.P.S. officer may suffer untold anguish in subordinating himself to men of this stamp. His bright ideas will arouse no enthusiasm and he will feel like an unprized errand-boy attached to a man who has reached the pinnacle of his career and wants only to enjoy it.

When feelings are raw, rivalry assumes a host of petty forms. Some I.P.S. officers are reported to go to extreme lengths never to appear before the collector "covered," that is, with their uniform caps on, so that they will not have to salute. Others, in order to underscore their collegiate status with the collector, will carefully change from khaki uniform to bush shirt and non-uniform trousers before attending a meeting with him. Some officers resent the automatic assumption of superior attainments on the part of the collector displayed by local people. Collectors are often asked to preside at cultural events or at prize-givings in schools, while the superintendent is rarely considered even though he has quite as much education. Wives, as well, are not immune from the sense of competition. They are often as sure as their husbands that the I.A.S. clique, and particularly *their* wives, regard police with contempt. Relations between I.P.S. and I.A.S. wives may be very touchy. The collector's wife may insist on

[14] Government of Bombay, *Report of the Officer on Special Duty*, p. 174.
[15] Some of these collectors were promoted to the I.A.S. in the late 1940's when, due to independence and partition, there was an emergency recruitment to fill vacated posts. These officers are now within a few years of retirement.

playing the role of district grande dame. Competition for chair-manship of a welfare committee, a cultural group, or a philan-thropic activity may be intense. If a superintendent's wife achieves it, the event may take on the significance of a palace coup. The pretexts may sound trivial, but among the intimate associations of an administrative elite playing upon the isolated stage of a small district town, the anguish is bitterly real.

Partly in response to these pressures a "joint foundational" training course was established some years ago at the National Academy of Administration, Mussoorie, for I.A.S., I.P.S., and Class I civil servants. Government hoped that if recruits spent several months together at the outset of their careers they could come to think of one another as brother officers and would not be quite as cliquish as in the past. Although the situation may be some better, clannishness is still palpable.

Initiative in lessening the strains of the collector-superintend-ent relationship must be assumed by the collector. He should be alert to an overbearing, peremptory attitude on his part. For he alone can remove the taint of subordination and make the super-intendent a colleague. The diplomatic skill required is enormous. It will not always be found in every collector, nor will every sit-uation allow ample scope for its use. Sometimes orders must be given; the dictates of reason and conscience on the collector's part cannot give way to a desire to propitiate. The superintendent has an obligation too: he must be willing to meet the collector's initiative halfway. He must possess the magnanimity to give the collector the benefit of the doubt and not to interpret every event as an indication of I.A.S. animus. In fact, of course, relations are more often than not entirely cordial. Bound together by a sense of duty, collector and superintendent get on with the job as re-quired. There are faults of course on both sides, and they will prob-ably persist. But hauteur on one side and testiness on the other, if allowed to grow, only aggravate an ambiguous structural arrangement.

CONCLUSION

Underneath the claims of professional vanity on both sides, there is an issue of much deeper significance—the place of the district in political and administrative life. Collectors tend to believe that the district is a useful level at which to exercise policy supervision and coordination; it provides an important mediating link between state government and growing village government. Here general principles are translated into action appropriate to the diversity of vast states. Those who support the proposal for reducing the authority of the collector implicitly support a view that districts are no more than links in a chain; they are not centers for unified and coordinated policy formulation and adaptation. The place of districts in Indian administration is in process of change, but whether districts will decline in importance or attain new stature is not yet clear. Resolution of the argument about the role of collector in law enforcement will significantly affect the direction of change. It is important to bear in mind that the uneasiness between collector and superintendent, regrettable though it is, is not simply a reflection of personal spite and overweening pride. It is a reflection of these shiftings in duties and responsibilities as government assumes new burdens and obligations. Indeed one might well doubt the vitality, intensity, and extent of India's political and economic development efforts if administrative arrangements produced a century ago by the British were to prove indefinitely serviceable. Strain between collector and superintendent is a function of change; it remains to be seen whether it will be a source of growth.

14 • *Police and the Politicians*

In a democracy the relation between any administrative agency, such as the police, and politicians is conditioned by the need to ensure the efficiency and impartiality of the agency, on the one hand, and its responsibility and accountability to the people, on the other. The achievement of these conditions requires delicate balancing. Efficient administration without responsibility is incompatible with the principles of democracy; accountability without efficiency calls into question the whole purpose of government. The duality of requirements must be understood. It is in the very nature of administration within a democratic political system that relations between politicians and bureaucrats will be made up of a series of uneasy and shifting compromises.

One of the curiosities of life in the world's great democracies is that although public accountability through elected leaders lies at the heart of the system, citizens of these states continually suspect and decry *political influence*. Perhaps their suspicions are healthy. Since Lord Acton was probably correct, suspicion is simply the eternal vigilance that is the price of liberty. Political control has certainly led to gross abuses in many lands. Police have been known to become the tool of self-serving elites. They have been given the job of preserving the stability that might otherwise be achieved through willing popular participation in political life. In democratic countries partisanship and political "bossism" have on occasion destroyed the morale of police forces, rendering them ineffective, and making them objects of contempt in the public mind. The United States has not been an exception. The "spoils system" is a term of opprobrium throughout the democracies. British and American children learn in school of the gradual emancipation of administration from politics.[1] But the

[1] A delightful capsulization of this point of view is to be found in the very last line of the "Munir Report," which was the product of a commission of inquiry in West Pakistan, 1954, into violent disturbances of the previous year. Having found evidence of political interference in police affairs, the report concluded: "But if democracy means the subordination of law and order to political ends—then Allah knoweth best and we end the report." Pakistan, Province of Punjab, *Report of the Court of Inquiry Con-*

denigration of political influence may be overdone. It obscures, by oversimplifying, a complex relationship. The law, which police are charged with administering, is not self-activating. Resources of the police are not without limit and so choices in enforcement must be made. Moreover, law must be applied to human situations which are chronically ambiguous. For this reason discretion is often written into laws. Who is to determine when to arrest, when to use lathis or nightsticks against an unruly crowd, when to shoot, when to prohibit the meeting together in a public place of five or more people, when habeas corpus is to be suspended, when prohibition is to be enforced at the expense of night patrolling, when a man should be cautioned instead of cited, or when a campaign against dacoits is to be especially pressed? Should such vital decisions be left to the police themselves or to the civil service? Or should responsibility be exercised by leaders chosen by the people in free elections?

It is probably fair to say that the balance of opinion in India today has tilted against the politicians and in favor of the bureaucrat. Generally Indians are very critical of the self-centeredness of politicians. They are convinced that politicians have their own good rather than the public's in the forefront of their minds. Even more haunting, however, at least among India's intelligentsia, are the memories of Kerala's experience with a Communist government from 1957 to 1959. The Communist government at the outset of its tenure announced a new police policy.[2] The causes of eventual dissatisfaction with the government were many, as were the causes of the violence that shook the state in the summer of 1959; nonetheless the documentation of partiality in the administration of justice was one of the critical factors turning the tide of opinion and impelling the central government to take over the governing of the state. The lesson which some observers drew from this experience was that law enforcement should be automatic. It should be removed from politics and entrusted to responsible civil servants.

The issue of state political authority over law enforcement is likely to become a focal point of concern once again now that the

---

stituted under Punjab Act II of 1954 to Enquire Into the Punjab Disturbances of 1953 (Lahore, Government Printing, Punjab, 1954), p. 387.

[2] The policy was enunciated by the chief minister at a press conference in Trivandrum, July 23, 1957. For the text of the statement, see Indian Commission of Jurists, "Report of the Kerala Inquiry Committee," *Journal of the International Commission of Jurists*, Winter, 1959, and Spring-Summer, 1960, Appendix B, pp. 208-212.

Congress party majorities have been reduced in several states as a result of the general elections in 1967, and opposition governments have been formed. With a Congress government at the center, it will be very easy for disagreements about proper political control of law and order to strain federal relations.

Complete divorce between politics and administration is impossible and certainly undesirable if democracy is to thrive. Is it possible, however, to establish broad guidelines for separating proper from improper political influence? How does one know when politicians have pushed too far? Are there distinguishing criteria for the improper exercise of public responsibility by elected officials? This issue is one of the classic concerns of democratic political theory. It can hardly be resolved satisfactorily in brief remarks. There do seem to be two principles, however, that will serve as a first approximation in isolating proper from improper control. First, directives from political authorities must be within the law. Political leaders must not urge policy upon administrators which is contrary to enactments of the supreme lawmaking body. However, unforeseen situations require the adaptation of policy and legal mandates. Administration works within law to serve general objectives perceived by legislatures. Interpretation, judgment, and discretion are required if policy is not only to be within the letter of the law but within its spirit as well. Second, then, directives from political authorities must serve the public interest. That is, policy must be set so as to fulfill general social ends and not particularistic ones of a personal, sectarian, or partisan kind. This is the rub. Definition of the public interest is a matter of individual judgment. It can never be cut and dried; it will defy precise definition. Guidelines for proper political control that one may specify do not, perhaps cannot, avoid the need to make judgments.

The point to underscore is that in approaching the subject of the police and politicians in a democracy, influence is inevitable and its propriety in particular situations never beyond dispute. It will always be a matter of honest disagreement among reasonable men. One cannot be dogmatically precise about criteria for its proper amount and kind. And disquieting though it may be, people should understand that judgments about police-political relationships will be unavoidably ad hoc, bound by specific situations and evaluations. Democratic life demands balancing of accountability and efficiency; balancing in turn requires shifting weight from one foot to the other.

The Police as an Issue

India's politicians are ready to condemn the police at the drop of a hat and do so loudly and fairly regularly. Politicians express the attitude that people must be continually defended from the injustices, exactions, and stupidities of the police. Police have served as the issue sparking some of the most unruly scenes in the state legislatures as well as the national parliament. Calling attention notices and adjournment motions are constantly being filed by legislators hoping to ventilate some alleged injustice perpetrated by the police. On these occasions tempers run high and walkouts by the opposition are common. Budget debates, especially in north India—Uttar Pradesh, Punjab, and West Bengal—have been disrupted and violent accusations flung back and forth across the floor. Often so many legislators wish to speak on the police, to recount iniquities in their own constituencies, that a rigid time limit has had to be enforced and many legislators have not been given a chance to speak. Probably the greatest emotion is generated over instances of police violence against private individuals in police stations or against groups, particularly students, in public places. At these times tempers know no restraints, and ruling party and police are lumped together as conspirators in a vast plot against the freedom of political parties and of individual citizens. In true opposition style, faults of the police are laid at the door of the ruling party. Some ruling party members may, in the course of debate, rise to defend the police, and they may do so with skill and genuine enthusiasm. Others, however, carefully dissociate government from the police and proceed to cite instances from their own experience of indefensible police behavior. Indeed, except for the few supporters of the police, it would be difficult to distinguish between ruling party members and opposition simply by reading spoken remarks made in legislatures about the police.

There are several recurrent themes in criticism of the police by legislators. Corruption is one. Members mention ubiquitous demands by police for a gratuity before complaints are recorded at the police station. If money is not forthcoming the complaint is rejected, lost, or mistakenly noted. Police are accused of being in the employ of wealthy and influential persons. Police suppress facts about crimes and minimize the nature of crime. The stock example is murders that are recorded as dacoities. Another theme is that police are an arm of the ruling party or, in factionalized states, of the opposing section of the party. Members recount in tremendous detail the harassment to which they or their friends were subjected by police acting on behalf of the political opposition. Police followed them about, asked questions at awkward moments, threatened supporters, or filed false charges against them. Police are also portrayed as grossly inefficient and unable to maintain even minimal conditions of security in rural areas. The picture one gets is of vast areas of the country completely helpless before the depredations of the armed dacoit or vicious goonda. The methods of the police, when they do decide to do their job, are portrayed as completely primitive, unscientific, and based largely on the use of threats and torture. Stories of venerable old men, helpless mothers, and sweet virgins manhandled by the police crop up again and again. Finally, police are often charged with being in collusion with criminals. The police force is a notorious sheltering place for known criminals and bad characters. Money and power count in the countryside and successful criminals have both. Therefore the police can be found covering up their misdeeds and willfully failing to investigate or prosecute.

The touchstone of debates about police is invariably the issue of public cooperation. Government admits many of the defects so dramatically charged. If specifics are given, it promises a prompt and thorough investigation. The skepticism with which this is greeted is monumental. But, government goes on, many of the defects found in the police are the result of a widespread lack of cooperation by the mass of the people. For example, if the public will not come forward with information, police have no choice but to deal with antisocial elements. Similarly, the uneducated policeman may be tempted to apply force to get a conviction if he cannot obtain cooperative independent witnesses. If the public in India would provide the ready cooperation of the English or Americans, then the Indian police would not need to stoop so low and new habits would have an opportunity to take root. The opposition, says the government, would better serve the cause of police reform by helping to develop increased cooperation rather than by continually browbeating the police with malicious, intemperate, and unfounded charges. The opposition gives this argument short shrift. The prerequisite for willing cooperation, they say, is a police force that enlists respect and trust. How can the people be expected to volunteer when police are so demonstrably partial, venal, brutal, and stupid? The government must undertake to reform the police throughout; then it can ex-

pect cooperation. In short, the government calls for increased
public cooperation as the precondition of police reform and the
improvement of public safety; the opposition asks for reform
first and then promises generous cooperation. In each case, the
protagonists use their arguments against the other side—the opposition to charge the ruling party with neglect of police affairs
and the ruling party to charge the opposition with irresponsible
and inflammatory criticism.

Government, opposition, and ruling party members usually join
hands in deploring the conditions of pay and amenities of lower-
ranking policemen. They describe these men as harried, overworked, underpaid, ill clothed, poorly housed, inadequately
cared for medically, and unable to educate their children. In this
case political expediency and genuine need combine to produce
at least the protestations of concern.

Indian policemen are pained by the hostility shown them in
legislative debates but are not inclined to blame their financial
difficulties on this. They do say that immediately after independence some politicians took out past grievances against the
police by pursuing a vindictive, miserly policy. But this has passed,
they believe, and the low budgetary allocations must be attributed
to the fact that police belong to a "non-plan" department. Resources are scarce and are allocated firstly for development and
welfare activities. The police must be content with the minimum
amount considered sufficient to maintain general order and stability. While the opposition may try to cut the budget, more
usually they accept what government proposes, bemoaning the
lack of return for their rupees, but seemingly willing to pay if it
will improve the situation in their area.

The police have rarely been made an election issue. If there
has been a dramatic confrontation between police and public in
an area or a particularly spicy instance of brutality, then the police may become a stump issue. By and large it seems that there
is little mileage to be gotten out of criticism of the police on the
hustings. The issue is tired, the particulars are repetitious, and
few people expect any significant changes to occur. Bread-and-
butter issues are more important. The only other occasion for
public ventilation of criticism against the police comes as a part
of a campaign of public protest. Then the police are singled out
as the arch villains, speaker after speaker mounting the bullock
cart to denounce repression and to liken the police to their
counterparts during British rule.

There can be no doubt that politicians are sensitized to the police as an issue, although not one to be used very much during election campaigns. Politicians can recite a catalogue of police faults automatically. And they will do so with very little urging. By attacking the police, they attack the government. In sum, the noise made by politicians about police is considerable. We must now see what it indicates about the nature of political control and its impact upon popular attitudes.

ACCOUNTABILITY AND POLITICAL INFLUENCE

Attempts by politicians to influence the activities of police are continual. A critical part of a politician's function is to mediate with administration on behalf of constituents. If he were not to do so, his position would be weakened severely. Any part of the administration is considered fair game. Among politicians there has not grown up a strong inhibition against influencing the course of criminal justice. Few people, certainly not I.A.S. or I.P.S. officers, seriously contend that contact initiated by politicians is not an important fact of life. Their reactions to it, their evaluations of its propriety, and their assessments of its effects vary considerably.

Most observers agree that immediately after independence, strained relations arose between politicians and administrators. Politicians were at last in the driver's seat; it was time to teach the stiff-necked bureaucrats who was boss. Morale suffered and some people questioned whether an efficient and impartial administration could survive at all.[3] In a few years the balance was righted and gross abuses were curbed. The interference that exists now appears to be the result of considerations of political profit and expediency and not an emotional attempt to establish dominance.

I.P.S. officers believe that pressure is greatest against lower-ranking policemen in positions of authority, notoriously the station-house officer. Non-police observers are not so charitable toward the I.P.S. and believe that politicians and ministers seek to enter the chain of command wherever their own pressure can be best applied and wherever they spy a weak link. No doubt the

[3] A. D. Gorwala, *The Role of the Administrator: Past, Present, and Future* (Poona: Gokhale Institute of Politics and Economics, 1952), p. 36, says "So far as one can judge, this kind of interference has constituted in many parts of the country a real danger to honest administration."

subordinate staff are the more exposed. And they may be penalized more easily than an I.P.S. officer. The threat of being transferred is particularly effective against them. I.P.S. officers join service knowing they will probably serve in other states; they are used to shifting from post to post. Subordinate staff serve in their home districts; they are surrounded with familiar things and with friends and acquaintances of long standing. It is undoubtedly harder for them to be completely objective and impersonal in the line of duty. The thought of being wrenched from this familiar environment causes great anxiety.

Interference comes from many different kinds of people, most of them playing a political role in the sense of dealing in power and influence in order to achieve a position of authority and possibly of wealth. Most pressure in quantitative terms comes from local bosses. These individuals may hold formal office, perhaps as chairmen of district political committees; more likely they have another profession and serve to link specific villages, regions, or castes with the formal echelons of political authority. These are "bosses" in the true sense; their authority is derived from their ability to deliver votes for their political patrons in exchange for which they receive patronage and favors. Their position locally is in turn dependent on their ability to do favors for their own flock. Members of legislative assemblies (M.L.A.'s) are probably next in importance in the contact hierarchy. They have direct links to ministers through political parties. Since police and law enforcement is a state subject, they are the shortest route between constituent and police affairs. Members of parliament are more out of touch with day-to-day enforcement concerns of their constituents, and their effective sphere of action is not state matters but national.

Influence is exerted in different ways. Rarely is an outright threat or even an explicit request involved. M.L.A.'s and state cabinet ministers simply call up a superintendent and reveal that such-and-such is pending and that they are interested and will watch closely. They may disguise their purpose by pointing out aspects of the matter they thought the superintendent would want to know. While no demand is made, the superintendent becomes sensitive to the fact that someone of importance is looking over his shoulder. If the politician is powerfully situated, the superintendent cannot forget his presence. Many decisions that administrators and police officers make are delicately poised between alternatives. It is only too human for the harried officer sitting in solitude at his desk to shrug at the moment of decision and decide to do something this way rather than that, knowing that no real harm is involved one way or the other—most matters are often terribly petty—and this way the chance of unpleasantness is avoided.[4] Pressure is apt to be much less subtly applied to subordinate policemen. These are men of scant education, possessing little poise in dealing with high levels of authority, from childhood tutored in the power of certain local figures. It would take a strong sub-inspector to hold out against the threat of a boss to take a matter to a minister or the inspector-general, particularly if the sub-inspector has seen the boss entertaining important officials and making trips to the state capital. How, he must think, can his word be taken against theirs about the real facts of a situation?

The success of political interference in achieving its objectives depends upon the character of leadership in the police and in a state's political parties. Most I.P.S. and I.A.S. officers realize their responsibility. They know that if they fail to defend a wronged subordinate, even once, morale within their organization will crumble overnight. This explains in part why the first reaction of I.P.S. officers to charges against subordinates is apt to be irritation or tired skepticism. They have heard them all too often and have investigated scores of times in vain for every charge that has proved to be true. They have decided, often without formulating the matter explicitly, that corruption and brutality can only be eliminated through their own information-gathering and action and that information coming from outside is largely worthless and often tendered for extraneous reasons. Therefore, they must look first to the morale of their force and pursue police malpractices in their own way within the confines of the department. It would be a mistake to believe, as many private individuals do, that their reluctance to take immediate and dramatic action against subordinates is based on condonation of malpractices. They are caught in a bind, and must protect the integrity of the honest maligned subordinate as well as the honest aggrieved citizen.

Leading political figures, especially ministers, also determine the tone of administration with respect to interference. Powerful men buck their demands from level to level, ever searching for the compliant individual. In a parliamentary democracy such as In-

---

[4] One I.P.S. officer told me that for just this reason he would prefer serving with the armed police. He did not then have to contend with politicians hovering around his back.

dia's the nexus between police and politics is the office of the home minister. A home minister must stand behind the civil servants he directs; he is also responsible to society for their activities. If he truckles to his own party men or influential supporters, police and other civil servants feel terribly exposed. This is particularly true of the members of the state services, the non-I.A.S. and non-I.P.S. men. The way in which a home minister balances these pressures upon him depends in part on his character, both as to courage and his value system in ascertaining the right in specific situations. Beyond that, it must also depend on the political situation in the state. It seems reasonable to suppose that where the home minister is himself secure and his party, or faction of a party, is in a strongly entrenched position, he can reject improper requests with greater impunity. If, however, these conditions do not exist, the temptation to use his power must certainly increase. This hypothesis would suggest that morale among administrative staff would tend to be worse in those states where the opposition was substantial enough to pose a genuine threat to the dominance of the party in power or where the home minister was fighting for his political life within his party or where a dominant party was split into two relatively evenly balanced factions. There is an opposing hypothesis, however, which must be taken into consideration. One might argue that where parties or factions of parties are evenly balanced, a situation of countervailing power is created and the administrator need not choose sides, indeed if he did choose sides the other group would immediately trumpet it from the housetops. In other words, in a pluralistic political situation opposing groups can effectively monitor one another's attempts at interference in administration, thus providing a willing ally to the hard-pressed bureaucrat. Very little attention has been given by students of administration and politics to the conditioning effect that the structure of political competition has upon administrative efficiency and morale. It is a neglected subject which deserves study.

There is impressive evidence that political pressure upon administrators not infrequently results in the transfer of a balky officer. A report from Bombay showed in the late 1950's that in ten districts studied, there had been on the average five collectors in five years. In sixty out of one hundred gazetted posts in these districts there had been five incumbents in five years.[5] Senior I.A.S. officers

[5] Government of Bombay, *Report of the Officer on Special Duty on Reorganization of District Revenue Offices* (Bombay, 1958), p. 90.

have admitted that political pressure is one of the major factors in the inability to keep officers in posts for more than two years. The result is that men are transferred very soon after they have learned the ropes in their new posts. Just when they are able to take charge, they are uprooted and sent someplace else to learn all over again. If pressure on I.A.S. officers can be so successful, can one doubt that its threat to lower-ranking officers is profound? Figures on transfers among subordinate officers would be difficult to obtain but could be pieced together from existing records. This is a subject that government might well be advised to investigate. One chief secretary told me that in two years he had had about ten "serious" cases of local politicians getting a subinspector transferred. In several cases he had been able to get the order countermanded. The success of the official in righting the balance was directly proportional to the support given him by the state's chief minister.

It is one thing to say that pressure exists, or even that it has resulted in policemen being penalized, it is another to say that it is pernicious in its effects. While most Indian observers believe that pressure is extensive, they also take pride in the fact that police are less a law unto themselves than they were under the British. The presence of political influence and the decline of police autonomy are not accidentally associated. Police are more accountable than they were; they are forced to be much more circumspect in their actions. Perhaps it is a good thing for police officers to temporize a bit in making a decision, considering carefully the range of effects that may result. Pressure may be worthwhile at this price.[6] Realizing that there will always remain an unresolved normative question about the relative value of administrative efficiency and political vitality, what has been the effect in India of political interference upon police administration?

The recent state police commissions unanimously viewed the extent of political interference with alarm. They either said so in words or implied it in proposals for isolating police activity from influence. The Kerala Commission was the most uncompromising in finding evil effects in political interference: "The greatest obstacle to efficient Police administration flows from the domination of

---

[6] Paul Brass, *Factional Politics in an Indian State*, pp. 227-228, has said: "Thus, any assessment of the impact of the Congress upon administration in Uttar Pradesh must weigh the political advantages—in terms of democratic development—which have resulted from Congress rule against the economic disadvantages which flow from a demoralized and inefficient bureaucracy."

party politics in the State administration."[7] And the Bihar Commission observed: "There is no doubt that some people try to exert political pulls and pressure, directly and indirectly, upon public servants in order to secure some favorable treatment and the Commission agree with the witnesses that growing and widespread meddlesomeness of some people in the day-to-day administration has shaken the morale of the public servants after independence."[8] The Commission obliquely criticized the ruling Congress party in Bihar state when it said that "in securing the desired adjustment between the members of the force and the representatives of the people, the political party in power has to play its role by taking steps to prevent political interference in administration."[9] The West Bengal Police Commission pronounced honest officers "helpless" against the pressures bearing upon them. The West Bengal Commission thought the matter so serious that it suggested officers keep a diary of soliciting phone calls and contacts and that it be read with care by inspecting officers.[10] The Commission even proposed that superior officers play the role of *agent provocateur*, sending bogus messages requesting special treatment and thereby determining which officers were susceptible to the outside approach.[11] The Maharashtra Police Commission recommended isolating whole classes of decisions from political interference through the promulgation of a "code of conduct prescribing the purposes for which alone political and social workers could approach a police officer for redress of public grievances. . . ."[12] The concern of the Uttar Pradesh Commission was shown in its suggestion that, because local influence in criminal investigations was so widespread, important cases should be referred to the state C.I.D.[13]

The picture that emerges is of a police administration habitually temporizing, avoiding responsibility, and deferring to people of influence. Especially at lower levels of authority, like the station-house officer, the ability to move vigorously seems to have become paralyzed in some areas of the country. Politicians can intrude, it would seem, with deadly effect if they choose. The result

[7] Page 12. And later the Commission observed: "The result of partisan interference is reflected in lawless enforcement of laws, inferior service and a general decline of police prestige followed by irresponsible criticism and consequent widening of the cleavage between the police and the public affecting the confidence of the public in the integrity and objectives of the Police Force. Police administration has not yet succeeded in extricating itself from political influence, with adverse results on law enforcement and consequent demoralisation of the force."

[8] Page 196. [9] *Ibid.* [10] Pages 142-143.
[11] Page 254. [12] Page 23. [13] Page 44.

is excessive sensitivity to the informal network of community power relations. This does not mean that politicians always do intervene in every police action. The larger proportion of police activities are undoubtedly done in conformity to right as it is perceived and duty as it is understood. Departmental sanctions and legal rules are generally controlling. But in a proportion of cases that many experts consider substantial, the will to act courageously and vigorously in conformity with law has been undercut by insistent political interference.

I.A.S. officials support this reading of the situation. Paradoxically, so do politicians. One of the stock charges against a ruling party in any state is that it has made the police its creature. To hear politicians tell it, police are appendages of politicians. The weight of official, political, and lay opinion alike is certainly that political influence has seriously damaged the morale and efficiency of the police.

These evaluations should not be accepted at face value. Politicians must pretend to be effective in interceding with administrators. They must appear omnipotent even when they are completely disregarded by conscientious officials. What is more, the rules of the political game require that the ruling party be castigated for doing what one would do himself if he had the opportunity. Politics in India thrives on charges of skulduggery; the police provide a convenient occasion. Within the ranks of the I.A.S. and I.P.S., evaluations of the effects of political intervention may vary according to the age of the officers. Men who joined service under the British or soon after independence remember when administrators talked only to administrators and did not have to be bothered by the noisy, hurried, and uncouth politicians. Administration was rational; it could be planned. With the coming of independence and full-fledged democracy, administrators found themselves struggling in an unfamiliar environment, one for which they had not been trained. Officers of that generation are apt to feel very keenly the loss of freedom they once enjoyed. Many older police officers talk about the lack of "respect" shown for the police today. Police, they intimate, are restrained from acting with the stern, though benevolent authority once employed. Politics is the culprit—and being less self-directed, less autonomous, and more accountable than formerly, police undoubtedly do feel hampered. To them this appears as a serious loss of administrative efficiency. Younger men, at least in my experience, do not complain quite as vigorously about political interference—although they do not discount its pernicious effects if allowed to go unchallenged. It is possible that the younger officers are more accustomed to the frenzy and motion of democratic political life. They perceive no loss of respect or prestige, no clipping of their wings, because a democratic environment is all they have known. They are not inclined to overreact to political contacts; they consider them normal and can discount them as part of the system. The point is that reports of the effects of political intervention depend upon expectations people bring to the situation, and this depends very much on their experience and training.

The public is convinced that political control of police is extensive.[14] Close to 50 percent of urban residents thought there was a "great deal" of political control of the police; 21 percent of rural respondents gave this opinion. About one person in seven in urban areas thought the police took sides at election times. One in twenty felt this way in the rural area.

The fault is not all on one side. Just as politicians seek to use police for their purposes, so policemen sometimes seek to use politicians for theirs. Policemen ask politicians to use their influence to obtain choice postings, to avoid being transferred, to mitigate disciplinary sentences, or to earn an advancement in rank. Most states have strict rules about policemen appealing for outside support. The rules are hard to enforce, however, because so little is put in writing. A head-constable may ask for help from a politician who in turn calls the superintendent. Neither the head-constable's request nor the politician's phone call is a matter of record. The superintendent can't even be sure the politician is acting at the request of the head-constable. He may have been responding to a plea from another member of the family or simply trying to ingratiate himself with the family. Superintendents and inspectors-general have repeatedly warned their subordinates in written circulars about the consequences of this practice. Superintendents will sometimes note solicitous intervention by a politician in the policeman's confidential record. Discipline in this regard should be strict, for an appeal to a politician may form the basis of a bargain to the detriment of the impartiality with which an individual performs his duty.

[14] See Chapter 8.

THE BASIS OF INFLUENCE

Indians are deeply suspicious of the impartiality of the police. They believe that police treat people unequally, especially discriminating against low-status individuals. They also think that political control of the police is extensive, even to the extent of having police interfere in elections. Politicians are able to get the police to do things other people can't. On the basis of this evidence alone, it would be wrong to conclude that political mediation is universally denigrated. Indians are profoundly ambivalent about influence-peddling. This ambivalence involves more than being reasonably confident that the system can be made to work for you even though the system as a whole is bad. There is a serious question whether Indians do not prefer a system based on personal intervention to an impersonal one where each man mediates for himself and the rule-book is king. An impersonal system may be so unreal to many Indians as to be unwelcome; its imposition would make them acutely uncomfortable. F. G. Bailey has noted that peasants fail to distinguish between politicians and administrators; they consider them part of the same tree. They cannot understand that each may have a different function.[15] Consequently, a politician who was unwilling to intercede, pleading a principle of functional division, would be thought a fraud. More than that, Indians by and large are exceedingly unsure of themselves in approaching people in positions of formal authority. Their world is a small one, characterized by face-to-face relationships with people they have known all their lives. Manipulation of a non-village administrative structure is beyond their capacity. Possibly they project village mores onto the larger scene. Just as village relations are intensely personal, so relations in the wider world must respond to the personal touch as well and it becomes necessary to appeal to a man of influence who has such relations with officials outside the village.[16]

[15] *Politics and Social Change: Orissa in 1959* (Berkeley: University of California Press, 1963), pp. 23-24.

[16] Eldersveld *et al.* found in Delhi state that there was a general expectation that assistance was needed in approaching the official hierarchy. The individual could not do it for himself, unaided. *The Citizen and the Administrator in a Developing Democracy*, p. 25. This view was somewhat more prevalent in rural areas, although cynicism was palpable in both. While most people thought they needed help, only 17 to 19 percent had actually solicited it. The expectation that help was needed was found to be greatest among people of low social status and income. The more education one has and the higher his status, the more confident he is that he does not need to seek outside assistance in their approach to the bureaucracy. See pp. 48-49.

This insecurity has resulted in the growth of a large class of intermediaries. Politicians play this role, but they are only one of the agencies. Across the face of India are thousands upon thousands of people holding no formal political office whose chief business is mediation with authority. These people are variously called. Sometimes they are "bosses"—men who control the rudiments of an organization, with subordinates dependent on them and a clientele above and below. There are also natural leaders who by virtue of traditional standing, education, wealth, or occupation are expected to intercede with government officials and politicians. There are also the "touts," mercenary individuals who live off intercession, having no other occupation, willing to mediate for a price, and encouraging people to file some action or make some demand upon government. They are provocateurs, urging action on their erstwhile clients so as to create the business they live on. Touts are a feature of the landscape around courts and police stations. The Bihar Police Commission referred to them as "a class of semi-educated gentlemen" who "endeavor to establish unhealthy contacts with police officers."[17] The Commission blamed them for a great deal of the faulty reporting of crime. In Uttar Pradesh they are known as *"dalals."* In 1963 the Uttar Pradesh home ministry issued orders that they were not to be allowed to hang around the courts of police stations and that any policeman found dealing with them would have the fact noted against him.[18] A deputy inspector-general was quoted as saying that if these "barristers" could be eliminated, 50 percent of the corruption in the police would be eliminated.[19] The function that all these people perform—whether politician, boss, or tout—is that of broker or mediator.[20] They cannot be wished away, however harmful one may think them, because they perform an es-

[17] Pages 102 and 103-104.
[18] *The National Herald,* April 9 and 17, 1963.
[19] *Ibid.,* April 17, 1963, p. 5.
[20] See F. G. Bailey, *Politics and Social Change,* especially, pp. 63-67, and then again pp. 150-151, when he distinguishes various kinds of intermediaries. He explains the need for mediation as follows: ". . . they are simply an ignorant people, they are frightened of the clerks through whom they must work, they do not know the proper approach, they can neither read nor write, and, above all, they believe that the only way to get their due is to employ some knowing intermediary: and he is likely to be the local boss. Once again our analysis comes down to the fundamental fact of an enormous social cleavage between the middle classes and the common people. The politician cannot reach his electorate: the voters cannot communicate with their politicians and administrators: the gap is bridged by the political brokers and their network" (p. 111).

sential function. They do for people what people do not think they can do for themselves. The deep-seated need for intercession with burgeoning government undoubtedly provides an opportunity for crass and self-centered individuals, but until this need ceases to exist someone will be found to minister to it.[21]

The public survey has shown that contacts with the police increase with an individual's income, education, and social position. One can understand that people with higher social status might be more willing to seek out police assistance of some kind, but it seems odd that they had also been contacted by the police for questioning more often than lower status individuals. Part of the explanation may lie with the broker phenomenon. Just as the literate peasant expects the local boss, educated teacher, or wealthy businessman to know the ropes of administration, so the police expect these same individuals to have their fingers on the pulse of village life. One frequently hears that police, making an investigation in a village, first seek out the natural leaders. Many people think cynically that this is done in order to obtain free food and accommodation from those who can afford it. However, since villagers look to these leaders for cues as to how they should themselves behave, success in a criminal investigation may depend on the attitude and cooperation of these leaders. These people are also more apt to have information, and to have the poise to give it. Mediation is, therefore, a two-way street; a broker's clientele is both official and nonofficial. Police may encourage brokerage by *their* expectations as much as the diffident peasant does by his.

Favoritism is the other side of the coin from mediation. Both are inevitable in a society where impersonal administrative structures are relatively new and unfamiliar to the mass of the people and where these people possess neither the education nor the experience necessary to approach them with confidence. At the same time, favoritism is the result of a pervasive and fundamental suspiciousness that characterizes many Indian social relations. Indians seem not only to be unsure of themselves in making official contacts but unable to conceive that any administration can be impartial. Politicians reveal this attitude chronically. Debates

---

[21] Charlotte and William Wiser, *Behind Mud Walls*, p. 24, note that many times these village intermediaries go to great lengths to perform services for their constituents. "Like a father, the leader intercedes and makes whatever settlement is demanded on behalf of his dependent." "When we are tempted to criticize leaders, we should remind ourselves of the innumerable times when they have shouldered burdens which most of us would be tempted to throw back upon the man who incurred them."

in state legislatures are shot through with charges and counter-charges about administrative nepotism and bias. Governmental decisions are never seen as having been taken on their merits. Each politician justifies interceding on behalf of his constituents by referring to the likelihood—the certainty—that the other side will gain an unfair advantage if he does not. Intercession is created by the fear of interference by others—the result is a classic vicious circle. So suspicious are politicians of the effects of special relationships based on family, caste, faction, or party that under the guise of offsetting these pressures they act in terms of them themselves. Not only does bribe force counter-bribe, or influence counter-influence, but the bare thought of their likelihood brings both. Favoritism undoubtedly exists in large measure; the tragedy is that it feeds upon itself.[22]

Mediation is a requirement of modernizing societies; it has advantages that seem obvious to most Indians; it is unlikely to die out until each citizen feels confident that he can make his own contacts with officialdom. At the same time, mediation is the result of traditional social patterns that breed an endemic distrust. The charge of illicit favoritism will echo in political debate, as well as in village and hutment, for a long time to come. This makes it difficult ever to know the real extent of favoritism;

[22] Many observers believe that chronic suspiciousness is a product of the extreme compartmentalization of Indian life. To the divisions of caste and kinship which have affected village India for generations has now been added the cleavage between modern impersonal styles of life and traditional, paternalistic ones. Trust, the basis of cooperation, hardly exists outside the immediate family. As a result, two peasants from different castes or different extended families who are fighting over a piece of land will not join hands to resolve their dispute without recourse to law, leeching intermediaries, or bribes. They cannot trust one another so far; one man's gain is another man's loss. So they both reinforce the system of mediation. W. H. Morris-Jones, who has called distrust a "striking general feature of Indian political life," describes it in these words:

"In the courts a man in India is innocent until he is proved guilty, but in social and political life the position tends to be reversed. One has noticed the wariness with which people encounter each other and the relative difficulty in establishing friendships except within 'community' groups. If we understand the character of caste, this is hardly surprising, for its little worlds are worlds of mental attitudes and styles of behavior. To have dealings of any intimacy with a man of a different world from one's own is an adventure into a dark unknown and is best avoided; personal relations, in the strict sense, are not contemplated in the scheme of Indian traditional life. In politics this has its counterpart in features such as the extraordinary extent to which the other man's motives are suspect and the enormous difficulties attending any attempt at concerted action." *Government and Politics of India*. London: Hutchinson University Library, 1964), p. 63.

it also makes it inevitable that individuals who depend on public regard for their position and livelihood must act in the very manner they deplore.

POLICE AND THE CONDUCT OF POLITICS

Politics certainly touches the police. Policemen feel it; politicians decry it; and the public believes it. But do the police touch politics? That is, do their activities intrude in any way into the conduct of political competition? Do they affect political fortunes? As one would expect, many people believe so. Politicians themselves loudly charge it. The most common claim is that the police have been directed by the ruling party to suppress opposition political activity. This is the stock charge whenever a public demonstration sponsored by the opposition has been controlled in any way by the police. Positions become polarized then, the opposition charging systematic repression and the ruling party criticizing the opposition for its disregard for law, its callousness toward the deluded demonstrators, and its disregard for public order. Even without these dramatic public confrontations, opposition politicians charge that they are being harassed by the police. Sometimes they criticize police surveillance at public meetings. Special Branch operatives of the state's C.I.D. attend public political meetings routinely and have often been seen surreptitiously taking notes. More seriously, opposition members say that the police deliberately make difficulties during campaigns. They are denied licenses to parade or to hold public meetings; they are shadowed and questioned at inopportune moments. Police are even charged with beating and threatening supporters of opposition members. Filing false accusations against politicians is often cited, and it is a most potent weapon. False accusations not only discredit the politician in the eyes of the public but they force the politician to devote time and slender resources to clearing himself. What is more, if he is convicted for a term in jail of two years or longer election law debars him for a time from running for public office. A spurious case, even if unsuccessfully prosecuted, can cost a man his political career.

It is impossible to determine how often such events occur. If the word of politicians themselves is taken, there hasn't been an uncoerced election in India since independence—except their own. Police officers will not admit sanctioning such tactics although they do admit having been approached to do so. A standard campaign tactic seems to be alerting the police to the criminal activity of the opposition candidate. Hints are made that surveillance will show that candidate X is involved in smuggling, illicit distillation, or the planning of dacoities. Police are urged to bring him in for questioning or to search his house. Police are caught in a very delicate position. Some politicians are unscrupulous and do have criminal connections; others deliberately seek martyrdom by agitating disruptively or unlawfully in order to dramatize their willingness to suffer for the people; and others foment unrest so as to embarrass the ruling party. Such men may deserve to be kept under surveillance; the police would hardly be doing their duty if they did not. But where does surveillance leave off and harassment begin? The question is not easy to answer. Where rules for political competition are as yet unclear and not entirely beyond reproach and where public disorder is a mainstay of electioneering, overcautiousness on the part of police officers may result in instances of genuine repression.

Police have the power to repress, they also have the power to succor. Politicians continually charge one another with using violence to sustain their positions. They also claim that their opponents shelter hooligans and criminals whom they use for underhanded political work. Meetings are broken up, supporters threatened, posters torn down, or campaign workers beaten. In Uttar Pradesh "political murders" have been laid at the door of the ruling party, with opposition members charging that the police will not protect them. In 1963 a full-scale debate in the legislature was held on this topic. Politicians do sometimes admit or quietly imply that they feel compelled to have strong-arm squads at their beck and call. They justify their actions with spread hands, saying that since everyone does it so must they. Self-defense requires collaboration with unsavory elements. It is not unusual for M.L.A.'s to charge one another by name with sheltering dacoits or criminals. Thus the police become involved in political fortunes in two ways: either because they fail to protect one side from criminal attacks of the other or because they hesitate to take action against known criminals sheltering under the wing of a powerful individual. Once again the police are caught in a cruel dilemma. Too much supervision of political behavior would be repressive; too little supervision would allow the unscrupulous politician too free rein.[23]

[23] Professor Paul Brass reports this conversation with a politician in Lucknow in the early 1960's, which he considers a fair appraisal of the situation:
"Home [Ministry] means power. Because, under the British, this was a police state, the Home Minister was supposed to be the next officer [after

By acts of commission and omission the police do play a part in political life. So prevalent seem to be the opportunities that they must make errors from time to time. There must also be situations in which they yield to improper pressure, thus affecting the interplay of political forces. It must be stressed, however, that the fault is not entirely theirs. As long as private violence is a part of politics, the police cannot avoid applying the sanctions of the law to politicians. As long as political competition is carried out contrary to law, the police cannot avoid involvement. To stand aloof from intervention would be as improper as hasty action. Therein lies the dilemma and the danger.

CONCLUSION

The relations between police and politicians are not easy in India today. Politicians are critical of the police, not without justification, and the police are angry or cynical about the self-seeking of politicians. There is appreciable evidence of successful political intervention in police affairs, some of which has produced injustices and weakened the morale of the force. The public at large believes political interference is efficacious, but this has not noticeably improved their confidence in either the police or politicians. In fact, it may have redoubled their anxieties about other people using influence to gain an unfair advantage.

Relations between politicians and administrators are in a time of testing, with accommodation among various elements yet to be worked out. The police have been discredited by their colonial past and present defects in practice; politicians have been discredited by their unscrupulousness, partiality, and parochialism. The problem for modern India is to establish a stable equilibrium between two imperfect forces so as to serve the public interest. There is room for improvement on both sides. Progress begins with this admission by all concerned.

---

the chief minister]. The most powerful officers in the district then and now are the District Magistrate and the Superintendent of Police. The S. P. is powerful because life and property are in his hands. Every day your supporters are coercing my supporters—the only relief is through the police. Then, people can be falsely implicated in dacoities; similarly, Home can give relief to people." (Brass, p. 213). Although the situation in Uttar Pradesh may be extreme, there is an undercurrent of violence and coercion in Indian politics which at the least impels the police into the limelight of political debate and at the most confronts them with invidious choices involving the application of restraint to people playing formal political roles.

15 • *The Police and Village Government*

POLICING in India is predominantly a rural affair. According to the 1961 census, approximately 82 percent of the people live in communities of less than 2,000 persons.[1] There are slightly over a half million of these communities. If crime is not inhibited and order preserved in the villages, in these scattered hamlets and clusters of hamlets, the police are failing in their responsibility.[2]

Determining the manner in which policing should be conducted in village India raises one of the historic concerns of Indian government: namely, how are the institutions of the village to be related to those of national authority? Imperial powers, indigenous and foreign, have wrestled with the problem for centuries. Today, India is caught up in a massive expansion of democratic institutions. Village government is being made part of the national democratic political system. Clearly the success achieved in spreading these institutions to the grassroots cannot help but affect police policy. Could it also be that police policies may affect the successful development of these institutions?

POLICING IN RURAL INDIA

In 1960, when figures were last made available for police strength, there was one unarmed policeman—the true civil constabulary —for every 1,450 people and for every 3.89 square miles of territory.[3] Since then police strength has grown, but so has population. Moreover, growth in police strength has been concentrated in the armed police. It is doubtful if the ratio of unarmed policemen to population has changed for the better since 1960. India has, therefore, three times as many people for each policeman as the United States or Great Britain. What is more, the ratio improves markedly for urban areas. India's major cities compare favorably

[1] Census of India, *Paper 1 of 1962*, pp. lxi and 5 ff.

[2] In 1961 there were 2,690 towns, accounting for 18 percent of the population. Over half the towns were classified as Class IV and V, i.e., ranging in size from 5,000 to 20,000. A town is any community with more than 2,000 people in it.

[3] For a detailed discussion of police strength, see Chapter 3.

with New York and London. The rural countryside with its vast expanses has been neglected relative to the cities. As near as these things can be figured, given the paucity and fragmentation of official statistics, there are about six thousand police stations. Each has a jurisdiction on the average of two hundred square miles and a population of seventy-five thousand people. Jurisdictions tend to be larger in the north, smaller in the south. The average distance of a police station from any village is approximately eight miles, although there are tremendous variations from place to place. There is one police station for every eighty-three villages. Each station will have a minimum complement of ten to fifteen men, constables and N.C.O.'s together.

In terms of personal contact with police, the survey shows that villagers have much less than urban people. About a third as many people in rural Mysore have gone to the police for help as in urban Bangalore, while about two-thirds as many have been questioned by the police. Among Kanpur immigrants from rural areas there is a similar difference in comparison with established inhabitants: about half as many have gone to the police for help and about two-thirds as many have been questioned. It is true, of course, that crime rates are lower in rural areas. For example, the survey shows that less than half as many rural respondents have been victims of a crime. There is less reason to have had contact in rural areas than urban ones. The distribution of policemen in each state reflects these facts.

Hesitancy to contact police is significantly more marked among rural respondents. Villagers in Mysore, for example, were more reluctant to contact than Bangalore respondents in the following situations: when a child was lost, a fight was likely to break out between two groups, they had been robbed of valuables worth Rs. 100, they had been robbed of valuables identifiable in the future, a bicycle had been stolen, a person had been killed accidentally, and they needed directions in an unfamiliar territory. Bangalore residents were more reluctant than rural ones when a person had been injured in a fall or by an animal, a person had been found beaten up, and they had been threatened with unjust eviction. Whenever there was a significant difference in responses between rural Kanpur migrants and established Kanpur residents, the rural migrants were always the more reluctant. Out of thirteen hypothetical situations listed, rural migrants were more reluctant on six. These were: a person injured in a fall or by an animal, a friend in danger of being attacked by goondas, a fight likely to break out between two groups, a man found beaten up, a person killed accidentally, and a person found who appeared to have been murdered. It would appear that the police have a major job to do in convincing rural people that ready assistance is available at the nearest police station.

In the south, rural people tended to be less willing than city folk to praise the police for doing a good job in catching criminals or in being ready to take sympathetic action. The proportions of outright negative responses were the same between rural and urban samples. In the north, migrant and established urban samples had the same proportions of positive and negative responses on these two items. Northern responses were generally less favorable than southern ones. One can conclude that in the south, at least, there is more doubt in rural than urban areas about the efficiency and responsiveness of the police.

The survey showed little difference between rural and urban people with respect to the sense of duty they articulated about cooperating with the police. Only on the item about volunteering information to the police about a crime committed in their vicinity was there an important difference. Over three times as many rural respondents said they would not volunteer and would wait for the police to come to them. The Kanpur samples did not show significant differences on any of the duty questions.

Contact with police tended to rise somewhat with education and income. The correlations were not large—on the order of 0.20—but they give some support for the proposition that upper class villagers are more willing to seek help from the police and are in turn more sought after by police when gathering information. Rural people have about the same amount of elementary knowledge of the police as urban people. However, they are less familiar with them in personal terms. They recognize few policemen on sight and they know few of them by name. The police seem to be more anonymous in the villages; they are not the fixtures they are in cities and towns.

Perceptions of security do not differ greatly between villagers and urbanites. There is, however, substantial thwarted demand for owning firearms, which is more intense among urban people. About 11 percent of the Mysore rural sample said their village had been troubled by dacoits. In all probability the proportion would be larger in the north.

The composite picture that emerges from the survey data is of villagers who have little contact with police, and much less than urban people; have no personal familiarity with them; are more reluctant to seek help from them than urban people; may be less willing to cooperate with police in criminal investigations; have little experience with crime personally; and have some anxieties about the safety of person and property but not more than urban people.

In villages the most familiar police agent is the chowkidar or patel. These are the men of the rural police. Their job is to patrol the village at night and to watch for disturbing or suspicious happenings at all times. They are basically watchmen. They link the village and the regular police, for they have the responsibility of reporting all crimes to the nearest police station. The post of watchman is often hereditary although promotion to it must be approved by the superintendent of police or the district collector. Village police are paid a pittance, and that irregularly. Their stipend is paid partly by the state and partly from local sources. There are more chowkidars in India than unarmed police. Almost every village has someone who holds the post. This would mean about a half million chowkidars in all, compared with a civil constabulary of about 300,000. Records of chowkidar strength are not carefully kept, so it is difficult to be precise.

The general consensus among observers is that rural police are far from being an effective police agency. They may not even be very effective watchmen. A chowkidar is considered a menial role in many parts of the country. Night-patrolling is an unpopular task. Rural police are thought to be in collusion with criminals, to suppress evidence of crimes or to misreport information deliberately for the sake of a patron, and to take their cues in tendering information to the police from the village headman or other influential personages. The recent police commissions criticized the rural police in strong language. They found it moribund as an effective ally of the regular police. Most police officers are pleasantly surprised when they find a chowkidar who will just stand guard over the scene of a crime and take steps to notify the nearest police station. Few officers consider them an effective deterrent against crime.

The public opinion survey revealed an enormous amount of dissatisfaction with the rural police. The survey data are unfortunately limited to a single district in Mysore. It may not, therefore, be representative. Respondents were asked whether they wished to have a permanent police officer stationed in the village in place of the chowkidar. Seventy-nine percent said they would prefer a regular police officer. Nineteen percent said they preferred the chowkidar. Two percent had no opinion—an unusually low proportion of "don't knows" for a rural sample. Rural people, at least in Mysore, quite evidently perceive a need for police services which is not being filled by existing institutions. It is significant indeed when villagers indicate a preference for the permanent presence in their village of an outside governmental agency, particularly the police. Police officers who have continually argued that there is considerable latent demand for police services in rural areas have certainly been vindicated.

Rural India is spottily and inefficiently policed. The impunity with which dacoits and highway robbers operate is a plain indication of this fact. The criminal situation would not *appear* to be as bad in the rural areas as the cities, but until crime reporting has been considerably improved, especially in villages, one cannot be sure. Villagers would seem to welcome the development of an efficient, reliable, trustworthy, and pervasive police system. To date, neither the state police nor the chowkidari system has met the need.

The Police and Democratic Decentralization

Whatever may be done to improve police operations in rural areas will be affected in large measure by the policy of democratic decentralization that has gathered momentum in recent years. Democracy has come to modern India in two waves. The first began with independence when the country inaugurated a representative parliamentary system ensconced within a federal structure. The second wave came a decade after independence with Panchayati Raj. The decision to broadcast democratic forms throughout the many layers of administrative authority was a courageous one. It was a leap in the dark; and the most certain sign of the continued attachment of India's leaders to the democratic credo. In essence democratic institutions were developed in order to harness the energies of the people to the arduous task of economic development. In the mid-1950's it became apparent to many people that agricultural and community development was lagging; they had not aroused the enthusiasm of the masses and generated self-sustaining progress. Rather than adopt a manipulative solution from the top down, India's leaders decided that willingness to participate in development could only be fostered through association of the masses in planning and implementation of development projects. Unlike so many developing nations, India did not decide that economic progress was the precondition of democracy and that until standards of living were permanently raised democracy had little chance. Democracy became the Indian vehicle for economic development; it was the essential ingredient of rapid social change that had been lacking. The new policy is like lifting by one's bootstraps, only on a colossal scale, for the decision was made that an unlettered, depressed, tradition-ridden people could be so caught up in the free play of democratic institutions that they would modernize both rapidly and willingly.

Village councils—panchayats—have performed adjudicating functions for thousands of years. Embracing this heritage, which had become somewhat dilapidated under British rule, the central government urged every state to enact legislation establishing a coherent, interlocking system of local governing bodies, running from village to district. Since 1958, when the movement got under way, Panchayati Raj has swept the country. By 1962 estimates placed the proportion of the rural population covered by panchayats at 95 percent.[4] Two hundred thousand panchayats had been established, each one covering about two and a half villages. The population per panchayat was approximately 1,400.[5]

Panchayati Raj calls for the involvement of local people, through elected representatives (*Panches*), in the planning and administration of development efforts. It implies a growing amount of local control of development activities, especially as they impinge in practical ways on the individual community. But economic development is not the whole story. The traditional role of panchayats as adjudicating bodies has not been forgotten. In fact the new panchayat legislation formalized it by establishing *nyaya panchayats* to perform the traditional function. Nyaya panchayats are composed of people elected from the village *gram panchayat* or several gram panchayats in a cluster of villages. In this way the functions of development administration and dispute adjudication are kept separate. Nyaya panchayats generally have both civil and criminal jurisdiction. Civil jurisdiction is limited by the value of the property involved, often not more than Rs. 250; criminal jurisdiction is limited to offenses whose fine is

[4] Government of India, *The Third Plan: Mid-Term Appraisal*, p. 86. Ministry of Community Development and Cooperation, Central Institute of Community Development, Mussoorie, "Seminar on Public Administration in Panchayati Raj at Savoy Hotel, Mussoorie, 9 to 13 April, 1962: Agenda Papers," p. 13.

[5] *Ibid.*

not large and where a jail sentence cannot be imposed.[6] Benefits from the nyaya panchayat system have been obvious, and grass-roots support throughout the country appears to be substantial. Panchayat courts are close at hand, uncomplicated, and relatively speedy. Emphasis is placed on conciliation, not litigation. Lawyers are usually barred from appearing before them. Informality is stressed; contending parties appear for themselves in the sight of the community. Nyaya panchayats relieve an already overburdened judiciary of a multitude of petty offenses and complaints.

The panchayat system touches the police in two ways: first, through its jurisdiction in certain classes of criminal offenses and, second, through its authority over the rural police. Nyaya panchayat criminal jurisdiction involves offenses common to the village. For example, they hear cases involving the performance of obscene acts or songs; petty theft; affray; fouling water in a public spring; voluntarily causing hurt; committing mischief or criminal trespass; and misconduct by a drunken person in a public place. Problems of coordination with the police arise because they have jurisdiction in these cases too. In some areas the police have taken the view that cognizable offenses within the purview of nyaya panchayats are no longer a police affair. Enforcement and investigation should be left to the villages and panchayat personnel. In other areas local police have undertaken to help the nyaya panchayats by turning over records to them, by urging attendance of witnesses, and even by acting as prosecutors before the panchayat courts. Police have a duty under the criminal law to investigate cognizable offenses; they cannot avoid this even though panchayat courts have joint jurisdiction with magistrate's courts. But police must not exercise their responsibility so as to contaminate village autonomy by intervening too largely in the conduct of panchayat courts. For their part, panchayat courts often recognize that they need help and seek to involve the police. They try to direct police investigations, demand that certain suspects be detained, or ask the police to compel attendance of people before them. The Study Team of the Law Ministry recommended that police pursue investigations independently and when finished turn over all reports to the panchayat court for

[6] The monetary limit for fines varies considerably. Government of India, Ministry of Law, *Report of the Study Team on Nyaya Panchayats*, April, 1962, recommended that the limit be placed at Rs. 50.

hearing and judgment.[7] In this way, they hoped, village self-direction, police responsibility, and public safety could all be ensured.

Panchayats also become involved with the police by virtue of their authority over the rural police and certain volunteer police bodies. In these cases panchayats defray part of the costs and have supervisory responsibilities for their operation. If panchayats exercise their authority conscientiously they soon find themselves needing to coordinate directives with the district superintendent of police or circle inspector, because the state police have supervisory powers as well. Dual authority causes ruffled feelings on both sides: the panchayat feels that the superintendent is overbearing, the superintendent feels that the panchayat is a nuisance, making an already bad situation worse. In a few places the panchayats have been given authority to issue executive orders with respect to public safety and criminal affairs. In Bihar, for example, the nyaya panchayats can issue prohibitory orders under section 144 of the Code of Criminal Procedure. And in Uttar Pradesh they can demand security for keeping the peace. The nyaya panchayats thus function as magistrates, promulgating orders that police must observe. The Study Team of the Law Ministry argued strongly against vesting such powers in nyaya panchayats. It pointed out that prohibitory orders deprived people of fundamental rights. In conformity with the principle of limiting panchayat jurisdiction to minor criminal matters, they felt that prohibitory orders raised too serious issues.[8]

The present policy of Panchayati Raj and the philosophy of democratic decentralization leads to greater interplay between local communities and the police. Hitherto direction of the police has been a state prerogative; local communities expressed their dissatisfaction through elected representatives to the state legislature. Local institutions of opinion-aggregation and decision-making cannot avoid becoming involved with matters of public safety if these matters are on the minds of their constituents. Members of panchayats are bound to feel that village democracy is truncated if basic conditions of life and property are completely outside their proper consideration. In deference to this feeling and in order to improve cooperation between police and community, panchayats have been given executive authority over village police. Some of these powers go back for many years. The pres-

[7] Page 103. [8] *Ibid.*, pp. 78-89.

sure for widening the ambit of supervision, especially to extend it to the state police, is considerable. Many politicians openly advocate substantial decentralization of police authority. Direction of the police, they argue, should be put more and more in the hands of district panchayats—the zilla parishads—and even local panchayats. An immense opportunity, they argue, for binding the police and the public more harmoniously together is being wasted. How strong this movement will become and where equilibrium between local control and state authority will be established are matters impossible to predict. As panchayat institutions become stabilized, the movement to make police more accountable locally can be expected to grow. Democratic decentralization has unleashed new political forces. It would be naive to believe these forces will not impinge upon police affairs.

At present police relations with panchayat institutions are correct but distant. By and large local officers are left to work out their own patterns of consultation and cooperation. Superintendents in some parts of the country have seized the opportunity to use panchayats to inform people about police problems. Others have tended to think of panchayats as distracting, fractious, and unimportant. They have held them at arms' length. Very few officers have been willing to see panchayats assume any practical control over the police. Police-panchayat relations are uncoordinated and unclear, with both sides hoping to use the other on their own terms.

Improving Police Operations in the Countryside

Police reform in rural India involves two issues which should be clearly distinguished. First, what should be done to improve the service provided by police? Second, what should be done to improve accountability of the police? The first question involves determining what can be done to either rural or state police to improve performance, as well as to resolve the problem of balance between them. The second question concerns the relations to be established between any police agency, however efficient, and representative institutions of popular government. These issues will be considered in turn.

The Gordian knot in improving police performance in the countryside is the rural police. Should they be retained and improved? Should they be retained but bypassed? Should they be abolished altogether, concentrating efforts at improvement entirely on the regular police? These are the alternatives, and they have faced police reformers since imperial and village forces first confronted one another. So far the alternative of preserving the police but doing very little to improve them has held the field. It has led to the present state of disrepair. The Police Commission of 1902-1903 and the recent state commissions unanimously advocated retaining rural police.[9] Although all of them found the existing rural police defective, they continued to believe that rural police served a useful function. There are four primary benefits often credited to the system of rural police. First, rural police deter criminal activity. They may be inefficient but to replace them in all of India's villages with full-time beat constables would be prohibitively expensive. Without village police, regular patrolling would cease to exist. In many cases village police have acted courageously in dangerous circumstances. They have alerted villages to imminent danger; they have organized defenses against dacoits; they have apprehended criminals. Second, rural police are a part of a village as no outside policeman can ever be. Therefore they provide a unique source of information. They monitor potentially dangerous events and can furnish precious clues to investigating officers. Third, rural police are an institution of self-help, lessening the dependence of the village on outside succor, and encouraging an attitude of self-sufficiency. The chowkidari precedent should be utilized and expanded, not allowed to fall by the wayside. Fourth, rural police, being a local police, are more trustworthy than outsiders. National and state police are too far removed from local control. No matter that the local force is inefficient, slightly corrupt, or even partial; it is still local, and therefore more responsive to local feelings. Indians believe, as many Americans and British do, that there is virtue in local control. This is a first axiom of political life, to which people are deeply committed emotionally. Better to be in the hands of the local chowkidar, is the thinking, than of a sub-inspector who knows nothing of the village, was himself brought up miles away, and who takes orders from remote authority. In summary, the rural police deter crime, furnish information, promote self-sufficiency, and promote freedom through decentralization of the police function. What is often not said but is clearly implied in commentaries

[9] The Uttar Pradesh Police Commission advocated abolition of the chowkidari system but then recreated a rural police under a new name and organization. The Police Commission clearly did not want to leave policing exclusively to the state police.

on the rural police is that their demise would represent an unacceptable break with the past. They are a traditional fixture of Indian life. Tradition would be bruised if rural police were summarily abandoned.

The argument against retaining village police is much simpler, and much more cold and calculating. The rural police force has not worked and it cannot be made to work at an acceptable cost. There is no point in preserving an outmoded institution lacking funds and prestige to attract able people to its service. Whether one likes it or not, effective policing begins with the state police. The lesson of the past two centuries of police development is that a central police force can provide far better protection than chowkidars. The rural police are and will continue to be a fifth wheel. Effort should not be directed to patching them up for reasons of sentiment but should be directed at improving the best instrument at hand.

The arguments put forward in favor of the rural police system need a long, hard examination. If the survey data from Mysore are representative, villagers seem to have very little confidence in their village police. They would prefer police constables. The outcry when a police station is moved is further indication of preferences. Policemen themselves applaud isolated instances of bravery and foresight on the part of chowkidars, but generally have little confidence in them. As a source of information most chowkidars are suspect precisely because they are so much a part of the villages they live in. Rather than intimacy bringing understanding, it promotes distortion. The chowkidars do inform the police about suspicious events or criminal happenings but these functions would probably be performed anyhow. It is doubtful if many of them are much more conscientious in this regard than any villager leader would be. When the going really gets tough, as in dacoit-infested parts of northern Madhya Pradesh or southern Uttar Pradesh, little help can be expected from the chowkidars. The only real deterrents are an increase in regular police patrols and large-scale clearing operations. Neither the public nor the police expect much out of the rural police in terms of practical accomplishments.

The recommendations of the recent police commissions press in two directions for reform of the rural police. They ask for an upgrading of the rural police enterprise and for establishment of new relations with village councils and the state police. The commissions are unanimous as to the kinds of things that should be done to improve performance, even if they do not agree about the relations rural police should have with other institutions. We shall take this matter up in a moment. In no case do the police commissions recommend turning all policing over to the state police. In order to improve rural police performance, the police commissions have made the following recommendations. Training of chowkidars must be more extensive, including provisions for retraining from time to time; pay must be raised and steps must be taken to ensure that it is paid regularly; ancillary duties, such as keeping records and attending on local officials, should be eliminated; a higher quality recruit should be found. Summing up the trend in official and lay thinking, the village police are probably here to stay, although the improvements that will be made in fact in their performance are problematic.

It is worth noting that there has been one experiment in abolishing rural police and putting an expanded constabulary in its place. In 1955 the government of Uttar Pradesh carried out this reform in two police circles, one in Bulandshahr district, the other in Pratapgarh district. Each constable was given a beat covering seven villages. In 1961 the Uttar Pradesh Police Commission concluded that it was still too early to evaluate the experiment. Several problems, however, had emerged. The jurisdiction of each constable was too large; the constable was not in close touch with the people and his contacts were much less effective than the chowkidars. The inspector-general of police at the time spoke unenthusiastically about the experiment. He said it was costly in manpower; it depleted reserves by scattering men all over the area making it more difficult to handle fairs, elections, security duties, and emergencies.[10] In India as a whole, then, there has been only one tentative attempt at radical solution to the uncertain compromise between rural and state police functions.

The other agency for improving police service in the countryside is the state-controlled, stipendiary police. What can be done to improve the operation of the state police in rural areas? Apart from improving many technical aspects of police work, the problem is basically one of coverage. We have already seen how lacking a police presence is in villages and how welcome it would be. Politicians continually ask government to appoint more constables and fewer officers of exalted rank. Such requests are a sly way of criticizing top officers and appearing to line up on the side of

[10] *Ibid.*, pp. 40-41.

the common man, but they also indicate what people do want—they want policemen nearby with the responsibility and competence to handle criminal situations. Where are such men to come from?

There are two answers to this question: they may come from expanded recruitment or from reassignment of existing personnel. The latter choice has the advantage of requiring no additional expenditure. Most people would say that reorganization of police tasks might produce a few more men for assignment to the field, but that the gain would be marginal. That is true. There is one very large pool of manpower already on the police rolls, however, which is rarely considered in this connection. That is the armed police. In 1960 two-fifths of all Indian policemen were armed police. If unpublished statements by officials are correct, since then there has been a substantial increase in their numbers, so that now perhaps half of all police are armed police. If they were all assigned to unarmed duty, the number of men available in the station houses would double. One should not expect of course that men currently in the armed police could feasibly be transferred to constabulary duties. They are simply not fit for the task. But recruitment patterns could be changed; savings in expenditure on armed police could be used for larger numbers of civil constabulary.

Given the evident need for better police operations in rural India dealing with crime prevention and investigation, the question of the utility of the armed police must be raised. It is anomalous, for example, that a U.P. inspector-general could complain that assigning constables to more villages reduced police strength for tasks involving crowd-control, security, and emergencies when half his force is composed of armed policemen whose work is predominantly of this kind. The experiment in Uttar Pradesh involved substituting reserves of unarmed constables for chowkidars, not armed reserves for chowkidars. What the inspector-general is indicating implicitly is that he is more concerned about performing these episodic tasks effectively than he is about meeting day-to-day needs in the villages. Many police officers and civil administrators—perhaps most—share this point of view. They are very concerned always to have enough reserves on hand so as to be able to intervene with overwhelming power to shut off dramatic unrest or disorder. They have few illusions about the adequacy of village policing, but they are not willing to improve village policing at the expense of armed reserves. The prevalence of this view causes, and will continue to cause, more than half of all policemen to spend their lives in military-style cantonments isolated from daily contacts with individual citizens. Surely one of the great curiosities of the Indian system is that organization of the police into armed and unarmed branches, so admirably fitted to the needs of a colonial regime, should have been continued without serious question a generation after independence. Recognizing the needs of the countryside for a more effective police presence, the utility of the armed police as opposed to an unarmed constabulary should be considered afresh. While the issue should not be prejudged, the sanctity of the armed police should no longer be allowed to stifle responsible study and discussion.

Let us examine briefly the merits of an armed police system. Armed police perform four valuable functions. First, they serve as a security force for public installations and property. This task must be performed; if armed police were not available, government would have to recruit a new force of armed guards for banks, treasuries, government offices, and so forth. Watchmen and guards are often recruited independently by government agencies in America or Great Britain; this is not the case in India. Second, armed police perform a deterrent function in times of public tension, incipient instability, or potential mob danger. They deter by their presence; they remind people that the ultimate sanction of force is near at hand and available to government. They also help manage large groups of people, such as at athletic events, fairs, and rallies. Third, they are the ultimate weapon in the hands of civil authority for restoring public order. When force must be employed, armed police are called upon to do it. They are trained in the use of force and are kept in sufficient strength so as to be able to cope with any reasonable threat. They are called out to quell riots and communal disturbances, to hunt bands of dacoits, and prevent infiltration along international borders. Fourth, armed police are a force-in-being to cope with any emergency, even if it does not involve the use of force. They are often used in times of natural calamities. They build dikes to prevent flooding, evacuate people from low-lying areas, distribute food in drought-stricken areas, dispose of threats to public health, and dispense medicines.

On the face of it, the maintenance of an extensive armed police apparatus seems to be at odds with British police philosophy upon which Indian practice has been so largely molded. In fact, it is not. The Indian police system is founded on the principle that a civil constabulary should be unarmed. This was an essential part of Sir Robert Peel's vision for the Metropolitan Police Force. There should be a division between those who use force and those who do not; moreover, those who do not should be the visible police agency. Existence of armed police in India does not reflect a difference in essential philosophy but a difference in social conditions. Britain can afford a police establishment predominantly unarmed. Large bodies of armed policemen in India can be seen as the logical extension to more turbulent conditions of the principle that an unarmed constabulary should be kept distinct from armed civil forces.

There are disadvantages as well to the armed police system. First, assuming that resources that can be allocated to police are fixed and cannot be expanded substantially, armed police drain away funds that could be used for a civil constabulary. The result is that one kind of policing is neglected for another. In practical terms, fewer men—and perhaps fewer men of higher caliber—are available for ministering to the mundane, daily requirements of individual citizens. Patrolling is neglected; a visible police presence disappears. Criminal investigating staffs become overburdened, unable to handle all the complaints that come to them. Short-cuts are adopted. Police begin to feel hard-pressed, submerged in a sea of requests. They act hastily, brusquely, unsympathetically. The net effect is for police intervention to become impersonal and spasmodic, associated with calamity and bringing serious dislocation, rather than being a persistent, welcomed, informal act. Second, the presence of armed policemen affects the discrimination with which officials respond to potentially threatening situations. It tends to engender an all-or-nothing philosophy. Knowing that armed police can be called in if the situation gets out of hand, officials give less attention to stabilizing situations at a lower level of violence. The unarmed police become little more than a trip wire to activate armed police. More attention is given to how force should be used and when than how its use might be prevented through more discriminating use of the civil police. Officials perhaps cannot imagine how the armed police can be dispensed with precisely because they have never been forced to try. The potentialities for prevention are insufficiently studied because overawing force is so ready at hand.

Many people would concede that expansion of the unarmed police would produce real benefits. They would be concerned, however, if these had to be achieved at the cost of reducing mobile armed reserves. Is this substitution required? The answer is probably yes. Resources for police are so slight that it is doubtful if the unarmed police can be expanded substantially while maintaining existing quotas of armed police. Indeed, current reliance on the armed police by both officials and politicians is an indication that these means for preserving public order are acceptable at the price. To put the matter another way: government would rather maintain social order through reliance on the armed police than spend a larger sum of money on experimental methods built on a different concept of police function. Due partly to lack of funds and partly to the inertial weight of past practice, responsible leaders are generally unwilling to try a new police policy if it requires substantial increases in expenditure. It follows, therefore, that a more pervasive civil constabulary, perhaps more highly trained, can only be developed at the expense of the armed police.

An exchange of this kind involves enormous risk. Can one be sure that an alert, dedicated, well-trained constabulary in intimate contact with half a million villages can so successfully deter crime and prevent public disorder that the size of armed reserves can be reduced? Can any official take this chance? Given the level of violence in Indian society, one should not expect them to be very willing to try. The existing system has the supreme virtue of being familiar; it has worked reasonably well in the past in the sense that public order has been generally preserved and outbreaks of violence quickly contained. Imputed gains from a pervasive civil constabulary may be worthwhile in theory, but they are not assured. A mistake in calculation could cause untold suffering among millions of people if law and order should dramatically break down. Furthermore, if the new constabulary is to be successful it must have more than increased numbers. Today's constables, who are so largely ciphers, cannot realistically be expected to shoulder major responsibilities. A new kind of constable must be created. Perhaps all this requires is to use the old material in new ways. But this requires training; the transition cannot be made overnight. Rather than trading one armed policeman for one unarmed constable, the proposition may entail trading several for one. The risks are thereby multiplied while the benefits remain a promise. The point is that there are indeed serious reasons why the approach to reform should not be headlong.

At the same time, faith in past practices should not be allowed to prevent exploration of the usefulness of new approaches. The fact is that no one *knows* if another policy would be more successful. The information to make this determination simply doesn't exist. The first requirement of reform is for a sympathetic examination of alternative possibilities and the second is for controlled experimentation. Given the concrete needs of the countryside and the unhappy state of police-public relations, are the risks to be found in study and experimentation so very great? Persuasive evidence for the utility of substituting unarmed for armed police can only be obtained through undertaking experiments in a variety of districts. In the short run, this may mean that budgetary outlays for unarmed police must be raised, without corresponding savings in the armed police. This is because the experiment may fail, and officials, knowing this, would be loath to reduce the numbers of armed police in the meantime. Although if the experiment were to succeed, savings could be effected at a later date. Success in the trial requires dedicated acceptance of the scheme by all relevant officials. Their attitudes, particularly their willingness to try new ways and to learn, are critical. They must be entirely committed; they cannot feel that they can fall back immediately upon old arrangements if things go wrong. This reasoning suggests that the areas of experimentation must be large—district size at a minimum. Districts form cohesive administrative units, as well as territories large enough to be uncontaminated by different practices across their borders, but not so large that help could not be rushed to the scene if the situation got seriously out of hand.

In summary, without substantial increases in funds for unarmed police, rural police needs cannot be met other than by exchanging armed police for them. Without hard information about the success of such an exchange, officials and politicians will be most unlikely to sanction such a scheme. And for very good reason. If police practices are to break out of the mold of the past, experimentation with new methods is essential. The willingness to be shown must begin to activate those concerned with police affairs. Politicians must realize, however, that even experimentation requires expenditure. Progress is not bought without cost.

The second major issue involved in reforming police operations concerns the manner in which control of the police should be exercised. Since there are two distinct police organizations in the field—rural police and state police—there are two aspects to the problem. For the rural police the question is whether they should be more strongly linked to the state police, hence to state-level political institutions, or attached exclusively to village institutions, particularly the panchayat network. The regular police are accountable to representative institutions at state level; for them the question is whether some of this supervisory power should be shared by panchayat institutions.

As far as the rural police are concerned, there is very little pressure to remove them from the supervision of village institutions. None of the recent police commissions considered this suggestion. At present they are subjected to dual control—responsibility for pay, appointment, and direction is shared by panchayats and the state, with the superintendent or collector acting as the state's agent. Village police are considered valuable precisely because they are tied to the local community; this bond, it is generally conceded, should not be severed. At the same time, few observers have much faith in the ability of local panchayats to raise, maintain, and direct the rural police without outside supervision. Accordingly the police commissions always recommended that the superintendent oversee the working of the rural police. This arrangement also guarantees that all police operations in a state are coordinated through a single agency. The system of dual control will undoubtedly continue, with the balance between village discretion and state police supervision struck differently in different parts of the country.

The more important and controversial question concerns the relations between state police and new local government institutions. Should accountability be shared by panchayats and state legislatures? Proposals for the kind of responsibility local bodies should exercise over regular police have never been carefully thought out. Discussion is always in terms of principle, and so it will be here. There are several arguments that are made in favor of sharing responsibility. First, if police were made accountable to local institutions, identification between police and community would be promoted. People would feel that police were in part their servants; they would consider them less as a remote, mechanical, faceless agency. The police would begin to become "our police." Some observers have noted that panchayats, whether old or new, often tend to work so as to keep police out of village affairs.[11] Village institutions tend to paternalism, believing that

[11] For example, see T. S. Epstein, *Economic Development and Social Change in South India* (Indian Branch: Oxford University Press, 1962), pp. 121-122.

responsibility for village concerns is theirs, even when criminal acts are involved. They resent the police and shield the village from police intrusion. If police were tied to panchayats, cooperation between police and communities would be promoted. Second, panchayat responsibility would force the police to become more sensitive to local needs. As matters now stand, local police officers are sensitized upward, not downward. Opinions of civilians are important only to the extent that they affect the way in which a man's work is perceived by his superiors. To local officers the views of a remote superintendent, based largely on written reports and statistical summaries, are infinitely more important than the opinions of local people. The police could be brought down to earth and attuned to local needs if panchayats had some directing authority over them. Third, panchayat institutions can only grow strong and command the allegiance of their communities if they are given real powers. There is no point in setting up panchayats if matters close to the hearts of the people continue to be handled exclusively by state or central agencies. Since police activities are fundamental, panchayats cannot avoid becoming concerned with the police.

There are disadvantages as well to be found in shared responsibility. First, panchayat members are likely to be too parochial in their outlook. They have neither the training nor the experience to direct police activities. Amateur intervention in police affairs will be quixotic and diverting. Local leaders may be in a position to note neglected needs, but they are hardly suited for making recommendations about solutions. Second, responsible police operations require more than parochial accountability, they require attunement to the principles of law. Police should never become completely responsible to men; it must be to laws as well. Accountability of the police both to laws and men is achieved through making them responsible to the men who make the laws. In the Indian case this means to state legislatures or the national parliament. Panchayats adjudicate criminal and civil matters, but they do not make criminal and civil rules. Third, control of police by local panchayats will lead to acute partiality and favoritism in police work. The besetting sin of village life is factionalism and the inability to see issues otherwise than in terms of persons. Public confidence in the impartiality of the police is none too strong as it is. People believe that rich and powerful persons can bend police to their desires. Evenhandedness can be obtained only by insulating local police from local pressures, not by giving local pressure formal access. Fourth, panchayat authority over the police would be irresponsible unless coupled with a corresponding duty of the panchayat to provide effective police services. Panchayats would be in the position of being able to criticize and direct without having to raise and maintain. Panchayats would have control without responsibility, particularly without financial responsibility. Panchayats and the government, or the legislature, would endlessly recriminate about whose fault ineffective or unfair police operations really were. Accountability requires pinpointing responsibility among representative institutions, not fragmenting it.

Official opinion is, so far, against any devolution of responsibility for the police upon panchayats. This conforms to the general predilection to reserve judgment about the viability of panchayats until they have gained more experience. None of the recent police commissions advocated devolution, and some of them indicated very serious reservations about the impartiality of panchayats. Police officers themselves are not in favor of it. Although politicians frequently do advocate giving some authority for the police to panchayat institutions, one cannot be sure they mean what they say. Loud espousal of local institutions is natural for politicians. Now that opposition parties have formed governments in several states, we shall see how sincere their protestations were about devolution of state power upon local bodies.

Unless the climate of opinion changes significantly with respect to the performance and capacities of panchayats, it is doubtful whether the insulation between police and local government will be broached. On the other hand, creation of Panchayati Raj is like riding a tiger—the trouble comes in getting off. If panchayats take root—as they seem to be doing—and succeed in gaining the allegiance of their constituents, the pressure to expand their functions will increase. If police remain unreconstructed at the same time, they will find themselves increasingly on the defensive. The best policy for the police, if they want to avoid being responsible to local institutions, is to become sensitive, impartial, and efficient on their own.

In my own view, it would be a profound mistake to make the police formally subordinate to panchayats at the present time. Such a policy would win spurious accountability at the expense of fairness and efficiency. However, police officers must avoid disdainful condescension toward these institutions. Panchayats are an opportunity for effective community relations work by the police. Very few officers are taking advantage of them. At district levels, for example, a great deal of goodwill could be earned if superintendents volunteered to present candid reports regularly to the zilla parishads about police affairs. Officers complain that the public knows little about their difficulties. Here is an opportunity to do some educating. The effort will be time-consuming and may very well lead to the creation of informal, implicit linkages between panchayats and police. Since initiative would be in the hands of the police, these dangers could be minimized. Successful liaison, the kind that creates mutual trust, demands that police pursue a policy of cooperation concertedly throughout their jurisdictions; establishment of liaison should not depend wholly on the personalities of individual officers. While officers must be allowed latitude in meeting local conditions, the nettle of cooperation must be grasped state by state. Panchayat leaders and other politicians are groping for a new relation with the police. For the moment, at least, initiative will remain with the police. If they are to give direction to panchayats, they must be willing to establish relations that are candid and continuous.

Rather than continue the past uncertain relation between the rural police and village institutions and the state police, I propose that panchayats be given exclusive responsibility for rural police. Rural police could be an admirable focus for development of local responsibility. Panchayats should be entrusted entirely to raise and direct a village police force as they see fit, and only if they see fit. One possible result could be that village police forces would disappear in many areas. Since the decision would be a local one, the demise of the police would hardly be marked by much mourning. Relations between the superintendent and local communities is asymmetrical with respect to control of police agencies. Panchayats cannot touch the state police but they do not have exclusive control over the rural police. Under the proposed scheme, panchayats would have responsibility for and control of their own police. To be sure, their functions would have to be spelled out by state legislatures so as to avoid conflicts with state police authority. Village police would have to remain primarily a guarding and reporting agency. America's mistake with the multiplication of autonomous local police jurisdictions must certainly be avoided. Panchayats may not now have the financial resources to support a village police force by themselves. This touches a larger problem of providing panchayats with their own taxing authority. A movement in this direction is already developing. Under the proposed scheme panchayats would be advisors to the state police about state police operations and the superintendent would be an advisor to panchayats about rural police affairs. The symmetry is tantalizing, and certainly seems to be much more in the spirit of Panchayati Raj than existing arrangements.[12]

[12] The Uttar Pradesh Police Commission's recommendations came very close to this, although they did not do away altogether with supervisory powers by the state police (pp. 41-42).

SIX

CONCLUSION

16 · The Police and the Political System: An Assessment

A POLICEMAN'S lot, as the saying goes, is not a happy one. While he must bear a large part of the responsibility for the reputation he acquires, it must never be forgotten that controversy and emotion are ineluctable parts of the work he does. He must restrain in society's name; he must encourage, and sometimes force, individuals to conform to society's regulations. For most people a policeman's contribution to their well-being is invisible. A policeman becomes real for them in most instances when he makes a demand of some kind. By the nature of his role he is not a mark for praise or gratitude, except occasionally and for a very small minority of a community's inhabitants. A policeman embodies authority, and although people understand the necessity for the role in the abstract, they are not likely to empathize easily with him or be drawn toward him by spontaneous liking. Evaluations of a police force must always be made within the context of its role. This is not to imply that policemen must always be unpopular and in the same degree. Improvement is possible for an unpopular force, just as a decline in popularity is possible for a very good force. Police-community relations are malleable. But a policeman's role limits how felicitous his relationship with the community can become; it imposes a floor, which cannot give way except by altering the nature of the role itself.

The thesis of this study is that a police force can exert substantial influence upon the nature of political life. We have seen how a police force may do so in principle and we have examined the operations of a particular police force in detail. We must now evaluate the impact that this particular police force may be having upon its encapsulating political system. In what ways do police operations in India impinge upon the functioning of the political system? In particular, does the police force operate so as to reinforce or subvert the maintenance of democratic political institutions?

The theoretical analysis suggested four modi operandi by which a police force could influence political life: (1) by the nature of its activity; (2) by the manner of its operation;

(3) by the nature of the organization; and (4) by the socialization of its members. Stated colloquially, a police force may affect the political system by virtue of what it does, how it does it, what it is or represents, and what it does to its personnel. I shall discuss these modalities one by one in evaluating the Indian situation. It must be understood, however, that this schema may not be exhaustive. Furthermore, Indian police may be affecting political life in ways undiscovered in the field research. This is a first attempt at applying a possibly incomplete theoretical plan to a very complex empirical situation.

The nature of the duty laid upon Indian police and the way in which it is operationalized are identical to American and British practice. In terms of what is expected of police, officers in India, Britain, and the United States could be exchanged and feel very much at home. The general activity of the Indian police is fully consonant with democratic life. They play no formal role whatever in politics. They are accountable to elected officials. In practice the chain of responsibility reaches from uniformed officers to permanent non-police civil servants to an elected minister to a legislature and ultimately to the people. Civilian control of the police has been firmly established; Indian officers would feel acutely uncomfortable if they were forced into playing a larger policy role. Like most dedicated civil servants, they are apt to be cynical about politicians and political machinations and to feel that police affairs could be administered more efficiently and more fairly if politicians would stay at home. Politicians are often perceived as nuisances, and few police officers believe that politicians act any more in the larger public interest than the police officers do. These sentiments should not be construed as indicating profound disenchantment with the system. They are, rather, the normal sparks produced by friction in a democratic system between free-wheeling politicians with no formal administrative charge and conscientious officials anxious to get a difficult job done well. Civilian control under elected officials is fully accepted by the police; I see no likelihood that the Indian police will assume political initiative.

The regulatory activities of the police with respect to day-to-day politics are by and large quite correct. Because politics has been conducted in a sometimes disorderly fashion, occasionally involving lawbreaking and serious threats to public order, the police have played a much larger role in political life than they like. They have been injected into politics against their will and not by design. They would be much happier if they were not forced from time to time to make very delicate decisions involving the holding of political parades, surveillance of politicians, use of force against partisan crowds, and separation of political combatants. No doubt the police have become especially sensitive to the activities of leftist politicians. They watch them closely and may occasionally deal with them more severely than with other groups. Again, I cannot fault the police for this because their operations have not been guided by manifest ideological commitment but by an earnest desire to maintain order. The fact is that unruliness and disorder have been repeatedly staged by these elements. They are not the only perpetrators of such actions—communal politicians are much more vicious—but they are certainly the most consistent. In mediating among political parties, or factions of parties, as well as in quelling riots, the police have undoubtedly made errors of judgment. An advantage may have unwittingly been given to one or another politician. It is also true that the deliberate use of police power in order to secure a political advantage has been solicited and sometimes been given. Although there are surely instances in which a personal political commitment by an officer decided policy, for the most part politicians themselves are the instigators. They seek to use the police for their own partisan ends. They do not scruple to employ unfair tactics against opponents, and to enmesh the police in their plots. But these events are relatively exceptional and when they do occur are by and large trivial in their effects. The freedom of Indian political life is so abundantly clear that one must conclude that the police have played a neutral role as mediators in a very delicate and demanding situation. It cannot seriously be contended that political fortunes have been generally affected by police activity.

The primary duty laid upon the police is to maintain order and preserve life and property. Their record in both has been mixed. Crime exacts a heavy cost each year, a cost that is not reflected adequately by official statistics because of serious deficiencies in crime reporting. The burden of crime to economic development is invisible, although it must be appreciable in aggregate terms. People are not generally anxious about their security and do not seem to fix upon insecurity as a major impediment to their greater happiness. This is not to say that conditions could not be substantially improved. In rural India especially, preventive activities are spasmodic and feeble; police effort is directed primarily at investigation and punishment. There is evidence to indicate that a more efficient police presence would be welcomed by many people. The record is also mixed with respect to dramatic incidents of public violence. Although the presence of public violence in Indian life is striking, it almost seems to have become routinized. It is usually quickly walled off and does not threaten the stability of the system itself. Given the pretexts for violence and the tendencies among some sections of the populace, the wonder is that the situation has been so well contained. The police have contributed to the limiting of violence, especially by the intelligence with which they have met it. Their record of restraint in the application of force to violent crowds has been admirable. At the same time, a nagging suspicion persists that not nearly enough attention has been given to administering an ounce of prevention. Police are understaffed particularly among those ranks which can assume responsibility on the spot. The bulk of policemen are either armed policemen living a military, garrison-type life or unarmed police constables who perform largely as ciphers. So great is the threat of violence that emphasis on containment by the government, civil service, and police is understandable. But, one wonders, might a more pervasive police presence in the persons of sensitive, educated, well-trained constables provide more detailed intelligence and prevent some of the disorder? The police are straining to contain a situation they cannot control. This is true for curbing crime generally as well as muting social violence. Like police forces around the world, the best they can do is minimize, to palliate. Countries rarely seem to be willing to bear the cost of really efficient police protection. In this, too, an Indian officer would feel very much at home in Great Britain or the United States.

Police perform very few administrative functions outside the scope of police duties narrowly defined. They do serve summonses, maintain elementary demographic records, and issue various kinds of licenses. Generally, however, police contact with the public occurs only when a matter of criminal law is involved. Policemen are increasingly engaged in investigating the improper activities of civil servants. Concern with administrative malpractices, particularly corruption, has grown appreciably in recent years. An elaborate system of investigating and complaint-receiving agencies has been set up. Very often the personnel of these agencies have been taken on deputation from the police. However, because control of these organizations is not in police hands, but rests with a civilian civil servant and a minister, the police force as such does not have authority to conduct investigations about administrative malpractices. The most notable exception to this rule is the Central Bureau of Investigation, which does have investigative authority over all central government departments and enterprises. Still, police control of administrative behavior through the power of investigation is minuscule and poses no threat to civilian control of government.

The primary function of the police in India is to enforce criminal law. They are not used for wider social regulation or for monitoring the general activity of citizens. As with most police forces, they have tremendous discretion with respect to the laws they choose to enforce. They are apt to deny this, but in practice choices must be made. Although they always act under law, their attention must be given to certain laws above others. They emphasize serious crimes, those which if allowed to go unpunished would produce a great hue and cry from the public. Their attention to criminal activity has been diverted somewhat by enforcement activities connected with prohibition and to a lesser extent laws against improper trading, particularly in food-grains. Police did not make this decision on their own, but were compelled by the promptings of civilian-established policy.

Police are only the initial point of contact between enforcement machinery and the citizenry. Functional specialization has proceeded as far within the criminal justice system in India as it has in America or Great Britain. Police are certainly not responsible for adjudication, although they are for prosecution in many inferior courts. Larger prosecuting staffs are being created, with the result that appearances by police as prosecutors are declining. Penal management as well is not in police hands. With the exception of the commissioners of police in five major Indian cities, police officers cannot make executive decisions under the law. Policemen can arrest for infringement of the law; they cannot exercise formal decision-making authority under it in particular cases. These powers are entrusted to magistrates or to collectors.

What the police do in India—the activities they undertake—adhere almost exactly to patterns familiar to people in the world's other great democracies. Indian police are bound by law, by civilian leadership, by freely competing political forces, and by the nature of their charge under law. They serve the community by preserving life and property through obtaining conformity to legal enactments. They play no formal political role and if they play one indirectly it is by accident, not design, in enforcing legal sanctions against obstreperous political elements.

Police affect a political system not only by what they do but by the manner they adopt. This comes about through the effect that police demeanor has upon public responses. Most immediately, police conduct affects relations specifically between the police and the public, with consequences for the way in which law enforcement is operationalized. At further remove, reactions to the human agents of law may transfer to the law itself, to the concept that laws per se are legitimate, deserving the customary loyalty of all citizens. Finally, reactions to the police may transfer to other agents of government and even to government itself. It is possible that alienation from a discredited police force could undercut regard for government generally. Could people retain respect for a system of government that allowed abuse of power by police, as well as meanness, corruption, and disregard of human feelings? In short, the manner in which police carry out their duties can affect the texture of civic regard.

The locus of initiative between police and public in India rests predominantly with the public. They contact the police for service; the police force does not as a rule seek out individuals in order to serve them. It can be argued that this is true for any police force—the bulk of their contacts for service will be initiated by the public. In the Indian case, however, the passivity of the police is particularly evident. People generally do not expect the police to go out of their way to help them. The survey showed that close to half of all respondents doubted even that the police sincerely tried to help people who came to them for help. Police are not thought of as an agency to which problems, say of a legal or official kind, can be taken. Although sufficient data are lacking on this point, it appears that nonenforcement or non-emergency demands are not often made on the police by the Indian public. The police are not generally known for their assistance in preventing crime or accidents. Police officers know that the public could materially contribute to crime prevention by foreseeing needs more properly and taking sensible precautions. But the police do very little to reach out and help the public in these matters, to give advice, and to demonstrate concern. The public has little opportunity to see the police display an active sympathy for them.

The police establishment is not compulsively secretive. Like all police agencies, since they deal in delicate or intimate aspects of human affairs, the Indian police will not open their files to every-one. But their procedures, operations, and housekeeping records are a matter of public record. Confidential material is readily shared with civilian administrators and politicians on the basis of the recipient's position and a need to know. The private citizen, as well as the foreign scholar, will find police officials cordial and candid. Indeed, police officers are anxious to be understood, consequently they are often pleased to show people what the world looks like from a police point of view. No doubt to most Indians police procedures and methods are a closed book. This, however, is not due to chronic secretiveness on the part of the police but to a lack of middle class assertiveness among Indians in deal-ings with large, authoritative organizations. Indian police affairs are as open as democratic life requires.

Public feelings toward the police are characterized by distrust. As official and unofficial commentators have noted for over a hun-dred years, Indians do not look upon the police as being sym-pathetic, friendly, or especially trustworthy. On the contrary, policemen have a reputation for rudeness, brutality, deviousness, dishonesty, and partiality. No doubt the suspicions are exag-gerated; most people learned them secondhand. Nonetheless, the presence of latent fears and great anxieties about police behavior erodes the chance to establish a cooperative relationship between police and public. Because suspicion is so palpable, it influences the ways in which people interpret what they see the police do; they see what they have been taught to see. On the other hand, a considerable proportion of people have seen individuals be-labored by the police or treated rudely and ill-manneredly. People also have considerable first-hand experience with police corruption and demands for a bribe before willing action has been taken. The fault, even here, does not lie exclusively with the police. For every favor given, one is received or asked for. For every bribe accepted, one is offered or acquiesced in. When police use force against crowds they may be acting as much from an intelligent apprehension of the needs of a situation as from a deep-seated delight in using force. The public is an important part of a police force's environment; police actions are condi-tioned by it. But having said this, the fact remains that the situa-tion urgently needs improving. Police continually complain of the lack of public cooperation, the undercutting of investigations, the inability to obtain truthful witnesses, the frequent resiling from testimony given to officers. Police even admit that because the public is uncooperative they must resort to other expedients in order to obtain convictions, expedients which may be improper or bordering on impropriety and which, when found out, like another turn of the screw, invite misunderstanding by magistracy and public. Police may not be entirely to blame for their predicament, but they are surely the most accessible point at which initiative may be taken in transforming police-public relations. One cannot reasonably expect the public to regenerate its attitudes spontaneously.

It should also be noted that suspicion, especially involving charges of partiality and dishonesty, touch all government servants and most politicians too. The problem is government-wide. The lack of confidence is sufficiently great to affect the success of government programs which require a ready, cooperative public response. Furthermore, it undermines the status of government agents and limits government's ability to harness enthusiastic action to any program. The police are only one among many agencies to feel suspicion's effects strikingly and to know its consequences for their own work and self-regard.

Police officials are anxiously aware of their reputation among the populace. As a result, they have undertaken various programs to improve their image. For example, they sponsor a variety of "days," parades, and reviews. They host sports competitions and enter their own teams in national or state meets. An interesting recent development is the organization of neighborhood councils, mostly in urban areas, made up of respectable people of the area, which meet with the police to discuss common problems. Police sponsor "courtesy weeks" and "safety weeks," aimed largely at schoolchildren. In some states they have organized boys' clubs and engaged in "*shramdan*," or the gift of labor to a community project. A few states and cities have established information offices and special squads to assist travelers and newcomers to urban areas. Police concern with creating better public relations has led to the development of press officers, responsible for releasing information to the press and acting as permanent liaison with them. Most officers are skeptical of the value of these schemes. They insist—rightly, in my view—that real progress can only be made if the rank-and-file policeman behaves more winningly in daily contacts. Public relations is not something tacked on to normal police work, it is part and parcel of routine activity. Special programs produce very little lasting effect. They should not be allowed to divert attention from the harder task of producing a thorough reform in everyday behavior.[1]

There can be no question that the manner in which police have operated has influenced public opinion, and that the influence has been for the worse. Their behavior year in and year out has kept alive deep suspicions about their rectitude and impartiality. The police daily reap the harvest of ill-will occasioned by hasty, brusque, inconsiderate, and improper actions. The quality of law enforcement and of authoritative contacts between government and public has been affected. The extent to which partial alienation has been transferred to other agencies of criminal administration is difficult to determine. It would be unfair, in my view, to blame suspicion about other enforcement agencies on the police. Lawyers, courts, and magistrates have their own peculiar ways of producing dissatisfaction and hostility. Does the sum total of disaffection or lack of ready cooperation hamper the development of deeply rooted democratic institutions? Is it likely to undermine the stability of the existing system? I cannot pretend to know. One does know that if the police, along with other public servants, were to overcome the habits of the past in their dealings with the populace, astonished delight would sweep the country. Government's problems would not all disappear, but its capacity for leadership would surely be enhanced. Negative expectations about the quality of response from government servants to human needs can considerably dampen appreciation of government's real and practical accomplishments. By the same token, charitable regard for the activities of government personnel can ease the disappointments occasioned by failure of government to surmount pressing problems.

Police influence political life by virtue of what they are. They

---

[1] Eldersveld *et al.* (*The Citizen and the Administrator in a Developing Democracy*) found that police officers were "self-consciously aware of public relations responsibilities" (p. 111). Every rank level was conscious of the interest of its superiors in improving public relations (pp. 109-111). In fact, among the organizations they studied, police and community development were the most sensitized to the problem of maintaining good public relations, more so than the health and postal services and the Delhi Transport Authority. Moreover, the authors concluded that doing differently in bureaucratic contacts can be effective in transforming a climate of opinion. It is true that an image once developed will persist, thwarting strenuous efforts to change it. Nonetheless, in time, their analysis indicates that "officials with democratic orientations who are actively involved with the citizens in the field, and not bureaucratically shut off from them, can and are having a tremendous impact on the attitudes and behavior of Indian citizens" (p. 176).

influence by example; they also create external economies, as for example with chemical and seriological laboratories or improved wireless communications; and they generate demand for skills or products of particular kinds. Although the net impact of the Indian police in these ways is difficult to estimate, there is no question that within the context of Indian development they constitute a modern, technologically oriented professional group. Police are organized in terms of functional specialties and a division of labor between line and staff cadres; merit is the criteria for advancement (perhaps not always observed in the lower ranks); courses of training are required for appointment; and leadership is exercised by a permanent officer corps recruited and posted on an all-India basis. Police have an intense interest in the development of communications facilities. They continually urge government to improve the quality of forensic laboratories and to distribute these and related skills into every district in the land. They have an abiding interest in sophisticated hardware of all sorts. Recently they have become concerned with the need to utilize modern data-processing equipment. They continue to generate demand for a variety of skilled people, many of them quite specialized, such as doctors, auto mechanics, electronics technicians, traffic engineers, and research chemists. The needs of police work compel officers to think in terms of national cooperation, regional interdependence, educational excellence, social stability, and complex, ramified governmental organizations.

Finally, police exert a formative influence by socializing people who serve with them. They teach one another to become something different from what they were. This may reinforce traditional ways or it may encourage new styles of life and new ways of thinking. The direction of effect depends on the kind of people taken into the organization and the elan of the organization itself. Unfortunately, almost nothing is known about the effect of recruitment to the police. We do know that different sorts of individuals are recruited for the officer cadre, N.C.O. ranks, and the constabulary. But we have hardly any information about what the organization does to the raw material it ingests. The training of officers has been designed to accomplish particular objectives relevant to fashioning a modern nation-state; they are to be intelligent, possessing a wide range of interests, to be merit-oriented, sensitive to human needs, adept at communication orally and in writing, honest, responsible, loyal to institutions rather than individuals, and dedicated to the development of a united India. Their training and subsequent posting, discipline, and promotion are predicated upon encouraging appropriation of these values. The extent to which these values are new to probationary officers or are brought to the organization and simply reinforced would be an interesting question to study.

The need for data about the effects of recruitment to non-officer ranks is particularly acute. Who are the men who join the police as constables? What families do they come from, what castes, how much effective education do they have, what occupational skills do they bring, what are their aspirations, what political affiliations are they drawn to, how modern are they, what predispositions do they carry into communal situations? One study in Delhi state has demonstrated a tremendous gap between supervisors and line personnel in terms of "democratic job perspectives."[2] Police staff demonstrated the greatest awareness of democratic norms, police constables showed the least. Of the five agencies studied, the gap between supervisors and line personnel was greatest in the police. This may be a tribute to the excellence of the officer corps as much as a criticism of the constables. Socialization to nation-building and development-supporting attitudes may be occurring in the lower ranks. It may not be immediately apparent to the educated, city-bred officers, policymakers, or scholars who are cut off from the constables by styles of life, language, worldly experience, and position. On the other hand, it may not be occurring at all. At lower levels the police organization may have been captured by the men it recruits; the organization exhibits their proclivities rather than successfully engendering new patterns of thought and action. The lack of information is overwhelming. This is a major area of research to which government might give attention in the future.

In summary, the Indian police force cannot be blamed for acting in ways that subvert the maintenance of democratic political forms. Its formal tasks and activities are regulated by law and in carrying them out the organization is accountable to elected officials. It is a modern social force in itself, and particularly at the I.P.S. level acts to develop an able, responsible group of policemen who represent the nation as a whole. The police are supportive of technological innovation, emphasizing those that knit the country more closely together. It is loyal to democratic institutions and has not sought to become an actor, assuming initiatives on its

[2] Eldersveld *et al.*, pp. 81ff.

own, in the conduct of political life. While, therefore, it cannot fairly be charged with subverting democratic processes, its potentialities for reinforcing the development of habits that undergird a democratic system have not been fully utilized. The police have not demonstrated to the people a pervasive, efficient, sympathetic presence, founded on the concept that police themselves must seize opportunities to serve the public in ways appropriate to the police function. They must be faulted, then, not for acting outside the prescriptions of democratic rule but for failing to fulfill the creative potentialities of civil servants in a democratic political system.

What is required of the Indian police if this wider opportunity is to be exploited? In my opinion, it is essential that the police develop greater numbers of more highly trained constables capable of assuming responsible initiative in day-to-day affairs. This development was the essence of Sir Robert Peel's reforms for the London police force in the early nineteenth century. In practical terms for India, implementation of this proposal would entail two changes: first, development of a different philosophy with respect to the functions of a police constable and, second, a shift in emphasis between armed and unarmed police. The police constable must cease to be a spear-carrier in the background of the police drama; he must become a major actor standing in center stage. Development of a more efficient, responsible constable probably would involve lesser expenditures on the armed police. This would happen for two reasons. Savings might thereby be realized that could be applied to the recruitment and training of new constables. Also emphasis in administration, both police and civil, would be encouraged to shift from containment to prevention. The fact that the armed police exist in such overwhelming numbers inhibits the more creative utilization of the unarmed constabulary. It is possible that additional funds could be produced by using fewer constables, if they were of a superior kind. For example, if two-thirds of existing constables could really assume professional police responsibilities, effective police coverage of the country would be considerably augmented. Constables would cease to be tied in bundles to police stations or district headquarters but would have their own mandate to be exercised as individual officers.[3]

[3] It might be noted that doubts about the utility of the existing constabulary are not hard to find among police officers. To illustrate, West Bengal's inspector-general proposed before the West Bengal Police Commission that

There are many reasons why reform along the lines suggested will not be embraced enthusiastically. These reasons explain why the situation is as it is. Resources are scarce, and they will continue to be. Police do not enjoy a high priority in the allocation of government revenues. The deadening effect of straitened financial circumstances, and the priorities implicit in current government policy, should not be underestimated.[4] Change itself is unsettling to many people, not the least to politicians and government servants. The existing system has the immense advantage of being established. It works—not perfectly, but reasonably well. Reform requires changes in laws, organization, regulations, training programs, institutions, command assignments, inter-rank relations. Are the advantages of change really worth the dislocation? Then, the exigencies of contemporary life will dampen enthusiasm for reform. India faces so many problems: a continuing emergency in food-grain production, the threat of military violence along the northern border, the sluggish pace of economic development, a burgeoning population, and divisive tendencies within the Indian union. With problems like these clamoring for solution, harassed officials will not give their attention unbegrudgingly to police reform. The receptiveness of the public for reform may be questioned as well. Are they really prepared to accept a pervasive police presence, even in the form of more responsible, better-trained constables? There is certainly reason to doubt this—many politicians will be exceedingly skeptical—although my own survey indicates a much greater receptivity than many people might imagine. It might be recalled that London's population did not at first welcome the Bobby with open arms, but a revolutionary change of heart was wrought in time. Finally, there are enormous practical problems to be overcome in the proposal. Can the proper recruits be found? Can they be trained adequately and maintain necessary esprit de corps during the transition? What will be the relation between superior recruits and older constables? How will

---

the number of constables be reduced by *two thirds* and the saving in pay applied proportionately to the remainder. Implicit in the suggestion was the notion that fewer constables of a higher order would more than substitute for the current arrangement (p. 132n).

[4] The words of the Police Commission of 1902-1903 should chasten the optimistic reformer: "[The Commission] realize that [their recommendations] involve a large expenditure; but they feel that the police department, which so nearly concerns the life of the people, has hitherto been starved; that the reforms they propose are absolutely essential; and it is worth while to pay for them the price required."

existing N.C.O.'s react to the new constables? What will be the command responsibilities of sub-inspectors and inspectors if autonomous constables are developed? In short, a new police scheme, despite its attractions, gives many hostages to fortune. If people are anxious to preserve the practices of the past, cogent reasons can be found.

The greatest obstacle of all, however, and the one which can be changed at least cost, is a failure of vision. In part the failure rests upon an inability to ask an unfamiliar question: namely, can a police agency play a formative role in political development? The role of the police in supporting a democratic regime must be seen not just as faithfully acting within certain boundaries. It must be seen in terms of helping to develop habits of thought and action in citizens required by resilient, freedom-conserving institutions. Once this potentiality is grasped, a new police philosophy—and practical programs as well—follow inevitably.[5]

Contemporary police philosophy in India is an ironic combination of British liberal tradition and British colonial practice. It involves subordination to the rule of law and popular accountability, on the one hand, and passive relations between police and public except in times of emergency, both personal and public, on the other. One can understand that the British might not have felt much urgency about reforming the Indian police during the last hundred years of their rule, especially during the twentieth century when they were preoccupied with containment of political self-assertion. But the philosophy of containment and passivity, quite proper as far as it goes, has endured after independence. Despite the fact that the unhappy relations between police and public have been documented again and again, reform has been approached through patchwork expedients. Pay has been raised, new offices established, fringe benefits improved, supervision reorganized, and new regulations unveiled. The effect has been predictable. In the words of one recent police commission, the situation "appears to have remained more or less the same since independence."[6] Is this good enough?

Leaders inside and outside the police must become accustomed

[5] I might add that narrow perceptions of how congruence is established between police and a democratic system is not a uniquely Indian complaint. The United States is in the throes of reconsidering the role of its police in socializing minority and disadvantaged persons.

[6] West Bengal Police Commission, p. 251.

to examining the opportunities for democratic tutelage that are contained in the police role. Standing proudly upon the heritage of accountability under law and neutrality in politics, they must begin to fashion a concept of police activity that will exploit present opportunities. And they must have the courage to undertake the experimentation necessary to provide information upon which future policy may be founded. In this way, the Indian police force of today will outgrow its role as passive instrument of government and, without ceasing to be responsible, will begin to play a creative role as well, a creative role that perhaps no other agency of government is so critically placed to assume in a developing democracy.

APPENDICES

APPENDICES

Appendix A

SURVEY METHODOLOGY AND ANALYSIS

Survey Methodology

The work of the survey was carried out by the Indian Institute of Public Opinion, New Delhi. According to specifications furnished by me and under my supervision, the Institute conducted the pretesting of the questionnaire, drew the samples, administered the questionnaire, coded the results, and prepared punch-card decks of data.

The Samples—Twenty-four hundred interviews were allocated to the public survey and twelve hundred to university students. The reasons for singling out university students for special treatment are explained in Chapter 12.

The nature of the public samples was dictated by the hypotheses the survey was designed to test. There were three of these: (1) that great differences exist between rural and urban people with respect to their experiences with the police and their evaluations of them; (2) that urbanization—measured in terms of length of residence in a major urban center—constitutes a formative influence on public perceptions of police activity; and (3) that important differences exist among regions of India, particularly between the north and south. I had previously done a pilot survey of the police and the public in Uttar Pradesh in 1964—two rural districts and Kanpur city—and hoped that these data could be used for a rural-urban comparison in the north. Accordingly, for the new rural-urban contrast I chose locations in south India, fixing finally upon the state of Mysore—Bangalore city and rural Tumkur district. As it turned out, the pilot survey was not sufficiently comparable with the new survey to warrant reporting it here and using it with the south Indian data. Kanpur city was selected for testing the effects of urbanization largely because it is a large, modern city with a large immigrant population that has developed in an *Indian* fashion. Unlike Bombay, Calcutta, or Delhi, it has not been touched deeply by cosmopolitan influences or imperial purposes. Like Nagpur, Ahmedabad, and Bangalore, it seemed prototypical of the kind of city many Indian communities are likely to grow into in the next few decades. By selecting

Kanpur from the north, the needed contrast with south India—at least for urban populations—was provided.

Urban and rural samples were drawn from the electoral rolls, which are lists of eligible voters. The Bangalore and Kanpur rolls had been revised within two years of the survey. Electoral rolls comprise the most extensive list of people available to the surveyor in India. One cannot use a phone directory or a list of water or electricity subscribers, as one might in the West. The alternative would be to use some variation of a geographic sampling technique, choosing interviewing points on the basis of a formula. Study of the merits of using electoral rolls indicated that they were much better than other available expedients. Professor S. Eldersveld, who directed the Delhi state survey in 1964, has commented about using electoral rolls:

"These lists were not completely accurate, as we subsequently discovered, but there was no feasible alternative open to us without the expenditure of tremendous time and money. Block-listing and house-listing, particularly in the high-density sections of the city would be impossible, if not misleading, because of the large numbers with no house address. Our experience suggests that, while not perfect, the electoral rolls are a fairly reliable list of the universe of adults."[1] Considering the representativeness that has been achieved when compared with the 1961 census results, the choice appears to have been correct.

Only males were interviewed, because women were not expected to be able to respond freely in a survey situation.

The electoral rolls were divided into groups of 1,000 names, using random numbers. The number of groups of names differed among *mohollas*, which are subdivisions of a city. In this way the number of respondents chosen from each area would be proportional to its population. From each batch of 1,000 names a certain proportion was selected, again according to random numbers, until the sample quota had been filled.

In Bangalore the sample was of 600 people; in Kanpur it was 800 second-generation urban residents and 400 migrants. We were able to draw 1,150 names using the electoral rolls, comprising the full quota of residents and 350 migrants. That is, the random-number technique produced migrants to urban residents in this proportion. The remaining 50 migrants were selected from areas of heavy migrant concentration using a formula for point-

[1] Eldersveld *et al., The Citizen and the Administrator in a Developing Democracy,* p. 146.

to-point sampling. Because of the problem of locating people on the electoral rolls and the possibility of refusals, an alternative list was drawn up at the same time, from which names could be substituted by the field survey teams.

Because a particular point was made of testing the effects of length of urban residence in the Kanpur sample, use of electoral rolls might have produced distortion. If the rolls had not been updated recently then very few migrants to the city would be sampled. In fact the Kanpur rolls had been revised in December, 1964, approximately eleven months before the survey. We felt that this was recent enough, especially when 50 migrant interviews (out of 400) were chosen by a geographical sampling technique which would not have this defect.

The rural sample was constructed somewhat differently. The basic unit for sampling was villages. The following criteria were employed to determine which villages to select from the district: (a) population of between 200 and 2,000; (b) not an important government center, such as a Block headquarters or a police station; (c) not located on a major road; and (d) dominant occupation agriculture. In this way I hoped to maximize the contrast between rural and urban regions and to sample people from "typical" rural villages. From district census data a list of appropriate villages was chosen. Using random numbers, twenty villages were selected, plus an additional fifteen to be used if cooperation of leaders in selected villages was not forthcoming. Using the electoral rolls from each village, names were drawn in proportion to population. The number of interviews in each village averaged about twenty.

Four universities were selected for study, with 300 interviews to be conducted in each. The universities were chosen on the basis of type and location. Universities were to be from both north and south, to represent universities administered by states as well as the central government, to be unitary as well as affiliating, and residential at least in part. Accordingly, the universities selected were Delhi University (north, central, affiliating), Allahabad University (north, state, unitary), Osmania University (south, state, affiliating), and Bangalore University (south, state, affiliating).

Within each university the sample was drawn from lists of matriculated students furnished by the registrars. The total enrollment of the university would be divided into groups of approximately equal size and a specified number of these groups selected by using random numbers. Then, from these groups a specified number of names would be drawn—usually ten—until the sample of 300 was constructed for each university.

The Questionnaire—A draft of the questionnaire was prepared by me and submitted to the Indian Institute of Public Opinion. The draft for the 1965-1966 survey was based on experience gathered in the pilot study of 1964. Pre-tests were conducted among approximately 200 persons. The questionnaire was designed to take about an hour to administer.

Copies of the two questionnaires will be found in Appendices B and C.

Interviewing—Interviewing was conducted in local languages by personnel familiar with the region. Most of the interviewers were part of the permanent panel of interviewers maintained by the Indian Institute of Public Opinion in various areas. Two bases of operation were established, one in Bangalore and one in Delhi. Direction and supervision were exercised from these locations.

Before interviewing was conducted in a village, the cooperation of the village leaders was solicited. Interviewing was only conducted after the purpose of the venture had been explained and approval had been obtained. The same was true of surveying in the universities. In all cases the office of the vice-chancellor and/or college principal was contacted and cooperation elicited. It might be mentioned that reception was almost invariably cordial, both in the villages and the universities. Very rarely were impediments placed in the way of interviewing teams.

The interviewing was carried out from November, 1965, to May, 1966.

Data Preparation—Most of the questionnaire items were pre-coded. The few open-ended responses could only be coded after returns had come in. A tentative list of codes for these items was set up by the I.I.P.O. and approved by me.

Statistical Analysis

Data Preparation—In order to utilize the data once they had been sent to the United States, it was necessary to recode and repunch. There were two reasons for this. First, our machines had difficulty in reading the Indian cards. Reading tolerances proved to be so small that very minor misalignment in punching caused the card to be rejected. The first step, therefore, was to duplicate the Indian cards, hand-punching those that the machine would not accept. Second, codes for the original data decks had been designed to convey the maximum amount of information from questionnaires to cards. If statistical analysis was to be done, other than sheer calculation of percentages, it was necessary to arrange responses into ordinal scales. For example, decisions had to be made about caste and occupation hierarchies. Which castes ranked above which others? And which occupations had the highest status? A rescoring program was written, from which we compiled a new, readable deck of punch-cards. The data on this deck were amenable to correlation and factor analysis.

Correlation Analysis—A Pearson product-moment was computed to determine the correlations among variables.

Most of the questionnaire variables produced nonparametric data. About two-thirds of all variables were dichotomous. When there were multiple answers, the data were at most interval scale and usually ordinal. Nonetheless, despite the advice of some respected textbooks in the field of statistical analysis, I have used parametric rather than nonparametric statistical tests. Experts in the field of statistics have discussed the uses and limitations of these two kinds of statistical tests for many years. Very recently a shift in authoritative opinion has been visible. Many statisticians now advocate the use of parametric tests even on data that violate parametric assumptions. I have followed the newer learning, as it might be called, in my own analysis. Suffice it to say, as a layman, that I have been convinced that with data of the sort produced by the survey, parametric tests are more rugged, more useful, and will not produce results that can seriously be faulted. As I shall discuss in a moment, when I did use parametric and nonparametric tests on the data, in this case to determine differences in responses between samples, I got identical results.

If the reader wishes to read several short discussions of the parametric vs. nonparametric statistics controversy, I suggest the following: George A. Ferguson, *Statistical Analysis in Psychology and Education*, 2nd ed. (New York: McGraw-Hill Book Co., 1965), Chapter 22; Fred N. Kerlinger, *Foundations of Behavioral Research* (New York: Holt, Rinehart and Winston, 1965), Chapter 14; Norman H. Anderson, "Scales and Statistics: Parametric and Nonparametric," *Psychological Bulletin*, July, 1961, pp. 305-316; C. Boneau, "A Note on Measurement Scales and Statistical Tests," *American Psychologist*, XVI, 1961, pp. 260ff.; and John L.

Horn, *Concepts and Methods for Correlational Analysis* (forthcoming from Holt, Rinehart, and Winston).

Factor Analysis—Factor analysis was performed on selected variables from each sample. The variables that were selected were ones that seemed to define a particular dimension of analysis, such as: contact with the police, feelings of insecurity, perceptions of police honesty, evaluations of police partiality and political control, respondent's sense of duty, respondent's personal recognition of policemen and his knowledge of the police. The factor analysis involved just under half of the total number of variables. The selected items were designated "core variables." Manipulation of the data showed that factor loadings of less than 0.40 were not stable.

The procedures used in the factor analysis have been prepared for computer uses at the University of Denver by Professor John L. Horn, Department of Psychology. Three steps were involved in the analysis. First, a correlation matrix was generated using data for the "core variables." Second, the matrix was manipulated for the principal axis factors by successive solutions without residuals. An algorithm of the principal axis factor analysis can be found in P. Horst, *Factor Analysis of Data Matrices* (New York: Holt, Rinehart and Winston, 1965), Chapter 7, section 4.2. Third, the solution from step two was used as the basis for an orthogonal rotation according to varimax criteria developed by Henry F. Kaiser, "The Varimax Method of Factor Analysis" (Berkeley, California: unpublished Ph.D. dissertation, 1956).

Factor analysis determined relations among the core variables; it left unanswered questions about relations among the total number of variables, except on a pair-by-pair basis. Since background variables were not included in the core variables, it was particularly important to determine how they related to the factors generated. This was done by means of an extension analysis which allowed us to find the factor loadings for all variables without having to determine a factor solution from a matrix composed of all the items, which would have meant a matrix about 130 by 130. The extension procedure was more economical in machine time and made for greater facility in interpreting results. The following steps were involved: (1) creation of a factor matrix for the core variables and calling it F (in fact this was already available as the product of the varimax procedure); (2) formation of F transpose F; (3) formation of inverse of F transpose F;

(4) multiplication of F times F transpose inverse; (5) creation of a correlation matrix using all the variables and calling it R; (6) reading X columns of R corresponding to the core variables; and (7) multiplication of X columns of R into F times F transpose inverse. These steps produced a factor matrix showing not only the original factor matrix for the core variables but the loadings of all other variables on those factors. Therefore, if a factor from core variables had been generated defining security-insecurity, one could immediately determine whether this factor was related to any other questionnaire item, for example, caste, income, education.

Tests for Significant Differences Between Samples—There were eight samples in the survey, four for the general public and four for university students. An important aspect of the analysis was to determine whether responses among samples were significantly different. For example, were people in Bangalore more anxious about their safety than people in Kanpur? Were students in Allahabad University more critical of the police than students in Osmania? Tests for significant differences among uncorrelated samples are a t-test for parametric variables and a chi-square test of proportions for dichotomous variables.

The t-test formula I have used is:

$$\tau = \cfrac{\bar{X}_1 - \bar{X}_2}{\sqrt{\dfrac{\Sigma(X_1-\bar{X}_1)^2 + \Sigma(X_2-\bar{X}_2)^2}{N_1+N_2-2}\left(\dfrac{1}{N_1}+\dfrac{1}{N_2}\right)}}$$

This is a conservative test for sample differences. That is, it may be used even with small N's with reasonable guarantee that significant results will be meaningful. It is a two-tailed test for uncorrelated samples with unequal N's. The results obtained may be read in conjunction with standard t-test tables. (See, for example, The Chemical Rubber Company, *C.R.C. Standard Mathematical Tables*, 12th ed., Cleveland, Ohio: C.R.C. Publishing Co., 1959.)

According to the assumptions of a t-test it should be used only on data that have a normal distribution. Since many of the survey variables were dichotomous, thus not having a normal distribution, most textbooks recommend using another test for sample differences. A standard test is to compute chi-square for the variables to be compared in each sample and interpret the results from a chi-square table as if there were one degree of freedom.

This was the procedure adopted in my analysis. The formula for chi-square is:

$$x^2 = \frac{N(AD-BC)^2}{(A+B)(C+D)(A+C)(B+D)}$$

Where A and B are the number of instances of each response in sample 1 and C and D are the number of instances of each response in sample 2, and where N equals A plus B plus C plus D.

Curiosity about the power of the two tests on nonparametric data led me to test for sample difference on all dichotomous items using both the t-test and the chi-square. The results were identical, thus supporting the new learning about parametric tests and nonparametric data. In short, a t-test could be used—at least for data of this kind—to determine differences between samples of unequal size even for dichotomous variables.

Appendix B

QUESTIONNAIRE ADMINISTERED TO THE PUBLIC

THE questionnaire used in the survey of public opinion and experience with respect to the police will be found below. The questionnaire items are presented in the order in which they appeared during the interview. The variable numbers, given at the left-hand side of the page, were added later during the analysis. In the text of the book, items are referred to by these variable numbers. The reader will notice that although the questions pertaining to background were asked at the end of each interview, they were listed first during the analysis. Thus the first question in the following questionnaire has been given the variable number of 21.

PREAMBLE

We are engaged in the Indian Institute of Public Opinion on several research studies ascertaining the view of the public in regard to matters which concern them intimately. We are doing at this time a study in particular of the ways in which the police can be of greater assistance to you and the community as a whole. For this purpose, we would like to know how you feel generally about them at present and where you think they can serve the community better. The results will be published in due course and we believe they will assist the government in framing policy for your better protection. Your cooperation, for this purpose, will be much appreciated.

Variable Number   *Item*

A. SECURITY-INSECURITY

FOR ALL:

21   Would you say that this is a safe or unsafe area to live in?

        Safe   Unsafe   Don't know

FOR CODE "2" RESPONSES:

21A   What makes you say this is not a safe area to live in?

        Reasons: ....

        Unable to specify (If vol.)   N.A.

22   In general, do you think it is safe to keep valuables, such as money and jewelry, in one's house?
Yes, safe   No, not safe

23   Is it safe to travel about this village/this neighborhood at night?
Yes   No

24   Is it safe to travel *outside the village/around this city* at night?
Yes   No

25   Do you *often* travel outside the village/around the city, i.e., outside this neighborhood at night?
Yes, often   Yes, sometimes   No

26   Do you own a firearm?
Yes   No

27   Do you think it would be a good idea to have a firearm for protection?
Yes   No   No opinion (Only if vol.)

FOR RURAL RESPONDENTS:
28   Have dacoits ever troubled this village?
Yes   No   N.A.

FOR CODE "1" RESPONSES:
29   How long ago?
Years: ....   Months: ....
Don't remember (If vol.)   N.A.

30   Have you ever been the victim of an offense or crime?
Yes   No

FOR CODE "1" RESPONSES:
30A   You were the victim of what kind of an offense or crime?
Kind ....
Unable to specify (Only if vol.)   N.A.

FOR CODE "1" RESPONSES:
31   Did you report the matter to the police?
Yes   No   N.A.

FOR "YES" RESPONSES TO ITEM 31:
32   Did the police catch the criminal?
Yes   No   N.A.

33   Do you know personally anyone (friend, relative, or neighbor) who has been the victim of an offense or crime?
Yes, know   No, don't know

For Code "1" Responses:

What kind of offense or crime?
Kind of crime: ....

Unable to specify kind (If vol.)   Not applicable

34   Was the matter referred to the police?

Yes   No   Don't know   N.A.

For "Yes" Responses to Item 34:

35   Did the police catch the criminal/offender?

Yes   No   N.A.

For Urban Respondents Only:

36   Do you think the police do a good job of regulating the traffic so as to reduce the danger to cyclists, motorists, and pedestrians?

Yes   No   N.A.

For Urban Respondents:

37   Are you concerned about women in your family moving about the street without an escort?

Yes   No   N.A.

38   Would you like to see the police display greater initiative in tackling everyday unpleasant situations?

Yes   No

If "Yes":

38A   In which of the following would you like them to display more initiative?

Maintaining queues

Coming to the aid of people harassed by drivers of hired vehicles such as scooters, taxis, and tongas, etc.

Assisting children, the old and infirm to negotiate traffic hazards like crossing a busy street

Coming to the assistance of unescorted ladies who appear to be subject to indecent overtures

Maintaining a check on Eve-teasers

Assisting people to find their way

Any other (specify) ....
N.A.

B.   PERCEPTIONS AND EVALUATIONS OF POLICE ACTIVITIES

39   Do you think the police do a good job in catching criminals?

Yes   No   Don't know

Would you tell me in which of the following situations you would contact the police for help and in which of them you would not because you wouldn't expect them to be helpful?

		Yes	No	Undecided (Only if vol.)
	Would you go if:			
40	A child is lost	1	2	3
41	A person has been injured by an animal or in a fall	1	2	3
42	A friend is in danger of being attacked by goondas or badmashes	1	2	3
43	A fight between two groups in the area is likely to break out	1	2	3
44	A house has been robbed of Rs. 100	1	2	3
45	A house has been robbed of valuables identifiable in the future	1	2	3
46	A man has been found beaten up	1	2	3
47	Cattle have been stolen	1	2	3
48	A bicycle has been stolen	1	2	3
49	A person has been killed accidentally	1	2	3
50	A person has been found who looks as if he had been murdered	1	2	3
51	A landlord is threatening eviction without good reason	1	2	3

52   If you were lost in a strange town or in a strange part of the country, would you go to a policeman to ask for directions and guidance?
Yes   No

53   Do you think that people, even when they need help, are *generally* reluctant to go to the police?
Yes   No   Can't say

54   Do you think the police *sincerely* try to help people who come to them for help?
Yes   No   Don't know

55   Do you know of any instance when offenses or crimes were committed but the people did not report them to the police because they were afraid of getting involved with the police?
Yes   No

For Code "1" Responses:

55A   What kind of crime or crimes they did not report?
      Kinds of crime: ....
      Unable to specify (If vol.)
      Not applicable

56   Have you ever gone to the police for help?
      Yes   No

For Code "1" Responses:

56A   For what reason did you go to the police?
      Reason: ....
      Can't recall reason (Only if vol.)
      Refusal to tell reason (Only if vol.)
      Not applicable

If "Yes" to Item 56:

57   How were you treated by the police?
      Courteously and sympathetically
      Rudely and unsympathetically
      Don't know/Can't remember
      Not applicable

58   Did the police register your case?
      Yes   No   Not applicable

For Code "2" Responses to Item 58:

58A   Why not? ....

If "Yes" to Item 58:

59   Were you satisfied with what the police finally did for you
      or do you think they should have done more?
      Was satisfied   Should have done more
      No opinion (If vol.)   Not applicable

For Rural Respondents:

60   Do you wish that there was a permanent police officer
      stationed in this village rather than the chowkidar?
      Yes   No

      There is already a policeman (If vol.)   N.A.

61   When the police come around asking questions about an
      offense or crime do they *generally* act courteously and fairly
      or are they *generally* rude and tricky?
      Courteously and fairly   Rude and tricky
      Can't say (Only if vol.)

62   Have you ever been questioned by the police?
      Yes   No

FOR CODE "1" RESPONSES:

> Were you treated courteously or rudely?
> Courteously   Rudely
> Not rudely but without courtesy (Only if vol.)
> Not applicable

64 Do you *know personally anyone* (friend, relative, or neighbor) who has been questioned by the police?
Yes   No

FOR CODE "1" RESPONSES:

65 Was the treatment courteous or rude?
Courteous   Rude   Not rude but without courtesy   N.A.

66 Do you think that serving as a witness in court exposes a person to pressures from both the parties in the case?
Yes   No

67 Have you ever been asked to serve as a witness in a police case?
Yes   No

FOR CODE "1" RESPONSES:

68 Did you serve as a witness?
Yes   No   Not applicable

69 How many times did you have to go to court?
Number of times: (Actual) 1, 2, 3, 4, 5, 6, 7 or more
Can't recall (If vol.)   N.A.

70 Did serving as a witness *expose you to pressures* from friends connected with the people involved in the case?
Yes   No   N.A.

71 Do you personally know anyone (friend, relative, or neighbor) who has *ever* served as a witness in a police case?
Yes   No

72 If you knew that the police were coming around here asking questions and looking for information, would you try to avoid being questioned and having contact with them?
Yes, would avoid   No, wouldn't avoid
It depends (If vol.)
Elaborate: ....
Unable to elaborate   Can't say (Only if vol.)

73 When the police present cases in the courts, do they twist and/or make up evidence in order to convict people?
Twist evidence   Make up evidence
Twist and make up evidence

Do not twist/make up evidence
No opinion (Only if vol.)

74   When the police take people to the police station for questioning, even those who aren't criminals, do they (police) often threaten them or beat them?
Threaten or beat only criminals
Threaten or beat even those not criminals
Threaten or beat no one
Can't say though people say so (Only if vol.)
Can't say (Only if vol.)

75   In order to get the police to do their duty and to help people, does it take money in the form of a bribe?
Yes   No   Can't say

76   Do you know of any instance when the police didn't take any action until they had received some money?
Yes   No

IF "YES":

77   Were the people in this instance known personally to you?
Yes   No   N.A.

78   If you needed help from the police for some reason, and you had to go to the police station, would you take money with you so that you could be sure of getting the help you needed?
Yes   No   No opinion (If vol.)
Depends (If vol.)
(Probe to obtain amplification for "depends")

....
....

79   Do the police *often* beat people up?
Yes, often   Yes, sometimes   No
Can't say/Don't know

80   Have you ever seen any policeman/policemen strike a person?
Yes   No

FOR CODE "1" RESPONSES:

80A   What was the situation/occasion?
Situation/Occasion ....
Unable to specify situation (Only if vol.)
N.A.

81   Do you know personally anyone (friend, relative, neighbor) who was threatened by a policeman?
Yes   No

82   Do you know personally anyone (friend, relative, neigh-
          bor) who was struck by a policeman?
          Yes   No

83   Do the police show favoritism?
          Yes   Yes, sometimes/Some policemen
          No   Can't say

          FOR CODE "1" AND "2" RESPONSES:

83A   What kinds of reasons make the police show favoritism and
          treat people differently? (Provision for Multiple Responses)
          (Interviewer: Please encircle for "Yes" responses only)

                                                                      Yes
            (i) Would wealth be a reason?   1
           (ii) Would land ownership be a reason?   2
          (iii) Would caste be a reason?   3
           (iv) Would religion be a reason?   4
            (v) Would political position be a reason?   5
           (vi) Would influence be a reason?   6
          (vii) Would occupation be a reason?   7

          What else would be the reason for the police to show
          favoritism and treat people differently?
          Reasons: ....
          Nothing   Unable to specify (If vol.)
          Not applicable

84   Are their any groups which you think the police treat worse
          than others?
          Yes   No   Don't know

          IF "YES" TO ITEM 84:

84A   Which particular groups have you in mind?
          Particular groups: ....
          Unable to specify   Not applicable

          FOR URBAN DWELLERS:

85   Are the police in general hostile to labor unions?
          Yes   No   Can't say   N.A.

          FOR ALL:

86   Is there corruption in the police? A great deal, some, a little?
          Yes, a great deal   Yes, some   Yes, little
          No   Don't know (If vol.)

87   Have you ever seen a policeman take money?
          Yes   No

87A   If you wanted to complain about something the police have done *whom* would you complain to?
Would complain to:
(Specify designation) ....
Unable to specify

88   Has it ever happened that you *wanted to complain about* something *the police* had done, but you *decided not to do it* because you didn't think it would do any good?
Yes   No

For Code "1" Responses:

88A   What was it that you wanted to complain about?
Nature of complaint: ....
Can't recall (If vol.)   Not applicable

89   Have you ever complained to *anyone in official position* about the behavior of the police?
Yes   No

For "Yes" Responses to Item 89:

Who did you complain to?
Person by status: ....
Can't recollect (Only if vol.)   Not applicable

90   Do you think that the police join hands with criminals? Often, sometimes, rarely, or never?
Often   Sometimes   Rarely
Never   Can't say (Only if vol.)

91   If the police know that someone is guilty of a crime but they don't have evidence to convict him, do you think the police would then be justified in beating him to obtain a confession?
Police would be justified   Police wouldn't be justified
Can't say/No opinion (Only if vol.)

92   Do you think that nowadays the behavior of the police in the way they treat people generally is getting better or worse?
Better   Worse
No change (If vol.)   Can't say/Don't know

93   Do you think that there is a great deal of political control of the police? That is, can politicians get the police to do what they want?
Yes   No   Can't say (If vol.)

94   Have you heard stories of cases where *politicians* of this area got the police to go after someone or stopped them from investigating someone?

Yes   No

95   Do the police take sides at election times?

Yes   No   Don't know (If vol.)

96   Do the police take sides between the factions in this village?

Yes   No

There are no factions in this village (Only if vol.)

Don't know   Not applicable

Compared to other government officials, are the police more or less (i) corrupt, (ii) courteous, (iii) sympathetic?

		More	Less	Same	No opinion
				(If vol.)	(If vol.)
97	Corrupt	1	2	3	9
98	Courteous	1	2	3	9
99	Sympathetic	1	2	3	9

100   Compared to people joining the army service, are those who join the police a higher type, lower, or about the same?

Higher   Lower

Same   Can't say (If vol.)

101   If you had been robbed and the *police caught* the person *who did it* but couldn't get him to confess, do you think the police should use physical force to make him confess?

Yes   No

Other opinion (specify) ....

No opinion (Only if vol.)

For All (Interviewer must not make any suggestion):

101A   What would be the *one most important thing* the police could do to improve their relations with the public?

One most important thing: ....

No idea (If vol.)   Refusal

102   Do you think that the common man has a duty to help the police by going to them with information about a crime *if he has it?*

Yes   No

103 How would you characterize the attitude of the people living in this area (village) toward the police? ....
....

Are they (possible suggestions)

Friendly   Cooperative   Indifferent
Suspicious   Uncooperative   Hostile
No opinion (If vol.)

C. PUBLIC DEMONSTRATIONS AND POLICE CROWD-CONTROL BEHAVIOR

104 Do you think that public demonstrations are or are not a useful way of getting the authorities to do the right things or to correct some wrongs?
Are a useful way   Are not a useful way
Can't say (Only if vol.)

105 Have you ever participated in a demonstration?
Yes   No

FOR "YES" RESPONSES:

106 How long ago did you do this?
Period: 1, 2, 3, 4, 5, 6, 7, 8 or more years
Can't recall   N.A.

FOR URBAN DWELLERS:

107 Have you ever participated in a strike?
Yes   No   N.A.

IF "YES" TO ITEM 107:

108 How long ago did you participate in one?
Period: 1, 2, 3, 4, 5, 6, 7, 8 or more years
Can't recall   N.A.

109 When demonstrators break the law, should the authorities arrest them right away or should they be considerate and tolerate them?
Arrest right away   Considerate and tolerate them
Don't know/No opinion (If vol.)

110 How would you describe the way police usually handle public demonstrations? Do they handle them:
Very haphazardly   Firmly but properly
Too firmly and harshly   With too much force
Depends upon the nature of the demonstration
(Specify) ....
No opinion (If vol.)

111   Have you ever seen the police use lathis or canes against a crowd?
        Yes   No

112   Have you ever seen a police firing?
        Yes   No

        FOR CODE "1" RESPONSES:
113   Approximately how long ago was it?
        Period: Year .... Month ....
        Unable to specify   N.A.

114   Do the police resort to firings *too often*?
        Yes   No

115   Has there ever been a police firing in this village or this town?
        Yes   No

116   Do you think that these days demonstrations are used too often?
        Yes   No   Can't say (If vol.)

D.   A CITIZEN'S DUTY IN MATTERS OF LAW AND ORDER

        FOR RURAL RESPONDENTS:
117   If there were dacoits camped near here, and you knew about it, would you go and inform the police?
        Yes, would   No, wouldn't
        Can't say (If vol.)   N.A.

        FOR URBAN RESPONDENTS:
118   If you come to know that a gang of goondas near here was going to commit a crime, would you inform the police?
        Yes, would   No, wouldn't
        Can't say (If vol.)   Not applicable

        FOR ALL:
119   If a crime had been committed near here and you thought you knew something that the police would want to know, would you go to them and tell them or would you wait for them to come around and ask you?
        Would go and tell   Would wait for them to come

120   Do you think that the police are underpaid?
        Yes   No   Don't know (If vol.)

120A   Have you ever had any contacts with the police? If so, what kind of contacts have you had?

Kind of contact: ....

Had contacts but unable to specify kind (If vol.)

Had no contacts (If vol.)

Possible Suggestions—Went to them for help, asked for information from them; reported a crime; was a victim of a crime that they investigated; was questioned by them in connection with a crime; had a cycling violation (or motoring violation); they inspected a license I had; know a policeman well; have been in informal groups where a policeman came and talked for a few minutes.

E. KNOWLEDGE ABOUT THE POLICE

121   Would you recognize on sight some of the policemen who are in this area?

Yes, most of them   Yes, a few

Yes, one or two   None   No opinion

122   Do you know any policeman by name?

Yes   No

123   Do you think that being in the police would be a good job or a bad job?

Good   Bad   Depends (If vol.)

Elucidate: ....

Unable to elaborate   Can't say/No opinion

Ask All Except "No Opinion" Cases:

123A   Why do you say so? ....
N.A.

124   What is the salary of a police constable?

Actual: ....

Correct response   Incorrect   Don't know

125   What is the title of the top police officer of this district?

Title: ....

Specified correctly   Specified incorrectly

Unable to specify

126   Where is the office of the top police officer of this district located? In which town and where in the town?

In which town: Name of town: ....

Correct response   Incorrect response

Don't know   N.A.

126A   Name of location in the town: ....

Correct   Incorrect   Don't know   N.A.

F. BACKGROUND INFORMATION

3   Sex:
        Male   Female

4   Age:
        Under 20   21 to 30   31 to 40
        41 to 50   Over 50

5   Education:
        Illiterate   Literate (Primary pass)
        Under-matric   Matric   Intermediate
        Graduate   Post graduate

6   Occupation: Actual: ....

        Artisan   Non-owner cultivator
        Retail trader   Domestic servant
        Owner-cultivator   Landlord
        Clerk and teacher   Unskilled worker
        Student   Housewife
        Unemployed   Agri. laborer
        Skilled worker   Retired
        Profession   Govt. servant

7   Caste of respondent: ....

8   Whether respondent is earner: Yes   No

9   Monthly income:
        Under Rs. 75 75 to 150   151 to 300
        301 to 500   501 to 750   751 to 1,000
        Over 1,000   Refused to specify N.A.

FOR OWNER-CULTIVATORS AND LAND-OWNERS:

10   Amount of land owned:
        Actual: .... in acres
        N.A.

11   Has respondent always lived in this village or area?
        Yes   No

FOR CODE 1 RESPONSES IN ITEM 11:

12   Which ancestors moved here:
        Parents
        Grandparents
        Beyond grandparents   N.A.

13   From where did parents or grandparents move in here:
        From a village   From a similar city
        From a town   From a bigger city
        From a smaller city   N.A.

For Code "2" Responses in Item 11:

14   How long ago did respondent move to this area?
       Less than 2 years ago   10 to 20 years ago
       2 to 5 years ago   Over 20 years ago
       5 to 10 years ago   N.A.

15   Did respondent move from:
       A village   A similar city
       A town   A bigger city
       A smaller city   N.A.

16   How long had respondent lived in the previous place?
       Less than 2 years   10 to 20 years
       2 to 5 years   Over 20 years
       5 to 10 years   N.A.

17   Has respondent been a member of the police?
       Yes   No

18   Has any member of respondent's family been a member of the police?
       Yes   No

For Code "1" Responses to Item 18:

18A   What is the relationship to respondent of the family member who was a member of the police? ....
       N.A.

19   Has respondent ever been charged with a civil or criminal offense?
       Yes   No   Refusal (If vol.)

20   Is respondent a member of a labor union?
       Yes   No

For Code "1" Responses:

20A   Which labor union?
       Name of labor union ....
          Unable to recall name (Only if vol.)
          Refusal to tell name (Only if vol.)   N.A.

Appendix C

QUESTIONNAIRE ADMINISTERED TO UNIVERSITY STUDENTS

The questionnaire used in the survey of university student opinion and experience with respect to the police will be found below. The questionnaire items are presented in the order in which they appeared during the interview. The variable numbers, given at the left-hand side of the page, were added later during the analysis. In the text of the book, items are referred to by these variable numbers. The reader will notice that although the questions pertaining to background were asked at the end of each interview, they were listed first during the analysis. Thus the first question in the following questionnaire has been given the variable number of 23.

PREAMBLE

We are engaged in the Indian Institute of Public Opinion on several research studies ascertaining the views of the public in regard to matters which concern them intimately. We are doing at this time a study in particular of the ways in which the police can be of greater assistance to you and the community as a whole. For this purpose, we would like to know how you feel generally about them at present and where you think they can serve the community better. The results will be published in due course and we believe they will assist the government in framing policy for your better protection. Your cooperation, for this purpose, will be much appreciated.

Variable Number	*Item*

A.   THE UNIVERSITY SETTING FOR LAW AND ORDER:

23   Do you live in a university residence of some kind, such as a hostel, or outside the university in private dwellings?
University residence/hostels
Outside university in private dwellings

For Those Living Outside the University:

24   Is the area you live in safe or unsafe? That is, is there
        much danger in living there: could you be easily robbed
        or hurt?
        Safe   Unsafe   Can't say   N.A.

For Those Living in University Dwelings:

25   Is it safe to keep valuables in one's rooms?
        Yes   No   N.A.

26   How would you describe discipline generally in the resi-
        dence halls/hostels?
        Good   So-so   Bad   N.A.

27   Is there thievery in the residence halls/hostels?
        Good deal   Little   None
        Don't know/Can't say   Not applicable

For all:

28   *In the university area*, is there *generally* safety and security
        for the student?
        Yes, safety and security   No

29   Have you been the victim of a crime or offense since join-
        ing the university?
        Yes   No

For Code "1" Responses:

29A   What kind of a crime or offense were you the victim of?
        Kind of crime: ....
        Unable to recall crime (Only if vol.)
        Refusal   N.A.

For Code "1" Responses:

30   Was the matter investigated?
        Yes   No

        I did not report it to the authorities (Only if vol.)
        Not applicable

For Code "1" Responses to Item 30:

30A   By whom was it investigated?
        Investigating officer's status: ....
        Don't know status (If vol.)   Not applicable

For Code "1" Responses:

31   Was the criminal caught and/or the property returned?
        Yes   No   N.A.

32   Do students ever engage in any offenses, i.e., criminal activity? Many, some, a few/or none?

Many   Some   A few
None   No opinion (Only if vol.)
Refusal (If vol.)

33   Do you think the university should have its own policing system?

Yes   No   No opinion (Only if vol.)

FOR ALL:

33A   What kinds of activities need to be controlled more effectively in the university area including residence halls/hostels?

Activities: ....
Unable to specify (Only if vol.)
Refusal to specify (Only if vol.)

34   Do you think the local police should be used *more* than at present to curb crime within the university?

Yes   No
Police not used (If vol.)   Refusal to answer (If vol.)

35   How would you describe the general attitude of the police toward students? Are police:

	Yes
Friendly	1
Cooperative	2
Indifferent	3
Suspicious	4
Uncooperative	5
Hostile	6
No opinion (Only if vol.)	9

36   How would you describe the general attitude of the students toward the police? Are students:

	Yes
Friendly	1
Cooperative	2
Indifferent	3
Suspicious	4
Uncooperative	5
Hostile	6
No opinion (Only if vol.)	9

Variable Number   *Item*

B.   PERCEPTIONS AND EVALUATIONS OF POLICE ACTIVITIES:

Would you tell me in which of the following situations you would contact the police for help and in which of them you would not because you wouldn't expect them to be helpful?

	Would you go if:	*Yes*	*No*	*Undecided (Only if vol.)*
37	A child is lost	1	2	3
38	A person has been injured by an animal or in a fall	1	2	3
39	A friend is in danger of being attacked by goondas or badmashes	1	2	3
40	A fight between two groups in the area is likely to break out	1	2	3
41	A house has been robbed of Rs. 100	1	2	3
42	A house has been robbed of valuables identifiable in the future	1	2	3
43	A man has been found beaten up	1	2	3
44	Cattle have been stolen	1	2	3
45	A bicycle has been stolen	1	2	3
46	A person has been killed accidentally	1	2	3
47	A person has been found who looks as if he had been murdered	1	2	3
48	A landlord is threatening eviction without good reason	1	2	3

49   If you were lost in a strange town or in a strange part of the country, would you go to a policeman to ask for directions and guidance?

      Yes   No

50   Do you think that people, even when they need help, are *generally* reluctant to go to the police?

      Yes   No   Don't know (If vol.)

51   Do you think the police *sincerely* try to help people who come to them for help?
Yes   No   Can't say (If vol.)

52   Do you know of any instance when offenses or crimes were committed but the people did not report them to the police because they were afraid of getting involved with the police?
Yes   No

FOR CODE "1" RESPONSES:

52A   What kind of crime or offenses they did not report?
Kinds of crime/Offenses: ....
Unable to specify (If vol.)
Not applicable

53   Have you ever gone to the police for help?
Yes   No

FOR CODE "1" RESPONSES:

53A   For what reason did you go to the police?
Reason: ....
Can't recall reason (Only if vol.)
Refusal to tell reason (Only if vol.)
Not applicable

IF "YES" TO ITEM 53:

54   How were you treated by the police?
Courteously and sympathetically
Rudely and unsympathetically
Don't know/Can't remember   Not applicable

55   Did the police register your case?
Yes   No   Not applicable

IF "YES" TO ITEM 55:

56   Were you satisfied with what the police finally did for you or do you think they should have done more?
Was satisfied   Should have done more
No opinion (Only if vol.)   Not applicable

57   When the police come around asking questions about an offense or crime, do they *generally* act courteously and fairly or are they *generally* rude and tricky?
Courteously and fairly   Rude and tricky
Can't say (Only if vol.)

58   Have you ever been questioned by the police?
Yes   No

For Code "1" Responses:

59   Were you treated courteously or rudely?
      Courteously   Rudely
      Not rudely but without courtesy (Only if vol.)
      Not applicable

60   Do you *know personally anyone* (friend, relative, or neighbor) who has been questioned by the police?
      Yes   No

For Code "1" Responses:

61   Was the treatment courteous or rude?
      Courteous   Rude
      Not rude but without courtesy (Only if vol.)
      N.A.

62   Have you ever been asked to serve as a witness in court in a police case?
      Yes   No

For Code "1" Responses:

63   Did you serve as a witness?
      Yes   No   Not applicable

64   How many times did you have to go to court?
      Number of times: (Actual) 1, 2, 3, 4, 5, 6, 7 or more
      Can't recall (If vol.)   N.A.

65   Did serving as a witness *expose you to pressures* from friends connected with the people involved in the case?
      Yes   No   N.A.

66   Do you personally know anyone (friend, relative, or neighbor) who has *ever* served as a witness in court in a police case?
      Yes   No

67   If you knew that the police were coming around here asking questions and looking for information, would you try to avoid being questioned and having contact with them?
      Yes, would avoid   No, wouldn't avoid
      It depends (If vol.)
      Elaborate: ....
      Unable to elaborate   Can't say (Only if vol.)

68   When the police present cases in the courts, do they twist and/or make up evidence in order to convict people?
      Twist evidence   Make up evidence
      Twist and make up evidence
      Do not twist/make up evidence
      No opinion (Only if vol.)

69   When the police take people to the police station for questioning, even those who aren't criminals, do they (police) often threaten them or beat them?
Threaten or beat only criminals
Threaten or beat even those not criminals
Threaten or beat no one
Can't say though people say so (Only if vol.)
Can't say (Only if vol.)

70   In order to get the police to do their duty and to help people, does it take money in the form of a bribe?
Yes   No   Can't say

71   Do you know of any instance when the police didn't take any action until they had received some money?
Yes   No

If "Yes":

72   Were the people in this instance known personally to you?
Yes   No   N.A.

73   If you needed help from the police for some reason, and you had to go to the police station, would you take money with you so that you could be sure of getting the help you needed?
Yes   No   No opinion (If vol.)
Depends (If vol.)
(Probe to obtain amplification for "depends")
....

74   Do the police *often* beat people up?
Yes, often   Yes, sometimes
No   Can't say (If vol.)

75   Have you ever seen any policeman/policemen strike a person?
Yes   No

For Code "1" Responses:

75A   What was the situation/occasion?
Situation/occasion ....
Unable to specify situation (Only if vol.)
N.A.

76   Do you know personally anyone (friend, relative, neighbor) who was threatened by a policeman?
Yes   No

77   Do you know personally anyone (friend, relative, neighbor) who was struck by a policeman?
Yes   No

78   Do the police show favoritism?

          Yes   Yes, sometimes/some policemen

          No   Can't say (If vol.)

FOR CODE "1" AND "2" RESPONSES:

78A   What kinds of reasons make the police show favoritism and
          treat people differently? (Provision for multiple responses)
          (Interviewer: Please encircle for "Yes" responses only)

                                                               Yes
          (i) Would wealth be a reason?   1
          (ii) Would land ownership be a reason?   2
          (iii) Would caste be a reason?   3
          (iv) Would religion be a reason?   4
          (v) Would political position be a reason?   5
          (vi) Would influence be a reason?   6
          (vii) Would occupation be a reason?   7

          What else would be the reason for the police to show
          favoritism and treat people differently?

          ....

          Nothing   Unable to specify (Only if vol.)
          Not applicable

79   Are there any groups which you think the police treat
          worse than others?

          Yes   No   Don't know (If vol.)

IF "YES" TO ITEM 79:

79A   Which particular groups have you in mind?
          Particular groups: ....
          Unable to specify group   Not applicable

FOR ALL:

80   Is there corruption in the police? A great deal, some, little,
          none?

          Yes, a great deal   Yes, some
          Yes, little   No, none   Don't know (If vol.)

81   Have you ever seen a policeman take money?
          Yes   No

81A   If you wanted to complain about something the police
          have done, whom would you complain to?
          Would complain to:
          (Specify designation) ....
          Unable to specify

82   Has it ever happened that you *wanted to complain* about something *the police* had done, *but you decided not to do it* because you didn't think it would do any good?

Yes   No

FOR CODE "1" RESPONSES:

82A   What was it that you wanted to complain about?

Nature of complaint: ....

Can't recall (If vol.)   Not applicable

83   Have you ever complained to *anyone in an official position* about the behavior of the police?

Yes   No

FOR "YES" RESPONSES TO ITEM 83:

83A   Whom did you complain to?

Person by status: ....

Can't recollect (Only if vol.)   Not applicable

84   Do you think that the police join hands with criminals? Often, sometimes, rarely, or never?

Often   Sometimes   Rarely

Never   Can't say (If vol.)

85   If the police know that someone is guilty of a crime but they don't have evidence to convict him, do you think the police would then be justified in beating him to obtain a confession?

Police would be justified

Police wouldn't be justified

Can't say/No opinion (Only if vol.)

86   Do you think that *nowadays* the behavior of the police in the way they treat people *generally* is getting better or worse?

Better   Worse   No change (If vol.)

Can't say/Don't know

87   Do you think that there is a great deal of political control of the police? Can politicians get the police to do what they want?

Yes   No   Can't say (If vol.)

88   Have you heard stories of cases where *politicians* of this area got the police to *go after someone* or stopped them *from investigating someone*?

Yes   No

89   Do the police take sides at election times?

Yes   No   Don't know (If vol.)

For Students from Rural Area:

90   Do the police take sides between the factions of your village?

Yes   No   Don't know

Not applicable

Compared to other government officials, are the police more or less (i) corrupt, (ii) courteous, (iii) sympathetic?

	More	Less	Same (If vol.)	No opinion (If vol.)
91 Corrupt	1	2	3	9
92 Courteous	1	2	3	9
93 Sympathetic	1	2	3	9

94   Compared to people joining the army service, are those who join the police a higher type, lower, or about the same?

Higher   Lower   Same

Can't say (If vol.)

95   If you had been robbed and the *police caught* the person *who did it* but couldn't get him to confess, do you think the police should use physical force to make him confess?

Yes   No

Other opinion (specify) ....

No opinion (Only if vol.)

For All (Interviewer must not make any suggestion):

95A   What would be the *one most important thing* the police could do to improve their relations with the public?

One most important thing: ....

No idea (If vol.)   Refusal

96   Do you think that the common man has a duty to help the police by going to them with information about a crime *if he has it?*

Yes   No

C. PUBLIC DEMONSTRATIONS AND POLICE CROWD-CONTROL BEHAVIOR

97   Do you think that public demonstrations are or are not a useful way of getting the authorities to do the right things or to correct some wrongs?

Are a useful way   Are not a useful way

Can't say (Only if vol.)

98   In your opinion, are student agitations necessary in order
        to get the university/college authorities to take notice of
        student grievances and needs?
        Yes   No   No opinion (If vol.)

99   Are student strikes a proper means of putting pressure on
        university/college authorities?
        Yes   No   No opinion

100   Have you ever participated in (i) a demonstration or (ii)
        a strike?

        Participated in a demonstration
        Participated in a strike
        Participated in both?
        Participated in neither

    For Participants:

100A   What was the occasion?
        Occasion: ....
        Can't recall occasion (Only if vol.)
        Refusal to tell (Only if vol.)
        Not applicable

101   When demonstrators or strikers break the law, should the
        authorities arrest them right away or should they be con-
        siderate and tolerate them?
        Arrest right away   Considerate and tolerate them
        Don't know/No opinion (If vol.)

102   Do you think that students generally are eager, indifferent,
        or reluctant to participate in demonstrations?
        Eager   Indifferent   Reluctant
        No opinion (If vol.)

103   In your opinion, are the student demonstrations at this
        university, which you have seen or have heard about,
        founded upon real and serious grievances or are many of
        them artificial and not based on widespread student
        concerns?
        Many founded on serious grievances
        Many founded on artificial grievances
        Can't say (If vol.)

104   Are there attempts among students to organize demon-
        strations from time to time?
        Yes   Yes, frequently   Yes, sometimes
        Yes, rarely   No, never

105   How would you describe the way the police usually handle public demonstrations? Do they handle them:

Very haphazardly   Firmly but properly

Too firmly and harshly   With too much force

Space for volunteered responses: ....

No opinion (If vol.)

106   Have you ever seen the police use lathis or canes against a crowd?

Yes   No

107   Have you ever seen a police firing?

Yes   No

108   Do the police resort to firings *too often?*

Yes   No

109   Do you think that demonstrations are used *too often?* or too frivolously, these days?

Yes   No   Don't know (If vol.)

110   How much interest have you in student politics? Do you have a lot, some, or only a little interest?

A lot   Some   A little

None   No opinion (If vol.)

D.   A CITIZEN'S DUTY IN MATTERS OF LAW AND ORDER

111   If you came to know that a gang of goondas near here was going to commit a crime, would you inform the police?

Yes, would   No, wouldn't   Can't say (If vol.)

112   If a crime had been committed near here and you thought you knew something that the police would want to know, would you go to them and tell them or would you wait for them to come around and ask you?

Would go and tell   Would wait for them to come

113   Do you think that the police are underpaid?

Yes   No   Don't know (If vol.)

114   Have you ever had any contacts with the police?

114A   If so, what kind of contacts have you had?

Kind of contact: ....

Had no contacts (If vol.)

Possible Suggestions—Went to them for help, asked for information from them; reported a crime; was the victim of a crime that they investigated; was questioned by them in connection with a crime; had a cycling violation (or motoring violation); they inspected a license I had; know a policeman well; have been in informal groups where a policeman came and talked for a few minutes; other.

E. KNOWLEDGE ABOUT THE POLICE

115   Would you recognize on sight some of the policemen who
        are posted in this area?
        Yes, most of them   Yes, a few
        Yes, one or two   None   No opinion

116   Do you know any policeman by name?
        Yes   No

117   Do you think that being in the police would be a good
        job or a bad job?
        Good   Bad   Depends (If vol.)
        Elucidate: ....
        Unable to elaborate
        Can't say/No opinion

        ASK ALL EXCEPT "NO OPINION" CASES:
117A   Why do you say so? ....
        N.A.

118   What is the salary of a police constable?
        Actual: ....
        Correct response   Incorrect   Don't know

119   What is the title of the top police officer of this district?
        Title: ....
        Specified correctly   Specified incorrectly
        Unable to specify (If vol.)

120   Where is the office of the top police officer of this district
        located? In which town and where in the town?
        In which town: Name of town ....
        Correct response   Incorrect response
        D.K.

121   Name of location in the town: ....
        Correct   Incorrect   D.K.

F. BACKGROUND INFORMATION

2   Sex: Male   Female

3   Age: Under 20   21 to 30   31 to 40
              41 to 50   Over 50

4   Years in the university: ....

4A   Name of secondary school: ....

5   How well did he do in secondary school: rank in class or
        class of school-leaving certificate:
        1st division   2nd division   3rd division

6-7 Degree earned to date (with dates): ....

8 Class/Division of degrees: ....

9 Course of study:

Arts	Medicine
Science	Law
Engineering	Commerce

Any other (specify) ....

10 Name of University: ....

10A Name of college: ....

11 Residence:

University facility   Private dwelling   At home   Other

12 Father's occupation: (or, if father is dead, supporting relative):

Artisan	Non-owner cultivator
Retail trader	Domestic servant
Owner-cultivator	Landlord
Clerk and teacher	Unskilled worker
Student	Housewife
Unemployed	Agricultural laborer
Skilled worker	Retired
Profession	Government servant

13 Caste of family: ....

14 Father's education: ....

15 Father's estimated income: ....

16 Home (Actual) ....

Urban   Town   Rural

17 Has home moved in lifetime of student:

Yes   No

18 If so, from where?

Rural	Town
Urban	N.A.

19 Has respondent ever been a member of the police?

Yes   No

20 Has any member of respondent's family been a member of police? If so, which relations?

Yes   No

21 Has respondent ever been charged with a civil or criminal offense?

Yes   No

21A Which of the following kinds of organizations do you belong to:

(Indicate as many as apply)

	Yes	No
(a) National political party or organization	1	2
(b) Student political party	1	2
(c) Cultural organization (those concerned with plays, concerts, art exhibitions, literary meetings)	1	2
(d) Religious association	1	2
(e) Social or sports clubs	1	2
(f) Professional or scientific association (those concerned with interests and problems of a career or field of study)	1	2
(g) Other type (which)	1	2

22 Do you hold a formal office in any student organization?

Yes No

IF "YES":

22A Which organization?

Organization: ....

N.A.

22B Which office:

Office: ....

N.A.

Selected Bibliography

GOVERNMENT DOCUMENTS—POLICE

Andhra Pradesh. *Report on the Administration of the Police of Andhra Pradesh State*, 1956, 1958, 1959.

Assam. *Report on the Police Administration in the State of Assam*, 1954-1961.

Bihar. *Report of the Police Commission, 1961*. Patna: Secretariat Press, 1961.

Bihar. *Report on the Administration of the Police in the State of Bihar*, 1953-1960.

Bombay City. *Annual Administration Report of Greater Bombay Police*, 1956-1960.

Bombay State. *Annual Report on the Police Administration Including Railways of the Bombay State, 1956-1958*.

Calcutta. *Annual Report on the Police Administration of the Town of Calcutta and Its Suburbs*, 1945-1949, 1953-1958.

Delhi State. *Annual Administration Report*, 1955, 1956-1957, 1957-1958, 1960-1961, 1961-1962, and 1962-1963.

Great Britain, Home Office. *Criminal Statistics, England and Wales, 1961-1963*.

Great Britain. *Royal Commission on the Police, 1962*. Cmnd. 1728.

Great Britain, Royal Commission on the Police. *Appendix IV to the Minutes of Evidence*, "The Relations Between the Police and the Public," 1962.

India. Ministry of Home Affairs. *Annual Report of the Delhi Special Police Establishment*, 1959-1963.

India. Ministry of Home Affairs. *Annual Report*, 1949-1964.

India. Ministry of Home Affairs. *Crime in India*, 1952-1960, 1963.

India. *Report of the Indian Police Commission, 1902-1903*.

Kerala. *Administration Report of the Police Department*, 1956-1962.

Kerala. *Report of the Kerala Police Reorganisation Committee, 1960*.

Madhya Pradesh. Police Department. *Report on the Police Administration of Madhya Pradesh*, 1954-1959.

Madras. *Report on the Administration of the Police of the Madras State*, 1950-1962.

Maharashtra. *Summary of Recommendations of the Maharashtra State Police Commission, 1964*.

Mysore. *Annual Administration Report of the Department of Police of the Mysore State*, 1950-1964.

Rajasthan. *Annual Police Administration Report of the State of Rajasthan*, 1955-1957.

U.S. Department of Justice. Federal Bureau of Investigation. *Crime in the United States* (Uniform Crime Reports), 1964, 1965.

Uttar Pradesh. *Report on Police Administration of the State of Uttar Pradesh*, 1956-1959.

Uttar Pradesh. *Report of the Uttar Pradesh Police Commission, 1960-1961*, 1962.

West Bengal. *Report on the Police Administration of West Bengal, Excluding Calcutta and Suburbs*, 1948-1959.

West Bengal. Home (Police) Department. *Report of the Police Commission, West Bengal, 1960-1961*, 1964.

GOVERNMENT DOCUMENTS—GENERAL

Assam. *Report of the Commission of Inquiry into the Goreshwar Disturbances*, 1961.

Bombay State. Home Department. *Report of the Commission of Inquiry on the Cases of Police Firing at Ahmedabad on the 12th, 13th, and 14th August 1958 and Government's Conclusions and Proposals for Action on the Report*, 1959.

Bombay State. *Report of the Officer on Special Duty on Reorganisation of District Revenue Offices*, 1958.

California. Governor's Commission on the Los Angeles Riots. *Violence in the City—An End or a Beginning?* 1965.

India. *Census of India.* Paper No. 1 of 1962 (Final Population Totals).

India. *Census of India.* Paper No. 1 of 1963 (Religion).

India. Lok Sabha Secretariat. *Report of the Delegation of Members of Parliament to Assam*, August, 1960.

India. Ministry of Education. *Report of the Banaras Hindu University Enquiry Committee, 1958*.

India. Ministry of Finance. *Commission of Enquiry on Emoluments and Conditions of Service of Central Government Employees, 1957-1959*.

India. Ministry of Home Affairs. Central Bureau of Correctional Services. *Social Defense*, January, 1964.

India. Ministry of Home Affairs. *Handbook of Rules and Regulations for the All India Services*. Third edition, Vols. I and II.

India. Ministry of Home Affairs. *Report of the Committee on Prevention of Corruption, 1964*.

India. Ministry of Home Affairs. *Report of the Committee on Traffic in Delhi, 1963*.

India. Ministry of Information and Broadcasting. *India: A Reference Annual, 1964 and 1965*.

India. Ministry of Law. Law Commission. *Fourteenth Report: Reform of Judicial Administration*, 2 vols, 1961-1962.

India. Ministry of Law. *Report of the Study Team on Nyaya Panchayats, 1962*.

India. Organisation and Methods Division. *Papers on Measures for Strengthening of Administration*, 1961.

India. Planning Commission. *Report on Indian and State Administrative Services and Problems of District Administration*, 1962.

India. Planning Commission. *Report of the Prohibition Enquiry Committee, 1954-1955.*

India. Planning Commission. *Report of the Team for the Study of Community Projects*, 1957. The report was written under the direction of Balvantray G. Mehta.

India. Union Public Service Commission. *Fourteenth Report of the Union Public Service Commission*, 1964.

India. Union Public Service Commission. *Notice.* February 29, 1964, and March 6, 1965.

India. University Grants Commission. *Report on the Problem of Student Indiscipline in India Universities*, 1960.

India. University Grants Commission. *University Development in India: Basic Facts and Figures*, 1963-1964 and 1964-1965.

Madhya Pradesh. *Report on the Disturbances Which Took Place at Raipur on the 26th and 27th August 1957*, 1958.

Madhya Pradesh. *Report on the Indore Firing Incidents, 1954*, 1955.

BOOKS

ADAM, H. L. *Oriental Crime.* London: T. Werner Laurie, n. d.

ALMOND, GABRIEL A., and VERBA, SIDNEY. *The Civic Culture: Political Attitudes and Democracy in Five Nations.* Boston: Little, Brown and Co., 1965. Paperback. Originally published by Princeton University Press, 1963.

ARTHUR, T. C. *Reminiscences of an Indian Police Official.* London: Sampson Low, Marston and Co., 1894.

BAILEY, F. G. *Politics and Social Change: Orissa in 1959.* Berkeley: University of California Press, 1963.

BANTON, MICHAEL. *The Policeman in the Community.* New York: Basic Books, Inc., 1964.

BEALS, ALAN R. *Gopalpur: A South Indian Village.* New York: Holt, Rinehart and Winston, 1963.

BEAMES, JOHN. *Memoirs of a Bengal Civilian.* London: Chatto and Windus, 1961.

BENDIX, REINHARD. *Nation-Building and Citizenship: Studies in Our Changing Social Order.* New York: John Wiley and Sons, 1964.

BLALOCK, HUBERT M. *Social Statistics.* New York: McGraw-Hill Book Co., 1960.

BOHANNAN, PAUL. *African Homicide and Suicide.* Princeton: Princeton University Press, 1960.

BRAIBANTI, RALPH, AND SPENGLER, JOSEPH J. *Administrative and Economic Development in India.* Durham, N.C.: Duke University Press, 1963.

CARSTAIRS, G. MORRIS. *The Twice-Born: A Study of a Community of High-Caste Hindus.* London: Hogarth Press, 1957.

CARSTAIRS, R. *The Little World of an Indian District Officer.* London: Macmillan and Co., Ltd., 1912.

CHAUDHURI, SASHI BHUSAN. *Civil Disturbances During the British Rule in India (1765-1857).* Calcutta: The World Press, Ltd., 1955.

CHETTUR, S. K. *The Steel Frame and I.* Bombay: Asia Publishing House, 1962.

CHIROL, VALENTINE. *Indian Unrest.* London: Macmillan and Co., Ltd., 1910.

COATMAN, JOHN. *Police.* London: Oxford University Press, 1959.

CORMACK, MARGARET L. *She Who Rides a Peacock: Indian Students and Social Change.* New York: Praeger, 1961.

COX, SIR EDMUND C. *Police and Crime in India.* London: Stanley Paul and Co., n. d.

CRAWFORD, ARTHUR. *Reminiscences of an Indian Police Official.* London: Roxburghe Press, n. d.

CURRIE, MAJOR-GENERAL FENDALL. *Below the Surface.* London: Archibald Constable and Co., 1900.

CURRY, J. C. *The Indian Police.* London: Faber and Faber, 1932.

DEB, R. *Principles of Criminology, Criminal Law and Investigation.* Calcutta: S. C. Sarkar and Sons, Private Ltd., 1958.

Delhi School of Social Work. *The Beggar Problem in Metropolitan Delhi.* Delhi: Delhi School of Social Work, 1959.

EDWARDES, S. M. *The Bombay City Police: A Historical Sketch, 1672-1916.* London: Humphrey Milford-Oxford University Press, 1923.

————. *Crime in India.* London: Humphrey Milford-Oxford University Press, 1924.

ELWIN, VERRIER. *Maria Murder and Suicide.* London: Oxford University Press. First edition, 1943; second edition, 1950.

————. *A New Deal for Tribal India.* New Delhi: Ministry of Home Affairs, 1963.

EMERSON, GERTRUDE. *Voiceless India.* New York: Doubleday, Doran and Co., Inc., 1930.

FERGUSON, GEORGE A. *Statistical Analysis in Psychology and Education.* New York: McGraw-Hill Book Co., 1966. Second edition.

FICHTER, JOSEPH H. *Police Handling of Arrestees: A Research Study of Police Arrests in New Orleans.* New Orleans: Loyola University of the South, 1964.

FORAN, W. ROBERT. *The Kenya Police, 1887-1960.* London: Robert Hale Limited, 1962.

FORSTER, E. M. *The Hill of Devi*. New York: Harcourt, Brace and Co., 1953.

GOODNOW, HENRY FRANK. *The Civil Service of Pakistan: Bureaucracy in a New Nation*. New Haven: Yale University Press, 1964.

GORWALA, A. D. *The Role of the Administrator: Past, Present, and Future*. Poona: Gokhale Institute of Politics and Economics, 1952.

GOULDSBURY, C. E. *Life in the Indian Police*. London: Chapman and Hall, Ltd., 1913.

GOURLEY, G. DOUGLAS. *Public Relations and the Police*. Springfield, Illinois: Charles C. Thomas, 1953.

HAIKERWAL, BENJOY SHANKER, and MUKERJEE, RODHA KAMAL. *Economics and Social Aspects of Crime in India*. London: Allen and Unwin, 1934.

HERVEY, H. *Cameos of Indian Crime*. London: Stanley Paul and Co., n. d.

HOLLINS, S. T. *No Ten Commandments: Life in the Indian Police*. London: Hutchinson, 1954.

HORST, PAUL. *Factor Analysis of Data Matrices*. New York: Holt, Rinehart and Winston, 1965.

————. *Psychological Measurement and Prediction*. Belmont, California: Wadsworth Pub. Co., Inc., 1966.

Indian Commission of Jurists. *Report of the Kerala Enquiry Committee*. New Delhi: January, 1960.

The Indian Law Institute, New Delhi. *Essays on the Indian Penal Code*. Bombay: N. M. Tripathi Private, Ltd., 1962.

IYER, V. R. KRISHNA. *Police in a Welfare State*. New Delhi: Asia Book Centre, 1958.

JANOWITZ, MORRIS. *The Military in the Political Development of New Nations*. Chicago: University of Chicago Press, 1964. Paperback.

JEFFRIES, SIR CHARLES. *The Colonial Police*. London: Max Parrish, 1952.

KABIR, HUMAYUN. *Letters on Discipline*. New Delhi: Ministry of Education and Scientific Research, Government of India, 1958.

————. *Student Indiscipline*. New Delhi: Ministry of Education, Government of India.

Kautilya's Arthasastra. Trans. by R. Shamasastry. First edition, 1915. Mysore: Mysore Printing and Publishing House, 1961.

KERLINGER, FRED N. *Foundations of Behavioral Research: Educational and Psychological Inquiry*. New York: Holt, Rinehart and Winston, 1965.

KHERA, S. S. *District Administration in India*. Bombay: Asia Publishing House, 1964.

KHOSLA, G. D. *The Murder of the Mahatma*. London: Chatto and Windus, 1963.

LAFAVE, WAYNE R. *Arrest: The Decision to Take a Suspect into Custody*. Boston: Little, Brown and Co., 1965.

LaPalombara, Joseph (ed.) *Bureaucracy and Political Development.* Princeton: Princeton University Press, 1963.

Majumdar, D. N. *Justice and Police in Bengal, 1765-1793: A Study of the Mizamat in Decline.* Calcutta: K. L. Mukhopadhyay, 1960.

Martineau, G. D. *Controller of Devils.* G. D. Martineau, Temple House, Broad Street, Lyme Regis, Dorset, U.K., n. d.

Matthai, John. *Village Government in British India.* London: T. Fisher Unwin, Ltd., 1915.

Mays, John Barron. *Crime and the Social Structure.* London: Faber and Faber, 1963.

Moon, Penderel. *Strangers in India.* New York: Reynal and Hitchcock, 1945.

Nehru, Jawaharlal. *Toward Freedom.* Boston: Beacon Press, 1958. Paperback.

Nigam, S. R. *Scotland Yard and the Indian Police.* Allahabad: Kitab Mahal Private Ltd., 1963.

O'Malley, L.S.S. *The Indian Civil Service, 1601-1930.* London: John Murray, 1931.

Parker, W. H. *The Police Role in Community Relations.* Chicago: The National Conference of Christians and Jews, 1955.

Preiss, Jack J., and Ehrlich, Howard J. *An Examination of Role Theory.* Lincoln, Neb.: University of Nebraska Press, 1966.

Rao, S. Venugopala. *Facets of Crime in India.* New Delhi: Allied Publishers, 1962.

Reith, Charles. *The Blind Eye of History: A Study of the Origins of the Present Police Era.* London: Faber and Faber, Ltd., 1952.

————. *A New Study of Police History.* London: Oliver and Boyd, 1956.

————. *A Short History of the British Police.* London: Oxford University Press, 1948.

Sarkar, Jadunath. *Mughal Administration.* Calcutta: M. C. Sarkar and Sons, Private Ltd., 1963. Fifth edition.

Sethi, R. B. *The Police Acts (Central and States).* Allahabad: Law Book Company, 1959. Second edition.

Sinha, Alakh K. *Thirty-Two Years in the Police and After.* Printed by the author, 1952.

Sleeman, Sir William Henry. *Rambles and Recollections of an Indian Official.* London: J. Hatchard and Son, 1844.

Smith, Bruce. *Police Systems in the United States.* New York: Harper and Bros., 1949.

Spear, Percival. *The Nabobs: A Study of the Social Life of the English in Eighteenth Century India.* London: Oxford University Press, 1963.

————. *Twilight of the Mughals.* Cambridge: At the University Press, 1951.

SRIVASTAVA, SHANKAR SAHAI. *Juvenile Vagrancy: A Socio-Ecological Study of Juvenile Vagrants in the Cities of Kanpur and Lucknow.* New York: Asia Publishing House, 1963.

STEAD, PHILIP JOHN. *The Police of Paris.* London: Staples Press, Ltd., 1957.

TAYLOR, COLONEL MEADOWS. *Confessions of a Thug.* London: Oxford University Press, 1916.

TUKER, SIR FRANCIS. *The Yellow Scare.* London: J. M. Dent and Sons, Ltd., 1961.

WALSH, SIR CECIL. *Indian Village Crimes.* London: Ernest Benn, Ltd., 1929.

WHITAKER, BEN. *The Police.* Harmondsworth: Penguin Books, Ltd.— a Penguin Special, 1964.

WILSON, O. W. *Police Administration.* New York: McGraw-Hill Book Co., 1963. Second edition.

WOLFGANG, MARVIN E. *Crime and Race.* New York: Institute of Human Relations Press, American Jewish Committee, 1964.

WOODRUFF, PHILIP. *Call the Next Witness.* New York: Harcourt, Brace and Co., 1946.

———. *The Men Who Ruled India.* Vol. I: *The Founders;* Vol. II: *The Guardians.* London: Jonathan Cape, 1954; paperback edition, 1963.

———. *The Wild Sweet Witch.* New York: Harcourt, Brace and Co., 1947.

WRAITH, RONALD, and SIMPKINS, EDGAR. *Corruption in Developing Nations.* London: Allen and Unwin, 1963.

ARTICLES AND PERIODICALS

ALLMAN, JAMES J. "The Public Attitude Toward Police," *The Police Chief,* January, 1963, pp. 8 ff.

"An Appropriate Police System for India," *Transactions,* April, 1964, pp. 1-89.

ANDERSON, NORMAN H. "Scales and Statistics: Parametric and Nonparametric," *Psychological Bulletin,* July, 1961, pp. 305-316.

BAILEY, F. G. "Politics and Society in Contemporary Orissa," in PHILIPS (ed.), *Politics and Society in S. Asia,* pp. 97-114.

BALBIR, K. K. "Sampurnanand Camp, Ghurma," *Central Police Training College Magazine,* November, 1964, pp. 42-52.

BANERJEE, T. K. "The Substantive Criminal Law Prior to the Indian Penal Code," *Essays on the Indian Penal Code,* Indian Law Institute, New Delhi, 1962, pp. 1-32.

BANTON, MICHAEL. "Social Integration and Police Authority." Reprint from *The Police Chief,* April, 1963, pp. 8-20.

BETTELHEIM, BRUNO. "Violence: A Neglected Mode of Behavior," *The Annals,* March, 1966, pp. 50-59.

BHANWANIMAL. "Traffic Problems in Jaipur City, and Their Solution," *Traffic Safety Week* (a souvenir booklet), 1963.

BRAIBANTI, RALPH. "Public Bureaucracy and Judiciary in Pakistan," in LAPALOMBARA, *Bureaucracy and Political Development*, Princeton: Princeton University Press, 1963, pp. 360-439.

———. "Reflections on Bureaucratic Corruption," *Public Administration*, Winter, 1962, pp. 357-374.

———. "Reflections on Bureaucratic Reform in India," in BRAIBANTI and SPENGLER, *Administrative and Economic Development in India*, pp. 3-68.

Central Police Training College, India. *The Central Police Training College Magazine*.

COHN, BERNARD S. "Some Notes on Law and Change in North India," *Economic Development and Cultural Change*, October, 1959, pp. 79-93.

COSER, LEWIS A. "Some Social Functions of Violence," *The Annals*, March, 1966, pp. 8-18.

CUMMING, ELAINE. "Phase Movement in the Support and Control of the Psychiatric Patient," *Journal of Health and Human Behavior*, Winter, 1962, pp. 235-241.

CUMMING, ELAINE, CUMMING, IAN M., and EDELL, LAURA. "Policeman as Philosopher, Guide and Friend," *Social Problems*, Winter, 1965, pp. 276-286.

DAVIES, AUDREY M. "Police, the Law, and the Individual," *The Annals*, January, 1954, pp. 143-151.

DRIVER, EDWIN D. "Interaction and Criminal Homicide in India," *Social Forces*, December, 1961, pp. 153-158.

DUTT, G. C. "Reflections on Crowd Control," *Indian Police Journal*, April, 1960, pp. 20-25.

DUTTA, S. C. "Use of Improvised Fire-Arms in Crime," *Police Science Congress*, pp. 103-105.

ELDERSVELD, S. J. "Bureaucratic Contact with the Public in India," *The Indian Journal of Public Administration*, April-June, 1965, pp. 216-235.

GLUEK, GRACE H. "Fine Art of Fasting," *New York Times* Magazine Section, Sunday, October 8, 1961, p. 106.

GORER, GEOFFREY. "Modification of National Character: The Role of the Police in England," *Journal of Social Issues*, XI:2, 1955, pp. 25-32.

GOULD, HAROLD A. "The Adaptive Functions of Caste in Contemporary Indian Society," *Asian Survey*, III, September, 1963, pp. 427-438.

———. " 'The Incident of the Fish': A Sociological View of Contemporary Indian Political Trends," *Studies on Asia*, 1963, pp. 155-170.

GOURLEY, G. DOUGLAS. "Police Public Relations," *The Annals*, January, 1954, pp. 135-142.

GRIMSHAW, ALLEN D. "Police Agencies and the Prevention of Racial Violence," *The Journal of Criminal Law, Criminology and Police Science*, March, 1963, pp. 110-113.

GUPTA, HARI OM. "Ticketless Travelling on Indian Railways," *A.I.C.C. Economic Review*, September 1, 1959, pp. 38-40.

HOODA, R. K. "Democratic Decentralisation and the Police," *Police Science Congress*, pp. 119-126.

Indian Police Journal, 1962 to date.

International Commission of Jurists, Indian National Section. "Report of the Kerala Enquiry Committee," *Journal of the International Commission of Jurists* (double number, Winter, 1959, and Spring-Summer, 1960, pp. 139-214.

JAGOTA, S. P. "Training of Public Servants in India," in Braibanti and Spengler, *Administrative and Economic Development in India*, pp. 69-93.

JHA, M. K. "Seminar on Juvenile Delinquency: The Role of the Police," *The Indian Police Journal*, April, 1966.

JOSHI, C. P. "The Kumbh Mela at Allahabad, 1966," *The Indian Police Journal*, April, 1966, pp. 13-20.

KAMISAR, YALE. "On the Tactics of Police-Prosecution Oriented Critics of the Courts," *Cornell Law Quarterly*, Vol. 49, 1964, pp. 436-477.

————. "When the Cops Were Not 'Handcuffed,'" *New York Times* Magazine Section, November 7, 1965, p. 34.

KARVE, D. G. "Police Administration in India," *Indian Journal of Public Administration*, Vol. II, No. 4, October-December, 1956, pp. 307-315.

KEPHART, WILLIAM M. *Racial Factors and Urban Law Enforcement*, Philadelphia: University of Pennsylvania Press, 1957.

KUMAR, RAVINDER. "The Deccan Riots of 1875," *Journal of Asian Studies*, August, 1965, pp. 613-636.

LAL, SHYAM. "A Study into the Problem of Copper-Wire Thefts in India," *Transactions*, April, 1964, pp. 121-138.

LEFF, NATHANIAL H. "Economic Development Through Bureaucratic Corruption," *The American Behavioral Scientist*, November, 1964, pp. 8-14.

LIPSET, SEYMOUR MARTIN. "University Students and Politics in Underdeveloped Countries," *Minerva*, Vol. III, No. 1, Autumn, 1964, pp. 15-56.

MAHURKAR, P. P. "Problem of Hunger Strike," *Transactions*, April, 1965, pp. 67-99.

MALIK, BALRAJ. "False Friends in Agra," *The Indian Police Journal*, January, 1966, pp. 79-86.

McNEIL, ELTON B. "Violence and Human Development," *The Annals*, March, 1966, pp. 149-157.

MILLS, JAMES. "The Detective," *Life* magazine, December 3, 1965, p. 90.

MINTURN, LEIGH, and HITCHCOCK, JOHN T. "The Rajputs of Khalapur, India," in BEATRICE B. WHITING (ed.), *Six Culture-Studies in Child Rearing*, New York: John Wiley and Sons, 1963, pp. 203-362.

MIRANDA, SHRI C.J.V. "Student Unrest," *Maharashtra Police Journal*, May-November, 1960, Vol. I, No. 1, pp. 68-82.

MISAR, B. J. "The Problem of Black-Marketing and Hoarding," *Transactions*, November, 1965, pp. 88-112.

MORGENTHAU, HANS J. "The Political Conditions for an International Police Force," *International Organization*, Vol. XVII, No. 2, 1963.

"Outbreaks of Communal Riots," *Transactions*, April, 1965, pp. 100-133.

PADAMANABHAN, DR. K.V.H. "Forensic Science in India," *Indian Police Journal*, July, 1965, pp. 14-22.

PADMAGIRISWARAN, J. "Bonafides of Investigation and Evaluation of Evidence by Law Courts," *Transactions*, April, 1964, pp. 139-149.

PELZ, DONALD C. "Survey Research in Public Administration," *The Indian Journal of Public Administration*, October-December, 1964, pp. 608-624.

"The Police Forces of India—Their Strength and Cost," *Transactions*, October, 1963, pp. 1-29.

PURI, M. L. "Rural Police," *Police Science Congress*, pp. 132-134.

QUINNEY, RICHARD. "Crime in Political Perspective," *The American Behavioral Scientist*, December, 1964, pp. 19-22.

"Railway Crime," *Transactions*, April, 1965, pp. 159-199.

RAMANNA, K. G. "Police Forces of India and Their Cost—A Preliminary Study," *Transactions*, October, 1962, pp. 1-8.

RAO, MALATHI. "Institutional Failure," *Seminar*, April, 1963, pp. 21-24.

"Role of Supervisory Officers in Police Administration," *Transactions*, November, 1964, pp. 21-52.

ROSENTHAL, DONALD B. "Administrative Politics in Two Indian Cities," *Asian Survey*, April, 1966, pp. 201-215.

SANTHANAM, K. "The Lessons of Aligarh," *Hindu Weekly Review*, October 16, 1961, p. 10.

SATPATHY, S. C. "Ways and Means of Minimising Automobile Accidents," *Transactions*, November, 1965, pp. 60-87.

SHILS, EDWARD. "Indian Students," *Encounter*, June, 1961, pp. 1-9.

SINGH, D. N. "Police and the Government," *Transactions*, April, 1965, pp. 1-29.

SINGH, D.P.N. "Kanjars of Rajasthan," *Central Police Training College Magazine*, November, 1964, pp. 80-89.

SINGH, M. M. "Minimum Wage for a Policeman," *Transactions*, October, 1962, pp. 8-23.

SINGH, S. V. "Internal Security," *Transactions*, November, 1964, pp. 1-20.

"Slum Culture and Crime," *Transactions*, November, 1964, pp. 143-186.

STINCHCOMBE, ARTHUR L. "Institutions of Privacy in the Determination of Police Administrative Practice," *The American Journal of Sociology*, September, 1963, pp. 150-160.

"Training of Constables in Modern Set-Up," *Transactions*, April, 1965, pp. 30-66.

VARGHESE, ABRAHAM. "Practice and Precepts in Police Work," *Transactions*, November, 1964, pp. 53-82.

VERMA, S. K. "Police Publicity—A Neglected Aspect of Police Public Relations," *Police Science Congress*, pp. 22-25.

WADHWA, P. C. "All India Services (Discipline and Appeal) Rules, 1955—Interpretation of," *Transactions*, November, 1965, pp. 113-143.

"Welfare in Police," *Transactions*, November, 1965, pp. 1-34.

WESTLEY, WILLIAM A. "The Escalation of Violence Through Legitimation," *The Annals*, March, 1966, pp. 120-126.

———. "Violence and the Police," *The American Journal of Sociology*, July, 1953, pp. 34-41.

WILCOX, WAYNE. "Politicians, Bureaucrats and Development in India," *The Annals*, March, 1965, pp. 114-122.

WILSON, JAMES Q. "Generational and Ethnic Differences among Career Police Officers," *The American Journal of Sociology*, March, 1964, pp. 522-528.

———. "The Police and Their Problems: A Theory," *Public Policy*. Cambridge: Harvard University Press, 1963, pp. 189-216.

WILSON, PATRICK. "Letter from Calcutta: Fire-Balls in the Air," *The Economic Weekly*, January 25, 1964, pp. 111-112.

REPORTS

BROWN, WILLIAM P. *The Police and Community Conflict*. Paper read before the National Institute on Police and Community Relations, Michigan State University, 1965. New York: National Conference of Christians and Jews.

Government of India, Ministry of Community Development. *Seminar on Public Administration in Panchayati Raj at Savoy Hotel, Mussoorie, 9 to 13 April 1962: Agenda Papers*. Mussoorie: Central Institute of Community Development, 1962.

Indian Institute of Public Opinion. "The Citizen and His Society: Attitudes of the Indian People Toward Government, Modernisation, and Each Other," *Monthly Public Opinion Surveys of the I.I.P.O.*, January, February, 1965.

McBride, Thomas F. *Report to the Ministry of Home Affairs of the Government of India.* New Delhi: U.S. Agency for International Development, 1965.

Parker, William H. *Report to the Ministry of Home Affairs of the Government of India Through the United States A.I.D. Mission to India.* (Typescript.)

Westley, W. A. *The Formation, Nature, and Control of Crowds.* Canada: Directorate of Atomic Research, Defense Research Board, 1956.

Wolfgang, Marvin E. *The Police and Their Problems.* Paper read before the National Institute on Police Community Relations, Michigan State University, 1965. New York: National Conference of Christians and Jews.

Unpublished Material

"Agrarian Unrest." Report of a study group of I.P.S. officers at the Central Police Training College, 1962. (Cyclostyled.)

Ali, Syed Aabid. "Higher Training for Police Service in India." Central Police Training College, 1963. (Cyclostyled.)

"An Analysis of the Burglary Problem in India." Report of a study group of I.P.S. officers at the Central Police Training College, 1963. (Cyclostyled.)

Bisht, T. S. "The Deputy Superintendent of Police—A Reappraisal of the Position in Police Administration." Central Police Training College, 1963. (Cyclostyled.)

"Causes of Failure of Police Prosecutions." Report of a study group of I.P.S. officers at the Central Police Training College, 1963. (Cyclostyled.)

Clark, John P. "The Isolation of the Police: A Comparison of the British and American Situations." University of Illinois, 1965. (Mimeographed.)

Clark, John P., and Haurek, Edward W. "A Preliminary Investigation of the Integration of the Social Control System." University of Illinois, no date. (Mimeographed.)

"Control of Police." Report of a study group of I.P.S. officers at the Central Police Training College, 1963. (Cyclostyled.)

Deb, R. "Role of Police in Combating Juvenile Delinquency in India." Central Police Training College, 1963. This is an edited version of a paper given at the National Academy of Administration, Mussoorie, October, 1963. (Cyclostyled.)

"Detection of Property Offences in India." Report of a study group of I.P.S. officers at the Central Police Training College, 1962. (Cyclostyled.)

Dwivedi, I. C. "General Elections and the Police." Central Police Training College, 1962. (Cyclostyled.)

Eldersveld, S. J., Barnabas, A. P., and Jagannadham, V. "The Citizen and the Administrator in a Developing Democracy: An Empirical Study in Delhi State, India, 1964." University of Michigan, 1966.

Gould, Harold A. "The Peasant Village: Centrifugal or Centripetal?" University of Pittsburgh, 1965. (Mimeographed.)

Hassan, Afzaluddin. "Home Guards." Central Police Training College, 1962. (Cyclostyled.)

Lambert, Richard D. "Hindu-Muslim Riots." Unpublished Ph.D. dissertation, Department of Sociology, University of Pennsylvania, 1951.

Mathai, John. "A Scheme for Reorganization of the Police Force." Central Police Training College, 1963. (Cyclostyled.)

Nizamuddin, A. R. "Unarmed Police for India." Central Police Training College, 1962. (Cyclostyled.)

Reiss, Albert J., Jr., and Bordua, David. "Organizational Perspectives on the Metropolitan Police." Unpublished and revised version of paper presented to the American Sociological Association, Los Angeles, September, 1963.

Roberts, Sherwood Stanley. "Indian Police." Unpublished M.A. thesis, School of Public Administration, University of Southern California, 1953.

Singh, D.P.N. "The Role of the I.P.S." Central Police Training College, 1963. (Cyclostyled.)

Spencer, Metta Wells. "Political Behavior of Indian Students." Unpublished M.A. thesis, Department of Sociology, University of California, Berkeley, 1964.

Subrahmanyam, K.V.V. "Departmental Proceedings—A Comparative Study." Central Police Training College, n. d. (Cyclostyled.)

"Superstition and Crime." Report of a study group of I.P.S. officers at the Central Police Training College, 1963. (Cyclostyled.)

Tandon, O. P. "Concoction of Evidence and its Effects." Central Police Training College, 1964. (Cyclostyled.)

Thomas, M. V. "Higher Positions in Police Administration: An Officer Cadre or a System of Promotion." Central Police Training College, 1963. (Cyclostyled.)

Verma, I. J. "Some Aspects of the Legal Handicaps to Police Investigation." Central Police Training College, 1962. (Cyclostyled.)

Index

accountability, 11ff, 364-66. *See also* police

Ain-i-Akbari, 38

Akali Dal, 258

Allahabad University, *see* survey

armed police, 36, 58-60, 62, 397-401, 420

arrest procedures, 169-70

Ayub Khan, 288n

badmash, 193

Bailey, F. G., 378, 379n

Banares Hindu University, 330

bandobust, 59

Bangalore University, *see* survey

Banton, Michael, 21n

Beames, John, 43

Bihar Mounted Military Police, 60

Bihar Police Commission, 250, 300

Bombay City, police development in, 46

Border Security Force, 70n

Braibanti, Ralph, 353n

Brass, Paul, 374

brokers, *see* mediation

brutality, *see* police

burglary, *see* crimes against property

Calcutta, 46

case diary, 151

cattle theft, 114

Central Bureau of Investigation, 52, 69n, 134-35, 294

Central Forensic Science Laboratory, 152

Central Reserve Police, 52, 69n

Central Vigilance Commission, 294

cheating, *see* fraud

chowkidars, 388

Code of Civil Procedure, 44

Code of Criminal Procedure, 44

collector, 350ff

collusion, *see* public, students

Commissioner of Police, 351

communalism, 259-60. *See also* violence

complaints, *see* police

confessions, 173-74

contact with police, 189, 208ff, 233, 326-29. *See also* public, students

Cornwallis, Lord, 41

corruption, 284; in the judiciary, 289-90; in the police, 201-202, 283ff

Cox, Edmund C., 89n

crime, 118; unreported, 130

crime against property, 108-10

criminal investigation, 130-32, 139-41; effectiveness, 124-27, 135; impropriety, 141ff; organization, 132-34; physical evidence, 151ff; problems, 135-36; procedures, 136ff; supervision of, 145-46; work loads, 137-39

Criminal Investigation Department, 132-34

criminal statistics, 101ff, 124ff; problems with, 97-101

criminal tribes, 110-11

crowd-control, 410-12; firearms, 268-69; politics of, 276-79; public reaction, 24-25, 272ff; student reaction, 339-40; use of force, 267-68. *See also* protest

curricula, 312-15

Currie, Fendall, 47n

Curry, J. C., 89n

Curzon, Lord, 47

dacoity, 48-49, 108, 111-12

darogha, 41-43

Defense of India Rules, 265-66

Delhi Special Police Establishment, 52

Delhi University, *see* survey

democratic decentralization, *see* Panchayati Raj

demonstrations, *see* protest, public, students, violence

district administration, 349-50, 362-63, 373-74. *See also* police

drugging, 109-10

duty, 213, 217-18, 229, 238-39; Great Britain, 157n; public sense of, 162-63, 196-97; student sense of, 340-44

Eastern Frontier Rifles, 60

Edwardes, S. M., 89n

Eldersveld, Samuel, 84n, 95, 238n, 417n, 428
electoral rolls, 428
Eve-teasing, 108

factor analysis, 432-33
fasts, 256-58
favoritism, *see* police
firearms, 120
First Information Report, 152-53
forensic laboratories, 152-53
fraud, 112-13

Gandhi, 244, 256, 269
Goodhart, A. L., 21n
goonda, 108
Government of India Act (1858), 40, 44
Great Britain, 63-64, 71n

hartal, 256-57
Henry, Edward, 48
Home Guards, 74

independence struggle, 244-45
Indian Administrative Service, 51ff, 81ff, 350ff
Indian (Imperial) Police, 49
Indian Institute of Public Opinion, 427
Indianization, 49
Indian Penal Code, 44
Indian Police Commission (1860), 45; of 1902-1903, 47, 351
Indian Police Service, 35-36, 81ff; pay and allowances, 85-86; recruitment, 82-83; relations with I.A.S., 51ff, 350ff; supervisory capacity, 137; training, 87-88, 362
India Reserve Battalions, 70n
Indo-Tibetan Border Force, 70n
Inspector-General of Police, 76-77; annual conference of, 53
intermediaries, *see* mediation

jail terms, 128
Jhabvala, R. Prawer, 301n
judicial inquiries, 269-70
juvenile delinquency, 117-18

kotwal, 38, 41

lathi, 267
lathi-charge, 267
Law Commission, on confessions,

173n; on police-public relations, 203; on witnesses, 153-54, 155n
law and order, *see* protest, violence
lawyers, police view of, 176-77
Lucknow University, 330

Madras, 44, 46
Maharashtra Police Commission, 20, 296
Malabar Special Police, 60
Masters, John, 48n
mediation, 378n, 379-80
Morris-Jones, W. H., 50n, 288, 359
Mullah, A. N., 142n, 145
Mullick, B. N., 99n
Munro, Thomas, 42n
murder, 106-107
mutiny, 44
Mysore, 54
Mysore Special Reserve Police Force, 60

Napier, Charles, 43
National Academy of Administration, 362
Nehru, J., 277n
neighborhood councils, 416
Nizamuddin, A. R., 78, 79n
nonenforcement police tasks, 20-21
nonparametric statistics, 431-32, 434
Nutrition Advisory Committee, 304
Nyaya Panchayats, 390-92

organized crime, 117, 291
Osmania University, *see* survey

Panchayati Raj, 389-91; police relations, 391-93, 401ff; rural police relations, 405-406
Parker, William H., 141n
perjury, 164ff
physical evidence, *see* criminal investigation
Plassey, Battle of, 40
police, 4; accountability, 350-51, 364-66, 370ff; adequacy, 370ff; British legacy, 45-50; brutality, 71n, 158, 177ff, 200-201, 277, 372; in cities, 38-39; and the collector, 350ff; communications, 80, 130-31; complaints against, 204-205, 355-57; constables, 140-41, 420-22; control of, 51ff, 392-93; corruption, 162, 204, 286ff, 372; and democracy, 28-30, 405ff; dis-

cretion, 21-22; effectiveness, 124ff; expenditures on, 61-62, 67-68; firings, 268-69; formative role, 12ff; history, 36ff; organization, 54-55, 77-79, 349-50; pay scales, 303-306; and politics, 16-28, 367ff, 382-84, 409-11; powers, 55-56; and the press, 245; public relations, 416-17; ranks, 76; recruitment, 326; reforms, 420-23; rural problems, 385-86, 393ff; social isolation, 184-86; socialization of, 26-27, 79-80, 418-19; strength, 60-66, 69, 76, 385-86; systematic characteristics, 35-36; and technology, 417-18. *See also* armed police, criminal investigation, judicial inquiries, Panchayati Raj, public, political control, politicians, students

Police Act (1861), 45
Police Commission, *see* Indian Police Commission
policemen, 88-96
political control, 202-203. *See also* police
political unrest, *see* protest
politicians, 367-70; and bureaucrats, 364-66
Prantiya Rakshak Dal, 74n
Preventive Detention Act, 56, 265-66
prison sentences, 129
prohibition, 116-17
prosecution, arrangements for, 174-75
protest, 253-59, 263ff; importance in national life, 279; public experience with, 275-76. *See also* violence
public, attitudes toward police, 142-43, 156-57, 159, 170-71, 199ff, 227ff, 386-88; contact with police, 129-30, 156, 170-71, 184-91, 193-97, 208ff, 225-27, 233ff; and crowd-control, 24-25; knowledge of police, 214-17, 239; and police corruption, 285-87; recognition of police, 229; sense of security, 118-20, 208, 231-33. *See also* duty
public opinion, *see* public, students
public order, *see* violence
Punjab, 44

Railway Police, 70ff
Railway Protection Force, 70-71

Ramanna, K. G., 64n
Reith, Charles, 13-14
riots, 108, 249-50. *See also* violence
Royal Commission on the Police, 4, 143n
Royal Irish Constabulary, 44
Rummel, Rudolph J., 250n
rural police, 37-38, 73ff, 388-89, 393ff, 405-406

Santhanam Committee, 284n, 294
satyagraha, 256
searches and seizures, 153-54
search witnesses, *see* searches and seizures
Section 144 of the Code of Crime Procedure, 266
security, *see* public, students
Shore, John, 306
significant differences, *see* tests for significant differences
Sind, 43-44
Singh, Tara, 258
Sleeman, William Henry, 48
Spear, Percival, 40n
Sriramlu, Potti, 258
States' Reorganization, 54
students, attitudes toward police, 319ff; careers with police, 326; contact with police, 319-21, 326-29; criminality, 317; curricula choices, 312-15; demonstrations, 333-37; indiscipline, 307, 318-19, 329ff; knowledge of police, 341-44; police in universities, 318-19; politics, 337-38; recognition of police, 341-44; sense of security, 316-18. *See also* survey, duty
Superintendent of Police, *see* police, collector
survey, 6-7; interviewing, 430; methodology, 427ff; questionnaires, 435ff; respondents, 22-24; samples, 5-6, 427-28, 308ff; sampling procedure, 428-30; statistical analysis, 431-34
suspiciousness, 381n

Taylor, Meadows, 39n, 48n
Telengana, 248
testimony, 164-65. *See also* witnesses
tests for significant differences, 433
theft, telegraph wire, 109; from

railways, 109. *See also* crimes against property
thuggee, 48
thugs, see thuggee
ticketless railway travel, 113-14
traffic, 187-88

United States, 14, 63-64, 288
University Grants Commission, 330n
university police forces, 318-19
university students, *see* students
unreported crime, *see* crime

Varghese, Abraham, 146n
vice, 114-17
Village Chowkidari Act (1870), 47
village police, *see* rural police

Village Volunteer Forces, 74-75
violence, 248ff; communal, 249, 251, 277; complicity of political parties, 279-80; effects on police, 262-63; manner of handling, 263ff; types, 253ff
volunteer police organizations, 74-75

West Bengal, 41ff
West Bengal Police Commission, 250, 296-97
Wiser, William and Charlotte, 295n
witnesses, 153-56, 158ff
Wolfgang, Marvin E., 98n
Woodruff, Philip, 360

zonal police reserves, 53